edited by
Leo Bormans

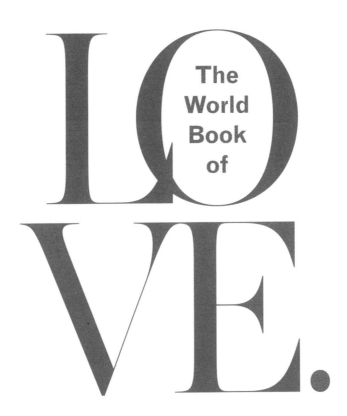

LOVE.
The World Book of

The knowledge and wisdom
of 100 love professors
from all around the world

LANNOO

www.theworldbookoflove.com

www.lannoo.com

© 2013 Lannoo Publishers (Tielt, Belgium), Leo Bormans and authors

Design: Kris Demey

Photography: Flickr collection Getty Images (selection by Kris Demey)

Special thanks go to Amoureus Lommel, pages 56 (© Jacky Geboers),

75 (© Robert Boons), 102 (© Leon Van Ham), 337 (© Jeroen De Wandel)

Photo of Leo Bormans © Yann Bertrand

The contribution of Martha Nussbaum is taken from *Upheavals of Thought: The Intelligence of Emotions*, New York: Cambridge University Press, 2011.

ISBN 978 94 014 2274 1

"The autumn moved across your skin
Got something in my eye
A light that doesn't need to live
And doesn't need to die
A riddle in the book of love
Obscure and obsolete
Until witnessed here in time and blood
A thousand kisses deep."

Leonard Cohen

I dedicate this book
to all people in the world
who will never read it,
but who hopefully experience
and share the power
and the warmth of love.

With special thanks to
Riet, Ine, Kasper, my father and my mother,
my friends and my family,
Yves, Maarten, The Embassy of Happiness,
De Heerlijckyt van Elsmeren
and all collaborators in this wonderful project.

Leo Bormans

For more background, updates, reactions and contact:
www.theworldbookoflove.com

The World Book of Love
Research into the heart of humankind

Where Hollywood stops, *The World Book of Love* will take you further and deeper into the heart of romantic love. Why and how do we fall in love? If we were to erase the word 'love', 90% of books, films, magazines and songs would disappear. We are searching for it in our houses, on the streets and on the internet. In the morning and at night. Google offers in a single second 8,930,000,000 results for our quest on 'love'. That's more than double what we find for 'sex'. **And still, a deadly silence follows** when you ask people to express something worthwhile, crucial and essential about the concept of love.

Though cultural differences occur, love itself has always existed. It is universal and can take many forms. **It is an extremely powerful emotional state.** But we all know: the fire doesn't burn forever. Up until recently the topic was not allowed to be studied at universities. ("Why should we spend money on researching something stupid like love?") Times have changed. Worldwide, thousands of sociologists, psychologists, anthropologists, neuroscientists, therapists and sexologists are studying interpersonal relationships and the how and why of romantic love. Their research brings us closer to the heart of humankind.

More than one hundred of the best researchers from nearly fifty different countries share in this book what we know about love. They talk to us about attachment, passion and commitment, about jealousy, abuse and pressure, from Darwin to science fiction, **from hidden secrets to open sex.** They explain the system and unveil the mystery. In a global and rapidly changing world, we can all learn from each other. From the Far East to the Americas and from Europe to Africa. Parental love, animals, marriage and divorce, teenage love and caring for the elderly. The world of love is full of wonder and surprise, pain and tears, despair and hope. Meet yourself and the ones you love in the mirror and the window of this book.

After the worldwide success of *The World Book of Happiness*, which was presented by European Council President Herman Van Rompuy as a New Year's gift to all leaders of the world, I have spent two years studying the international scientific research into love. We succeeded in engaging the most brilliant scientists and unexpected newcomers to describe in their own words what we ultimately know about love. Each was given a maximum of 1000 words to convey their message to you and the world. They are convinced we can learn to be better mates, friends, parents and lovers. Their insights are founded on research-based knowledge and enable a cross-fertilization of ideas within a global vision on universal love. They succeeded in transforming information into knowledge, and knowledge into wisdom. I thank them all from the bottom of my heart and I hope that this book, in one way or another, will contribute to more love and to a more lovable world. **Their words will probably hit you like Cupid's arrows**. But remember, Cupid is the son of the gods Venus (love) and Mars (war). His arrows are dipped in both sweetness and conflict, in both harmony and misunderstanding.

Welcome to *The World Book of Love*.

Leo Bormans
Author & Editor-in-Chief

8

live 2 love

love 2 live

Contents

"Passionate love and sexual desire are cultural universals."

Passionate love forever?

Dr **Elaine Hatfield** was born in Hawaii in 1937. For her lifelong cross-cultural research on love she has received distinguished scientist awards. Together with her husband Richard L. Rapson, she has published important studies on love and sex. She introduced the difference between passionate and companionate love. Do they last forever?

Today, scholars from a variety of theoretical disciplines – including psychology (social, cultural, and evolutionary), neuroscience, anthropology and history – have finally begun to provide answers to some of the important questions about passionate love. In doing so, they are employing an impressive array of techniques, ranging from the study of primates in the wild, to the scrupulous analysis of brain scans. In addition to the modern marvels of technology and analysis that have been implemented in this search for understanding, historians have managed to contribute a great deal through what is commonly known as 'bottom-up' history. Rather than examining just the lives of kings and queens, this 'bottom-up' method sheds light on the lives (and loves) of the majority through demographic data, architecture, medical manuals, church edicts, song lyrics and the occasional journal. As a consequence of this vast array of methodologies, scholars have managed to construct a variety of answers to questions that have fascinated (and stumped) previous generations of researchers. Let us consider a few of those answers here.

What is passionate love?

Passionate love is an extremely powerful emotional state that is generally defined as a state of intense longing for union with another. It is a complex emotion that is marked by its extreme highs and lows, as well as its tendency to cause the afflicted person to think obsessively about the person for whom they desire. Requited love (in which the object of desire feels the same way in return) is associated with fulfilment and ecstasy; unrequited love (in which the object of desire does *not* feel the same way in return) is often linked to feelings of emptiness, anxiety or despair. Passionate love may also be called 'obsessive love', 'infatuation', 'lovesickness' or 'being-in-love'.

How tightly linked are passionate love and sexual desire?

Recently, social psychologists, neuroscientists and physiologists have begun to explore the links between love, sexual desire and sexual behavior. They have found that (at least in the West and probably throughout much of the world), passionate love and sexual desire are closely linked. If young people are passionately (or romantically) in love with someone, they almost always feel a stirring of sexual desire for their beloved. Of course, young people need not be in love to desire someone sexually. The popularity of casual sex certainly attests to this.

How long does love last?

Passionate love is a fleeting emotion. It is a high, and one cannot stay high forever. Starting shortly after marriage, passionate love is shown to steadily decline, with long-married couples admitting that they feel only 'some' passionate love for each other.

Fortunately, there may be a bright side to this seemingly grim picture. Where passionate love once existed, companionate love is thought to take its place. Companionate love is said to be a gentle emotion, comprised of feelings of deep attachment, intimacy and commitment. Some researchers have argued that, as passionate love decreases, companionate love actually increases. It should be noted, however, that there is conflicting evidence both for and against the role of companionate love in romantic relationships. For instance, the study we just described provides no support for this contention. Couples reported that both romantic and companionate love tended to decline (and to decline equally) over time.

Elaine Hatfield & Megan Forbes

How long has passionate love existed, and does it exist everywhere?

Passionate love is as old as humankind. The Sumerian love fable of Inanna and Dumuzi, in which Inanna (the Sumerian goddess of love, sex, and warfare) takes Dumuzi (a shepherd) as her lover, was spun by tribal storytellers in 2000 BC. Although there was a time when anthropologists assumed that passionate love was purely a Western concept, today most scholars agree that passionate love and sexual desire are cultural universals.

Culture can, of course, have a profound effect on how people view love, how eager they are to experience such tumultuous feelings, and whether or not they assume such love is a prerequisite for marriage, or if marriages should be arranged on the basis of more practical factors.

Historians have also documented how profoundly a society's attitudes toward love, sex, and intimacy can alter over time. Consider China, which possesses an ancient culture. Its historical record begins 4000 years ago in the Xia (or First) Dynasty. These historical records document that, throughout time, Chinese citizens have embraced very different attitudes toward romantic and passionate love, have ascribed very different meanings to 'love', have desired very different traits in romantic partners and have differed markedly in whether such feelings were to be proclaimed to the world or hidden in the deepest recesses of the heart.

Though cultural differences undoubtedly exist, both within and between cultures, love itself is universal. What we should take away from this broad array of research is that love can take many forms. It can be all-encompassing and -consuming, or gentle and nurturing. It can last forever, or it can flitter away. All that is for certain is that it exists, and it exists everywhere.

The keys

→ **Passionate love is an extremely powerful emotional state that is generally defined as a state of intense longing for union with another. It is closely linked to sexual desire.**

→ **Some researchers argue that both passionate and companionate love tend to decline over time, whereas others claim that compassionate love takes the place of passionate love.**

→ **Though cultural differences exist, love itself is universal and can take many forms.**

Elaine Hatfield is Professor of Psychology at the University of Hawaii and Past President of the Society for the Scientific Study of Sexuality. In recent years she has received distinguished scientist awards for a lifetime of scientific achievement (e.g. from the Association for Psychological Science). Two of her books have won the American Psychological Association's National Media Award. Recently, Elaine Hatfield and Richard L. Rapson (who are husband and wife) have collaborated on the books *Love, Sex, and Intimacy: Their Psychology, Biology, and History* and *Love and Sex: Cross-Cultural Perspectives*.
Megan Forbes is a graduate student in Social Psychology at the University of Hawaii. Her special research interests include passionate love, equity theory, mate selection, and virtual (online) relationships.

"Look for someone who means more or less the same by the word love as you do."

What does "I love you" mean?

Reading studies on love, you always come across his name. One psychologist said: "For me his name sounds like Freud or Maslow when we are talking about love." His 'triangle of love' is widely recognized as one of the best models explaining the concept of love. But today, **Robert J. Sternberg** also adds our personal 'stories of love' to the triangle in his quest to understand the meaning of these three most popular words in the world: "I love you".

Often two people say they love each other, only to find out later, to their regret, that they meant different things by these words. Having invested time, money and, most of all, emotional resources into the relationship, they may wish that they had understood earlier on that love meant a different thing to each of them. When people say "I love you", what do they mean? According to my duplex theory of love, love has many different meanings. Whether a couple succeeds in their loving relationship depends, in large part, on whether the meanings of the two individuals are compatible.

The triangle of love

The first part of the duplex theory is a triangle. The idea here is that love has three basic components: intimacy, passion and commitment. Intimacy comprises trust, caring, compassion, communication, understanding, empathy and a feeling of bonding. Passion comprises excitement, energy, enthusiasm and a magnetic feeling of being drawn virtually inescapably to an individual. Commitment comprises the decision to enter and stay with the relationship over a long period of time, come what may, perhaps indefinitely.

Different combinations of intimacy, passion and commitment yield different kinds of love. Absence of any of the three components is non-love. Intimacy alone is what we commonly view as liking. Passion alone is infatuation. Commitment alone is empty love. Intimacy plus passion without commitment is romantic love. Intimacy plus commitment without passion is companionate love. Passion plus commitment without intimacy is fatuous love. And intimacy plus passion plus commitment is consummate or complete love.

Time courses

The three components of love have different time courses. Intimacy tends to be low when a couple first meets. As time goes on, if the relationship succeeds, intimacy tends to increase. If the relationship fails, intimacy begins to decline. If the relationship succeeds, eventually intimacy tends to asymptote. With time, intimacy may decrease if one or both members of the couple begin to keep secrets. Starting to keep secrets is like opening a door that is then hard to close again.

Passion shows the time course of an addiction. At first, even one exposure to the addicting individual brings on intense waves of pleasure. As time goes on, future exposures may result in habituation: one no longer feels the same 'wow' that one felt early in the relationship. After some amount of time, passion may asymptote at a lower level than it had reached at its height. But if one loses the person, one may go into withdrawal, much as one would if one suddenly stopped consuming an addictive substance to which one had shown some degree of habituation (alcohol, nicotine, caffeine, etc.) It then will take a while to get over the withdrawal symptoms.

Commitment generally increases with time in successful relationships, reaching an asymptote at some point, such as when a couple decides to marry. In successful relationships, the commitment will stay at this asymptote, or possibly go even higher. In failed relationships, the commitment may vanish altogether.

intimacy

passion

commitment

More satisfaction

We have created a questionnaire that measures each of the components of love in a particular relationship. Our research has shown that there are two conditions that tend to lead to greater happiness and satisfaction in love. First, there is a tendency for couples to be happier, the more they experience of each intimacy, passion and commitment. But at the same time, there is a moderating influence. Couples also tend to be happier to the extent that they show matching patterns of triangles. That is, couples are more successful in love to the extent that the balance of intimacy, passion and commitment each of them wants is the same. If one person, for example, wants a lot of passion but not much intimacy, and the other wants a lot of intimacy but wishes to hold off on the passion, the couple may find their relationship distressed.

Love is a story

One might wonder exactly from where triangles of love originate. Their origin is in stories of love. Almost from the time one is born, one is exposed to many and varied stories of love – in one's parents' relationship, in the relationships of parents of friends, in books, on TV, in movies and, of course, in one's own life. Each story has two protagonists, who may play similar or complementary roles. The stories evolve over time and may change as time goes on. People have hierarchies of stories. In other words, they do not just have one preferred story, but rather a hierarchy of preferences. One tends to be happier in love stories that are higher in one's hierarchy. If one is in a relationship with someone with a story that is not so high in the hierarchy, the relationship is threatened if one or the other partner meets someone who evokes a story higher in one's hierarchy. Stories are differentially adaptive, with some tending to lead to worse outcomes than others.

There are roughly two dozen different stories of love that are fairly common. Examples of common stories of love are the following: (a) the fairy-tale story, in which a prince and a princess live happily ever after; (b) the business story, in which two business partners view their relationship much like a business, with gains and losses; (c) the travel story, in which partners travel together through time and try to stay on the same path; (d) the police story, in which one partner is constantly seeming to conduct surveillance on the other; (e) the horror story, in which one partner abuses the other; (f) the collector story, in which one partner collects lovers.

We have created a questionnaire that measures each of the stories of love in a particular relationship. Our research has shown that couples are happiest when their stories are adaptive rather than maladaptive (e.g. the travel story vs. the horror story) and when their profiles of stories match – that is, when the stories that are higher and lower in the story hierarchy are the same or similar for both partners.

So?

People mean different things when they say "I love you". You will be happiest if you are with someone who means more or less the same thing by these words as you do.

The keys

→ **Love has three basic components, situated in a triangle: intimacy, passion and commitment. Different combinations yield different kinds of love.**

→ **The three components of love have different time courses. You are happier the more you experience of each and the more your balance looks like your partner's.**

→ **We all have a hierarchy of preferred love stories. We are happier when we experience love higher in our personal hierarchy and when our stories match.**

Prof **Robert J. Sternberg** is a psychologist and psychometrician and Provost at Oklahoma State University (USA). He has been President of the American Psychological Association and is member of the editorial boards of numerous journals, including American Psychologist. Sternberg has a BA from Yale University and a PhD from Stanford University. He holds ten honorary doctorates from one North American, one South American and eight European universities. He is a Distinguished Associate of the Psychometrics Center at the University of Cambridge. His main research includes higher mental functions (including intelligence and creativity) and love and hate. He is the author of numerous articles (including "A Duplex Theory of Love") and books (including *Cupid's Arrow* and *Love is a Story*).

Predictable changes

Dr **Josip Obradović** and Dr **Mira Čudina** have analyzed the emotional evolution of nearly one thousand married couples. What influences their passion, intimacy and commitment over the years? Be prepared for the predictable changes in your love life.

To measure love we used the well-known Robert Sternberg's scale. It measures three love dimensions: passion, intimacy and commitment. Numerous variables were defined as potential predictors of the intensity of love and we tried to assess what traits and circumstances would best predict a person's love experience in marriage.

Passion changes

There are several personal traits and relational factors that enhance passion in marriage. It could be generalized that the more extrovert, agreeable, emotionally stable and highly self-esteemed partners are, the more intensely passion will flourish in marriage. Also, younger marital partners are more passionate. But the relationship of passion and the length of marriage is complicated. Passion is very high at the beginning of marriage, but after five years it starts to sink. It reaches its lowest level around the tenth year of marriage, while after the fifteenth it increases, but without ever returning to the level of newly-wed bliss. Children also play a part here. The greatest passion is experienced by married couples without children. After the first child is born there is a clear drop in passion, but with no further change after the birth of the second. Oddly, passion even increases in couples raising three children.

Intimacy changes

Similarly to the determinants of passion, determinants of intimacy are 'good' personality traits. Partners who are extroverts, agreeable and emotionally stable will achieve more intimacy in marriage. The same is true for high self-esteem and physical attractiveness. Young marital partners experience high intimacy, which drops after a while but then recovers. Having children interferes with intimacy too, but much less than with passion.

Intimacy is most intensive in childless couples. It drops for a while after the first child is born but increases again rather quickly.

Commitment changes

Marital partners' extraversion and agreeableness increase commitment as much as their self-esteem and physical attraction. Young partners are very committed to marriage, but commitment drops steadily with age, reaching a low between the 30th and 40th birthday. Afterwards, it increases again rather quickly. Evidently, there is a low commitment when partners are resolving some personal issues and the decisions on their future life course are taking place. Similarly, there is a distinct relationship between commitment and length of marriage. Commitment is very high at the beginning of marriage, but soon it starts dropping and reaches its lowest low between the sixth and fifteenth anniversary. After that, it starts to increase again and is much higher after 25 years of marriage than at the beginning. Obviously, times can be difficult during the low commitment period, some issues are resolved and the decision to stay together is questioned. But, after that decision is reached, the commitment gets stronger with time. The arrival of the first child threatens commitment somewhat, but after the second or third child is born, commitment is much stronger.

Neither passion nor intimacy nor commitment correlates with educational level. But economic hardship endangers these three aspects of love tremendously.

The keys

- → **The best candidates are agreeable, open, extravert, emotionally stable and self-confident people.**
- → **Be aware of the changes time and age will bring to your marriage. Be ready for it and prevent it.**
- → **Unpreparedness for the first child could cost you dearly in terms of loss of passion, intimacy and commitment. Prepare, organize, seek support.**

Josip Obradović (BA in Psychology, PhD in Sociology) is Professor at the Faculty of Croatian Studies, University of Zagreb (Croatia). He is specialized in family psychology and sociology of marriage and family.
Mira Čudina (BA in Psychology, PhD in Psychology) is Professor Emerita at the Faculty of Croatian Studies, University of Zagreb. She is specialized in emotions, motivation and adolescent development. Together they have co-authored many research papers on marital processes, particularly marriage quality, and the university textbook *Psychology of Marriage and Family*.

"To fall in love is stressful."

The Love Lab

Prof **Donatella Marazziti** proved for the first time that romantic love is underlaid by a biochemical abnormality. The world was shocked. Some critics argued that she destroyed the poetry of love, reducing it to a molecular game. But her Love Lab is still exploring the mystery of love and step by step disentangling its biological mechanisms. On top of that: Donatella fell in love with love and that changed her life drastically. This is her story.

My scientific meeting with love was serendipitous. In the mid 1990s I was interested in both obsessive-compulsive disorder and serotonin and was looking for a physiological model that could permit me to explore this condition in large populations. One day, while talking with my boss, suddenly **I realized that romantic lovers were similar to patients suffering from obsessive-compulsive disorder,** as both were thinking of the same subject over and over again. Therefore, I decided to measure a peripheral marker of serotonin and found that it decreased to the same level in both patients and romantic lovers. I must be truthful: the results came out in 1996, but I waited until 1999 to publish them, as I controlled them several times. However, my doubts were not scientific, because the experiments were correct, but I was aware they could have a great impact by showing, for the first time, that a typical human emotion, that is to say, romantic love, might be underlaid by a biochemical abnormality.

I decided that I was strong enough to cope with the eventual problems raised by my paper and sent it to *Psychological Medicine* that accepted and published it a short time after commending the topic and the findings. As suspected, the media attention on my paper was enormous and I had to participate in different TV programs and interviews all over the world. Generally speaking, the majority of the comments were positive, only a minority argued that I wanted to destroy the poetry of love and reduce it to a molecular game. However, I knew and I know that **love is not 'only' the result of different molecules and biological systems, but it is 'also' as such.** In addition, I am sure that its beauty and wonder are not decreased when you become aware that some biological systems are implicated in its expression. Further, my aim was to demonstrate that the peculiar thinking of obsessive-compulsive patients shares a biochemical abnormality with the way of thinking of romantic lovers, but love, obviously, is much more, and it is not far from the scientific domain to assume that it may depend on one neurotransmitter only.

Journalists

On a personal level, I had to change some aspects of my life. First, I had to meet a lot of journalists and had to speak in front of laypeople, where I had to adapt my language in order to be understood. For this reason, I learned that **sometimes it is important to promote knowledge and increase awareness outside the scientific setting**. As a result, I decided that I could write a book summarizing all the scientific findings on love, a book that did not exist at that time. And I had liked to write since I was a child. Through a series of unexpected and fortunate events, I found a great editor who published my first book entitled *The Nature of Love*, which was also translated into different languages. In the following years, I wrote another one entitled *E vissero per sempre gelosi e contenti* (*And they lived for ever, jealous and happy*), an essay on jealousy.

Neurohormones

Second, on a scientific level, love became my main interest and expanded to the point of including jealousy, attachment and social relationships, as I realized that they are basic mechanisms fundamental for human wellbeing. After serotonin, we measured some neurohormones in romantic lovers and concluded that to fall in love is stressful, as shown by the increased cortisol levels. Interestingly, **testosterone concentrations went in opposite directions in the two sexes**, increased in women and decreased in men, as if women and men have to become more similar in order to meet. These findings are in agreement with the notion that to fall in love is a basic emotion not different in the two sexes. At the same time, I performed some studies in jealous subjects and found a decrease of serotonin in obsessively jealous subjects. In addition, I realized how complex and poorly understood normal jealousy is, which is also quite heterogeneous, as we identified at least five subtypes.

The next research focus was on oxytocin. It took some time to set up a reliable method to measure this neuropeptide, but now we use it every day. The main publication on this topic was one showing that **oxytocin is related to the anxiety linked to romantic attachment**, that is to say oxytocin is necessary in order to be relaxed when attached to the partner. It was then evident that to fall in love, to love and to be attached to somebody is beneficial. In terms of brain functions, some of the benefits of love may be due to the production of neurotrophins, substances that are involved in the survival, differentiation and functioning of neurons. Interestingly, we found that one of these neurotrophins, the so-called brain-derived neurotrophic factor (BDNF) is related to romantic attachment, but differently in the two sexes. In fact, only in women does it seem that high concentrations of BDNF are correlated to low avoidance characteristics. In other words, women became less shy towards the romantic partner and more prone to social relationships in general. In another study of mine, women proved quite sensitive to the effects of male armpit extracts (pheromones?) up to the point of changing their serotonin levels and displaying some impulsivity and attachment features. At the moment, in my laboratory several studies are in progress to explore further biological aspects of love, and the whole group of co-workers shares with me a great and genuine enthusiasm for this topic. I can say that I am in love with love.

Benefits

Third, on a personal level, studying love changed me profoundly. I was forced to revise my personal life and realized that I was very lucky. I had two fantastic parents who brought me up while enhancing my self-esteem and promoting my freedom and my choices. Moreover, my partner loves me as I love him since the beginning of our story a long time ago. As long as I go on exploring love, I am more and more fascinated by it, the more I study it, the more I respect it. I think that **to love and to be loved represents the most extraordinary experience for a human being,** but it requires care, attention, alertness, flexibility, disposition to change. Nature has provided us with the appropriate equipment to develop love and to get all the benefits that it can give us, that is to say, the deepest joy of our existence. And I think that science, while exploring its mystery and one day, perhaps, disentangling its biological mechanisms, might permit us to love in the best way we can.

The keys

→ **A typical human emotion, romantic love, is underlaid by a biochemical abnormality similar to patients suffering from obsessive-compulsive disorder.**

→ **To fall in love is stressful, as shown by the increased cortisol levels. But ultimately our brain functioning shows that to love and to be attached to somebody is beneficial.**

→ **Love is an extraordinary experience but it requires care, attention, alertness, flexibility and disposition to change.**

Donatella Marazziti is Professor of Psychiatry in the Department of Psychiatry, Neurobiology, Pharmacology and Biotechnology at the University of Pisa (Italy), where she graduated in Medicine and Surgery. Again at the University of Pisa, she specialized in Psychiatry and then in Biochemistry. She has won various national and international prizes and is on the editorial board of different specialized magazines. She has written around 350 scientific papers, eight books, two bestsellers and one novel.

Product of the West?

"There have been very few studies of romantic love in non-Western societies to date because anthropologists, psychologists and historians have simply assumed that romantic love is a Euro-American contribution to world culture, transmitted to other parts of the world by European exploration and colonization." Hsu-Ming Teo **says they are wrong.**

From the 1950s to the 1990s, American scholars often argued that love is found only in the United States and in societies whose belief systems derive from the Western European cultural tradition. Many other European scholars were quick to agree that romantic love is a relatively localized phenomenon which originated with the doctrine of courtly love that arose in southern France around the twelfth century. In this, they were following the lead of the French literary critic Denis de Rougemont. In his 1940 landmark work *Love in the Western World*, Rougemont argued that Western culture is distinct from all other cultures because it invented and celebrated romantic love, by which he meant a conception of love which idealizes the beloved and combines ideas of altruism, friendship, eroticism and intense passion. Rougemont maintained that romantic love was later incorporated into, and became a necessary part of, conjugal love. It is this ideal and practice which, many Western scholars in the twentieth

century believed, have become universal today through the global spread of Western culture.

Rougemont relied on French troubadour literature for his thesis, but other historians have rejected this argument, observing that literary and musical

*" In pre-modern Wales a young man expressed
his love for a woman by urinating on her dress."*

evidence is no indication of its widespread acceptance or practice in general society. The French
historian Philippe Ariès, for example, argued in his
work on childhood that there was little evidence of
affection in European families or courting couples
throughout most of European history. English
historians and sociologists concurred, suggesting
that romantic love and affective family ties
appeared only in the eighteenth century, concur-
rent with, and perhaps even indirectly prompting,
the processes of modernization – the agricultural
and industrial revolutions, and the social changes
brought about by these economic shifts.
**Love is made to serve the ends of Western
exceptionalism, and to function as a cultural
marker of 'civilization'.**

Recent efforts by anthropologists to revise this
negative assessment of non-Western love have
been numerous but not particularly varied. All
continue to judge non-Western societies according
to modern Western definitions of romantic love.
Western scholars define romantic love according to
Western cultural norms and expressions, then set
out to find it (or fail to do so) among non-Western
cultures and tribes. But this is problematic because,
even in the West, expressions of love and the rituals
of romance change over time. Red roses and a box
of chocolates may signify romance and love these
days; in pre-modern Wales, however, a young man
expressed his love for a woman by urinating on
her dress in a practice known locally as *rhythu*.

For many scholars, it is useful to recognize that
while feelings of love may be universal, the expressions and rituals of romantic love are culturally
specific and change over time. This acknowledgement breaks out of the cul-de-sac of considering
whether love is universal or Western, and instead
allows scholars to examine historically specific
cultural practices of love.

Hsu-Ming Teo is a cultural historian based
in the Department of Modern History, Macquarie
University, Sydney (Australia). She has recently
edited a book and a special journal issue on
the popular culture of romantic love in Australia.
Her publications include *Cultural History in
Australia* and *Desert Passions: Orientalism
and Romance Novels*. She has written
the award-winning novel *Love and Vertigo*
and is an editorial board member of the *Journal
of Australian Studies* and the *Journal of Popular
Romance Studies*.

"Don't wait for love to fall onto you."

Architects of love & sex

Imagine architects and engineers building houses and bridges based on fairy tales, myths, gossip and stories. Their constructions would be a disaster. Nevertheless, these are still the basics of the most important constructions in our life: love and sex. Prof **Emil Ng Man Lun** has done lifelong research on the architecture of love and has been awarded with the Gold Medal in Sexology from the World Association for Sexual Health. Does he know how we can become better architects of our own love life?

Long-lasting romantic and sexual love is losing its supporters in the modern world, East and West, as reflected by the rapidly rising divorce rates, marital age, rates of brief sexual relationships and the lowering reproductive rates. An important reason for this is the lack of serious, formal and practical education on sex and love. **Sex education in schools is bad enough in many countries, but worse for lessons in love,** because it is more difficult to teach, being thought to distract pupils from their more important training for future careers. Love problems are also not seen as immediately dangerous as sex is, which can cause sexually transmitted diseases, abortion and sex crimes.

Hence, most of the love and sex education people can get is informal. There are the popular media, fairy tales, legends and fictions which propagate lots of myths and misbelief. For example, nearly all fairy tales and love stories with happy endings end with the wedding ceremony or somewhere there, giving the false impression that the couples could "live happily ever after" without much more effort. **Love legends and fictions beautify and glorify everything in love,** including jealousy, hate, possessiveness, suicide, etc., which are in real life very destructive to love relationships.

Misleading messages

The more serious everyday education on love and sex can come from popular philosophy, psychology and spiritual teachings. But they often are just as confusing or misleading. Sam Vaknin, for example, in his book *The Pathology of Love*, labels romantic love and sex as a form of psychosis or addiction. Ayn Rand puts it just as another form of selfishness, "It is one's own personal, selfish happiness that one seeks, earns and derives from love." The Shinju or 'double suicide' teaching of Japan raises it to a level that condones even stalking, violence and suicide. The Christian Bible sanctifies it way above human capacity to "always protect, trust, hope and persevere", irrespective of conditions. The psycho-analyst Erick Fromm, in his very popular book *Art of Loving*, tries to purify love from sex, ascribing the sexual element only a transitional role in the growth process of love to its 'ideal' form, which is simply asexual altruism or love of God. Many other love philosophies elevate love to insurmountable heights of abstraction and complexity, mystify it as some-thing illogical, unpredictable and unmanageable, as Jennifer Smith says in her *Statistical Probability of Love at First Sight*: "**Love is the strangest, most illogical thing in the world.**" The implication is, and many people also believe, that it is better to leave love to chance or fate, or take it just as a gamble or luxury.

To restore hope and confidence in long-term love and sex, all those controversial contra-dictory messages about it must be removed. Yes, long-term love and sex is difficult to achieve, and there is always some room for chance or fate, but what successes are not? A long-term successful career is just as rare and needs the same conditions, but we do not, therefore, create complicated theories to say the wish for it is a psychosis, an illusion, a trivial transitional stage in life and so on. That could only give us reasons not to work for it. Yet, a good long-term love and sex career may be even more important than a good life-long job career, for it is about survival of the species, not about the self.

Five principles

If we admit that romantic love and sex is another career we have to succeed in life, we should apply the same methods and efforts to achieve it, starting with intelligence, hard work, dedication, good emotional and life management skills. Finer details cannot be given here, but five important principles are:

1. **Start preparing for it from the beginning of life.** Start training early for a good personality, because you will need it not only for your future professional career, but also to enter a good love and sex relationship and to maintain it.

2. **Know what you want early.** Make your criteria of a good ideal relationship and partner(s) early and they should be as clear and concrete as possible. Do not follow set models, including those prescribed by tradition or the majority, for everyone's needs and conditions are different. The criteria can be changed at times to adjust to external changes but it should be done infrequently, so that your partner(s) or prospective partner(s) can adjust to your changes also.

3. **Seek and approach your ideal partner(s) actively.** Same as for a good job, go out to find it, don't wait for it to fall onto you. You need to have good observation power, appropriate sensitivity, the skills to make your approach and the wisdom to know when to persist and when to give up – peacefully and elegantly.

4. **Learn from failures.** Few people succeed at their first attempt(s), no matter how well prepared or trained. Heal your wound fast and do not blame only the others. See what you could have done better so that you can have a greater chance of success next time.

5. **Continuous education and evaluation.** As for any long-term jobs nowadays, this is essential for long-term love and sex relationships also. Mind, body and environment change at every stage of one's life and relationship. Intelligent and well-planned adjustments are required to maintain love satisfaction.

Practical education

It may take quite some time for the world to clear up the mists and start this type of practical education on romantic love and sex, but there is a growing trend in China for the popular media to do it already. Television stations in many major cities have put out matchmaking programs in which gentlemen (or ladies) can come in front of the camera to state their criteria of an ideal love partner and meet, on the spot, a dozen or more ladies (or gentlemen) to matchmake and start dating with one if successful. These are long-running programs that have been on for years with high ratings. China, with its pluralistic culture and long history of practical and open-minded philosophy on sex, love and marriage, seems to be taking the lead to come out from those self-made sex-love conundrums and overcome the many serious difficulties that have ensued.

Love letters

Although a harsh critic of
the monogamous marital
system prevalent in our
modern societies and a firm
supporter of a pluralistic
system, Prof Emil Ng Man
Lun has been happily
married with "his one and
only love and sex partner
for over forty years (and our
love is still growing)".
For their fortieth wedding
anniversary, he published his
love letters from Hong Kong
to his wife in Vietnam during
the war in the period 1969-1972.
They could meet in Vietnam for
the first time and for one week
only in 1971. The book has become
popular in China as a live
demonstration and education
material on how love relationships
should be taken care of as one's
life vocation.

We all need serious, formal and practical education on romantic and sexual love.
Most of our education has come from the popular media, fairy tales, legends and fictions, whereby love and sex can be debased as a form of psychosis or possessiveness, over-glorified to condone even destructive behaviors such as stalking, violence and suicides, sanctified way above human capacity, to "always protect, trust, hope and persevere", irrespective of conditions, bleached to become totally asexual, philosophized to insurmountable heights of abstraction and complexity, mystified as illogical, unpredictable and unmanageable, better left to chance or fate, shrugged off as an entertainment or luxury, or taught impractically through slogans and truism. There is a growing trend in China and abroad now not to treat love and sex in any of those distorted ways. It is taken as another lifetime career to work on, with all the care, rationality and skills required to become architects of our own love and sex life.

The keys

→   **A lot of the popular or serious teachings about love that we have been receiving are misleading and destructive.**
→   **A successful love life needs intelligent and practical aim setting, good planning and relentless efforts to make it work and grow. Follow the five principles.**
→   **We all need serious, formal and practical education on romantic and sexual love to become better architects of our own love and sex life.**

Emil Ng Man Lun is Honorary Professor and Associate Director at Hong Kong University Family Institute (China). He completed his initial training in 1977 at the University of London. Since then he has authored or co-authored more than twenty books in Chinese, seven in English and more than one hundred papers on the topic of psychotherapy, love and sex. He is Founder President of the Hong Kong Sex Education Association (1985) and Asian Federation for Sexology (1990) and was President of the 14th World Congress of Sexology (1999). Consultant in various local, international governmental or non-governmental organizations, including the World Health Organization. He received the Sexologist of Asia award from the Asian Federation for Sexology (1994) and the Gold Medal in Sexology from the World Association for Sexual Health (2003).

"A compromise makes a good umbrella, but a poor roof."

The economics of love

What can economists tell us about love? A lot. They study valuable search strategies, the economic effect of marriages, how one plus one can be three and why we exchange expensive wedding rings. "The economics of love does not disenchant the miracle of love", says economist **Hanno Beck**. "If you use it in a clever way, it helps you to make the best out of your love life."

One may say that people choose love and their mates by gut feelings, not by a mathematical calculation. This might be true, but to dismiss the idea of comparing the advantages and disadvantages of love might be premature: after the first storm of emotions is over, one may take a second look at his decision – only fools rush in. And why not improve a decision made in the heat of the moment by (re-)thinking it?

Why (not) marry?

What are the disadvantages of a long-term-relationship? First, a long-term relationship means a loss of freedom: having a relationship means making a compromise, and a compromise is something that no party involved wanted that way. A compromise makes a good umbrella, but a poor roof. There is a second disadvantage of a stable relationship and that is the loss of options. If you are single, you are free to search for a partner, which is not an option if you are married.

On the other hand, there are a lot of advantages from a stable relationship. First, **a couple is able to increase its productivity**: a couple has the possibility to specialize on what each of them is good at. If two partners with different skills match, there is room for specialization. One partner, for example, specializes in housekeeping (because he or she is very good at this task and likes it), the other partner focuses on child-rearing (because he or she is very talented at entertaining children). In this way the output of this cohabitation will be maximized. This idea was first described by the economist David Ricardo who discovered that the division of labor between nations increases overall welfare for all countries involved, and what is true for countries is also true for loving couples. From this point of view, the advantages of a relationship coming from the division of labor depend on the differences between the partners: the larger the differences between them, the greater the yields from the division of labor.

Moreover, there is a second advantage of a stable relationship: intimacy. From an economic point of view, **a relationship is like a company**. It takes inputs (two partners, lots of compromises, one or two grains of love) which you need to produce a certain output. In the case of love, the output is not a well-run household but another unique output: intimacy. This very exclusive output cannot be provided by means of markets: a loving, caring partner, somebody who understands your sorrows and fears, familiarity – something which can only be produced within a stable relationship by means of two people knowing and caring for each other.

Similar or opposite?

From examining those advantages and disadvantages, we can answer one of the most important questions concerning love: should two birds of a feather flock together or do opposites attract? Starting with the idea of opposites that attract, as we found out, the economic advantage of this arrangement comes from the division of labor: the more dissimilar two people are the greater the advantages from the division of labor will be. From this point of view, opposites attract because they are able to reap large benefits from their dissimilarity, i.e. the gains from specialization.

But looking at the second big advantage from a relationship, the production of intimacy, it is perfectly clear that birds of a feather flock together. If two people are very similar in what they feel, think and like, the need for compromises will be much smaller and conflicts of interest will not be as large as in the case of opposite partners. This is an important prerequisite for the production of harmony and intimacy.

Modern times

The answer lies with the progress of modern technology: vacuum cleaners, ready-to-serve-meals, dishwashers – all of those inventions made it much easier for singles to look after their households without any help. As a consequence of this, a typical pattern from ancient times is not valid anymore: the man specializes in earning money, while his wife focuses on the complex task of housekeeping. This ancient pattern of marriage was intended to maximize the benefits from specialization.

Technical progress has made it much easier to run a household. As a consequence, the idea of an arranged marriage loses its attractiveness, the gains from specialization diminish and the advantages from marrying someone with a rather different character decrease. The advantages from the 'opposites attract' idea have vanished.

This leaves us with the 'birds of a feather' approach. **The outputs of a relationship (intimacy, harmony and love) cannot be delivered by technology or the market.** As one no longer needs specialization within a marriage, and harmony and love can still only be delivered by a stable relationship, from an economic point it is clear that the best approach is to go for a bird of the same feather.

A look at history affirms this conclusion: decades ago, the arranged marriage was the common model, nowadays, people choose their mate not by the advantages they can derive from specialization but by their romantic feelings. Nowadays, the question of whom to couple with is not a matter of specialization; it is a matter of romance.

The keys

- → **Disadvantages of a marriage are a loss of freedom and options. Advantages are increased productivity, welfare and a unique output: intimacy.**
- → **With modern technology the advantages from the opposite-attract idea have vanished.**
- → **From an economic point of view it is clear that the best approach in modern times is to go for birds of the same feather.**

Hanno Beck is Professor of Economics at the Pforzheim University of Applied Sciences (Germany). His research areas are the economics of everyday life, behavioral economics, media economics and financial markets. He has published numerous articles on several economic topics and a successful book on the economics of love. His personal love goes to his family and friends, his dog and his guitar.

Happy singles

"I've always loved living single", says Prof Bella DePaulo, "except for all the stereotyping and discrimination (I call that *singlism*) and the over-the-top hyping of marriage, weddings, coupling and romantic love (*matrimania*)." She has made a thorough study of the love and life of singles. And she didn't find misery at all.

Because of the ways in which marriage and romantic love are celebrated in the media and even in some academic writings, I assumed that I was mostly alone in my love of single life. Maybe other people wanted out of single life, but I did not. I'm not single because I haven't found just the right partner or because I have issues. Single life suits me. It is, for me, the most meaningful and productive way to live. I'm single at heart.

Once I began to do research, I was amazed at what I found. The beliefs that single people are miserable, lonely and loveless and want nothing more than to become unsingle are just myths. Those kinds of claims are grossly exaggerated, or just plain wrong. The scientific data do not support them. **One of the reasons that so many single people do so well is that they embrace bold and broad meanings of love**, big enough to encompass so much more than just romantic love. It is not just in their words that single people honor the many important people in their lives. Several surveys have shown that single people are more likely than married people to be there for their siblings, parents, neighbors and friends.

A favorite example in my collection came from the late Ted Sorensen – husband, father and renowned speechwriter for US President John F. Kennedy. When the *New York Times* asked "Was your working relationship with J.F.K. the great love affair of your life?" he replied "Yes, of course." Sorensen was married, but his fervent embrace of work as a source of love and purpose is a lesson to us all, regardless of our relationship status. In fact, it may be single people who most value work that speaks to their soul. A study of high school students found that those who would stay single into their late twenties already valued meaningful work more than those who would end up married. Nearly a decade later, that had not changed.

The title *Liberty, A Better Husband* comes from the diary of Louisa May Alcott. The author was writing about the single woman of antebellum America, who "envisioned her liberty as both autonomy and affiliation… Her freedom enabled her to commit her life and her capacities to the betterment of her sex, her community, or her kin." For generations of women and men devoted to the cause of social justice, **the meanings of love and passion have always transcended diamond rings and red roses.**

Who is the love of your life? Maybe that love is a 'what' rather than a 'who'. Or maybe your love is big enough for more than just one kind of person. If you open yourself to love in its biggest, broadest meanings, you are likely to live your best and most meaningful life.

Bella DePaulo (PhD, Harvard) is a social psychologist and a visiting Professor of Psychology at the University of California (USA). She is the author of more than one hundred scientific publications and has written several books, including *Singled Out: How Singles Are Stereotyped, Stigmatized, and Ignored, and Still Live Happily Ever After*. For years she has been writing the Living Single blog for *Psychology Today*.

" The love of your life may be a 'what' rather than a 'who'."

"In the search for 'perfect' love,
we may end up alone
in what can be a very lonely world."

Private lies

Trust and fidelity are highly valued in relationships, but in most cases, adultery doesn't end in divorce. We learn to deal with it. Prof **Julie Fitness** finds out how: love means having to say you are sorry – and meaning it.

When I began my studies in social psychology in the 1980s, I was struck by how little scientific research had been carried out on what is arguably the most important social context for all human beings: close relationships. Even more surprisingly, there was almost no research on the features and functions of what laypeople would surely argue is the most important feature of close relationships: feelings and emotions. Since that time, there has been a growing recognition amongst psychologists of the ways in which our relationships with other people give life its structure, while emotions like love, hate, jealousy, joy, anger and grief give life its meaning.

Breaking rules

My studies have demonstrated that **infidelity is not the only kind of betrayal that may happen in relationships.** Individuals feel betrayed when their partners break relationship rules, whether through deception, abuse, disloyalty, thoughtlessness or unkindness – any kind of behavior that signals a lack of love and a devaluing of the relationship. We have also demonstrated that any type of betrayal can, ultimately, be forgiven. However, forgiveness is a process that takes time, patience, commitment and a deep understanding of human feelings and frailties.

Loving effort

Of the various factors that appear to help partners find their way through the painful aftermath of betrayal, one of the most important involves the sincere expression of contrition and remorse by the betraying partner, and this goes far beyond verbal apologies. In fact, simply saying 'sorry' is the least costly part of winning forgiveness, and the most easily cheapened with repetition. **What makes the difference is behavior.** Essentially, an individual who seeks forgiveness must actively demonstrate that she loves her partner and that she is willing to work hard to regain his trust and to repair the damage she has done. This may take time, as one elderly respondent explained to me in an interview about how he betrayed his wife some thirty years ago. He noted that it took over two years of patient, loving effort to rebuild her trust in him, and to demonstrate his commitment to her and the relationship. Several comments from divorced respondents who had either not forgiven, or not been forgiven, by their ex-spouses, emphasized the same point; that in the initial aftermath of betrayal, it may feel as though there is no way through the pain, anger, shame and guilt, and the response is to end the relationship. With the benefit of hindsight, however, several of these respondents now believed that they could have worked through the pain and saved a loving relationship that had been important to them (and frequently, their children). They just didn't know how, or whether it was even possible.

Sorry enough

In fact, there is an important factor that can help partners achieve this goal, and it involves what psychologists have called 'emotional intelligence', or the ability to attend to, understand, and manage both one's own and others' feelings and emotions. The particular aspect of emotional intelligence that was most strongly and positively related both to forgiving and to being forgiven in my studies concerned respondents' abilities to accurately recognize, understand and talk about their own and others' emotions. Overall, the results suggested that **emotionally intelligent offenders and forgivers are better equipped** to work their way through the many and varied feelings and emotions that accompany the experience of betrayal, and to find their way back together again. For example, more emotionally intelligent offenders correctly perceived their partners as being deeply hurt and angry, and in need of acknowledgement, remorse, and compensation for the offence. Less emotionally knowledgeable offenders, on the other hand, appeared to focus on their own shame and to perceive their partners' emotions as hateful; consequently, they acted destructively and aggravated the offence. Further, more emotionally intelligent victims seemed better able to judge when their partners were 'sorry enough' and had earned renewed trust and forgiveness. Less emotionally intelligent victims assumed the worst about their partners' motivations and felt overwhelmed by feelings of distress that they assumed would last forever.

Adultery

About 10 % of married people in America (12 % of men and 7 % of women) say they have had **sex outside** their marriage during the past year. This number hasn't changed very much over the past forty years. But recent figures show an increase in older (60+) and younger (-35) couples.

Signal of care

In summary, I have learned from my research that maintaining loving relationships is difficult when bad things happen, but that the price of giving up can be very high. Ironically, in the search for 'perfect' love, we may end up alone in what can be a very lonely world. Realizing that we are imperfect, that we and our loved ones make mistakes, and that the strength of our emotions is actually a signal of how much we care, is the first step to forgiveness and relationship repair. It is also important to know that **the ability to better understand feelings and emotions can be learned**, and that the rewards of such emotion understanding include a deeper capacity for empathy and compassion, both for oneself and for one's loved ones.

The keys

→ **Forgiveness is a process that takes time, patience, commitment, and a deep understanding of human feelings.**

→ **Simply saying 'sorry' is the least costly part of winning forgiveness, and the most easily cheapened with repetition. What makes the difference is behavior.**

→ **Realizing that we are imperfect, and that the strength of our emotions is actually a signal of how much we care, is the first step to relationship repair.**

Julie Fitness (PhD, University of Canterbury, 1991) is Professor of Psychology at Macquarie University in Sydney, Australia. Her research interests include emotions, betrayal, revenge and forgiveness. She has also published on topics such as the emotionally intelligent marriage and the causes and consequences of familial rejection. She is Editor of the journal *Personal Relationships*.

"Hell is the realization of the incapability to love."

The five facets of love

"Love is a feeling so complete that to divide it into components would seem to be blasphemy", says Prof **Mikhail Epstein**, one of the great critical thinkers of the century. "The mission of love is to unite two beings into one whole. But precisely for this reason it is so important to understand what love consists of, not to take it merely for one of its constituents."

A little boy was telling his mommy he loves her *at all*. She corrected him: not at all, but very much. Again, he said: no, *at all*. I love my toy horse and toy car very much, but I love you *at all*. That is where she understood that he loves all of her. He loves all of what she is. This can be considered the most important quality of love. We can single out five most distinctive components of love: desire, inspiration, pain, tenderness and compassion.

1. Desire. This is the most obvious, physiologically motivated and most bespoken side of love. Desire in love, however, is different from other kinds of physical desire because of the impossibility of its complete gratification: its object is infinite. Moreover, desire does not want to be satisfied, it craves its own continuation and growth. Love is a cultivation of desires rather than fulfilment.

Another peculiarity of loving desire is its dialogical openness to the other's desires, as distinct from lust which is directed at the other as an object. True desire cannot be satisfied merely physically because it depends on the will of another person and interacts with others' wishes and reluctances, converses with their 'yes', 'maybe' and 'no'. **I desire someone else's desire, which desires me.** This is the *golden rule* in erotic desire, which excludes violence and coincides with the golden rule in ethics: "One should treat others as one would like others to treat oneself."

2. Inspiration. If desire is the joyous and torturing dependence on another person, then inspiration is a freedom from one's own identity, freedom to become someone we have never been before. For many, if not for the majority of people, love is the only experience of inspiration in all their life. Even if a human being is a 'worm on earth' and not a 'son of heaven', nobody can take this sense of flight and lightness away from a person in love. No poet or artist can rival the lover in this soaring inspiration. Love can only happen between creative personalities, not because they compose poetry or music together, but because they create each other in the process of love itself.

3. Pain. The strength of love is its ability to gain or lose *everything*: the bet on infinity. Therefore, suffering is inherent in love and occasionally even becomes the synonym of love: "he is suffering because of her", he is in pain, agonized without her. Why does the experience of love, even a happy one, always bring the feeling or at least the anticipation of pain? And why does this agonizing feeling aroused by another person often indicate a symptom of emerging love for this person?

One becomes fully dependent on the person he loves, which immediately makes him a captive or hostage. Imagine that a person's heart is situated outside of the body, hanging on a thin string of blood vessels. This makes an organism extremely fragile and vulnerable, subject to the whims and fancies of its external heart. Love does not come without pain, and to relieve this pain there are two choices: to become numb, less sensitive and loving, or become more loving, to spill blood and to imbue the outer heart with this blood and thus to assimilate it.

4. Tenderness. Of all five facets of love, this is the most difficult to describe. Tenderness is self-giving, it bestows on the beloved everything that has been insatiably appropriated by desire and inspiration, while protecting every step she takes, taking care to spare her any pain or trouble. Tenderness is an attempt to shield the loved one from the gusts and blows of hostile environments and, even more importantly, from the crude and rapacious approaches of the lover himself.

5. Compassion. The subject of compassion is the weakness of the beloved, his short-comings, suffering, ignorance, ineptitude, inability. It is dangerous to confuse compassion with love, but it is even more dangerous to exclude the feeling of compassion from love. Love without compassion can be passionate, inspirational, tender, romantic, but it is missing the sense of the lover's weakness, which it can infuse with its strength.

Some say that weakness is more lovable than strength and that we become more deeply attached to weak individuals because the main capacity of love is to give to the loved one everything we possess. This does not imply, however, that love is aroused by weakness; the essence is that love can perceive weakness even in strength and when infatuated with it, one starts to feel compassion for it.

After falling in love with a strong, good-looking, intelligent, lucky person we start to sense his vulnerability of which he can appear unaware, or that he hides from himself. If this suppressed weeping about the mortality of the loved one, the inevitability of a separation from him is absent from our embraces and kisses, then this means that our love has an undeveloped taste. It is unsalted, not imbued by blood and sweat, which mortal creatures share while clinging closer to each other.

Union

It is impossible to say which one of these five components is more important. It is impossible to predict which of them will trigger falling in love. It is probable that men more frequently enter love with desire and women with compassion. Some individuals are guided by inspiration and others by tenderness. No matter which facet leads to love, it can only become love by uniting desire, inspiration, pain, tenderness and compassion. I define my personal life credo in a banal and arithmetic manner: **"All that contributes to the growth of love is good, all that leads to its destruction is bad."**

As the years pass, less time is left to waste on anything else that is not love. Quarrels, reproaches, arguments, discussions... It is a matter of being on time to love, embrace, snuggle closer and spread warmth... And hurry, desperately hurry with this love before the source of it extinguishes in you, before you have lost the means to embody it. According to Dostoyevsky, hell is the realization of the incapability to love.

The keys

→ **The five most important components of love are desire, inspiration, pain, tenderness and compassion.**

→ **Don't take love for one of its parts. Love only becomes love by uniting these five facets in one complete feeling.**

→ **All that contributes to the growth of love is good, all that leads to its destruction is bad.**

Mikhail Epstein is Professor of Cultural Theory and Russian Literature at Emory University (Atlanta, USA) and Professor of Russian and Cultural Theory at Durham University (Durham, UK). Born in Moscow, he moved to the USA in 1990 and joined Emory faculty in 1991. He is especially interested in the practical extensions and applications of the humanities and their creative contributions into the areas of their study as programmatically advanced in his latest book *The Transformative Humanities: A Manifesto*. He is the author of 29 books and more than 600 articles and essays, many of which have been translated into 17 languages. Mikhail Epstein has won national and international prizes, including the Liberty Prize, awarded for his outstanding contribution in the development of Russian-American cultural connections.

Body to body

" We express love and communion by connecting our bodies."

Love seems to come in many forms and is expressed in many different ways according to whom we love: romantic partners and spouses, children, parents and siblings, friends, colleagues, teammates, total strangers, one's country or even humanity. It can be intense or fleeting and diffuse. But why do we call them all 'love'? Dr Rodrigo Brito researches what they all have in common: our body.

Love is the general name people give to feelings that drive them to form and to maintain intimate bonds of whatever kind. People experience this feeling as a desire (or satisfaction) to transcend their own individual selves and to merge or fuse into a 'communion' with those whom they love (also called attachment, bonding, or communal sharing). This communion may be idealized, but in their daily interactions, people express it by either connecting their bodies – directly or indirectly, in a great variety of ways – or by using metaphors based on physical connections. So what are these varied forms of physical connection?

1. First, there is direct physical connection. The mother-child bond is probably the strongest one in humans and many other mammals: mothers are physically connected to their children even before they are born; they then breastfeed, kiss, and cuddle them. Romantic partners feel they 'melt' their bodies into one another during love-making, 'becoming one'. Kissing, cuddling, hugging and touching are used to express love (or at least some form of affection) and to establish some level of communion in many relations with romantic partners, friends, neighbors, colleagues and even strangers. And 'blood-brotherhood' in many societies throughout history is an unbreakable bond, established through the mixing of bodily substance.

2. Next, there are a number of indirect forms of physical connection that also produce the feeling of being bonded to others, which is, at the very least, associated to a diffuse feeling of love. One is through **sharing food and drink**. To prepare food for others and eat it with them, to share food from the same recipient, to drink together, these are recognized worldwide as acts that bond people together in communion. Similar sharing may occur with smoking, including peace-pipes and joints.

3. Another form is through **closely synchronized movements**, such as in rhythmic dancing and military drill, which produce the feeling in participants that their bodies are part of a single, larger body, containing all of them together. An intriguing experimental finding in psychology is that mere physical warmth (of air temperature) makes us feel more socially connected to someone in the same room with us, which suggests that we use any sign of physical proximity (such as warmth) as a sign of social connection.

Trust and affection

In most of these forms of physical connection, and foremost in mother-child relations and close physical bonding of all sorts, including sex, a cocktail of hormones (most famously oxytocin) is a mediator with multiple roles, producing pleasure, enhancing trust and affection and helping to 'fix' the mental representation of close relationships in the brain.

Naturally, cultural rules define with whom, when and how we are allowed to touch, cuddle, kiss, have sex (romantic or otherwise), breastfeed, share food, drink, or smoke, dance or otherwise synchronize movements, or any other form of direct or indirect physical connection. **We would not wish to love everyone and anyone the same way and with the same intensity.** Indeed, across cultures, people tend to feel more love and communion with their family in general than with other people, and family tends to claim priority or even exclusivity over other relations. Likewise, romantic partners and spouses in many cultures are given exclusive rights to sexual love. But, given the availability of so many different ways of expressing love and being bonded with others, with different degrees of intensity, it is relatively easy to express more love by sharing it around in diffuse forms, without compromising the limits established by one's culture. So: connect your bodies. Don't be afraid to touch, kiss, and cuddle (within the limits of what is appropriate in your culture). Share the love around. Cook for your family and friends, eat and drink with them; feel the taste of connection. And celebrate your connections by dancing in synchrony or close coordination to whatever style of music appeals to you.

Rodrigo Brito is a lecturer in Psychology at the Lusophone University, Lisbon (Portugal). He obtained his PhD from the Free University of Brussels (Belgium) and has lived, studied and worked in half a dozen different countries, learning others' cultural ways of expressing love and affection. Together with colleagues in social and experimental psychology from around the world, he tests hypotheses derived from anthropological ideas about the universal structures of social relations, focusing in particular on communion and bonding.

Confucian love

Confucius lived in the sixth century BC. "But his ideas are still pretty much the mind-set of almost all East Asian people", says Dr Yong Huang. He is an expert in the concept of Confucian love: love with distinction.

Confucianism maintains that we should start with family love and then expand it to others, but this is not unique about the Confucian conception of love, as many other philosophical traditions would also agree on it. Rather, what is unique about Confucianism is its conception of love with distinction. This is often understood to mean that our love should be strongest towards our family members and should gradually decrease when expanded to others. Its true spirit, however, is that there should be different kinds of love for different kinds of moral patients, since our love, to be appropriate, has to take into consideration the uniqueness of each of the objects of our love. We can see this most clearly in Mencius' (the most famous Confucian after Confucius himself) distinction among three kinds of love: "a superior person loves things but is not humane to them. He is humane to people in general but is not affectionate to them. He is affectionate to his parents, humane to people, and loves all things." Here, love, being humane and affection are not three different degrees of the same love, but three different kinds of love, appropriate to three different kinds of moral patients: things, humans, and parents.

Hate

Although Confucius himself did not use the term 'love with distinction', it is clear that for him our love of different objects of love should be different, each appropriate to its unique object. For example, Confucius claimed that "only a humane person knows how to love people and hate people". In other words, from the Confucian point of view, 'hate', just like 'love', is a kind of love in a more general sense. On the one hand, the most fundamental meaning of humaneness is to love, and so the humane person who knows how to love and hate is a loving person; on the other hand, 'hate' here does not have any connotation of ill will. It is rather one's profound feeling of regret that one's beloved moral patient lacks what he or she should have and one's strong desire to help that person become a good person.

Internal

There is, related to this, another unique feature of Confucian love: to love a person is not merely to be concerned about the person's external well-being. As a matter of fact, it is more important to take care of the person's internal well-being. Thus, when a person is not virtuous, a truly loving person ought to do all that is possible to help the person to become virtuous. Confucius has a famous saying, which is often regarded as a version of the Golden Rule: "One who wants to establish oneself shall establish others; and **one who wants to prosper oneself shall help others prosper**." However, there is something unique here. The Golden Rule, as commonly understood in the Western tradition, requires us to do unto others what we would like to be done unto; however, it does not require us, desiring to follow the Golden Rule, to make others also follow the Golden Rule. For example, it does not require us, desiring to help others in need, to make others help (their) others in need. In contrast, Confucius made it clear that if we want to be upright in character, fond of rightness,

sensitive to what other people say, observant of other people's facial expression and mindful of being modest, then we ought to help others be upright in character, fond of rightness, sensitive to what other people say, observant of other people's facial expression and mindful of being modest. In short, if we want to be superior persons, we ought to help others become superior persons; and if we don't want to be inferior persons, we ought to help others to not become inferior persons. In Confucius' view, this is the true meaning of love.

Yong Huang is Professor of Philosophy at Kutztown University of Pennsylvania (USA). He is the author of five books and over a hundred journal articles and book chapters. He is editor-in-chief of *Dao: A Journal of Comparative Philosophy* and *Dao Companions to Chinese Philosophy*.

" *Love and affection are different kinds of love.* "

*"Our genes did not program us
to remain in love."*

The pyramid of love

"Human love relationships are probably the most complex things in the known universe", says Dr **Robert M. Gordon**. He reviewed the existing theories and research. For him, no one theory explained it all. This led him to develop his own integrated meta-theory to help understand romantic love and why it is so difficult: the pyramid of love.

What we call 'love' is the result of several conflicting irrational forces. In relatively healthy people, the conflicts are minimal and are resolved with insight and healthy values. In more disturbed individuals, love relations are highly conflictual and regressive and often characterized by egocentricity, hostility and defensiveness.

Five levels

There are five main factors in human love relationships: species traits, individual traits, relational internalizations, beliefs and current context. This theoretical model explains why love can be so irrational. Love relations are primarily based in primitive instincts. They are subject to problems of temperament and problems from poor parenting. They are subject to cultural biases and expectations and to situational stresses. Love is attacked from all angles. Visualize these five factors as a pyramid, moving from our common human biological instincts to our current psychological issues.

1. **At the base of the pyramid is the most powerful influence on our behaviors, our species traits**, which we possess as a result of millions of years of natural selection. They define how we love as a human species (as compared to other animals). What we, as humans, find attractive in a mate are physical features and emotional triggers that used to be associated with survival, protection and reproductive ability. They helped the species survive for millions of years, but have little to do with the survival of a couple's love today. A woman may be attracted to a powerful man or a man may be attracted to a beautiful woman, but these qualities have nothing to do with the ability to maintain a loving relationship.

2. **The next level is individual traits.** We are all born with different temperaments or traits. Researchers have consistently found, for example, that extraversion, neuroticism, aggressiveness and impulsivity are largely inherited traits. People who are too aggressive or impulsive will have intimacy problems.

3. **Next is the influence of our parents, our earliest attachments and family dynamics.** These relational internalizations become part of a person's unconscious personality. An infant's attachment style is likely to be unconsciously repeated in later love relations. A secure attachment to a sufficiently mothering figure and parents who help a child deal with aggression and sexuality, and provide a healthy self-concept are just some of the interpersonal prerequisites to loving maturely. Childhood neglect and abuse does damage to personality and the capacity to trust. A person who is naturally resilient may later learn to love maturely with psychotherapy, despite an unhappy childhood.

4. **The next level is our learned beliefs from cultural norms and personal romantic experiences.** After we look at ourselves as human animals, then as individuals with innate personality traits and then as influenced by parenting, we now look at the period from later childhood into adulthood and the influence of cognitive learning. People often think that marrying someone who fits an ideal family or cultural stereotype, or someone the opposite of a toxic parent or last lover, is the solution to their mistakes in romantic choices. These beliefs are often superstitious and biased. A relationship is more likely to be successful if the couple shares beliefs that promote altruism, honesty, fairness and mutual concern.

5. **The final level is the current psychological context.** The time in a person's life or current emotional circumstances can produce conditions for an over-idealization of another. A situation in a person's life can create a need for a certain kind of relationship. Later, when the condition changes, the romance fades. Love based on a true appreciation of the other's qualities is more likely to last.

CURRENT ENVIRONMENT   PSYCHOLOGY

CONTEXT

BELIEFS

RELATIONAL
INTERNALIZATIONS

INDIVIDUAL TRAITS

SPECIES TRAITS

GENETIC HISTORY   BIOLOGY

THE 5 LEVELS	UNHEALTHY LOVE	HEALTHY LOVE
CURRENT CONTEXT	Attraction is based on current fears and insecurities	Attraction is based on appreciation of the good qualities of the other
BELIEFS	Superstitious, irrational, unfair beliefs and concrete, selfish values	Strong sense of fairness and altruistic values
RELATIONAL INTERNALIZATIONS	Attachment traumas, toxic internalizations of parenting figures cause fears, distortions and provocations in intimacies	Secure attachment in infancy and a good enough childhood allows for a healthy capacity for sustained love
INDIVIDUAL TRAITS	Too much aggression, irrationality, egocentricity, unreliability and defensiveness	A healthy personality has the ability for sustained passion, concern and commitment
SPECIES TRAITS	Attraction is primarily based on primitive triggers	Attraction is not primarily based on primitive triggers

As you move up the pyramid, you are moving from evolutionary history to current psychological context. All these combined levels contribute to the irrationality of romantic love. Reliance on instinctual triggers, immature personality traits, toxic internalizations and attachment traumas, irrational beliefs about love objects and a stressful current context that distorts the value of another are all factors that disturb relationships.

Personal growth

Falling in love is instinctual. It is an over-idealization of another which serves to induce reproduction for the survival of the species. We are genetically programmed to have a sex drive and to find a desirable mate. However, our genes did not program us to remain in love. For that, we need concern and tenderness. Concern and tenderness are dependent on a person's emotional maturity, which results from a normal temperament and having had adequate parenting. Typically, after a period of idealization of the beloved, tensions in the relationship mount. We regress in intimacy. Old hurts and emotions emerge. If emotional maturity does not take over what passion started, the relationship will wither in time.

Love relations are an opportunity to unconsciously repeat the past or grow from it. We can all learn to love better with personal growth. Personal growth takes time and hard work. We earn it with commitment, openness to constructive feedback, emotional insight into our own flaws, a capacity for concern and remorse, a sense of responsibility for our actions and situation in life, and a willingness to be a better person.

The keys

→ **There are five main factors in human love relationships: species traits, individual traits, relational internalizations, beliefs and current context.**

→ **As you move up the pyramid, you are moving from evolutionary history to current psychological context. All these combined levels contribute to the irrationality of romantic love.**

→ **To remain in love we need concern and tenderness. We can all learn to love better with personal growth. That takes time and hard work.**

Robert M. Gordon is a Diplomate of Clinical Psychology and a Diplomate of Psychoanalysis in Psychology in the USA. He is a Fellow of the American Psychological Association, and served on its governing council for many years. He was President of the Pennsylvania Psychological Association and received its Distinguished Service Award. As a scientist-practitioner, he has authored many scholarly articles and books in the areas of psychotherapy, love relationships, forensic psychology, ethics and assessment. His work on love relations is further developed in his books, *I Love You Madly* and *An Expert Look at Love, Intimacy and Personal Growth*. When not practicing psychology, Robert Gordon loves sailboats, fly-fishing and his motorcycle.

Compassionate love

Recently, research has focused on a type of love that can be experienced not only by romantic partners, but also other close others (e.g. family and friends) and even for strangers or all of humanity. Susan Sprecher and Beverley Fehr **research the benefits of compassionate love.**

Social scientists have identified and studied many types of love, even if the lion's share of scholarship has focused on romantic/passionate love and companionate/friendship love. Compassionate love has been defined as an attitude toward someone, containing feelings, cognitions and behaviors that are focused on caring, concern, tenderness and an orientation toward supporting, helping and understanding the other. Compassionate love shares features with related constructs including empathy, agapic love and compassionate goals. **This type of love may be unique in terms of the far-ranging benefits** that can accrue from both giving and receiving it, and because it can be experienced for a range of targets, including the self.

Strangers

We recently created a scale that measures compassionate love. The Compassionate Love Scale (CLS) can be used, in alternative versions, to assess compassionate love for diverse targets. Example items in the version focused on strangers/humanity include "I spend a lot of time concerned about the well-being of humankind"; "It's easy for me to feel the pain (and joy) experienced by others, even though I don't know them" and "I feel considerable compassionate love for people from everywhere". The other versions have similar items except that the focus is on a specific close other (e.g. "When I see X feeling sad, I feel a need to reach out to him or her") or close others in general (e.g. "I often have tender feelings toward friends and family members when they seem to be in need"). Evidence has been found for the reliability and validity of the scale in its various forms.

In our research with the Compassionate Love Scale, we have found that people who score high on compassionate love for strangers/humanity also score high on self-report measures that assess empathy, helping behaviors directed to others, volunteer behaviors and spirituality/religiosity. Compassionate love for close others is further associated with the provision of social support. Not surprisingly, people report feeling more compassionate love for close others than for strangers or all of humanity; highest scores are found when completing the scale for a romantic partner. The experience of **compassionate love is positively associated with satisfaction and commitment** in romantic relationships, as well as with other types of love experienced for one's partner. We also have found that those who are high in compassionate love use more compassionate breakup strategies when a relationship ends.

"Central features are caring, trust, helping and understanding."

Direct investment

In additional research, we have examined how laypeople (not experts) conceptualize compassionate love. In our research, participants were asked to list features of compassionate love. Other participants were asked to rate how central each feature was to compassionate love. Features that were listed as central to compassionate love were caring, trust, helping and understanding.
Given the many benefits of both giving and receiving compassionate love, it would seem important to **develop interventions to increase this type of love** – both for close others and for non-close others and indeed humanity in general. Research has begun on intervention strategies, conducted by a variety of scholars. For example, in tightly controlled laboratory experiments, priming attachment security through a variety of ways (e.g. recalling personal memories, seeing a picture of a supportive interaction) can lead to greater pro-social emotions (empathy, compassion) for another in need. Security priming has also been found to reduce prejudice toward disliked groups. In field research conducted at Santa Clara University, it has been found that humanitarian immersion trips can lead to increases in compassionate love for others. In research conducted in medical settings, meditation has been found to increase compassionate love for others.

In sum, we encourage people to increase this type of love and to experience it for many others. Efforts to increase the experience of compassionate love reflect a direct investment in the personal and social well-being of humankind.

Susan Sprecher is a Distinguished Professor in the Department of Sociology and Anthropology at Illinois State University (USA), with a joint appointment in Psychology. Her research, which has spanned over thirty years, has focused on a number of issues concerning close relationships and sexuality, including most recently on compassionate love. She was Editor of the journal *Personal Relationships* and has coedited several books or handbooks, including *The Encyclopedia of Human Relationships*.
Beverley Fehr is Professor at the Department of Psychology, University of Winnipeg (Canada). She is Past President of the International Association for Relationship Research and has served as Associate Editor of the *Journal of Personality and Social Psychology*. Her recent work includes the edited book *The Science of Compassionate Love: Theory, Research and Applications*.

"In only 5 % of mammalian species we see something like pair-bonding."

Darwin's bedroom

Charles Darwin's book *On the origin of species* (1859) has fundamentally changed life sciences, explaining the diversity of life by common ancestry and processes like natural selection and reproductive success. What's the influence of his theory on our concept of love? Dr **Peter B. Gray** looks at love from a Darwinian perspective.

In a longer contemplation of the pros and cons of marriage, Charles Darwin commented in his journal: "Only picture to yourself a nice soft wife on a sofa with good fire and books and music perhaps." While that imagination may not stew many fires of romantic passion, we can surmise from biographies and further self-reflections of his that Darwin deeply loved the woman who would ultimately become his wife, Emma, and their ten children, also suffering great sorrow upon the death of his beloved daughter Annie when she was ten.

Bonobos

Love serves the ultimate of evolutionary ends: reproductive success. For humans, this means that love can stoke the basis of deep, long-lived friendships, a couple's romantic passion, a mother's care for her children and a father's desire to sacrifice for his kids. Love acts as an emotional glue to tie people together in the relationships that can enhance an individual's social status (as friendships often do, whether during adolescence or in an adult work place), formation of a long-term socio-sexual bond (the typical context in which humans typically reproduce) and in the devotion of a parent to her or his children (perhaps the greatest of human sacrifices of self and effort to aid another being).

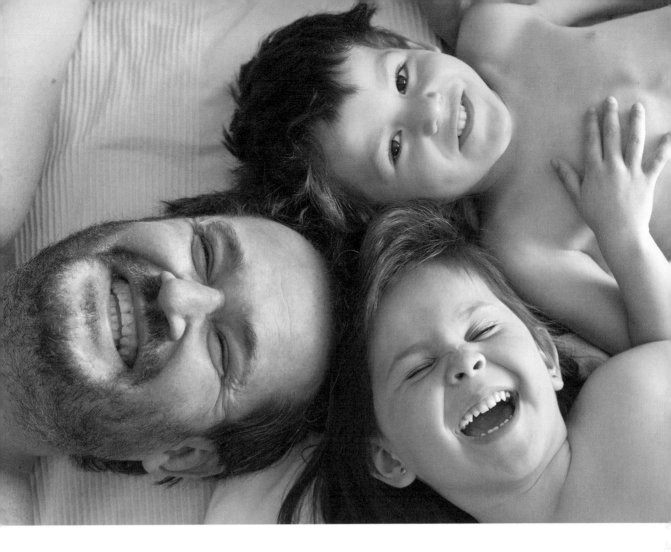

Evolutionary tinkering with highly conserved, and yet modifiable, physiology is the way by which evolution employs love to enhance reproductive success. Our physiology is very similar to that of other creatures on evolution's green Earth: **we are nearly genetically and physiologically identical with our closest living relatives, chimpanzees and bonobos, and yet we appear to love in both similar and different ways.** For a mammal, the physiology of love most readily begins with mother-offspring attachment, including the roles of hormones oxytocin and prolactin, and neurochemicals such as dopamine and endorphins. These systems operate in all kinds of pleiotropic (having multiple effects) ways, with oxytocin facilitating uterine contractions at birth, milk ejection during lactation and emotional positivity and calm, all effects that reinforce the same outcome of a mother's acts enhancing the survival prospects of her young. For dopamine, its effects range widely too, many having more straightforward survival (e.g. in feeding) effects, but also helping emotionally orient an individual toward rewarding behaviors of tending to one's romantic partner or dependents.

Testosterone

The physiology of pair-bonding and paternal care likely piggy-backed onto that regulating maternal care, though also with some male-specific modifications. After all, for mammals, maternal care is species-given, whereas pair-bonding and paternal care are relatively uncommon, occurring in around 5 % of mammalian species. These pair-bonding and paternal minorities in the mammalian class include us humans, though not our closest living ape relatives, an indication that **these relationships arose recently**, likely within the past 2 million years among our African ancestors. The contemporary variation in human male social behaviors (e.g. male-male competition and alliance formation, courtship, formation of long-term pair bonds, providing parental care) map on to variation in male testosterone levels, with family men having lower testosterone levels than their single, childless counterparts. This is one illustration of the physiological attunement of human males to these evolutionarily-derived relationships. The specifics of how our plastic physiology articulates with socio-ecological features of our worlds (e.g. whether polygyny is allowed, where pair-bonding relationships are more fluid, where parents may not have the emotional or material resources to provide for their children) vary around the world and across the life course, although the scope of that variation fundamentally has a human-specific and evolved stamp upon it. As the British singer David Gray put it, in his song "Shine", about love lost: "It don't come down to nothing except love in the end". That end, as Darwin has helped us understand, is reproductive success.

The keys

→ **Love serves the ultimate of evolution ends: reproductive success.**

→ **Love acts as an emotional glue to tie people together, helping to orient individuals toward rewarding behaviors of tending to one's romantic partner or dependents.**

→ **Pair-bonding and paternal care is relatively uncommon. They likely piggy-backed onto maternal care with some male-specific modifications.**

Peter B. Gray is Associate Professor of Anthropology at the University of Nevada, Las Vegas (USA). He received his PhD in Biological Anthropology at Harvard University. He has co-edited one book (*Endocrinology of Social Relationships*) and co-authored two others (*Fatherhood: Evolution and Human Paternal Behavior* and *Evolution and Human Sexual Behavior*). His research focuses on the evolution and endocrinology of human sex differences, sexuality, and parenting.

"We can leave the mono-plane or rollercoaster for a sturdy boat built for two."

The roller coaster of love

What makes a stable, plain-sailing romantic relationship? Why does one friend experience tumultuous dramas with each new partner, when another can't open up enough to get beyond a second date? Dr **Erica Hepper** examines the rollercoaster of love and finds out what the role of our personal attachment style is.

Life would be dull if everyone were the same, but it can be hard work understanding the different ways that people approach and experience love. My research explores one reason why these individual differences might be so ingrained: because a person's sense of who they are (their identity) and how positively they feel about themselves (their self-esteem) is wrapped up in their relationships.

Psychologists call the ways that different people approach close relationships our 'attachment style'. Our different relationship experiences while growing up (e.g. with parents) are thought to influence our attachment style as well as our identity. So, knowing a person's attachment style tells us something about how their identity and self-esteem depends on their adult relationships. Whereas some people feel good about themselves no matter what their partner does, others feel like they are riding a rollercoaster, with every compliment flinging them sky-high and every criticism crushing them to rock-bottom. Knowing your *own* attachment style may be helpful for understanding why you sometimes do certain things, and for overriding those instincts when they could cause arguments.

Your attachment style is made up of levels on two dimensions: avoidance of intimacy and anxiety about abandonment. **Avoidance and anxiety are two types of insecurity**, and having low levels of both is known as being secure. People can be high, low, or anywhere in between on avoidance and anxiety (just like height). Let me explain what it's like to have high or low levels of each attachment dimension, and what my research suggests it means for your self-esteem.

A sturdy boat

Secure attachment is feeling comfortable with getting close to a partner and having them depend on you, and being confident in coping with life, but also seeking support when you need it. People with secure attachment styles tend to have had more consistently positive past relationships. This taught them that they are worthwhile and deserve love, and that it's possible to take on challenges successfully. So, **people who are relatively secure tend to have high self-esteem**, which generally stays around the same level and recovers quickly from experiencing failure or criticism. Secure people's self-esteem is like sailing on a sturdy boat: the ride is pretty calm, but even when the waves come, the boat is strong enough to cope.

Solo in a mono-plane

High avoidance is feeling uncomfortable with closeness: you tend to avoid opening up or getting close to people, and don't trust or depend on anyone but yourself. People with higher avoidance often had less warm or affectionate past relationships; this taught them that to be worthwhile and avoid rejection, they must hide emotions, keep their distance, and tackle the world alone. Crucially, this means that highly avoidant people's self-esteem becomes dependent on proving their independence and success. Because of this, **people with high avoidance may be ambitious and put work before relationships**. Their self-esteem may go up if they succeed in work, sports, or personal goals, but is not affected by other people. Avoidant self-esteem is like flying solo in a mono-plane: it is separated from others and has to work hard to stay airborne.

Flying solo has its downsides, and relationships involving highly avoidant people are often not very satisfying. It can take time to break down these emotional barriers, especially because avoidant self-esteem depends on being independent, and so distance feels rewarding, whereas closeness feels threatening. If you or your partner is high in avoidance, understand that it's a protective strategy, and be patient. People usually become less avoidant over time in a relationship. Encourage this process by trying to respond positively when an avoidant partner opens up or shows emotion, and not pushing them too far.

Peaks and troughs

High attachment anxiety is feeling constantly worried that others will abandon you – you tend to doubt your own worth, need reassurance and want to be too close to others. People with higher anxiety often had inconsistent or overprotective past relationships; this taught them that their own needs are unimportant, they are unworthy of consistent love and they can't cope without others' protection. Crucially, this means that **highly anxious people's self-esteem is pretty low and depends on receiving others' love and approval.** Their self-esteem goes up hugely when they notice any signs of love, such as a compliment or hug, but soon crashes down when those signs wane or they notice any hints of rejection. Highly anxious self-esteem is like the aforementioned rollercoaster: constant peaks and troughs.

Not surprisingly, rollercoaster self-esteem makes for rollercoaster relationships: highly anxious people tend to be clingy, possessive and jealous, have more arguments, and often break up and then get back together with the same partner. Again, it takes time for these patterns to calm down as a relationship progresses. Encourage this process by reassuring an anxious partner and not playing 'hard-to-get'. The good news is that people usually become less attachment-anxious with age.

Secure relationships

Naturally, most people will find their experiences less extreme than these examples, or may relate to more than one attachment style – it's possible to have high avoidance *and* anxiety. But understanding where these reactions come from in their extreme may help us to recognize tendencies in ourselves and our partners – and to be kind to ourselves and each other when experiencing them. Arguments or stress often make people revert to their 'default' attachment style, even in a very secure relationship. If you feel an automatic avoidant or anxious response in yourself, take a breath and remind yourself that you don't have to listen to that insecure instinct. The best way to increase a partner's attachment security (and decrease their avoidance or anxiety) is to be a secure partner and provide consistent love and support. Over time, partners can help each other move towards attachment security and stable self-esteem, leaving the avoidant mono-plane or anxious rollercoaster in favor of a sturdy boat built for two.

The keys

→ **Your attachment style is made up of levels on two dimensions: avoidance of intimacy and anxiety about abandonment.**

→ **Knowing a person's attachment style tells us something about how their identity and self-esteem depends on their relationships.**

→ **Partners can help each other. The best way to increase a partner's attachment security is to be a secure partner and provide consistent love and support.**

Erica Hepper, PhD, is a social/personality psychologist at the University of Surrey (UK). She is a member of the International Advisory Board on Attachment and Human Development. Examining relationships has been something of a personal mission for her and, as a highly avoidant person who married a highly avoidant partner, understanding the effects that attachment styles have on close relationships and identity has been both enlightening and personally helpful.

Giver's glow

"I first heard of something like 'helper therapy' from my Irish mother. On my boring 'off days' as a child, Molly Magee Post told me, 'Stevie, why don't you just go out and do something for someone?'" says **Dr Stephen G. Post**. **He is studying the relationship between love and giving.**

No, she did not say, "Stevie, go read a book", or "Stevie, go clean up your room". I read a lot anyway, and kept an orderly room. Heading across the street I would give old Mr. Muller a hand raking leaves, or help Mr. Lawrence fix his mast. It always felt pretty good. Such simple actions, but they bring together spiritual, moral and health psychology in a common chorus, and it may be one of the few things that constitutes universal truth.

In a community, volunteering is a good way to recreate social networks. People who volunteer tend to report better health, greater happiness, lower anxiety levels, deeper meaning, and even sleep a little better. **Helping is a buffer against helplessness and an affirmation of self-efficacy** – I can do this! Find something to do that is meaningful, draw on talents and strengths in order to feel effective, and have faith that, even if at first you are not quite inspired, your capacity of joy will eventually catch up with your actions. These days we have so many researchers concluding that the brain is essentially a social organ with its cells and pathways wired for empathy, for experiencing the joys and sufferings of others as if they are our own. Inhibit giving and inhibit flourishing.

Freedom of love

Virtue, as the saying goes, is its own reward. Pay it forward, no need to pay it back, and hope to inspire others to go and do likewise. But in giving, there is a glow, an inner benefit to the giver that can be seen in buoyancy and effervescence, and this is something that we can depend on pretty well. Reciprocity, in contrast, is never reliable, however much we should all be gracious recipients when others seek to return kindness. **We have to break free of 'I scratch your back, you scratch my back' mentalities** that require a response in kind. This iron law of reciprocity hangs over our necks like a sword of Damocles, keeping us from the inner freedom of love without limits.

Helping others rarely stands alone. Studies show that it brings with it an internal freedom, a sense of meaningful agency, joy, hopefulness and peace. It is impossible to imagine love not giving rise to a spontaneity and liberation from all those emotions that weigh us down; it is impossible to imagine loving without joy and delight in the beloved; it is impossible to imagine loving without having hope in them and for them; and it is impossible to imagine loving in any sustained way without an inner peace and gratification that, by its nature, denies violence in emotion, word, intention, or deed.

"Give and grow, give and glow."

Glow stick

The 2010 *Do Good Live Well Study,* released by United Healthcare and Volunteer-Match, surveyed 4500 American adults. 41 % of Americans volunteered an average of 100 hours a year. **68 % of those who volunteered in the last year reported that volunteering made them feel physically healthier.** In addition: 89 % report that "volunteering has improved my sense of well-being"; 73 % agree that "volunteering lowered my stress levels"; 92 % agree that "volunteering enriched their sense of purpose in life"; 72 % characterize themselves as 'optimistic' compared to 60 % of non-volunteers; 42 % of volunteers report a 'very good' sense of meaning in their lives, compared with 28 % of non-volunteers. How wise it is to do what one can to contribute benevolently to others!

This 'giver's glow' as I term it, has healing properties. Inner wholeness, nirvana, true peace – these are all related to the activity of self-giving love. A glow stick is a translucent plastic tube containing substances that, when combined, make light through a chemical reaction.

After the glass capsule in the plastic casing is broken, it glows. The brokenness is part of the process. Give and grow, give and glow.

Stephen G. Post is Professor of Preventive Medicine and Founding Director of the Center for Medical Humanities, Compassionate Care, and Bioethics at Stony Brook University School of Medicine (USA). He is the author of 200 articles and 17 books on love, altruism and compassionate care, including the bestseller *The Hidden Gifts of Helping*.

"Love is free from attachment."

The oriental perspective

"Being brought up in the oriental culture and being an oriental medicine therapist and clinical psychologist, my perspective on 'love' is heavily influenced by Hinduism and Buddhism", says Dr **Bijay Gyawali**. "From this perspective, love is the highest form of happiness."

I guess 'love' is the most used and misunderstood term in the world. There are innumerable interpretations of it. However, it is widely accepted that love is a positive energy and force. It is subjective rather than objective and thus it is to be felt. For me, love is the highest form of happiness. In other words: love brings happiness and happiness heightens love.

Me and mine

Usually when people speak about 'love' they are referring to the relation that exists between the opposite sexes, husbands and wives and young men and women, also between parents and children, family members, countrymen and so on. In fact, this is not true love, but the attraction and attachment that are bound to bring suffering and hatred. Love is

something universal that brings peace and prosperity to the entire human being.
It is free from attachment, far away from the sense of 'me' and 'mine'. It is unlimited and unconditional. It is spontaneous and pure. True love brings happiness, contentment and satisfaction. When you are in a loving state of mind, only then can you love everyone and every creature of the universe without discrimination. **Love unites rather than divides.**
There is no logic in love, it just happens. Love is like a stream that comes out from the infinite source: the pure heart.

The conditioned mind with the sense of 'me' and 'mine' confines you within boundaries rather than making you universal. In this mental state, people limit themselves to loving only their parents, spouse, children, grandchildren, their own relatives and at most their countrymen. It is actually selfishness rather than love. When people are caught in attachment, they get worried about accidents that could befall their loved ones even before such things actually take place. When such accidents do occur, they suffer terribly. Instead, if they were in true love, there could be equanimity within. Love promotes harmony within and around. Love that is based on discrimination with the sense of 'mine' and 'others' breeds prejudices. People become indifferent or even hostile to those outside their own circle of love. Attachment and discrimination are sources of suffering for others and oneself.

Karuna and Maîtri

Kindness and Compassion are the forms of true love. Kindness and compassion can be equated with the terms *karuna* and *maîtri* used in Hindu and Buddhist philosophies. According to these philosophies, *karuna* has the capacity to remove another's suffering whereas *maîtri* brings happiness to others. **It is a universal law that when you take care of others' happiness without attachment, you are bound to be happy.** *Maîtri* and *karuna* demand nothing in return. They are not limited to one's parents, spouse, children, relatives, caste members and countrymen. They extend love to all people and all beings. In *maîtri* and *karuna* there is no discrimination. And because there is no discrimination, there is no attachment and if there is no attachment, there is no suffering, tension or pain.

Actually, 'true love' is the true nature of human kind. It is nowhere else but within ourselves. Anyone can attain true love within if they try a little. It is effortless effort that makes it possible to attain true love. Effortless effort is possible when one becomes merely the witness of the happenings within and around. To be the witness, meditation is essential. Meditation is possible when we lead a simple and pure life.

The keys

→ **When love is about attachment ('me' and 'mine') it is actually selfishness rather than love.**

→ **Love is the true nature of humankind and is bound to bring happiness. Kindness and compassion are the forms of true love.**

→ **Love promotes harmony within and around. It is not limited to some persons but it extends to all people and all beings.**

Bijay Gyawali is a clinical psychologist and acupuncturist from Nepal. He completed his studies at the International University of Health and Welfare in Tokyo (Japan). He is the founder Vice Chairperson of the Acupuncture, Acupressure and Moxibustion Association of Nepal. He is the author of two books about oriental medicines. Now he is completing his doctorate research in Japan on post-conflict mental health impacts of civil war in Nepal.

*"Never get trapped
in this form of false love,
it's far less than you deserve."*

The Stockholm syndrome

Battered wives, victims of child abuse, hostages in a robbery…
some of them experience feelings for the aggressor that look
like love. This is called the 'Stockholm syndrome'.
Psychiatrist **Frank Ochberg** originally defined the term and
has lifelong experience in dealing with post-traumatic stress,
serial killers and victims. As a Red Cross volunteer, he has assisted
families at sites of earthquakes, floods, fires and aircraft disasters.
He unveils the system behind this false feeling of love.

Sometimes love arises in bizarre, unexpected situations and we psychiatrists are asked to
explain. Such was the case in the mid-1970s when Kristin, the bank teller, became attached
to Olsson, the bank robber, who held her hostage in a vault for six days and nights.
The term 'Stockholm syndrome' was born.

We called it a syndrome because of three observations: strong positive feelings from
the captive toward the captor, reciprocated positive feelings from the perpetrator to the
hostage, and antagonism from both of them toward the authorities responsible for hostage
rescue and prosecution of the captor. I was a government psychiatrist working with the FBI
during this era, training negotiators in resolving deadly incidents, interviewing survivors
who had been kidnapped or held hostage and, on occasion, consulting in the command

---

What is the Stockholm syndrome?

One quarter of all hostages and victims seem to express some empathy
or positive feelings towards their captors. Some of them even try
to defend them. A minority falls in love with them. This is called
'the Stockholm syndrome', after **a robbery** in Stockholm (1973) in which
bank employees were held hostage for six days.
The term is used for many other cases of unexpected affection and also
refers to some feelings of later generations after colonial experiences,
such as the Indian and the British or the Algerian and the French.

---

center during extended sieges, like the time in 1977 when Dutch Moluccan terrorists held
hostages in a school and on a train. From a humanitarian point of view, we valued
the Stockholm syndrome, since it included a bond of affection felt by the captor and
we could use this to save lives. We trained negotiators to look for and to encourage
the development of this attachment.

Permission to live

I explained the progression of the syndrome as, first, a period of sudden, unexpected,
terrifying capture. Shots were fired. Screams were heard. Conventional life was turned
upside-down. Captives were forbidden to talk, to move, to use a toilet, to speak. They were
like infants, totally dependent on a parent-figure for the necessities of life. Afterward, many
told me, in various ways, "**I knew I was going to die.**" They didn't just think they would
die. They knew it. But following that sense of utter helplessness, they eventually were
given permission to move, to speak, to eat. These 'gifts of life' were given by the same
powerful and terrible figure who caused their peril. The hostage denied the cruelty of
the captor. They experienced, instead, the ultimate kindness: permission to live.

I assumed this feeling (usually described to me in halting sentences) was somewhat like
gratitude, but also like the blissful relief of pain or terror. I also assumed that this emotion
is the precursor of all the varieties of human love: love of mother, love of friend, love of
a romantic partner. One former hostage said, of his young kidnapper, "He was like my
teenage son" and I saw a warm smile as this fatherly feeling was recalled. Another said

"They gave us blankets; they gave us cigarettes. You know they are killers. But they come off human. You have to fight a feeling of compassion." When the age and gender are appropriate, the connection can become romantic, as it appeared to be with Kristin in Stockholm and with heiress Patty Hearst toward Cujo of the Symbionese Liberation Army.

Powerful person

We have had several decades to explore siege and hostage dynamics, and we still find Stockholm syndrome in certain situations where hostages are (1) terrified, (2) infantilized, (3) allowed the elements of sustenance, (4) afforded time and opportunity to develop a bond. Once this relatively rare situation became known and highly publicized, the term Stockholm syndrome was applied to many other cases of unexpected affection, such as the loyalty to an abusive athletic coach or the tolerance of a battered wife.

These ironic attachments have elements of the Stockholm syndrome. A powerful person occupies a parental role, and does so with lethal or symbolically lethal force. The punishment is swift, severe and associated with loss of life or livelihood or career. There is nowhere else to turn (at least not in the mind of the one who is so completely dominated). But then, there is a period of relief. There is a path toward the coveted goal. There is life after a belief of death or its equivalent. The traumatic bond that results is beyond reason and, often, beyond conscious awareness.

False love

This may feel like love to the subjugated survivor. But I warn you, if you are trapped in this form of false love, it is not healthy and far less than you deserve. There is nothing wrong with you if you live in such a trap and you find it very difficult to escape. But there is something tragically wrong with life spent in emotional bondage. Many have escaped with the help of friends and of experts from womens' shelters and victim advocacy groups. More subtle, insidious captivity in hostile work environments requires enlightened intervention and legal protection. The necessary help begins with a path to a secure and safe place and it concludes with training in self-esteem and self-protection.

Stockholm syndrome is not true love. It is temporary comfort when a conviction of certain death changes to hope for survival. Stockholm syndrome is meant to apply to hostage and kidnap situations, but elements are found whenever ironic affection arises as bullies grant respite from abuse. Remember that freedom and dignity are our ultimate goal. With freedom and dignity we can experience mature, dependable love.

The keys

→ **Stockholm syndrome is characterized by strong and reciprocated positive feelings between captive and captor and antagonism towards the outside authorities.**

→ **The term is applied to many other cases of unexpected affection, based on strong emotions as permission to live, extreme gratitude, relief after an expectation of death, etc.**

→ **This may feel like love but is not true love. Only with freedom and dignity can we experience mature love.**

Frank Ochberg is Clinical Professor of Psychiatry, formerly Adjunct Professor of Criminal Justice, and Adjunct Professor of Journalism at Michigan State University (USA). He is a founding board member of the International Society for Traumatic Stress Studies and recipient of their highest honor, the Lifetime Achievement Award. Ochberg developed, with colleagues, the Academy for Critical Incident Analysis, 'Gift From Within' (a charity for people with Post Traumatic Stress Disorder) and the Committee for Community Awareness and Protection (responding to serial-killer threats). He also founded the Dart Center for Journalism and Trauma to help journalists understand traumatic stress and traumatic stress experts understand journalists.

Love under stress

"Daily stress is a secret enemy of love", says Dr Guy Bodenmann. **He has been studying for more than twenty years the impact of everyday stress on the functioning of close relationships, enrolling more than two thousand couples in cross-sectional, longitudinal and experimental studies, from their workplace to their bedroom.**

My primary goal was to comprehend mechanisms how everyday conditions undermine love and why the relationship quality of initially happy couples deteriorates over time. A second goal was to develop prevention strategies and methods for couple therapy based on these findings. Our research findings reveal that love is often destroyed by stress, on the one hand, and poor dyadic coping, on the other hand. These are the most important findings of our studies.

1. Negative daily hassles. Chronic minor external stresses (such as daily hassles that pile up in everyday life) increase the likelihood of tension and conflict in couples, eroding positive feelings towards the partner (i.e. affection, tenderness, love), and leading slowly but steadily to alienation between the partners and the loss of love.

2. We are not aware. This process often is outside of conscious awareness and couples do not realize the harmful effect of daily stress until it damages their relationship quality seriously.

3. We get lost. Chronic external stress has a negative impact on couples functioning by means of four mediating processes: (1) decreased time spent together, leading to a reduction of shared experiences, weakens the feelings of togetherness ('we-ness'), decreases self-disclosure among partners, and jeopardizes dyadic coping; (2) increasing negative communication, hostile interaction and withdrawal as usual reactions of stressed spouses poison family life and drive partners apart; (3) an increased risk of psychological and physical problems such as sleep disorders, sexual dysfunction and negative mood burden on the partners and disturb the balance between partners; and (4) an increased likelihood that negative personality traits will be evident in stress situations, as subjects are less able to mask them, (e.g. rigidity, avarice, dominance, intolerance) dismantles the previous positive view of the partner.

4. The others can make it worse. Marriages that are subjected to chronic external stress (stress at the work place, stress with neighbors, stress with family of origin, etc.) have a greater probability of ending in divorce. Thus, often external stress spilling over to the close relationship is an initial trigger for a negative development of close relationships and dissolution.

7. Share experiences. Partners engaging in mutual self-disclosure about stress experiences in their everyday life, listening to each other, trying to understand the partner's experience and trying to help him or her cope effectively with this bad experience (by showing empathy, understanding, encouraging the partner or believing in the partner) are happier in their relationships.

8. More than words. Another important finding of our studies is that love is more strongly related to mutual support (dyadic coping) than just to positive communication (paying compliments, giving gifts, showing affection towards partner) and that both positive aspects are stronger predictors than hostile or negative communication.

9. Support each other. Stressed partners recover faster from external stress when the other is showing interest and providing support and this both on a psychological as well as a physiological level. Cortisol level, as a physiological correlate of stress, decreases faster when the partner is supportive.

5. Cope together. On the other hand, the better the partners are able to cope 'together' with stress, the higher their chance for advantageous marital satisfaction and stability. Our studies have shown that couples engaging in dyadic coping (provided by one partner to another or common efforts to deal with the stressors) were reporting more frequent feelings of love, higher marital quality, lower stress experience and better psychological and physical well-being.

6. Work as a unit. Dyadic coping revealed to be a significant direct predictor of relationship satisfaction and stability, but also to be an important moderator of the verbal aggression-increasing impact of stress in couples. The negative impact of external stress spilling over to dyadic interaction and increasing the risk of verbal aggression was alleviated by dyadic coping.

Guy Bodenmann is Professor of Clinical Psychology at the University of Zurich (Switzerland). Stress and coping in couples is one of his main research interests. He is a member of the editorial board of numerous international journals (including the *Journal of Social and Personal Relationships*) and has developed the Couples Coping Enhancement Training (CCET).

" Daily hassles erode our positive feelings."

"Love is including and excluding at the same time."

Seven fundamentals

"From a sociological perspective, love is conceived primarily not as an emotion but as a social relationship. It is oriented towards significant others and their reactions", says **Prof Wolfgang Glatzer. His love advice is based on seven fundamentals of social cohesion.**

Love is a relationship between two or more people based on a decision taken by two or more people. It has a strong place in everyday life for regulating relationships between people. Sometimes conflicts arise from love because the loved ones are privileged and the non-loved are frequently disadvantaged. Sometimes love creates chaos, but life without love would be unbearable. Love is only one feature in the fundamentals of social cohesion, which are necessary for living together. In addition to love:

1. **We cannot live without trust.** We have to trust that, under regular conditions, people around us tell us the truth and do not act maliciously.

2. **We cannot live without reliability.** It is important that we keep our promises.

3. **We cannot live without recognition.** We want to be recognized and others expect to be recognized by us.

4. **We need reciprocity in our social networks.** If we give goods, services or attention to somebody, we expect some kind of reciprocal answer.

5. **Solidarity is fundamental** as a value. In the course of life, everybody can get into need and everybody can be in the position to provide support.

6. **Security is a basic need** of individuals and it is the task of individuals and societal institutions to provide this.

7. **Fundamental needs exist for fairness and justice,** violation of which will create problems for individuals and society.

What is necessary in life is a balance of all these fundamental components of needs and values. Everybody has to develop their own 'cocktail' of aspirations and emotions and everybody has to define the role that love will have in this comprehensive context. It is never possible to fulfil all our needs at the same time to their maximum.

The function of love is ambivalent: under normal conditions, love is a principle that brings order into our world, but sometimes it does the opposite and creates disorder. Order is created by love relations as it is impossible to maintain personal relations with everybody we meet in life. Love is a principle that includes some people and excludes others. The exclusion principle works, especially when a couple falls in love and marries: inclusion with the partner and exclusion of potential partners outside the couple. Having children often reduces couples' relationships outside the family. Love implies simultaneously the inclusion of the loved and preferred ones and the exclusion of the less-loved and non-loved.

Recommendations depending on these insights?
Love yourself because you are unique and it is good for you. Love your life because it is precious and will not last for ever. Love your boyfriend and/or your girlfriend because it can be a great feeling and you need their love. Love your relatives: it is good to know that you have a support network in life's emergencies. Love every member of humankind, especially the disadvantaged: we are all human beings and we all need charity and solidarity from time to time. Do not forget that life needs more than love, though love is a need of highest significance for life.

Wolfgang Glatzer is Professor of Sociology at the Goethe University in Frankfurt am Main (Germany). He has published various books on quality of life. He has been President of the International Society for Quality of Life Studies and is a member of the editorial board of the *Journal of Happiness Studies*.

"You need to love someone a lot to be able to leave them alone."

Love is giving what you don't own

"Together with happiness, love is just about the most important thing in life. The word quickly conjures up the idea of the 'one and only' person with whom we are ready to share the rest of our days. Reality requires of us a painful correction", says Prof **Paul Verhaeghe**. "Love is giving what you don't own."

Visibly the distrust that marks contemporary life has reached as far as our love life, and we seek to shield ourselves against the eventuality of the 'one and only' failing to fulfill expectations. Separations abound, and just about every marriage today is undergirded by a legal contract. Almost imperceptibly, a reduction has occurred: from love to matrimony, in the context of confusion between eroticism and love. It is precisely this confusion that causes misery. Eroticism is focused on sexual desire, on tension and release. In this process the other person is not so terribly important, he or she is a means rather than an end. And therefore ultimately exchangeable. In love, things are exactly the opposite: the other is in the center, often exalted as the adored one, the true one for whom one is prepared to sacrifice everything. Sex plays a less prominent part in the picture and may even be experienced as detrimental to the sublimity of love. How can we understand this drastic difference?

This is less difficult than it seems. **The basic model for love is not the erotic relationship between a man and a woman,** but rather the original relationship between mother and child. The way we have experienced this relationship will very strongly influence all our later love relationships. Consequently, it is more than worth the effort to rethink the basic characteristics of this relationship.

Exclusivity

In the beginning the love relationship between a mother and her baby is both total and exclusive. Even after parturition, the two continue to form a single unit, in which the one means all for the other, and vice versa. Instead of a relationship between two distinct individuals, there is rather a fullness, a closed-in-on-itselfness, where outsiders are by definition outsiders. The figure that experiences this the most acutely is the father. Each brand new father has to wise up to the fact that he is now a father, offsetting the feeling that he has lost his wife – she has become a mother – and that he is kept out of a relationship that he barely understands.

Herein lies the basis for something that, in the adult love relationship, will provide inevitable difficulties: the (requirement) of exclusivity. The other has to be everything for me, and only for me, every third figure is automatically threatening, ranging from a new brother or sister for the child or the mother-in-law for the brand-new mom. The parent's attention to the other child or the child's attention to another care figure is unbearable. **Rivals are not tolerated, one must and will take first place.**

This requirement of exclusivity becomes even more important when the all-embracing relationship between mother and baby is broken by the demands of life. The physical separation gradually becomes a mental separation, resulting in the emergence of an initially insatiable desire. Insatiable, because the original fullness can never be restored. The best way of putting it, I heard from a toddler: "Mama, I wish you were a mushroom, then I could live inside you."

Mirror love

Once the original unity is broken, the love relationship shifts indeed to a relationship, with giving and receiving. But **whatever one gives or receives, it will never be sufficient to restore the original unity.** It is here that we find the basis for a uniquely human trait: the creativity with which we keep searching for constantly shifting solutions, once we have understood that there is no definitive solution to our desire.

The prerequisite for this understanding is clear: we must loosen ourselves from our mothers, in order to build elsewhere, later, a new relationship with someone else, with a place for our own individuality and that of the other. If this breaking loose has not taken place properly, then the subsequent love relationship will be very compulsive; with my demanding that

I and only I fulfil the desire of the other, and that the other responds to my and only my demand. This is mirror love, which, for two reasons, is doomed to failure. This is a desire that no one can totally meet, and the demand that someone else do this is to fail to recognize the role of the other as other.

Illusion

In contrast to this is mature love. The best words I have heard put to this was by someone at the end of his psychoanalysis: "You need to love someone a lot to be able to leave them alone." Leaving alone, not immediately paralyzing desire by filling the other's inner lack with one's own content.

That is, allowing someone to be genuinely different, and thereby facilitating a relationship on the basis of difference. **In mature love one receives something that can never be given in tangible form**, one gives something one does not oneself possess. As the French psychoanalyst Lacan once put it: "L'amour, c'est donner ce qu'on n'a pas."

The tragedy of our materialistic age is that we grow up with the illusion that everything is for sale, that the value of something depends on the cost and the packaging, and that a contract offers a guarantee. Love is living proof of the contrary.

The keys

→ **Almost imperceptibly, a reduction has occurred: from love to matrimony, in the context of a confusion between eroticism and love. This confusion creates misery.**

→ **The basic model for love is the original relationship between mother and child, with a demand for exclusivity.**

→ **We must loosen ourselves from our mothers, in order to build elsewhere, later, a new relationship with someone else, with a place for our own individuality and that of the other.**

Paul Verhaeghe is a clinical psychologist and psychoanalyst. He works as a professor at the University of Ghent (Belgium) and is particularly interested in the relationship between social change, identity and psychological problems. His books are an international success. His *Love in a Time of Loneliness* has been translated into eight languages. When not reading or writing in his free time, he enjoys gardening and long distance running.

"Bring out the best in each other."

The Michelangelo phenomenon

"Over the years, my collaborators and I have found that love can be strengthened to the extent that romantic partners are able to help shape individuals closer to the kind of person they themselves desire to be", says Dr **Madoka Kumashiro**. Discover the Michelangelo in yourself and in the one you love.

Michelangelo allegedly remarked that, as a sculptor, he chipped away the outer layers of stone to unearth the ideal form lying within. Analogously, the Michelangelo phenomenon theory suggests that people also often need such a skilled sculptor to help reveal the ideal form lying within – the 'ideal self', or the kind of person they most aspire to become. Romantic partners are often in the best position to be such a sculptor, given their considerable influence over their partners over an extended period of time.

However, romantic partners can bring out both the best and the worst in an individual, with lasting effects. For example, if Mary desires to be more assertive, John's encouraging behaviors may make her gradually feel more comfortable voicing her opinions, even in his absence. On the other hand, if John believes Mary will always be timid, he will likely engage in behaviors that may make her even more apprehensive about voicing her opinions. Thus, **a romantic partner's expectations may create a self-fulfilling reality**: partners can draw out certain qualities from each other and influence attitudes and behaviors towards each partner's most cherished goals.

The ideal self

What are the consequences of a romantic partner drawing out qualities that are considered desirable, undesirable, or irrelevant to the individual? Our research finds that to the extent that individuals move closer to their 'ideal self', they also feel better about themselves and the relationship which enabled this transformation to occur. Conversely, individuals in relationships that draw out undesired or irrelevant characteristics and goals are likely to feel worse about themselves and their partner. Thus, we find that romantic relationships can be strengthened or weakened to the extent that each partner feels closer or farther away from their ideals within the context of their relationship.

Of course, it would be naive to claim that both partners can always find the time, energy, and motivation to be supportive while pursuing their own goals. In fact, modern relationships can be particularly problematic given that both partners are likely to be actively pursuing their own challenging goals while also trying to meet the needs of others, such as children. Frequently, one or both partners will have to make considerable sacrifices or give up on some goals. Under these situations, **the key to a stronger relationship is to find a solution that will allow individuals to continue to pursue their ideals**. For example, individuals often have multiple visions of a desired future, each with various alternative means of reaching them. Individuals also sometimes enjoy daydreaming about some fantasy goals rather than actively pursue them. In such cases, individuals may focus on one set of goals over others, be flexible about how they pursue their goals, or make sure they are pursuing their goals in a way that shows consideration for their partner's well-being. Finally, desired characteristics and goals are likely to change over the course of a lifetime; relationships can thrive to the extent that partners recognize such changes and adjust their behaviors accordingly.

Personal growth

The Michelangelo phenomenon is not the only theory to propose that romantic partners may play an integral role in an individual's quest for personal growth. Complementing our findings, other research shows that love can be regarded as attachment; similar to young children who use their primary caregivers as a 'secure base' from which to engage in personal explorations, romantic partners appear to serve as such a 'secure base' for adults to continue their personal explorations. Other research also suggests that well-being is enhanced to the extent that individuals are able to meet their fundamental psychological needs, which include needs for autonomy and belongingness. Although it is often thought that these two are opposing needs, research findings show that **the best kind of relationships are those in which close relationship partners are able to provide both love and autonomous support.**

Love is often viewed as restricting the self and requiring one to make undesired changes. Findings from our research suggest that in loving relationships, both partners bring out the best in each other and use the relationship as a solid foundation to experience personal growth and achieve their most important personal goals.

The keys

→ **One of the best types of love is one in which partners help each other move closer to the kind of person they each aspire to become.**

→ **Partners may not always have time or energy to support each other's most important goals, and such goals also may change over time, so it helps to be flexible and considerate.**

→ **Fundamental human needs include needs for both relatedness and autonomy – relationships benefit when the two needs complement each other.**

Madoka Kumashiro is Assistant Professor of Psychology at Goldsmiths, University of London (UK). While pursuing her PhD at the University of North Carolina at Chapel Hill under the direction of Professor Caryl Rusbult, who originally proposed the theory of the Michelangelo phenomenon, she became interested in integrating the previously disparate fields of self and close relationships. She has published many journal articles and book chapters on 'the self' in interpersonal contexts.

What we want

*"We simply see people we like
in a warm and positive light."*

If you ask singles how their desired romantic partner should be, they are usually able to provide a fairly clear-cut picture. But does this match with their final choice? Dr Lars Penke researches whether we need to know what we want.

Most often, stated preferences do not match actual partner choices at all. For example, when participants in speed datings say they want a warm or wealthy partner before the event starts, this has nothing to do with whom they choose to see again, despite people's astonishing ability to judge these attributes fairly well within seconds. Similarly, identical twins, who share their family upbringing and all of their genetic background, are very similar in their self-reported romantic preferences. Their actual romantic partners, however, are so dissimilar that they almost appear to be randomly chosen. Indeed, comparisons with less genetically similar fraternal twins indicate that actual romantic partner choices are about the only aspect of life where people do not differ partly due to genetic influences. The same is not true for reported preferences or any other psychological trait, all of which are substantially heritable.

Sometimes some of these self-reported preferences reflect the partners these people end up with reasonably well. However, this mostly happens for rather trivial attributes like age, or when preferences for characteristics like religiosity, ethnicity or education can be very much traced back to expectations and influences from the family and cultural environment. Overall, **people do not seem to know very well what they want when falling in love.** For psychologists, this is not too surprising, as they know that people have very limited insight into what is really going on in their minds when they make decisions. Also, unlike most other decisions in life, romantic partner choices usually need to be mutual – it is not enough that one person finds someone who suits his or her preferences; the other person has to be interested as well. Finally, it is important to understand what people really mean when they report they want an 'attractive' or 'kind and understanding' partner. Let us stick with these two examples for a moment.

Attractive

For both men and women, physical attractiveness is one of the prime factors that make them interested in seeing each other again after first sight. We now have a good understanding of which objectively measurable features make bodies and faces attractive, including symmetry, masculinity-femininity, smooth skin and otherwise a lack of deviation from the norm. However, **perceived attractiveness in real life boy-meets-girl situations is affected by many other factors,** including what is available in their surroundings and whom others find attractive. Furthermore, attractiveness to a potential partner can be substantially increased by behavioral signals of interest and contact-readiness, conveyed by dress and styling, a confident and approachable appearance, flirtatious behavior, smiling and eye contact. It might well be that these often highly targeted signs are what people really want when they say they prefer an attractive partner.

Kind

In a similar manner, people looking in a prospective partner for kindness, understanding, warmth and trustworthiness, attributes that are always on top of self-reported preference rankings, might not necessarily pair off with someone with a general personality trait of agreeableness or cooperative tendencies towards everybody. For one, people generally regard trustworthiness the most desirable attribute in people in general, not only romantic partners. It is simply a prerequisite for social interactions, especially with strangers. **People also tend to categorize others into rough groups of good or bad,** or friend or foe, and then assign overly positive attributes to people they like. This includes assigning obviously contradictory attributes like 'modest' and 'assertive' or 'flexible' and 'orderly' to the same individual, and often goes hand-in-hand with judgments as 'warm' and 'kind'. People simply see people they like in a warm, positive light. In addition, there is evidence that people do not necessary want their romantic partners to be kind and understanding towards everybody, but specifically towards them. Overall, it seems like people who say they want a kind and warm partner are not necessarily looking for the

general personality trait of agreeableness, but for someone who simply loves them back.

So, all in all, **what people say they want in a romantic partner does not reflect well on whom they end up choosing,** especially when self-reported partner preferences are taken at face value. It seems that people lack insight into why they fall in love with someone. This does not mean, however, that romantic partner choice is random or just a result, as has been claimed, of proximity and opportunity. Instead, a lot more subtle, but nonetheless functional, processes seem to be at work when people fall in love, including adjustments of preferences to environmental demands and to one's own popularity as a romantic partner, and female shifts in partner choice criteria across the menstrual cycle that balance sexual attraction and affiliative motives. It is just not necessary that we can fully reflect on them to fall in love.

Lars Penke is a lecturer in the Department of Psychology at the University of Edinburgh in Scotland (UK). He has studied attraction, romantic partner choice and sexual behavior from an evolutionary perspective using a variety of methods, including detailed behavioral observations and speed dating designs. He is co-founder of the Personality and Social Relationships network.

"The prescription of Dr Love?
Eight hugs a day and use the 'L'-word."

The chemistry of love

His lab discovered in 2004 that the brain chemical oxytocin allows us to determine whom to trust. This was world news. Dr **Paul Zak**'s work on oxytocin and relationships has earned him the nickname 'Dr Love'. How does he deal with that?

My current research has shown that oxytocin is responsible for virtuous behaviors, working as the brain's 'moral molecule'. This knowledge is being used to understand the basis for civilization and modern economies, improve negotiations, and treat patients with neurologic and psychiatric disorders.

It took some time getting used to being called 'Dr Love'. My graduate students started calling me Dr Love as a bit of a joke. But, then I was 'outed' as Dr Love by a journalist whom I hugged after an interview for a magazine. I had become Dr Love. I'm a scientist and I spent ten years running laboratory experiments searching for the brain chemicals that make human beings moral. Our human nature is kind and cruel, generous and stingy, tolerant and dismissive. But why? I discovered that the neurochemical oxytocin was released after nearly any positive social interaction, even between strangers, and caused people to tangibly care about others. Wow! That's big news.

Touch

I had even developed a way to infuse synthetic oxytocin safely into people and showed I could turn on these caring, moral behaviors like turning on a garden hose. But we can't create a more compassionate world with drugs, so I looked harder – what else would turn on the oxytocin-care brain circuit? My team and I found that touch released oxytocin. So, some years ago I tried a little experiment on myself: I'll hug everyone.

It turns out that just announcing that I hug everyone put a big smile on people's faces and then, like a strike of lightning (or oxytocin!), they opened up to me. I found that every interaction I had got better. **When our brains release oxytocin it signals that the person in front of us is safe** and we can trust them. I found my relationships were richer and my life happier. Oxytocin motivates attachment to romantic partners and parental care for offspring so it is sometimes called the chemical of love. We care about people because we are predisposed to love others.

Philia

Oxytocin is an evolutionarily old brain chemical. This means love is an essential part of our human nature. We need love, we crave love. But, just like you cannot force someone to love you, **you cannot make your own brain release oxytocin**. You can only care for others and stimulate oxytocin release in others. So, give the gift of love. And give it indiscriminately. In 95 % of the thousands of people I have tested, they will reciprocate and show you love in return. And the 5 % who don't, probably need the love more than all the others.

Let Dr Love offer you a prescription: eight hugs a day. Offer to give eight people a day hugs and you'll start a virtuous cycle of caring and compassion, the first step in the creation of a more loving world. Your second prescription is to use the 'L'-word. Tell those around you that you love them. For friends, co-workers and neighbors, the love I'm talking about is 'philia', meaning that you truly care about their well being. Go ahead and put it out there, there is solid science behind it. Once you do, love will come back to you many times over.

And it can all start with a hug.

The keys

→ **Oxytocin is an evolutionary old brain chemical. It is the brain's moral molecule.**

→ **Oxytocin motivates attachment to romantic partners. It is released by touch.**

→ **Give the gift of love: give eight hugs a day and tell people you truly care about their well- being.**

Paul J. Zak is the founding Director of the Center for Neuroeconomics Studies and Professor of Economics, Psychology and Management at Claremont Graduate University in California (USA). He also serves as Professor of Neurology at Loma Linda University Medical Center. He is credited with the first published use of the term 'neuroeconomics' and has been a vanguard in this new discipline. Dr Zak is the author of the bestseller *The Moral Molecule: The Source of Love and Prosperity*.

"Paired monkeys spend up to 20% of their day simply sitting next to each other."

Animal love

Scientists have always been afraid of being accused of anthropomorphism: projecting human qualities onto animals. But now they openly talk about something like romantic love in animal behavior. Prof **Charles T. Snowdon** is a renowned specialist in the field, having studied the behavior of monkeys for more than thirty years. A love story of titi, marmosets and tamarins.

The night before he died, Alex, a language-trained African grey parrot, said "I love you" to Irene Pepperberg, his trainer and collaborator of several decades. However, the vast majority of non-human animals cannot express love through language. How then can we determine if love exists in other animals?

In the absence of language, we can pay attention to behavior to evaluate love. In reality, this is not much different from observing relationships in other humans who speak a different language and with whom we cannot communicate. **We easily recognize several behaviors that indicate a loving relationship.** Do partners prefer to be with each other when given a choice? Do they demonstrate affectionate behavior towards each other?

➤

Do they show emotions of distress when they are separated and emotions of joy and relief when they reunite? Do they protect or guard their partners in the presence of others of the same sex? Do they stay together for relatively long times? Do they share with each other or give gifts?

If we accept these acts as signs of love in humans, then why not use the same criteria with other species? The vast majority of humans live in monogamous relationships, and it is in monogamous species that we can see the closest similarities in loving behaviors. In titi monkeys, small monkeys from South America, pairs frequently sit side by side with their tails twined together. When they are given a choice between their mate and another animal of the same sex, they choose their mate. They even prefer to be with their mate when given a choice between their mate and their own infant.

Marmosets and tamarins

In another group of South American monkeys, the marmosets and tamarins, paired monkeys spend up to 20 % of their day simply sitting next to each other and grooming each other by combing through each other's hair. When separated for a brief time these monkeys produce plaintive sounding calls. When they are reunited, they quickly run to each other, groom and often engage in sexual behavior. Marmosets and tamarins are very much like humans in showing frequent sexual behavior even at times when the female is not fertile or is already pregnant.

These monkeys are aggressive when strangers approach, with both males and females cooperating to keep strangers away. **They spend time cuddling, grooming and engaging in sex** after an encounter with a stranger. In the wild, marmoset and tamarin pairs stay together for several years at a time, with breakups found only at times of environmental stress when pairs have lost their infants. We see the same results with other monogamous primates and monogamous mice where a male and female stay together over several years.

Marmosets and tamarins give special calls when they discover food and they readily share food with others. Marmosets have special teeth that allow them to gouge holes in tree bark which then leads to sap running out. All family members share the sap that was created by one animal's work. In formal experiments in captivity, these monkeys work together to solve a common problem to find food and will continue to cooperate even if only one animal gets all the food. They will even donate food to their mate, pulling on a tray that brings no food to them but does give food to the mate.

The love hormone

Another form of cooperation is childcare. In monogamous animals, childcare is divided and coordinated between both parents, with fathers doing much of the physical work of carrying infants when mothers are nursing. Fathers also step in at weaning to offer solid food to infants, distracting them from nursing on the mother. Infants can even reach into the mouths of fathers to take food.

Many hormonal changes accompany pair behavior in animals. In a tiny rodent called a vole, we find monogamous species that form tight and long lasting relationships with mates and polygynous species where long-term relationships are rare. In monogamous female voles, when the hormone oxytocin is present in the brain, they take an immediate liking to whatever male they are with and will avoid other males. A similar hormone called vasopressin has a similar effect in monogamous male voles. In monogamous monkeys, pairs that spend more time cuddling, grooming each other and having sex have much higher levels of oxytocin in their bodies than pairs that are not so affectionate. Oxytocin has been called the 'love hormone' and it appears that physical contact and frequent sex are important to maintain love-like behaviors and hormones in these monkeys.

Close contact

In marmosets, becoming a father leads to greater fidelity to his mate and many hormonal changes. When presented with the scents of a novel female, non-fathers react with sexual arousal and rapid increases in testosterone, but father marmosets are indifferent to the wiles of a novel female. When presented with the scents of his own infant, a father's testosterone levels plummet within minutes, while his oestrogen levels rise.

The close behavioral interactions between males and females seen in monogamous species are rare in animals that do not have monogamous relationships. However, even in these species, there are close social bonds in some cases between mothers, daughters and sisters and in other cases between fathers, sons and brothers. There is close physical contact, grooming and sharing of resources as well as anxiety when individuals are separated. Thus, the behaviors of heterosexual love seen in monogamous mates may also be seen as brotherly and sisterly love in other species.

Love is not unique to humans but can be found in many other animals when we know how to look for it.

The keys

→ **The vast majority of humans live in monogamous relationships, and it is in monogamous species that we can see the closest similarities in loving behaviors.**

→ **Oxytocin has been called the 'love hormone' and it appears that physical contact and frequent sex are important to maintain love-like behaviors and hormones in monogamous monkeys.**

→ **Love is not unique to humans but can be found in many other animals when we know how to look for it.**

Charles T. Snowdon is Professor of Psychology and Zoology at the University of Wisconsin, Madison (USA). He is highly respected for his lifelong work with monkeys. For more than thirty years he has studied the behavioral of pair-mates, paternal care and hormones in monogamous monkeys. Currently, he is applying some of the ideas and methods from monkey research to the study of human romantic relationships.

Love is love

> *"Love is not love,*
> *except when it is."*

"Lots of psychologists have written to say that love is not love, that really it's something else. Some say that love's a throwback to a state called attachment. Others concentrate on how we are descended from apes. A third idea is social exchange. All of these ideas have something to them. But sometimes love is love", says Prof **Keith Oatley**.

My colleague Maja Djikic and I have written about this. Love is not love, except when it is. Often, perhaps especially when we've been alone for some time, we can feel a void, a lack of meaning in our lives. Then we meet someone who seems marvelous, who seems to glow in a way that can border on the divine. In that person's presence, we can feel transformed, less mediocre, more alive. We can come almost to worship that person and that person's acceptance of us gives our life meaning. At the same time, when things work well, that other person thinks and feels something of the same about us. So what can we do? We can give that person our love as a gift. You may be fortunate enough to have been loved but, remember, it's a gift. As such, it's something you, too, can give.

In this way, love isn't something we need. It's something we can bestow, and we can bestow it on sexual partners, on friends, on family members, on offspring. If we are fortunate enough to have had such love bestowed on us, it's more likely that we will have enough solidity and meaning inside ourselves that we can bestow love on someone else. **Love that is love isn't just about you.** It's based on knowing the other person. Anger often signals something that's gone wrong in a relationship that needs to be repaired. Working through it without too much blaming enables you to know the other person better.

Romeo and Juliet

Patrick Hogan has shown that of all the stories in the world, in every kind of society, the love story is the most common. In a prototypical form, two young people long to be united, but a father opposes the union. In a tragic version, the lovers die, but in a cheerful version, the father is reconciled, and the couple live – as the story-world saying puts it – happily ever after. The best known tragic love story is *Romeo and Juliet*. You need look no further to see the steps needed to fall in love. First, you must be open to the experience. Then you see a stranger across a room. You are attracted. Perhaps your eyes meet. Then there's an interval during which, in both potential lovers, fantasies build. After the interval, there is a meeting in which each confirms by something said or unsaid that the other has taken the same steps and has been thinking and feeling in the same way. In *Romeo and Juliet*, there is even the sense of Romeo worshipping Juliet. He reaches out his hand to touch her, and starts to speak a sonnet – a verse-form specially formulated to express love in which he says he sees her as a saint. **As each step is taken, projection increases.** Neither of the lovers knows anything substantial about the other.

The worshipping is unlikely to last because the other person is a human being with a particular personality, particular habits, particular wants and needs. What one has to do, then, while soaring on the transformation, is to begin to withdraw the projections and start to bestow one's love on the other, not as a saint to be adored, but as someone to be understood and valued for who that person actually is. Many people have never gone through these steps of falling in love. If you're among them, perhaps you should be grateful. But there are other (and probably better?) ways of coming to love someone. Unlike so much of literature, which is about conflict, love is about being able to join with another to do something that neither person could do alone, perhaps even be someone that neither person could be alone.

The keys

- → **There are different theories about love: attachment, evolution or social exchange. But sometimes love is love: a gift, to give and take.**
- → **Real love is based on learning to know the other person as he or she is.**
- → **Finally, worshipping and projection can be steps towards a unique understanding and appreciation of the other.**

Keith Oatley is a psychologist and Professor Emeritus at the University of Toronto (Canada). He was an undergraduate at Cambridge (UK) and completed his PhD at University College London. With his partner, developmental psychologist Jennifer Jenkins, and Dacher Keltner, he is a co-author of the standard textbook *Understanding Emotions*. All three of his novels are love stories, including *The Case of Emily V.*, which won the 1994 Commonwealth Writers Prize for Best First Novel.

The six colors of love

The famous Canadian sociologist Alan Lee developed in the 1970s a typology of love, widely known as the six colors of love. Since then, Dr Félix Neto has conducted worldwide research on love, using these colors. What is the influence of gender, generation and culture on love? Storgè, Ludus and Eros will tell us.

Lee identifies six socio-ideologies or styles to reflect the diversity of human ways of loving. He regards these styles as a natural component of learning and experience, arguably influenced by culture and society. He uses the metaphor of a color wheel on which to place the many 'colors' of love. As with color, there are primary love styles and secondary, and even tertiary, mixed. Attention has focused on six relatively independent styles of love. The primary styles include Eros (romantic love), Ludus (game-playing love), and Storgè (friendship love). Compounds of two of each of the primary styles form the three secondary styles: Pragma (practical love), Mania (obsessive love) and Agapè (altruistic love). What does my research show?

"Our love styles show some striking variations."

1. Gender. Consistently I have found two gender differences in love styles. Men show themselves more ludic and more agapic than women. Men are more likely to report a willingness to sacrifice their own needs for those of their loved ones. This may be due to traditional gender roles that require men to be providers and protectors, or simply reflect an ideology that men inherit from societal norms. The greater presence of Agapè in men may be attributed to a more idealized, romantic concept of heterosexual relationships in that gender.

2. Generation. We extended research on love styles over the entire life span by assessing the views of three generations of female family members. The findings show that the three generations of women do not share substantial similarities in most love styles. The effect of generation is significant on Eros, Storgè, Pragma and Agapè. In keeping with the erotic style, students emphasize more the physical side of love, including an ideal of physical beauty, they experience intense emotions (without the demanding, possessive quality of mania) and they are more self-confident in their relationships than their mothers. However, grandmothers don't differ from their daughters and granddaughters on the erotic style. This may be surprising given that passion is consistently described as less important in one's older years. This phenomenon may be a result of society's limiting view of sexuality as solely the act of intercourse. While aging can affect one's physical health and therefore sexual expression, it does not necessarily affect one's erotic style.

The present study does indicate that erotic love orientation can be experienced just as intensely by elderly adults as by middle-aged and young adults. Such a report indicates that Eros may not be a fragile and ephemeral experience, as has been previously suggested. This finding suggests that the erotic style encompasses the life span, rather than being a phenomenon largely confined to the youthful years.

3. **Culture.** One view of love is that it is a cultural phenomenon, a learned affect or behavioral response resulting from experiences and culture. Because culture provides meaning and shapes experiences, it is important for researchers to illuminate the influence of culture on love and relationships. We have examined to what extent the model of the Love Color Wheel was able to account for data gathered across a large set of countries, from Africa (Angola, Cape Verde and Mozambique), Asia (China-Macao), South America (Brazil) and Europe (France, Portugal and Switzerland). The findings support the hypotheses that (a) factors involving strong personal feelings, such as Mania, Eros, and Agapè , are largely similar cross-culturally and (b) factors involving strict rules and, consequently, low affects, such as Pragma, Storgè and Ludus, are dependent on cultural influences. Thus, the general picture to emerge from the results is that while there are similarities between cultures in love styles, there are nevertheless some striking and interesting variations.

Félix Neto is Professor of Psychology at the University of Porto (Portugal). His research interests include the relationship between culture and well-being. He has published 16 books and around 250 scientific articles on social psychology and cross-cultural psychology.

The colors of love

Lee's model is a typology of love, expanding the view that there are many ways to love, not all of them fully romantic. The model posits 6 types.

TYPE	DESCRIPTION
Eros	Represents romantic love in its most common form. It is often characterized by a sudden and potent attraction to the physical appearance of the ideal beloved, as well as an urgent desire to be emotionally intimate and express open, intense and passionate feelings.
Ludus	Almost opposite to Eros, this type is aware of beauty but holds to no beloved ideal. Ludus understands love as a playful non-committal game generally involving multiple partners and characterized by emotional detachment. In some ways it is the style least like romantic love.
Storgè	A slow developing friendship which grows naturally over time through the mutual enjoyment of shared interests and activities and matures into a committed love. It manifests as a calm, companionate, comfortable love with a built-up reserve of stability.
Mania	Obsessive, insatiable and intense emotional involvement are distinguishing features of this type. Similar to the ludic lover, the manic lover believes almost anyone will do; however, unlike the ludic lover, the manic lover is unable to be detached and let go. Because they are doubtful of their own desirability and lovability, they become intensely and possessively preoccupied with the beloved.
Pragma	This is a logical, practical, common sense outlook to love associated with people who deliberate over a calculated 'shopping list' of social and personal attributes of their partners. These individuals do this to ensure compatibility and a workable marriage partner who fits neatly into their social milieu.
Agape	An altruistic, dutiful, giving and selfless approach to love. Since Agape is indicative of will, rather than emotion, head rather than heart, this lover is able to be deeply compassionate and, regardless of benefits or difficulties, is able to give the gift of love without any expectation of reciprocity.

Black and white

"South Africa offers an unusually interesting perspective from which to investigate aspects of love because of its multicultural nature", says Dr Hilton Rudnick. **How do Blacks, Whites, Mixed-race people, Indians and Asians look at love in a globalizing world?**

South Africa offers both first world and developing world populations living side by side and culturally influencing each other. For our research, we divided the population into four broad ethnic groups (Black, White, Colored and Indian/Asian), and sought to look at the criteria they used in choosing partners. Although these kaleidoscopic groups co-exist, they are not fully integrated due to history, past regulation (apartheid) and, in some cases, choice.

Black South Africans are the dominant (80%) racial group in South Africa, though within these racial categories there are multiple tribes, language groups and regional cultures. For example, Professor of Psychology Nhlanhla Mkhize argues that **the African self is pluralistic and in constant dialogue with the universe.** The dialogical self changes organically in tune with environmental influences and is subject to influence from intersecting cultures. In contrast, the worldview of the White South African is thought to be primarily individualistic, while the Mixed-race South African is more difficult to pin down. Finally the Indian/Asian group tends to emphasize the preservation of their own culture and be less porous to competing worldview ideologies. We wondered if there were differences in how these ethnicities chose their partners. We interviewed nearly 400 students (average age 23) from the University of Johannesburg.

Romance

We utilized Lee's model of the Colors of Love (see box on page 108). The typologies tend to be usefully descriptive but somewhat limiting. All people are richer than their type, and some nuance is lost in defining someone in regard to a particular type. Nevertheless, when we looked at how the dominant type measured up against ethnicity, the results were interesting.

Eros, the love style most closely associated with conventional romantic love, was endorsed as a primary style by about 46% of Whites and Coloreds and 40% of Blacks. For Indian/Asians, however, Agape was their most endorsed style (28%) with Eros second (25%). Clearly **across most cultures in South Africa, romantic love is regarded as the ideal way to choose a partner.** Agape, the most selflessly giving style, was the second most endorsed style across the entire sample (about 22%). What the research indicates

"Lovestyle is related to lifestyle."

is that most people across the cultural groups yearn for romance – chemistry, devotion, physical attraction and intensity. Ludus, the lovestyle least like romantic love was endorsed as a primary style by only 6 % of the sample. It was represented highest in the Indian/Asian group where it accounted for 11 % of the sample.

Affluence

Putting cultural differences aside, we also investigated how men and women differ when it comes to love. The differences were clear, but not that profound. As might be expected, men were significantly more Ludus than women, more into the conquest of love than being in for the long haul, though not dramatically so. In a similar vein, women were more Storgè than men, more willing to base a love relationship on a deep friendship than men are.

From a socioeconomic perspective, there was also a clear and significant trend. We utilized five categories (Upper to Lower) of socioeconomic groups that the individual was raised in. In the first four categories, upward of 80 % of individuals indicated that love was the primary decider of who they would marry. Only in the last category, the most financially challenged group, did this drop dramatically to about 55 %. The same group was significantly more likely to be Ludus, possibly indicating that permanent relationships were less a focus where financial strain was an issue. This could indicate that **socioeconomic history is a better predictor than ethnicity and gender** in determining the centrality of love in the partner selection equation. It suggests that lovestyle is in some way related to lifestyle, and that with increased affluence, marrying for love is increasingly foregrounded.

Satisfaction

Looking at the overall results, we suggest that, in developing countries, globalization is impacting on the way in which people make their decisions in regard to partner selection. Whereas there are strong indications that mate selection in Africa was previously a matter of collectivism, pragmatics, convenience and parental intervention in selecting a partner, this has shifted to be more in line with Western values of marrying for love. **The Black population seems to be moving strongly in this direction.** Only the Indian/Asian group differs from this practice, though even in this group, the majority of participants still regard love as the foundation of marriage. While on the surface this does appear to be a liberating idea, the statistics regarding failed marriages are well known. To complicate the issue, in other research we did, there was very little difference in the satisfaction of marriages for those who married for love and chose their own partners, versus those who had partners chosen for them. Clearly the marriage equation is a complicated one to unravel. Love as a basis for marriage seems, to the Western world-view, to be almost too obvious to debate. Yet Lee's model and the way it identifies multiple forms of love indicates that there are many ways to give expression to love. It also indicates that, while there are some minor (though significant) differences in the way different ethnicities choose their partners, by far the bulk of people, for better or worse, see romantic love as the cornerstone of marriage.

Hilton Rudnick is a psychologist and former academic from the University of Johannesburg (South Africa). His PhD sought to find the links between Western psychotherapy and traditional healing in South Africa. He has published in several local psychological journals on various topics in applied psychology. Hilton is currently Managing Director of Omnicor, a South African company that specializes in psychological services.
Kety Pavlou, PhD, is a researcher and looks at love from a cultural perspective.

"We are primates, clothed in culture."

Free choice?

A father has a discussion with his daughter about her plan to marry.
She argues "I know what I'm doing and it's my own, free choice."
Dr **Carlos Yela** doubts. In love matters we are not as free,
nor as rational as we would like to believe.

We are not as free because we are subject to a wide range of biological and sociocultural factors that are beyond our control, which we are frequently unaware of:

→ We have discovered that **we love like 'dressed-up chimpanzees'**: a small primate, clothed in 'culture', which has developed the 'primary affective bonds' we share with other species, converting them into a complex bio-psycho-social amalgam we call 'love'. We remain a member of the animal kingdom, with biological needs and neurochemical processes that affect us more than we imagine.

→ We have understood that we **love as members of a given culture** in which we learn, for example, which kind of love is standard (e.g. passionate) and which is taboo (e.g. playful), or what the relationship between love, sexuality and marriage (or stable relationships) should be. In Spain, for example, we have confirmed that most people disapprove of sex without love (especially among women even today), love without sex and marriage without love. This was not the case at other times in history, nor is it so in other cultures.

→ And we have discovered that **we love as social beings**, that throughout the 'romantic socialization' process (which begins with children's stories), we learn how, when, with whom, why and where to fall in love, what that should mean to us, and what the consequences should be. Loving passion does not mean the same (and does not have the same consequences) in different societies.

We are not so rational as our loving behavior (including what we think, feel, say and do) is largely at the mercy of errors in the other's perception (from cognitive bias to the process of idealization as we fall in love), of intense emotions (passion, as one of the key elements of love, at least in the initial stages) and of romantic myths (absurd, impossible and/or irrational beliefs about what love supposedly 'is' and 'should be', adopted and shared without question by our collective society). Love is one of the most important aspects of human life, but it is also one of the areas shrouded in most clichés, myths, false beliefs and misunderstandings. Some myths are especially damaging as they create unreasonable expectations that sooner or later will result in disappointment. Some of these are:

→   **The belief that falling in love should necessarily lead to a stable relationship** (what we have called the myth of marriage or living together).

→   **The belief that true passion should last forever,** and that falling in love and love are basically the same. If you don't feel the same dizziness after 1000 days (and nights) of living together, it's because you don't really love your partner and you should break off the relationship, whether or not it's satisfying (myths of eternal passion and of falling in love-love equivalence).

→   **The belief that you can only feel true love** (including physical attraction and passionate desire) **for a single person** and, therefore, if you feel an attraction for another person, it's because you no longer truly love your partner and you should break off the relationship, regardless of how satisfying it is (myth of exclusivity).

If ignorance, unrealistic expectations and misunderstandings are behind so much suffering in loving relationships, some knowledge of all these processes might prove to be a powerful tool for making things better (e.g. let's not marry while we still haven't passed the 'falling in love' phase, let's not break off a relationship just because of attraction for another, let's not break up because the level of passion decreases, etc.). Bearing in mind that nobody today doubts the importance of and need for good sex education, let's go for good 'love education' as well. The social obligation of research on love must involve an attempt to apply the available knowledge to solving personal or relationship problems, and on generally improving the well-being of people and their quality of life.

The keys

→ **We are not so free because we're subject to a wide range of unconscious biological and sociocultural factors: being an animal, a member of a given culture and a social being.**

→ **We are not so rational because our loving behavior is largely at the mercy of perception, emotions and romantic myths. Some of these myths are damaging.**

→ **Some knowledge of all these processes might prove to be a powerful tool for less failure and more well-being in our relationships. Let's go for good 'love education'.**

Carlos Yela (PhD in psychology) is Lecturing Professor at the Universidad Complutense de Madrid (Spain). His main areas of research are related to social psychology and include the psychological, biological and sociocultural analysis of romantic love. He has published more than thirty papers in a range of national and international journals and contributed to a number of international publications, such as the Encyclopedia of Applied Psychology. He is the author of *El amor desde la Psicología Social: ni tan libres, ni tan racionales* (*Love Seen from Social Psychology: not So Free nor So Rational*).

"What comes first: love or desire?"

Love & desire

Very specific brain scans uncover the secrets of love step by step.
Dr **Stephanie Cacioppo** builds further on the lifelong research
of **Elaine Hatfield**, analyzing now detailed brainscans.
She has recently been named a rising star by the Association for
Psychological Science. For *The World Book of Love* they combine
their insights and discover the specific interaction between love
and desire. What comes first?

Although love and desire are two of the most powerful subjective feelings one may
experience in a lifetime, there are still debates about the nature and origin of these two
phenomena. For decades, scholars from a variety of disciplines have tried to disentangle
these two experiences. Several studies have found behavioral similarities as well as
differences between love and desire. From a psychological viewpoint, love is defined as
a complex mental state involving basic and complex emotions as well as chemical, cognitive,
rewarding, and goal-directed behavioral components. More precisely, the scientific
definition of passionate love that we have formulated states that love is "a state of intense
longing for union with another. A complex functional whole including appraisals or
appreciations, subjective feelings, expressions, patterned physiological processes, action
tendencies and instrumental behaviors", while sexual desire is most appropriately defined
as "a longing for sexual union".

Brain activity

From a neuro-functional viewpoint, recent evidence from both human and non-human animal studies investigating the biochemistry and brain activity of love and desire shows a strong correlation between these two phenomena. Recently, neuroscientists have begun to collect some data indicating that these processes may be very similar in a variety of cultures. For instance, fMRI (Functional magnetic resonance imaging) studies in humans find that both love and sexual desire spark increased activity in the subcortical brain areas that are associated with euphoria, reward and motivation, as well as in the cortical brain areas that are involved in self-representation and social cognition. The co-activation of subcortical emotion-related areas and higher order cortical areas that mediate more complex cognitive functions (e.g. body image, mental associations and self-representation) reinforces the top-down neuro-functional model of interpersonal relationships and the potential role of past experiences on future emotional feelings and behaviors. Interestingly, neural differences also exist between desire and love. Notably at the subcortical level, the posterior-to-anterior insula pattern, from desire to love, suggests that love is a more abstract representation of the pleasant sensorimotor experiences than desire. More precisely, comparing love with sexual desire, activity has been shown to be diminished in the ventral striatum, hypothalamus, amygdala, somatosensory cortex, and inferior parietal lobule. Those reductions are in keeping with sexual desire as a motivational state with a very specific, embodied goal, whereas passionate love could be thought of as a more abstract, flexible and behaviorally complex goal that is less dependent on the physical presence of another person. Love is associated with a more intense activation of the ventral Tegmental Area, and a specific recruitment of activity in more dorsal regions of the right striatum, two dopamine-rich regions involved generally in motivation, reward expectancy and habit formation.

Emotions and pleasure

Those findings reinforce the importance of specific goal-directed incentives if one is looking to fall 'head over heels in love'. The activation of these subcortical dopaminergic-rich areas during experiences of passionate love is in line with psychological studies defining love as a rewarding, positive, and motivating experience. Interestingly, the anterior part of the insula has been shown to be activated significantly by feelings of love, whereas the posterior part of the insula is activated significantly by feelings of sexual desire. This posterior-to-anterior insular distinction between sexual desire and love reinforces the neuro-functional characteristic of a posterior-to-anterior progression of integrative representations of affective bodily feelings to an ultimate representation of all feelings. This is in line with the view that love is an abstract construct, which is partly based on the mental representation of repeated past emotional moments with another. This specific pattern of activation suggests that love builds upon a neural circuit for emotions and pleasure, adding regions associated with reward expectancy, habit formation and feature detection. In particular, the shared activation within the insula, with a posterior-to-anterior pattern, from desire to love, suggests that love grows out of and is a more abstract representation of the pleasant sensorimotor experiences that characterize desire.

From these results, one may consider desire and love on a spectrum that evolves from integrative representations of affective visceral sensations to an ultimate representation of feelings, incorporating mechanisms of reward expectancy and habit learning. Although love is not a prerequisite for sexual desire, these recent neuroimaging meta-analyses suggest that desire might be a prerequisite for love. Whether desire has to be conscious or subconscious is a question scholars need to further investigate in future research.

The keys

→ **Love is a rewarding, positive and motivating experience.**

→ **Love is a more abstract representation of the pleasant sensorimotor experiences than desire.**

→ **Although love is not a prerequisite for sexual desire, recent neuroimaging meta-analyses suggest that desire might be a prerequisite for love.**

Stephanie Cacioppo (née Ortigue) is a Professor at the University of Geneva (Switzerland) and received her PhD in psychology and cognitive neuroscience from the University Hospital of Geneva and the University of Savoy (France). Author of over fifty scientific articles, her work focuses on social neuroscience, neurology, implicit cognition and, in particular, the consciousness of the interacting brain in social settings. She serves on the editorial board of NeuroImage and is the past Editor-in-Chief of the peer-reviewed scientific journal *Psyche*. She also currently serves on various committees for three major non-profit societies in neuroscience, including the Society for Social Neuroscience, Cognitive Neuroscience Society and the Association for the Scientific Study of Consciousness.
Elaine Hatfield is also the author of the text "Passionate love forever". See page 16.

"Exotic is erotic but similars attract."

The perfect match

Some people find their love thousands of miles away. Exotic is erotic. But most of us just marry the one next door. In her lab, Dr **Cindy Meston** examines different effects on our way to the perfect match.

1. The proximity effect. Familiarity breeds liking. As it turns out, some amount of familiarity creates liking whether you're talking about a person, a drawing, a word in an unknown foreign language, a song, a new product being advertised, a political candidate, or even a nonsense syllable. Proximity is often the first step in becoming attracted to someone. We often marry people who are living in the same neighborhood. In classrooms with assigned seating, relationships develop as a function of how far people are seated from each other. Students assigned to a middle seat are more likely to make acquaintances than those who are seated at the end of a row. With alphabetical seating, friendships form between those whose names start with nearby letters. The more frequent a person's exposure during the early period of introduction, the more positive the response. Why? We often respond to anyone or anything strange or novel with at least mild discomfort, if not a certain degree of anxiety. With repeated exposure, our feelings of anxiety decrease. The more familiar we are with someone, the better we are able to predict his or her behavior and thus to feel more comfortable around the person.

2. The exotic effect. The previous effect doesn't contradict the fact that, *initially,* a certain amount of 'mystery' can be sexually motivating. Once people are in close proximity, eye contact becomes critical. In one study, forty-eight women and men came to a lab and were asked to stare into each other's eyes while talking. The effect of mutual gaze proved powerful. Many reported that deep eye contact with an opposite-sex stranger created feelings of intense love.

Too much familiarity, however, can backfire. Traits that are initially deemed positive can become a source of annoyance. Men who were once described as 'funny and fun' become 'embarrassing in public'. An attractive 'spontaneity' transforms into an unattractive 'irresponsibility', 'successful and focused' into 'workaholic' and 'strong willed' into 'stubborn'.

Just as overexposure can douse the fire of sexual attraction, its opposite – novelty – can stoke its flames. Psychologist Daryl Bem sums it up with the phrase "the exotic becomes erotic". Indeed, in college classes in which instructors ask women to list the qualities they find sexually attractive, 'mysterious' invariably emerges on the list.

3. The matching effect. There is no doubt we are attracted to people who are different from ourselves. However, when it comes to actually choosing a long-term sexual partner, it is more the rule than the exception that 'similars attract'. Several studies have shown substantial similarity between husbands and wives in their attitudes about faith, war and politics, as well as similarities in their physical health, family background, age, ethnicity, religion and level of education. Dating and married couples are similar in physical attractiveness, and young married couples even tend to be matched in weight! The 'matching hypothesis', as named by social psychologists, is so strong that observers react negatively when they perceive couples who are mismatched on levels of attractiveness. There is one notable exception: a beautiful woman and a not so attractive man. In this scenario, consistent with evolutionary hypotheses, people judging the mismatched pairs ascribe wealth, intelligence or success to the man.

Why do similars attract? One motive for seeking a close physical match to oneself is a fear of rejection. People prefer those similar to themselves in overall 'mate value' or desirability on the mating market. Going for someone substantially more desirable is often a losing proposition for both women and men. And, if a person manages to lure a more desirable mate, there are costs involved – such as needing to be ever vigilant of mate poachers. Finding someone who shares similar attitudes and beliefs is attractive because it provides a validation of what we already believe. That is, a partner who shares our opinions provides

Higher dating potential

The Meston Lab research team went to several theme parks in Texas to examine whether riding a roller coaster, which increases SNS* activity, might be a way to enhance women's sexual responses. The researchers asked the women to look at a photograph of a man and then fill out a brief questionnaire that asked how attractive they thought the man was, how much they would like to kiss him, and how willing they would be to go on a date with him. Even though all the women viewed the same photograph of an average-looking man, **the women who had just gotten off the roller coaster rated the man as being more attractive** and having higher dating potential than the women who were waiting in line to take the ride did. It appears that attraction increased as a result of residual SNS activation from the roller coaster ride.

Pragmatic daters and maters may wonder whether the findings from the roller coaster study mean they would have a better chance of attracting a mate if they frequented locales that offered dancing instead of lounging, or if they hung out at a gym instead of a coffee shop. The answer is not so straightforward. In real-life dating situations, it depends on whether there is at least some initial level of attraction. If so, then yes, perhaps. But, if the woman does not find her pursuer in the least bit appealing, then even having her run a marathon would not make her want to go on a date, much less have sex with the person.

* SNS is our sympathetic nervous system which mobilizes our body's nervous system in a fight-or-flight response.

evidence that we must be correct. 'Balance' is a pleasant emotional state, a harmonious feeling that occurs when two people like each other and agree about some topic. It is much easier to maintain a pleasant balance if you start out agreeing on most topics. Finally, similarity foretells long-term relationship success. It leads to emotional bonding, cooperation, communication, mating happiness and lowered risk of breaking up. So, although opposites *sometimes* attract, when it comes to mating, 'birds of a feather flock well together'. I do think love has a lot to do with finding the right 'match', which is very individual and related to all sorts of personal past experiences. My favorite definition of love is from Plato's Symposium where Aristophanes describes love as the reconnection with one's severed half.

The keys

→ **Proximity is often the first step to becoming attracted to someone. Familiarity breeds liking.**

→ **Too much familiarity can backfire. The exotic is erotic.**

→ **Although opposites sometimes attract, similarity often foretells long-term relationship success.**

Cindy Meston is Full Professor of Clinical Psychology at the University of Texas at Austin (USA). She directs the Sexual Psychophysiology Laboratory, which is one of the few laboratories in the world devoted exclusively to the study of women's sexual health from both a psychological and physiological perspective. Her research has often attracted the attention of the international media. She currently serves on the editorial boards of several scientific journals and is Past President of the International Society for the Study of Women's Sexual Health. She has published over 100 peer reviewed articles and book chapters on women's sexuality, and given over 200 professional presentations on human sexuality.

Passive love

" We enhance our self-worth in close relationships."

If the need for love is universal, how does culture play a role in shaping its manifestation? Digging to the heart of love, cross-cultural psychologist David Dalsky has a close look on *amae* in Japan. Some call it childish, others call it passive.

Researchers have found that, in Japan, the need to feel good about oneself may not be important for psychological, sociological, and anthropological reasons. In traditional Japanese culture (compared to Western cultures) people are socialized from a young age to value group membership more than individual self-expression; therefore, the goal of preventing failure becomes more important than striving for individual success. In light of this, some researchers have argued that the **Japanese have a fundamental motivation for avoiding failure** and trying hard to achieve this, rather than promoting their self-worth.

On the other hand, another group of researchers have argued that a relational context needs to be considered when studying positive self-image in modern-day Japan. For example, when doing well in a task such as a university exam, studies have found that the Japanese will attribute their success to external causes (e.g. "I must have been lucky"), but expect their friends to make an internal attribution for their success (e.g. "you are a smart person"). In this way, positive self-feelings are indirectly enhanced through relationships. My own cross-cultural research proposes a unique way in which people may enhance positive self-feelings in relationships; namely, when the self of a person theoretically includes another person's self in terms of resources, perspectives, and identities (i.e., self-expansion), Japanese as well as Americans will enhance their self-worth in close relationships through the exchange of compliments. I call this process 'mutual self-enhancement'.

Let's keep it this way

How does all of the above relate to the manifestation of love through relationships in Japan? Starting from the beginning of one's life, it could be said that the love between a mother and child is strengthened and deepened instinctively at the breast, a phenomenon that forms a lifelong bond. In a country such as Japan, where group goals are prioritized over individual ones and interdependency reigns, the dependency feelings experienced by the child in this relationship can extend into adulthood and, what's more, permeate throughout society. This feeling is called *amae* in Japanese, a word that may be roughly translated into English as 'passive love'. *Amae* **is a feeling that offers a positive attitude toward interdependence** in Japan. It is behaving childishly so that others will indulge the individual to feel at one with others and his or her surroundings. As it is mainly characteristic of the relationship between a Japanese parent and child, *amae* is difficult to translate into other languages, suggesting that it may be a uniquely Japanese phenomenon (although some research suggests that *amae* can be identified in other cultures – even Western cultures such as North America). If we are to learn something from the Japanese about love, *amae* may hold some of the keys. Love can manifest itself differently depending on culture: what seems like childish behavior in one country, may be adaptive behavior in another. As long as it isn't extreme, don't be afraid of relying too closely on others, for love can be grown and nurtured in the bonds of interdependency. Exercising your inner child with the right people can lead to self-expansion and feelings of love.

David Dalsky is an Associate Professor in the Center for the Promotion of Excellence at Kyoto University (Japan), where he teaches courses on culture and academic writing. He was awarded a fellowship from the Japanese Ministry of Education for doctoral research in cross-cultural psychology and this project received the Outstanding Dissertation Honorable Mention Award from the International Academy for Intercultural Research.

"I can't imagine my parents ever making love."

Beyond shame

Three in five people prefer making love in the dark, global research tells us. For most of them, it is simply more exciting. One in five, however, is ashamed of his or her own body. Developmental psychologist **Willem Poppeliers** provides training worldwide, aimed at remedying this situation from a young age. A healthy sexual relationship is within everyone's reach.

Reduced to its simplest terms: a dynamic, lively relationship is love plus desire. Our love life is the sum of a desire for life and desire for love. Desire for life forms the relational component of our love life and desire for love the biological component. Together, they form the cultural package that we have received right from conception and birth.
For love to work well, a free and safe sexual environment is necessary. But without social and cultural protection a human child cannot survive (in any society). It needs warmth, protection, love and autonomy in order to come to full adulthood, to enter as an adult into a satisfying relationship with a partner and then be able to go on and care for children. Beyond guilt, shame and fear. For this, five basic conditions need to be fulfilled.

1. **Feeling free and safe.** To grow into sexually mature persons, we must be totally present in our bodies. Feelings of guilt about bodily excitement and shame about our body parts do not belong here. Early in life, babies and toddlers experience sexual feelings. Parents need to accept this and respect it as something belonging to the child. They have to realize

that these childhood sexual experiences are necessary for growing into a sexually well-integrated adult. The child discovers that its sexual organs are an integral part of its body of which it can be proud.

2. **The ability to self-regulate.** Self-regulation is the supreme state of inter-subjectivity and consists of four components: imitation, empathy, mentalization and regulation. The abilities to imitate and to show empathy are innate qualities. By imitating others and being able to move into the person of another, children learn to fit into their wider human environment. Imitation and empathy are, however, not sufficient in order to achieve full maturity. It is a known fact, for example, that in intimate violence, it is precisely empathy that partners use to touch and wound each other's most vulnerable properties. For loving relationships, more is needed. To this end, children learn mentalization and self-regulation. Mentalization is the capacity, within a relationship, to see the other person as an autonomous, self-thinking, feeling and acting being. From there we can experience the other as someone with their own history and their own world, separate from our own.

3. **Touching and being touched is elementary.** Sexual fulfilment within body contact is very different from sexual gratification. Gratification is short-lived, it is masturbation *à deux*. Sexual fulfilment stems from a loving relationship in which both partners are able fully and unconditionally to surrender to each other. They feel physically touched, both inwardly and outwardly. Each in their different way, sexual partners feel touched in the mind (consciously and durably), in the heart (satisfaction and autonomy) and in the sexual organs (desire and satisfaction) and share this feeling with one another.

4. **Discovering the feminine and the masculine.** Femininity and masculinity are a continuum. The distinction between men and women is not absolute, and indeed cannot be. How else would we be able to form loving relationships? In neurological and hormonal respects, men and women resemble each other more than is generally supposed. Thus, oxytocin, vasopressin, testosterone and estrogen occur in both sexes. In particular, it is about men discovering the female in themselves and women the male. This rule also applies to homosexual relationships.

5. **Respecting each developmental phase.** Many adults say they cannot imagine their parents making love to one another. But the fact is that their parents shared their love. Sexuality plays a role in each stage of development, but each time with a different meaning and nuanced expression. During the first revelation stage, the child needs the proper genital mirroring and validation that belong to this stage (curiosity, innocence, excitement and regulation), but does not need adults to impose their own sexuality. Before puberty,

children learn that their sexuality belongs to their own personal world and is respected by parents. With puberty and adolescence, young people enter the period of exploration and experimentation and learn, with the help of their environment (educators, friends, and teachers), how to combine sexual desire and intimate love. The parents remain in the background with a regulating presence: the inner security of the first phase continues. In the period of adulthood, the formation of relationships takes place, after which children are often born. At this stage, the partners discover that openness and receptivity are the main ingredients in a love relationship and that it is not just about satisfying each other's emotional and bodily needs. In the following phases, their own children grow up and in turn, need mental, emotional and genital mirroring in order to learn that their sexuality belongs to their experiential world. With increasing age and until death, curiosity about the desire for love remains alive, with the desire for sexual intercourse decreasing and that for affection increasing. Desire for life is more internalized. But any kind of love is always a form of desire for life.

The keys

→ **Our love life is the sum of drive for life (relational aspect) and desire for love (biological aspect). For this, a free and safe sexual environment is necessary, without guilt, shame or fear.**

→ **In relational education, learning to empathize is not enough. Equally important are mentalization and self-regulation.**

→ **Sexuality plays a role in each stage of development, but each time with a different meaning and expression. Adequate mirroring and validation are crucial elements here.**

Willem Poppeliers is a developmental psychologist and bioenergetic analytic therapist. He is the founder of the Foundation for Sexual Grounding Therapy (FSGT) and trains Sexual Grounding therapists and trainers, who teach courses and training sessions in Mexico, France, the Netherlands, Switzerland, Austria, Germany and Ukraine. He has written several articles and a book about this.
Theo Royers is a sociologist and bioenergetic therapist. He is the chairman of the FSGT. He also works as a researcher at a national research institute. He has written and collaborated on over 200 articles and books.

"In our love of God,
we should love everybody."

Live to love

"The real love is love towards God, who is the creator of the universe. Love towards God is not only worship or prayer. Along with this love, the love towards God's creatures is obligatory because love is the foundation of the universe", states Dr **Rauf Yasin Jalali** from Pakistan. And he describes the sexual part in detail: from the bath and foreplay, to the manipulation of the genitals.

The goal of our life should be to love everybody because that is the prerequisite of love towards God. Love, and the love between spouses, is the most important aspect of our everyday life. The element of spirituality should be felt in our daily expressions of love. Partners should know what the other one feels, likes and dislikes. Everybody has a sense of joy of exquisitenesses and everyone has fondness for gorgeousness.

It starts with hygiene. Neatness of body, house, surroundings and imaginations is extremely significant. The cleanliness is actual beauty. Partners should be more conscious about this. Their mouths, hair and bodies should be aromatic. During sexual intercourse, spouses should not consider that penis and vagina are meeting. They should believe that their hearts are entering in each other. They should become one soul. That is spiritual sexual intercourse. To achieve the pride of spiritual sex, I would like to mention here some simple ways of behavior that lead to an enjoyable love and sex life. I am hopeful that if, partners put into practice the following manners in their everyday love life, their love will last till their last breaths and the rates of divorces and separations will seriously diminish.

Start with a bath

Both partners may take a bath, use nice perfumes, eat cardamom and aniseed or take any fine chewing gum. Sexual arousal may occur suddenly as a response to sexual attraction, or gradually after looking, touching, stroking, kissing and other foreplay activities. The foreplay enhances sexual enjoyment. The early stages of sexual activity may take place in any position, but in later stages, the couple will usually take the position in which penetration occurs. **Foreplay varies gradually from gentle to rapid and forceful.** The man may smell, kiss, lick, suck, bite and explore the parts of the female partner's body with the tongue and lips. This often occurs in sequence of contact with different parts of the body: hands, arms and armpits, lips, tongue, eyes, nose, forehead, ears, cheek, chin, neck, breasts, nipples, abdomen, feet, shin, thighs, buttocks and genitals.

A good manipulation of the partner's genitals is of great importance. The man may lick and suck the woman's labia and the clitoris, which helps to vigorously arouse the woman sexually. Inserting the tongue into the vagina, and moving it in and out of the vagina is a replication of the movements of the penis. The woman should also lick the breasts, lower abs, inner thighs and perineum of the man. She may suck the man's testicles and penis wildly, subject to the social values of society and religion. Pressing and rubbing the genital areas against the partner's genitals helps to prepare the genitals for penetration. **The couple may adopt any position that allows coitus to take place.** The penis might be inserted gradually; just the tip at first, then progressively more of the penis is inserted in a series of small forward movements and half retreats. This spreads the vaginal lubricants over the penis, and enables the vagina to accommodate it easily.

During the sexual intercourse, the man's penis moves repeatedly in the woman's vagina and out again. Rhythmic hip movements do this, so the genital areas move apart and then together again. Both of the partners may move their hips, or one of them may move while the other stays still. Sometimes the range of movement is small, so the penis stays within the vagina for long duration. Sometimes large strokes, so the penis leaves the vagina completely, and then is thrust back deep inside it, hence more enjoyable. **In the intercourse, the couple may use many kinds of movements:** large and small, gentle and forceful, fast and slow. Either or both partners may take the initiative and changes of movement may be gradual or unexpectedly fast. The couple may also choose to stop and then begin again several times. At the same time, they usually continue many of the actions of love-making that preceded intercourse: kissing, fondling and other activities. After the orgasms and ejaculation, the couple may go to the completion with kisses and caresses.

Broken glass

This deep love urges us to contemplate on all the different aspects of nature that usually lead us to have a deeper faith in God, the creator who created all this beauty around us. In our love of God, we should love everybody. But our world is similar to the shop of a glass-blower, where glasses are present everywhere. So, we should be careful at every step, otherwise the heart's flask of human being will be injured. If this happens, along with the broken glass, we will get the retribution of our carelessness. Our souls will be wounded.

We should learn a lesson from the sun, moon, stars, day, night and the whole universe. Everything provides services for human beings. Trees do not eat their own fruits and do not sit under their own shadows. Their fruits and shadows are for us. They produce oxygen for us, which is necessary for life. Rivers and seas do not drink their own water, it is there for us. The human being is the most eminent part of creation. I state here with pain in my heart that humans have become the enemy of the humans. We have divided ourselves on the bases of color, race, language, religion and regional limits. **We have started to hate each other. That is not our path. Our path should be only love and love will result in unity.** So, as humans we should become one community. If we look at people with our spiritual eyes, we can observe that all people of the world are standing in one circle. If anybody hands thorns to another, those thorns will go round the whole circle and will come back into the hands of that person who first introduced them. Those thorns will injure everyone's hands. If someone gives flowers to another person, those flowers will go right round the entire circle and will come back into the hands of that individual who provided the flowers first. Those flowers will provide good fragrances and pleasure to everybody, along with the donor. We should live to love.

The keys

→ **The real love is love towards God, who is the creator of the universe. Along with this love, love towards God's creatures is obligatory because love is the foundation of the universe.**

→ **Spiritual sexual intercourse is expressed through respectful and detailed sexual behavior and practice from foreplay to orgasm.**

→ **This deep love urges us to contemplate on all the different aspects of nature that usually lead us to have a deeper faith in God, who unites all human beings in love and understanding.**

Rauf Yasin Jalali, MD, PhD, is Professor of Sexology in Rawalpindi (Pakistan). He is Director of the South Asia Institute for Human Sexuality (SAIHS) and is often called The Love Guru. He has been awarded the Medal of Excellence from Colombo University and has been involved in the world of sexology for more than three decades. He worked with various international universities and colleges as Dean & Professor of the Human Sexuality Studies Program. Dr Jalali is Lifetime Professor of Sexology, affiliated with the Academy for Sexology in South Africa. He is a well-known poet as well, involved in the rich tradition of Urdu poetry, which is very popular in Pakistani and Indian culture.

"Because a love is unconventional in a society does not mean that it is not genuine."

Love between men

"It is difficult for many people to understand how two men can love each other passionately and romantically the way that a man and a woman can", says Dr **Frank Muscarella**. "While it is true that the world is given many fewer examples of romantic relationships between men, they have existed across history with those of men and women."

Working on the assumption that passionate and romantic love between men can and does occur, my research has focused on the possible evolutionary foundation of this love. Theorists believe that the romantic love that exists between a man and a woman has its evolutionary origins in the love that a mother shows her offspring. The loving attention that a mother shows her offspring increases the likelihood that they will survive. With evolution, mating pairs of males and females that shared such loving attention produced offspring more successfully. In essence, there was natural selection for the loving behavior between the males and females because it increased the bonding between them, which, in turn, contributed to more successful reproduction. The emotional and psychological complexity of this loving behavior varies across species, but certainly has reached its highest point in humans.

Survival

A commonly asked question is how could loving behavior between males have evolved since it does not lead to reproduction. Emerging research on the evolution of humans suggests that loving behavior between all individuals, not just men and women, may have played an important role in early human survival. Human ancestors are believed to have lived in small, highly cooperative groups. Evidence from species closely related to humans such as chimpanzees and bonobos, as well as evidence from humans across cultures and across history, suggests that **sexual behavior between individuals reinforces bonds** between the individuals which, in turn, keeps the group together. Thus, it is now believed by some that, among our human ancestors, both reproductive and non-reproductive sexual behavior may have served as a form of social adhesive to strengthen relationships in the group, which, in turn, contributed to its members' survival and ultimate reproduction.

Alliances

The alliance theory of the evolution of male-male sexual behavior in humans holds that in the evolutionary past, male-male sexual behavior reinforced alliances between males. These social alliances contributed directly to the males' survival because their allies helped them to secure food and fight off enemies. They contributed to reproduction indirectly because the allies helped them live long enough to ultimately secure a female mate and reproduce. **Males who engaged in some male-male sexual behavior may have survived and reproduced more successfully** than males who never engaged in male-male sexual behavior because they had fewer and weaker alliances and, thus, reduced their chances of getting food or fighting off enemies. Males who engaged in exclusive male-male sexual behavior would not have reproduced. In this model, all contemporary males are descended from males who could respond erotically and lovingly to some males, sometimes, under some conditions. Several researchers theorize that, as humans moved from hunting and gathering societies to agricultural societies, cultures changed and some sexual behavior that was once acceptable began to be seen as problematic and was prohibited.

Romance

I think that the existence of the contemporary gay male subculture characteristic of the West arises from the interaction of several factors. One is that, due to normal variation in same-sex interest, a small percentage of men are largely or exclusively sexually attracted only to other men. The second is that **industrialized nations do not require a husband-wife, male-female couple for individuals to live and thrive**. This allows men romantically attracted only to men to live their lives with other men with the same interests. Finally, Western industrialized societies do not encourage, or actively discourage, three of the four recognized categories of male-male sexual behavior: status stratified (between master and servant), gender-stratified (between a man and someone who plays the role of a woman), and age-stratified (between adult and juvenile). This has left, as the primary accepted outlet for male-male sexual, romantic relationships, the fourth type, which is the egalitarian type. And, indeed, contemporary male-male relationships in Western societies are largely between adult male peers.

Culture

The most significant lesson I have drawn from my research is the importance of culture in determining whom and how we love. The capacity to engage in loving, sexual behavior with individuals of the opposite and same sex may be a fundamental element of the sexual nature of humans. However, anthropological and historical research suggests that it is culture that has the largest influence on how loving sexual relationships are expressed for most of the individuals in a particular society. Those who do not conform are often labeled criminal, or sick, or both. However, just because a love between two consenting adults is unconventional in a society does not mean that it is not genuine, profound and personally fulfilling to them. Fortunately, in numerous contemporary societies, this fact is being recognized, and many individuals will be allowed to find the love that is most important and sustaining to them.

The keys

→ **Research on the evolution of humans suggests that loving behavior between all individuals, not just men and women, may have played an important role in early human survival.**

→ **The capacity to engage in loving, sexual behavior with individuals of the same sex is part of the sexual nature of humans.**

→ **It is culture that has the largest influence on whom and how we love and on how loving sexual relationships are expressed for most of the individuals in a particular society.**

Frank Muscarella is Professor of Psychology at the Barry University in Miami Shores, Florida (USA). He is director of the master's degree program in clinical psychology and chair of the psychology department. His research is in the area of evolutionary psychology and human sexuality. He is author of various articles on sexual behavior and orientation, including "The Alliance Theory".

The motor of love

Cupid's arrows don't only hit our heart, they are aimed at our brains as well. Brain scans of people who are deeply in love surprisingly show activation in brain areas that are associated with 'rewards and goal acquisition'. What might be Cupid's goals and rewards? Prof **John Rempel** finds out. Love is a motive.

Love – it is a word that carries with it a richness of meaning and a depth of power that is unprecedented in human experience. It is regarded as the essence of the divine and the foundation of our most cherished relationships. There have been countless novels, treatises, sermons, poems, songs, dramas and works of art centred on the experiences and effects of love. Yet, love, as a concept, has proven notoriously difficult to define. For all its importance, love is a rather imprecise concept with multiple meanings, diverse targets and varied expressions. It seems that we know a lot about what it feels like to experience love and what love looks like in action, but there is much less clarity about what love actually *is*.

Four universal points

In a thoughtful philosophical analysis of love, Rolf Johnson (2001) proposed four points on which students of love virtually all agree. First, love has an object. Among other things, this means that love is something that flows out from us towards something else. Second, we value that which we love – the object of our love is meaningful and precious. Third, the lover is drawn or inclined toward the love object. Thus, there is a motivational component to love. And finally, love is something that we feel, often with extraordinary intensity. These points fit remarkably well with how Dr Christopher Burris and I have defined love. Quite simply, we believe that love is a motivational state in which **the goal is to preserve and promote the well-being of the loved one** – in short, love, in all of its varied forms, shares the common foundation of wanting what is best for the thing we love.

If love, at its core, is a motivational state, how then do we make sense of the various forms that love takes, and how does seeing love as a motive in any way capture the depth and intensity of its expression? The answer lies in recognizing that the desire to protect and enrich the lives of the ones that we love can emerge from a variety of profound, even transformative, experiences. For example, consider passionate love – the intense longing lovers have to unite their lives with their romantic partner. How can they not want to protect and enrich the life of the soulmate who fills them with excitement, desire and euphoria? In the same way, the desire to preserve and promote another's well-being can be rooted in the warmth, joy, and contentment of companionship and shared activities. The rewards of a mutually enriching friendship can foster lifelong bonds. Surely these rewards can also inspire the yearning for such companions – be they partners, friends, or siblings – to experience the best that life has to offer. Consider also children who rely on their parents to meet their needs for nurturing, caring and support. Would anyone question the deep concern that children have for the well-being of the caregivers on whom they depend?

Personal rewards

Of course, for all of these types of love, the well-being of the loved one is associated with the acquisition of personal rewards. To be sure, there is a clear desire to preserve and promote what is best for the one we love, but there is also something to be gained from their well-being. Yet, there is one type of love that can be considered 'pure' in that it does not include any additional goals beyond wanting what is best for the other – altruistic love. This is **love that gives without asking anything in return**, it inspires compassion, caring and self-sacrifice, it is the type of love ascribed to God. Indeed, some would contend that such love could only be ascribed to God – that humans are utterly and inescapably selfish and cannot be motivated solely for the well-being of another. Against such cynicism, research on altruistic motivation and compassionate love indicates that people, and even animals to some degree, can experience empathy – an emotional state characterized by feelings of tenderness, compassion, warmth directed towards another – and that empathic experiences can motivate people to benefit others, even when there is little to gain and much to lose. When it comes to altruistic love, sometimes it is 'all about them'.

Is there any evidence that love is a motive? Research on this topic is just beginning but there are some promising studies suggesting that motivation is central to how people understand and experience love. In a brain imaging study of people who were deeply in love, Arthur Aron and colleagues (2005) found that participants exhibited activation in brain areas, such as the ventral tegmental area, that are associated with rewards and goal acquisition. In another recent study, Kevin Hegi and Raymond Bergner (2010) found that participants were least likely to conceptualize Person A as loving Person B if Person A was not "invested in the well-being of the other for his or her own sake" and that the presence of this motive was rated as most essential to a good relationship. In some of our own research, we are also finding that **people are least likely to consider an experience as love if the motivation to benefit another is absent,** even if intense positive feelings for, and extremely positively evaluations of, the other are present.

Powerful force

Given this emerging research, there are good reasons to believe that love is indeed a motivational state brought on by powerful cognitive and emotional experiences. Yet, in the final analysis, does knowing this really matter? We think it matters a great deal. By recognizing that love is a motive, we can begin to understand why it is such a powerful force in people's lives. Unlike intense emotions or profound appreciation, **the desire to promote and preserve another's well-being demands action.** This is the true power of love – the power to inspire change, not only in how people think or feel about each other, but in what they want to do for each other.

The keys

→ **Love, in all of its varied forms, shares the common foundation of wanting what is best for the thing we love.**

→ **Empathic experiences can motivate people to benefit others even when there is little to gain and much to lose.**

→ **The desire to promote and preserve another's well-being demands action. This is the true power of love.**

John K. Rempel is Chair of the Psychology Department at St. Jerome's University in Waterloo (Canada). His primary research is focused on understanding the basic processes involved in close relationships and he has conducted studies on a wide range of interpersonal phenomena including trust, power, love, hate, conflict, empathy, sexuality, restorative justice, sexual violation, evil and partner influence on healthy decision-making.

"Love... feels like God."

Soap bubbles

Imagine we are all floating around in our personal soap bubbles. What happens when we feel love for someone? Prof **Chris Burris** uses the image of soap bubbles drifting across the sky to reflect on love.

One of the more curious discoveries that we have made in our research over the years is that experiences of different types of love not only have distinct motivational and emotional signatures, but that they also affect people's very sense of self in different ways. To explain, let me go back to when I blew soap bubbles as a kid (which, sadly, seems like a really long time ago).

Self and other

Imagine that you are contained in a kind of 'psychological soap bubble' that is floating through the environment. Other people are likewise surrounded – each by his or her own bubble. By using animations that portray these bubbles, we've learned that when someone experiences altruistic love for another, it's as if the lover perceives his or her own bubble as sticking to the beloved's bubble: They're traveling together, for sure, but they remain two distinct bubbles. In contrast, when someone experiences a non-altruistic form of love for another, such as erotic love, it's as if the two bubbles respectively containing self and other

not only stick together, but also merge into a single bubble. Thus, both altruistic and non-altruistic love experiences involve a sense of being connected to another person in a way that shifts one's own course. **One is no longer free-floating and detached from others.** At the same time, the sense of self as distinct from the other appears unique to altruistic love. In contrast, the self is lost in the other in the case of non-altruistic love and is perhaps lost entirely if the one bubble born of fusion of the two is ruptured by breezes and barbs in the psychological environment.

I beg you to trust me here: I never would have resorted to soap bubbles when talking about love unless it truly seemed to capture what our research participants were experiencing when they reflected on a past love episode. But if the metaphor is to provoke anything other than nostalgic yearning for childhood pastimes, we must consider what implications it may have for our understanding of love. To put it simply, why should we care?

The One

We have already conducted one study that suggests that confrontation with a person in need (a circumstance that is particularly likely to trigger altruistic love and its emotional signature, empathy) can evoke mystical episodes that are typified by a sense of oneness, absorption into something larger, and distortion of space and time – episodes that are often set forth as subjective evidence for the reality of the divine. Is it possible, then, that the experience of altruistic love – the love that bonds one's own 'self bubble' to another's – is typified by a sense of unity and self-transcendence that is the essence of mystical experience? Given that mystical experiences are one of the recurrent foundational elements across the faith traditions of the world, it is probably no accident that altruistic love is often accorded a special significance in religion – significance that, for example, moves the bodhisattvas of Mahayanan Buddhism to forgo the release from self of nirvana out of compassion for the suffering unenlightened. From a psychological perspective, there is no paradox. The very experience of altruistic love for the needy (and, hence, some sense of attachment to them) may be accompanied by a sense of transcendent oneness via release from the sense of self as separate.

We do not yet have data to address the question of whether non-altruistic forms of love can foster a similar sense of mystical oneness. Given the fusion results I mentioned above, however, it seems not at all surprising that erotic union has been portrayed on occasion as a path leading to spiritual transformation – as in Hindu Tantra, for example.

Many a theologian has asserted that God is love. A few have declared that Love is God. As a social scientist – indeed, even as a psychologist who studies religion – I must humbly throw up my hands, lacking the tool set to verify or dismiss the truth of either claim. Nevertheless, given the research findings that my colleagues and I are slowly compiling concerning the mystical properties of the experience of altruistic love for another, I am willing to make this more modest, cumbersome assertion: "Love can feel like what many people would call God."

The keys

→ **When someone experiences altruistic love, it's as if the lover perceives his or her own bubble as sticking to the beloved's bubble.**

→ **When someone experiences a non-altruistic form of love, such as erotic love, it's as if the two bubbles respectively containing self and other merge into a single bubble.**

→ **Love can feel like what many people would call God.**

Christopher T. Burris is a social psychologist and Associate Professor of Psychology at St. Jerome's University in Ontario (Canada). Colleague John Rempel and research assistant Kristina Schrage helped shape the ideas that he presented here. More broadly, his research deals with a range of topics including love and hate, religion and spirituality, evil and sexuality and consciousness and the self. When not 'playing academic', he can usually be found hovering behind binoculars, looking for birds.

Surviving life threats

"My project was not exactly dedicated to love", says Dr Marek Blatný. His work deals with the quality of life of childhood cancer survivors and their families. "But at once I realized it is, in fact, all about love."

Together with paediatric oncologists and clinical psychologists we are looking for areas where the quality of children's and adolescents' life is degraded due to the late effects of treatment and we are looking for ways to make up for the reduced life quality to these children. Within the project, we pay attention not only to the child patients but to their parents and siblings as well.

We were intrigued by the early results of the research: in many aspects of quality of life, the child cancer survivors did better than healthy children. Childhood cancer survivors, when compared with healthy children, reported worse physical performance and less involvement in leisure activities, but better emotional well-being and overall life satisfaction. Our explanation focuses on the fact that, after the experience with the life-threatening disease and the demanding and exhaustive treatment, everyday worries seem less serious to these children than to their peers. The survivors reported higher perceived quality of life in one more area: relationships with parents. **Survivors felt stronger involvement and greater warmth from their parents than children in the general population.** In the follow-up research we even found that for younger children (under age 12) the warmth of parental upbringing works as a protective factor against the impact of severity of the late effects of treatment on the experienced quality of life. In other words, although the children were suffering from serious consequences of anti-cancer therapy, the warmth of parental love was able to compensate for these effects and make up for the handicaps.

Parents

The testimonies of parents corresponded with how children and adolescents experienced their situations. According to current psychological knowledge, even adverse life events or even traumatic experiences may have certain positive aspects, for example, one may realize the value of life and the importance of loved ones. We asked parents what changes the illness of their child had brought to different areas of their lives, and we asked them to evaluate both negative and positive experiences. Among the positive aspects of this experience as viewed by the parents, **they predominantly cited improvement of interpersonal relationships** – greater love for their children, deeper relationship with the partner, the experience of support from relatives, friends and acquaintances, but also help and support from colleagues at work or directly from the employer. Naturally, some parents had had a bad experience, their relationships had fallen apart or they had lost

" The warmth of parental love compensates a lot."

are neglected. What they experience is characterized by major changes in life, especially requirements for independence and being overwhelmed with strong feelings such as fear, anxiety and feelings of guilt with which they are often left alone. Some healthy siblings in our research have also reported that they lacked greater presence of their parents or a chance to talk about their problems, but at the same time they never demanded more attention from their parents at the expense of their sick sibling. They suffered most from the disease of their siblings, their suffering, fear of their death, their absence and inability to be with them, and they wished them to be healthy and together again.

Once more, **it was compassion and love that emanated from the siblings' utterances.**

Well, I thought I was not involved in research on love… But we do know that love is present in every moment of our lives and, if we suffer, it is especially due to lack of affection. It is just important to be reminded of this fact every now and then.

Marek Blatný is Director of the Institute of Psychology of the Academy of Sciences of the Czech Republic and Professor of Social Psychology at Masaryk University in Brno (Czech Republic). His research includes longitudinal studies on general lifespan development and on the quality of life of children surviving cancer.

their jobs, but positive experiences significantly prevailed.

Siblings

At the time of the diagnosis, maximum care, attention and support are understandably given to the sick child. Also, parents receive support from medical staff, psychologists and other parents from the beginning. Sometimes the healthy siblings of sick children and their needs

"Love is wanting to make each other happy."

Infatuation is a disease of the eye

"Two concepts are always confused: Infatuation and love", says Prof **Alfons Vansteenwegen**, holder of the Gold Medal Lifetime Achievement of the World Association of Sexology. "Infatuation is a disease of the eye", he says. But what comes after?

Infatuation is a state in which one is overcome by an intense feeling of attraction to someone else. This is not the result of effort and cannot be brought about by willpower. You fall in love like you catch the flu. You see the other person not as he or she is, but as you will like him or her to be. For everyone else, the other is still the same; for the love-struck, the other is fantastic, amazing, unique, extraordinary, perfect and source of all goodness. This is called projection. Infatuation is an eye disorder, a soft psychosis.

Infatuation is compelling. It is something you cannot just shake off. It is an obsession, you are possessed by it. In a sense you are less free. Infatuation is accompanied by passionate attraction and extreme emotions. One is constantly driven towards the other. In this sense, infatuation is a driving force, a motivator. It drives people towards each other. Infatuation also energizes. It makes people creative. It intensifies perception. Mutual infatuation makes sexual intercourse function like clockwork.

Infatuation strives for reciprocity. One wants an exclusive emotional bond with the other. Heartbreak is the pain of the distance to the beloved or of unrequited infatuation. Mutual infatuation is a feeling of fusion but not, as yet, a realistic relationship. The disease of the eye heals itself with cohabiting. The other person turns out different to what one dreamed him or her to be.

True love in living together is giving love: making your partner someone special. It is about commitment to each other. When a relationship no longer works just like that, this demands commitment from the partners. Commitment is not easy and always involves an 'in spite of'. Cohabiting partners differ in everything and still want to live together. "Despite the fact that you're not what I dreamed you were, I still want to live with you." This is commitment. It implies a free choice. True love expresses itself in a number of ways of handling each other.

1. **Sharing words.** Giving real attention to each other and making time for each other's ways of giving love. Love lies in talking things through with each other. In the knowledge that you, as a partner, interpret every word based on your own history and that therefore each partner interprets words in his or her own different way. Understanding the difference in the meaning given to words and coming to shared meanings, dual constructs, is a form of love.

2. **Sharing feelings.** Love is also expressed in the exchange of feelings and in compassion for each other. One can never put feelings completely into words. One can, though, place oneself in one's partner's own world and give weight to those of the partner's feelings that are different to one's own. Love then becomes, creating a truly shared feeling, *à deux*.

3. **Enjoying together.** Love expresses itself in the desire to constantly bridge the sexual difference, in seducing and being seduced, in the enjoying of each other and of being with each other, together.

4. **Resolving problems together.** Love is also reflected in the resolution of differences, frictions and irritations. Negotiation is the backbone of a modern relationship, where the partners are equal in value, forgiving each other and even after injuries making up with each other, having the patience and tolerance to repeatedly begin anew with the partner. Being kind is also a form of love.

5. **Collaborating.** Living together always encompasses a number of tasks: income earning, housekeeping, looking after children, providing food, housing and clothing, etc. Love expresses itself in taking a balanced share of these tasks. It involves taking responsibility for one's own tasks and performing them correctly.

Love is therefore all about (intentionally) making the partner happy. A refined form of this is, for example, humor: getting the partner to laugh. This is done in both verbal and non-verbal communication between partners. Words alone are not enough. A loving behavior must also be there. To make the intentions clear, words of love become indispensable.

Love expresses itself in a real involvement with the partner. This involvement may also include strong confrontation. Love does not make partners similar, but helps them tolerate the differences. It expresses itself in the fact that people continue to live together, despite everything. To be able to give something away, you must first be able to keep it. **A 'yes' in living together is possible only if there is also room for a 'no'.**

There is a love that gives too much, where the giver damages him or herself by giving the other person exactly what they ask for. Exaggerated sacrifice makes us bitter and leads to hostility. Giving love, properly balanced, feels great, provides deep satisfaction and makes both partners ultimately satisfied.

And yet, there is one aspect of love that falls outside of all of this. In a cohabiting relationship people want to be emotionally involved with each other. They want to feel attracted to and desire each other. This part of love, the warm and positive feelings for each other, can also temporarily disappear and then return; at times the form of so-called 'flashes of love'; at times, in deep sexual involvement and gratifying intimacy. They are the basis of the will to live together and the urge to share joys and sorrows.

The keys

→ **Infatuation and love are not the same. Love is a powerful and motivating feeling. One sees the other person, not as they are, but as one would like them to be.**

→ **True love is giving: sharing words and feelings, enjoying things and solving problems together, working together. This requires dedication and commitment.**

→ **Love is feeling good with each other and wanting to make the partner happy. Not only with one's words, but also with one's behavior.**

Alfons Vansteenwegen is Professor Emeritus Psychology, Sexology and Psychotherapy at the University of Leuven, KUL (Belgium). In 2011 he received the Gold Medal Life Time Achievement of the World Association of Sexology. He is the author of some 350 scientific and clinical publications and of several international bestsellers, including *Tijd maken voor liefde* (*Making Time for Love*) and *Liefde is een werkwoord* (*Love Is a Verb*).

"Love leads to love."

The neuroscience of love

High-tech brainscans show, in detail, what happens in our brain when we are in love. Prof **Andreas Bartels** conducted the first human brain imaging studies on love and contributed to the discovery of universal biological mechanisms of love across the animal kingdom. They seem to control the darker sides of our psyche as well.

Love cannot be grasped easily. It is the most complex and at the same time the most simple, the most exhilarating and sometimes the most devastating states of mind. Love is the consequence of a genetically encoded biological mechanism in the brain with a very simple function - to bond individuals - yet with the most curious and far-reaching consequences in all aspects of our personal lives and also in the evolution of species and of intelligence.

Personally, I am particularly struck by what hard biological science has begun to discover about love in the last decade or two, and it looks as if this is only the beginning of one of the scientifically most important periods in our understanding of human nature – which, after all, may not be so uniquely human as we may like to think. I was lucky enough to contribute to our understanding of the mechanisms of love by conducting the first human brain imaging studies on love, together with Semir Zeki. These studies showed that, in the human, maternal and romantic love involve the same brain regions, which are the ones rich in receptors for the love-hormones oxytocin (OT) and arginine-vasopressin (AVP). Our study also showed that love-mechanisms in the human are tightly related to those found in animals.

Reward system

From an evolutionary perspective, love, or in more functional-biological terms, social attachment or bonding, is key to the existence of species like humans, as our babies' survival depends entirely on parental care, which is only possible through love. It is therefore no surprise that the brain's mechanisms that have evolved to ensure parent-child bonding are powerful and under genetic control.

Artists, writers, even historians have long recognized that love is inherent to human nature across times and cultures. Curiously, psychologists and scientists have only very recently begun to realize that love is indeed a biological property and therefore scientifically researchable, rather than a human artefact that can be normalized, or even repressed, for cultural, religious or legal reasons.

The basic mechanisms of love are very simple, clear and powerful: they involve the core of the brain's reward system, where the two neuro-hormones oxytocin (OT) and arginin-vasopressin (AVP) are sufficient and necessary, together with dopamine, to induce lifelong bonds between individuals. The brain regions and hormones involved with love are universal: they are the same in parent-child attachment, in pair-bonding, in same-sex or opposite-sex love, and they are preserved across species, such as voles, sheep and humans.

Love hormones

A single gene (e.g. that encoding for the receptors of OT or AVP in the brain's reward system) can make the difference between species that are capable of forming pair-bonds and those that cannot. Transfer of that gene from one species to another can change the second species from lonely wolves to cuddly couples, the latter making up 3-5 % of vertebrate species.

But how do we 'fall' in love? Mechanistically speaking, when love-hormones are released in the brain. This allows the reward system to form a long-lasting association between the presence of a particular individual with highly rewarding feelings. Love is therefore the consequence of a special learning mechanism in the brain that is highly specialized and exclusive to social stimuli, as associations to non-living objects cannot be formed by it.

In animals, a single dose of the love-hormones can induce a lifelong pair-bond, or bring about the strong attachment of a mother to its child in virgin females to stranger pups.

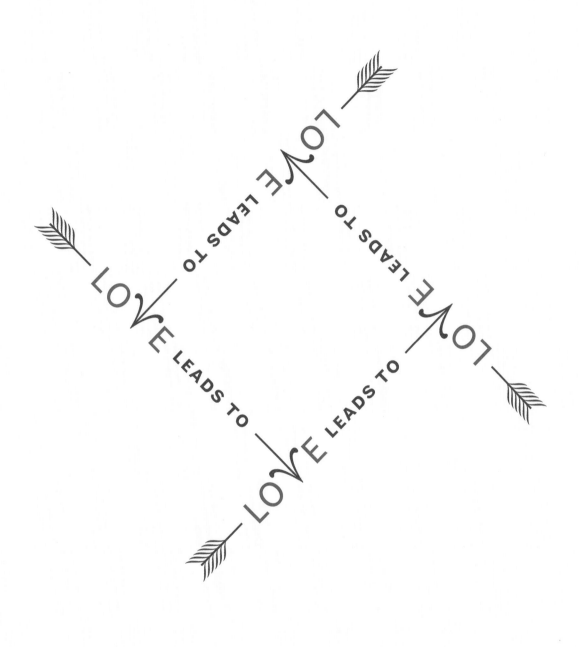

Conversely, blocking the love-hormones receptors in the brain will prevent pair- and mother-child bonds to form, in the latter case leading to carelessly abandoned pups and forever lonesome animals. Luckily, so far, such experiments have only been carried out in animals – but the mechanisms are the same in humans. Outside the lab, the highest dose of love-hormones are released during orgasm, birth, or breast-feeding, and to lesser extents also during eye contact, social touch and in various social situations.

Dark sides

Curiously, also individual differences, in the extent to which we bond, are controlled by this mechanism. Genetic variations, but also life experiences, mostly during childhood, can influence the density and location of love-hormone receptors in the brain, which affect various aspects of our social behavior. For example, **a single genetic variation can halve the chances of getting married and double the frequency of relationship crises in humans.** Other studies have shown that children who received only little love, for example, if they grew up in poorly organized orphanages, have indeed lower concentrations of love-hormones in their blood and are more likely to have pro-social deficits. In the lab, animals that received more or less love and care as puppies, will, once grown up, spend more or less time with their own offspring and with their partner. Love, therefore, leads to love, and lovelessness in a family or in a society can, tragically, be transmitted to the next generation - through genes as well as through experience.

The mechanisms of love go far beyond attachment - they also control the darker sides of our psyche. Once bonded, animals' aggressions in rejecting approaches from others, or in protecting their offspring, are also mediated by 'love-hormones' and dopamine. Beyond causing attachment, **these hormones also boost social exclusion, xenophobia, racism and selfishness.** This happens because the love-mechanism also mediates our feeling of belonging to a certain social group or race - which implies also knowing and showing who is not part of it. These varied and complex functions of the love-hormones are mediated by brain areas beyond the reward system, located in various limbic, memory-related and pre-frontal brain regions.

Our brain imaging studies showed several of these regions, including those associated with negative emotion, fear and aggression, and also regions related to critical social assessment. These regions were inactivated when our participants viewed their object of desire – but not when viewing their friends or strangers.

Evolutionary motor

Research on love has also revealed a surprise: it turns out that its mechanisms are high-jacked in addiction - replacing the person of desire by a substance. Similarly, research suggests links to autism, depression and other social deficit disorders. Treatments involving the love-hormones OT and AVP may not be far off – yet interfering with a system of such complexity may easily backfire.

Beyond my fascination with the mechanisms of love and their far-reaching consequences, I have a final speculation: **love is the key to the all-important transfer of knowledge between generations.** Only love-enabled species communicate for long enough periods and during the brain's development. Love is therefore directly related to our capability to learn and, therefore, to the huge brain size of love-blessed species. In introducing enormous social complexity to life, love gave rise to new evolutionary pressures related to partner-choice, to pro-social behavior, fairness and trust, but also to deceit and exclusion. Love is therefore not only the driving force in much of our achievements in life, but also the evolutionary motor driving our brain size, intelligence and culture.

The keys

→ **The basic mechanisms of love are universal, simple, powerful and tightly related to those of animals. They involve the core of the brain's reward system.**

→ **Love (and hate) is the consequence of a special learning mechanism in the brain that is highly specialized and exclusive to social stimuli. It is transmitted through genes and experiences.**

→ **Love is not only the driving force in much of our achievements in life, but also the evolutionary motor driving our brain size, intelligence and culture.**

Andreas Bartels leads a research group at the Center of Integrative Neuroscience in Tübingen (Germany). He uses all available human brain-imaging techniques to research neural mechanisms of visual perception, particularly those of visual motion, faces and emotion. Together with Semir Zeki, he performed the first human brain imaging studies of romantic and maternal love. He studied Zoology in Zurich, completed his master's in computational modeling at the Salk Institute, San Diego (USA) and obtained his PhD in neuroscience at University College London (UK). He loves life, climbing and good humor.

Love and conflict

"The long-term interaction between people generates the inseparable companion of intimacy: conflict", says Ayça Özen. **Successful partners succeed in dealing with their differences in a constructive way.**

We all search for the other we would love, accompanied with the wishes that our feelings are reciprocated. It gives meaning to our lives. When, and if, we find the right person, we are inclined to think that we deserve everlasting happiness. However, in real life, probably the most difficult stage starts after people begin to live together with their beloved ones. The first days of the relationship engender a honeymoon effect, which makes us feel like we are living the most ecstatic time of our lives. Regardless of the feeling of eternity, every good thing has an end. Thus, the question arises of how to maintain a long and satisfying relationship.

Unavoidable

Conflict, as an unavoidable part of human life, can have a detrimental effect on our relationships and on our well-being, unless the parties in a relationship handle it constructively. If conflict is an inevitable part of intimate relationships, the way in which a person or couple responds to conflict situations and how they regulate their emotions in these situations become critically important because their behavior will affect their adjustment and/or satisfaction. Furthermore, since two people constitute the relationship, how the other party responds becomes critical.

Whether the self is perceived as it is, is accepted and cared for by the partner and whether the partner is emotionally available when needed and responsive to our needs, is very important for both sides to feel understood and, thus, to feel secure in the relationship.

There are certain cornerstones that are important for handling conflict and, thus, maintaining a long-term relationship. Deficiency in communication and problem-solving skills gives rise to distress in people's lives. If partners run away from conflict and negotiation of conflictual issues, conflict resolution will be hampered, the potential for future conflict will accumulate and the satisfaction of the partners will decrease. Similarly, if partners handle conflictual issues in a destructive way, this may prevent resolution of conflicts and produce negative effects like anger and resentment, which will further undermine any constructive resolution attempt.

Constructive

Many researchers studying conflict have discovered that moderate levels of conflict may indeed be functional, although conflict is generally perceived as something that is negative and to be avoided. Just imagine a relationship in which you agree on everything, from the type of movies to watch, to eating habits and leisure time activities. It might be enjoyable at the beginning of the relationship. You may feel like you have found your soulmate; someone who understands you perfectly. However, as time passes, you may get bored because your partner is almost your mirror image. In life, we sometimes want to have differences; in this way we can challenge ideas, get challenged, and learn something new from the other. Conflict enables

catharsis and provides a refuge from the boredom of the daily routine. If differences can be discussed in a constructive manner and if agreement and harmony are achieved between partners, then conflict may carry the relationship one step ahead. However, if we handle issues and problems destructively, become the demanding party in the relationship or avoid discussing the differences, we can be punished by losing the miraculous relationship and our partner. Thus, we should communicate our differences constructively to achieve happiness in our lives. Love is something that we should not only cherish when we find it, but also something that we should nurture through a constructive approach to conflicts.

Ayça Özen is a research assistant at the Department of Psychology of the Middle East Technical University in Ankara (Turkey). Her research focuses on attachment, conflict and emotional experiences in romantic relationships and friendship.

" Conflict may carry the relationship one step ahead."

"Intentions are part of love."

The salt of life

"If love is the salt of life, what about the production of this salt?" asks Prof **Benedetto Gui**. He is an economist and takes us in four steps through 'the technology of love', to help us 'produce' and 'consume' love more abundantly.

A full day without a touch of love is really insipid. It does not need to be the romantic meeting of an enamored couple, or a mother embracing her baby; a bit of sincere regard for others can flavor our daily relationships with colleagues, or relatives, as well as apparently insignificant interactions with vendors or fellow bus travelers. As we know, benevolence benefits first those who practice it; and reciprocation – sometimes even a simple word of gratitude – greatly boosts satisfaction, but must be waited for with patience.

I have learned these simple truths – such I deem they are – thanks to upbringing and life experience. Still, I would not have given them much weight were it not for a spiritual leader who took the commandment of love very seriously in both personal and civil life. I was attracted by the daring idea that love has a role to play even in economic life, even more so since I could see it practiced by people committed to making it real in business enterprises and non-profit organizations alike. At that time, economic science was not interested in love. Its traditional orientation bent towards materialism and individualism. With some worthy exceptions, **concern for others was viewed as either unnecessary or even harmful to economic efficiency.**

Bakers and nurses

The last decades, however, words such as 'altruism', 'regard', or 'reciprocity' have broken into the writings of economic theorists. Meanwhile, research has shown that happiness depends little on how much we consume: what really matters are interpersonal relationships, things that had no place in the vocabulary of economics.

One contribution economic analysis can offer to understanding love concerns how it is 'produced' and at the same time how it 'produces' its benefits. Let me try to show how. Consider two people who may be engaged in any sort of activity and view their interaction as a productive process. What is produced? If the two are bakers working in a team, the obvious output is bread; if, instead, one is a nurse and the other a patient, the obvious output is therapy. However, other possible outputs of the interaction are in the 'love' category: the junior baker can be helped and encouraged, rather than blamed; the patient, on top of a drug, can receive emotional support; the senior baker and the nurse, in turn, can obtain gratitude.

→ **Comment one: the most precious 'products' of our activities may not be the most apparent.** How we interact with colleagues or clients can also be 'productive' – not of conventional, but of 'relational' goods; and each member of an organization, technicians included, is a human relations manager as well.

Chatters

What about the inputs of such productive processes? Take two chatters, who in the usual view produce nothing. If the interaction yields 'relief from sorrows' for one or both of them, an important input of the process is their friendship, which also belongs in the 'love' category.

→ **Comment two: friendship ties, mutual trust, the memory of shared experiences… are instances of 'relation-specific human capital' that facilitates all forms of cooperation.** But it is especially fragile. An occasional quarrel or a simple change of residence are sufficient to dissipate it.

There is more to personal interactions. Their outcomes depend on intentions, which are a sort of catalyst of interpersonal processes. Intentions, too, may belong in the 'love' category: while fixation on one's own objectives maintains human relations at a mere instrumental level, attitudes of gratuitousness open the way to deeper forms of interpersonal communication.

→ **Comment three: as gratuitousness rests on both convictions and cultivation, loving attitudes prevail where people are aware that human flourishing requires overcoming egoism and orient their behavior accordingly.**

Favorable context

Last, human interactions occur in a social milieu which too has a bearing on their unfolding, just as a chemical reaction is affected by the temperature of the environment. How bystanders are expected to react, what comments friends will make, or how others recently acted in similar occurrences all encourage or discourage other-regarding behavior.

→ **Comment four: as love is not the easy way to go, it greatly benefits from a favorable context.** A reciprocal promise of love is harder to maintain without contact with couples who try to remain faithful to it; and volunteers gather among themselves to reinforce their motivation.

This much as to the 'technology of love'. I hope greater mastery of this technology will help us 'produce' and 'consume' love more abundantly.

The keys

→ **Our interaction with colleagues and clients is also some kind of 'production' of valuable relational goods. It can also create human capital that facilitates all forms of cooperation.**

→ **Loving attitudes prevail where people are aware that human flourishing requires overcoming egoism and orient their behavior accordingly.**

→ **As love is not the easy way to go, it greatly benefits from a favorable context.**

Benedetto Gui is Professor of Economics at the University of Padova (Italy). His research interests include the economic behavior of cooperative, non-profit and social enterprises; the economic implications of interpersonal relations; and the role of non-instrumental motivations in economic organizations. He serves on the management board of the journal *Annals of Public and Cooperative Economics* and collaborates with the network of enterprises 'Economy of Communion'.

"Children's interest in love is natural and healthy."

Curious children

Children are curious to know everything about love and sex.
And they always want to know more. The Internet feeds this desire
with a bewildering and morally challenging variety of pictures,
material and chatlines. Parents and teachers don't know how to
react. Sometimes they don't even dare to say anything.
Prof **Mark Halstead** encourages us not to lose our grip. For several
years he was the only Professor of Moral Education in England.

When ten-year-old Jack told one of my researchers "I *looove* my mom", his strong emphasis
on the word 'love' indicated how important his intimate emotional attachment to his mother
was to him. It also suggested his ability to distinguish between this powerful feeling and
the lesser loves of his life like his dog, his favorite football team, his computer games
and the girl who sat next to him in science lessons. But the unusual intonation he gave to
the word also hinted that he was hesitant, almost embarrassed, to talk about his feelings
of love, as if he felt that such talk was a sign of weakness. The ambiguity in his response
was typical of many boys of his age – and older. The ten-year-old girls in the same research
project had no such inhibitions. They chatted freely and with considerable sophistication
in their focus groups about the various love relationships in the soap operas they watched
and they readily discussed such philosophical issues as the difficulty of being in full control
of their own lives and whether love could enable people to give up drink or drugs.

Fill the gap

Love is a powerful feature in the lives of children, but also something of a mystery to them.
They are bombarded with messages about love from popular music, TV shows, films,
magazines and the Internet. They laugh and joke about love, they make fun of it in their
playground songs, they tease their friends about it, yet many cherish it deep in their hearts

as the ultimate value, the route to personal fulfilment, the thing that gives meaning and purpose to people's lives. And always they want to know more. They want, for example, to know about passion and commitment, about the complexity and irrationality of love, about what it feels like to be in love, about what makes love last and about how to deal with the feelings of insecurity that looking forward to love can bring.

The primary educator of the child is the family and it is in the context of the family that the child first learns about love – through experience, through observation and through being told about it. But **the school has an important supplementary role in teaching children about love**. First, the school can fill in gaps in children's knowledge, understanding and experience, thus compensating for the impoverished home life of some children. Second, the school can broaden children's horizons by helping them to imagine possibilities beyond their current experience. Third, the school can develop children's critical understanding, so that they start to make sense of the diversity of attitudes and values to which they are exposed in their lives (including the ubiquitous porn sites on the Internet) and make judgments about what is good and bad, right and wrong, wholesome and degrading.

Confrontation

Yet, love is all too often a neglected topic in most schools. Like values education more generally, it is squeezed out of the curriculum by other targets and priorities. Sex education tells children more about the dangers of sexual infections and teenage pregnancy than it does about the fulfilment of a loving relationship or the joy of having a baby. Drama has enormous potential for exploring the pleasure of family life, but research suggests that much more time is spent on family conflict than family love (perhaps because it is thought to make better drama). Even literature, potentially a major source of insight into love in all kinds of human relationships, is taught differently these days, with more emphasis on style and technique at the expense of content. **The dominant ethos of many classrooms involves discipline and control more than love and respect** for children, and this negative atmosphere ends up generating confrontation, rather than caring. In any case, many teachers seem embarrassed by the thought of teaching about love; even to use the term 'love' in connection to pupils is questionable these days because of fears of abuse and inappropriate relationships. The result is that children may be denied the opportunities they need to think through their attitudes to love and left exposed to the haphazard array of influences that society brings to bear on them without the apparatus to make sense of them. In such circumstances, how will they grow into mature, loving adults?

The value of love

My research leads me to believe that children's interest in love is natural and healthy. Teachers ought to be in a position to develop this interest in a way that is sensitive and helpful without being intrusive, respects individual and cultural differences and does not expose children to premature cynicism and world-weariness. Teachers could explain the sublimity and power of love, its fragility and capacity for self-deception, its way of encouraging people to see beyond their own interests and needs and to care for others. Literature, media studies, drama, history, religious, social and moral education could all provide rich and diverse opportunities for critical reflection on love. To do this, however, would require a massive shift in current educational thinking and the development of a more loving ethos in schools. But first, teachers themselves need to learn to reflect on the value of love in their own lives – and this has important implications for the way they themselves are trained.

The keys

→ **Children are curious about love and sex. That's natural and healthy. Parents and teachers should educate them: filling the gaps, broadening their horizon and developing their critical judgment.**

→ **Many teachers seem embarrassed but they ought to be in a position to develop the interest in love and sex in a sensitive and helpful way.**

→ **We need a massive shift in current educational thinking, developing a more loving ethos in schools. Teachers themselves need to learn to reflect on the value of love in their own lives.**

Mark Halstead was Professor of Moral Education at Plymouth University for many years. He is now Emeritus Professor at the University of Huddersfield (UK). He has written widely on many aspects of values education. He studied in Oxford and Cambridge, worked as a journalist in Lebanon and as a lecturer in Saudi Arabia and has been a visiting professor at several North American universities. His PhD topic was the education of Muslim children in the UK and that has remained a major research interest alongside values in education.

Loving parents

The second World War changed the life of Michel Meignant **dramatically. He was born in Paris in 1936 and his Jewish grandparents were killed in Auschwitz. His family horrors have given him the energy to fight his whole life, to make sure this would never happen again. Introducing love and sexology, he became the first 'amorologist' in France and produced several popular documentaries on love. His final advice is for the parents…**

The most important discovery is that human nature is essentially good. At birth, we all have the capacity to love, after receiving love. When one is fortunate enough to have had a mother who went through a happy pregnancy without going through a difficult birth, all human beings are ready to love and to be loved. But during the course of life, one should not be perverted by psychological and mental violence. **It is necessary to have been raised and educated in a non-violent environment** without traumas. It is especially important for those who have children to bring up, that they avoid spankings, shouting and humiliation. This is difficult if one has been exposed to physical and mental violence. This is why I have developed positive parenting and why I created the Loving Parents' Foundation.

In 1980, Sweden was the first nation in the world to forbid spanking and any corporal punishment. In 1990, the United Nations enacted a bill enforcing 'A child's rights'. Since 2005, the Council of Europe has requested that all European states put forward legislation forbidding corporal and psychological punishment, accompanied by aid to develop positive parenting. In 2012, already 29 out of 47 European states enforced this law and around ten more other states around the world did so too. This explains, in part, why those suffering in the world dream of coming to Europe to find love. Love is founded on the development of empathy; in other words, the true feeling within one's self of what another is feeling. **Empathy is a natural feeling which is at the base of love.** A non-traumatized child has this capacity. Happy are those under a lucky star who have not been subjected to educational violence.

Using two new methods has been life-changing in my therapeutic practice and has permitted me to cure disorders that impede the natural process of loving. EMDR therapy, which integrates neuro-emotion by alternate bilateral stimulation (ocular and other movement), was discovered in 1987 by the American psychologist Francine Shapiro. It enables the start of a natural adaptive treatment of painful and blocked information (for example post traumatic shock), mobilizes the psychological recourse, and restores lack of confidence in oneself. Lifespan Integration is a simple method

"Avoid spanking, shouting and humiliation."

permitting a fast cure for patients suffering from trauma and/or mistreatment during childhood. The process of Lifespan Integration treats the split states in oneself and re-establishes by 're-associating' the global system of a patient's personality. Lifespan Integration combines the activation of the imaginary with a timely string of events of the states in oneself. This facilitates the neuronal integration and is a fast cure for adults who have suffered complex traumatisms and/or mistreatment and neglect during their childhood.

When parents come to realize that they find it difficult to control themselves, they should seek help. The development of positive parenting is an answer for those in need of help.

Michel Meignant (PhD) is a specialist in relationships and human sexuality. He lives in France and is President of the French Federation of Psychotherapy and Psychoanalysis and Vice-President of the World Council for Psychotherapy. He is the permanent representative in the Council of Europe of the European Association for Psychotherapy. Several of his books and documentaries have received awards for their outstanding quality.

*"If you show your 'true color',
you also face the possibility of rejection."*

One-night stands

Rock star Rolling Stone Mick Jagger is said to have had sex with more than 4000 women (and some men). We all know some people who always turn up with a new lover. Some pretend to have found 'the right one', again and again. Others just never stop their hunt for love and sex. Dr **Bente Træen** unveils their drive and their fears.

As a researcher, I have repeatedly learned that a basic motive underlying people's sexual actions is the search for love. Through sexual actions, people hunt for someone to love and to be loved by. In sexuality, people thus seek more than physical pleasure.

Beyond the bodily exercise people mutually exchange tenderness and intimacy. Experiencing these emotions and sensations also triggers feelings of falling in love and infatuation, even in short-time encounters, such as one-night stands. Love hunters are attached to the myth of romantic love, but cannot find it. They are not practiced lovers – **they take the opportunity to have sex when offered to them.** Their partners lack the qualities they seek and they themselves cannot express emotion towards the partner. This means they experience a lack of intimacy, but it doesn't mean that they are not looking for it. Beyond the physical sexual activity, there is the hope of finding love and the security of a committed relationship.

Ideal love

The committed relationship is regarded as a central arena for personal fulfilment and self-realization. Couple relationships are nowadays much more dependent on feelings and sexuality than they were before. The ideal is that love and sex belong together and sex is perceived as particularly rewarding and satisfying when emotions are present. According to the ideal, love should be expressed in a sexual way to be perceived as genuine, which implies an obligation for the partners to feel passionately about each other. However, in maintaining a committed relationship and not merely entering into it, the ability to become intimate, and to endure intimacy over longer time periods, may be more important than staying passionate. It is argued that **love develops to the degree to which intimacy does**, to the degree to which the partner is prepared to reveal concerns and needs to the other, that is to be vulnerable in the face of the other. This may seem simple at first glance, but is anything but simple in reality. Because, if you show your 'true color', you also face the possibility of rejection.

Fear of rejection

It is during childhood that we learn that love is connected to the fear of rejection. Loving someone will therefore always imply a potential risk of being rejected. As loving is closely connected to fear of being rejected, most individuals are likely to possess some degree of fear of intimacy. In some individuals, this fear is, however, more pronounced, which may reflect a general and basic insecurity in life. To find mutuality in love you must be able to receive love and believe you are worthy of being loved. In this context, **you must have the ability to appreciate yourself**. The quest for self-appreciation is directly connected to the construction of the self. Self-appreciation has two dimensions: other's appreciation of 'me' (external self-appreciation) and 'my own' appreciation of 'me' (internal self-appreciation).

Fear of intimacy

Loss of self-appreciation may be the result of a long-term process. A sudden crisis may, however, also result in feelings of being worthless and reduced self-appreciation. For others, the loss of self-appreciation may be caused by the events surrounding the breakup from a previous commitment relationship. As self-appreciation is of such vital importance to human functioning, the logical thing to do is to avoid situations that may threaten it. Some people seem to hunt for love continuously but never find it. They 'consume' partners at high speed. Some of them claim they are particular and afraid of losing their freedom.

From an analytical point of view, however, statements about the desire to get close and the anxiety of doing so, draw attention to the phenomenon 'fear of intimacy'. Rather than having sex for the sake of novelty and pleasure, one may question the position of fear of intimacy in persons with higher partner turnover. The concept 'fear of intimacy' does not imply a pathological personality. **All people are likely to possess some degree of fear of intimacy.** However, it can be hypothesized that some individuals may have entered into a vicious circle, where they are filled with negative expectations towards their own constructed 'self' and seek and find partners who are likely to confirm these negative expectations. The result may be inadequate psychosocial functioning.

Self-appreciation

To reject a partner before being rejected oneself may be seen as a coping strategy. An experienced low internal self-appreciation may, to some extent, be compensated with the external self-appreciation received from the partner(s). From the outside, they may appear sexually over-active or 'promiscuous', **on the inside, they may feel emotionally and relationally powerless.** Intimacy is about enduring the continuous exposure of one's inner world to another person over time. This is what people with a high partner turnover do not seem to cope with, and that leads us to the hypothesis that fear of intimacy out of the fear of rejection is underlying their behavior.

To break the vicious circle and achieve a change in the direction of experiencing loving and being loved, the person must learn to appreciate him/herself and gain insight into own needs in life. In encounters with a person with high partner turnover, you could ask the following question: "What was it this partner had that you needed in your life?" For some, this may be the start of a new beginning.

The keys

- → **In sexuality, people seek more than physical pleasure. But loving someone always implies a potential risk of being rejected.**
- → **To find mutuality in love you must be able to receive love and believe you are worthy of being loved. This requires sufficient internal and external self-appreciation.**
- → **People with a high partner turnover lack self-appreciation and are afraid of intimacy because they fear rejection. Rejecting a partner before being rejected yourself may be seen as a coping strategy.**

Bente Træen is a Full Professor of health psychology at the Faculty of Health Sciences, University of Tromsø (Norway). Her first research focused on adolescents' sexuality. Meanwhile, she has written scientific papers and popular books on different aspects of relationships and sexuality, including sexual well-being, sexually transmitted infections and the use of pornography.

"Love doesn't stop at the border."

We are the world

In January 1985, "We are the world", one of the century's most famous songs, made a strong global call for help and love for the hungry people in Northern Ethiopia during the worst famine in decades. At the same time, Dr **Sandro Calvani** was working in Makallè (Ethiopia) as a humanitarian relief coordinator for Caritas International. With children dying in his arms, he found that the lyrics of the song were dreams worth turning into reality. He then dedicated his entire professional life to deepening the understanding of what 'love the world' actually means.

"We are the world, we are the children. We are the ones who make a brighter day. So let's start giving. There's a choice we're making. We're saving our own lives."

"Love the whole of humankind like yourself and your family" is a sublime message proposed by most religions, by great leaders, by inspired songs and poems. The process of transforming such a timeless dream into everyday reality is the amazing experience of most expatriates in all parts of the world. The art of loving other peoples more than your own people is the common character of extraverted expatriates.

Extraverted expatriatism is the whole complex system of ideas, life styles, experiences, values, aspirations, economic and social policies that are expressed – or at least are inspired – by people who live and work in countries other than the one in which they were born, who grew up and were educated in yet other countries. Expatriates do not move to another country for good, as migrants do. Instead they strive to live and work in as many countries as possible. Be they missionaries or corporate executives, university professors or United Nations officials, doctors without borders or globetrotter artists, modern extraverted expatriates are truly the most genuine expression of expatriatism when they know well and feel at ease with the culture and the life of at least a dozen countries where they have lived and worked.

Wall Street

Extraverted expatriatism is both an ideology and an idealism. The ideology of expatriatism proposes the belief that there is no credible reason to love your own people more than other peoples. The idealism of expatriatism is the hope and the vision of a truly peaceful humankind where all human beings on Earth have equal rights and love and respect each other, irrespective of their nationality.

Everyday's life experience – be it in a remote African village or Wall Street in New York – gives evidence that, today, all the personal choices and situations of an individual or of a country affect other people in other countries without stopping at the nations' borders. Therefore, the distinctions proposed by old-fashioned political science and practice between home affairs and foreign affairs are *de facto* disappeared. All most relevant issues which affect peoples' quality of life and their pursuit of happiness in the modern economies and societies are already international. To characterize global interdependence as a 'foreign' matter is just a poor attempt to hide the evidence that **all 'homelands' are already amalgamated in only one true homeland, which is our planet.**

The world has become globalized faster than most people's capacity to perceive and understand how many old borders have vanished. Many people are uneasy or afraid of exploring the thousands of connections that have transformed the old 'us' and 'them' into a unique togetherness of the human race. Since no country can hope to be wealthy, happy and safe alone, the dream of loving other peoples as much as your own – like any other form of love among humans – has become a convenient must. Extraverted expatriates do not preach about elimination of fear and hatred among peoples: they just live togetherness as an everyday normality. Where they succeed to effectively teach love for all, they do it by example.

Third culture kids

A great majority of expatriates fall in love with and marry a person of another culture. Children of expatriates' couples are called 'third culture kids' or 3CK. 3CK youth have spent a significant period of time in cultures other than their parents' nationality and, often, they are unable to answer the question "where are you from?", a label that many 3CK consider a bit obsolete. 3CK integrate into their personal culture elements of all the cultures where they have lived and therefore naturally feel able to love many different peoples whom they feel to be their own.

Extraverted expatriatism is the art of learning and live universal love. It is a form of love easy to learn. If you truly love your own family and your country, you can easily learn to love other peoples too. To love other peoples contributes effectively to your happiness and maximizes the joy you will experience in loving your own partner, your family, your country. Expatriatism is an expansion of patriotism, not its contrary. Radical and extremist patriotism cause conflicts. Extraverted expatriatism expands people-loving attitudes beyond borders. When you love a person you want his/her happiness and never forget about him/her. When you love everybody on Earth you become happy to forget about yourself.

The keys

- → **There is no credible reason to love your own people more than other peoples. The world has become globalized faster than most people's capacity to perceive it.**
- → **Extraverted expatriatism is the art of learning and living universal love. It is easy to learn. If you truly love your own family and your country, you can easily learn to love other peoples too.**
- → **To love other peoples contributes effectively to your happiness and maximizes the joy you will experience in loving your own partner, your family, your country.**

Sandro Calvani is Director of the ASEAN Centre of Excellence on United Nations Millennium Development Goals at the Asian Institute of Technology in Bangkok (Thailand). As a United Nations' diplomat and head of UN missions for 32 years he has lived and worked in 135 countries around the world. He has written 20 books and 600 articles on sustainable development, human rights and on his experiences in humanitarian aid. He teaches Humanitarian Affairs in International Relations at the Masters Course on International Relations at Webster University. He has four children who live and work in the other four continents.

HOW DO
you
WANT ME TO LOVE
you
SO THAT
you
FEEL LOVED BY
me
?

Your kind of love

"I see a great deal of relational unhappiness because love is expressed in a way the other person doesn't understand as love",
says **Dr** Charlie Azzopardi.
He offers two golden rules.

People speak about love as if there's only one kind of love and as if everybody understands the same thing by the word 'love'. Love is so personal that when a hundred people speak about it they are speaking about a hundred different kinds of love. Practically, people speak about their own love, and about their own way of loving and being loved. Some people express it through their commitment, others through romanticism, sex or doing practical things in the house. Those who have children tend to confuse love for the partner with love for the family, which are two different kinds of love. When I say a love relationship, I mean any relationship character-ized by love, whether it is parent-child, husband-wife, boyfriend-girlfriend, friendship and so on. There are two important things one has to do in order to secure a love relationship.

1. Make sure you express your love in a way the other person understands as love.
Some myths prevail here and can lead to lots of disappointment. One of these is that "S/he knows I love her/him", assuming that the other knows about one's love. It is absolutely untrue – your

partner, child, parent, friend, etc. know you love them when you say it, when you show it in a way they understand it. When you do something to show your love to someone, make sure that the person is getting the right message of love. So many people fall into the trap of taking love for granted and stop expressing their love clearly to each other because "of course he knows I love him".

I have seen husbands and wives expressing their love in many strange and repelling ways. For example, through jealousy by prohibiting the partner to have a life outside the relationship. Initially it may be perceived as protection, eventually it becomes suffocation. In this way, love is not perceived as such by the partner anymore.
So, you have to ask people you love questions like: "How do you want me to love you so that you feel loved by me?"; "How can I show my love to you?"; "What do you expect me to do to show you that I love you?"

2. **Make sure you are clear about how you expect to be loved by others.**
Many people think that their partner magically knows when they need love and what kind of love they need. Such expectations are sure ways down the disappointment alley. Some very common misconceptions in this regard often include the idea that the partner should take the initiative, and that "if I tell him how to love me then, that's not coming from him/her, it's not spontaneous". People don't know what you need and how you need it unless you tell them. If you need love, which we all do, you have to learn to ask for it so

that people around you learn to love you in a way you understand as love. The truth is that the way we expect to be loved changes over time. Make sure you keep updating your loved ones about the way you want to be loved.

Dr **Charlie Azzopardi** is a systemic practitioner with more than twenty years of experience working in the field of mental health in Malta. He has published several articles and books on marital problems, addiction, adolescents and parenting. He developed a new therapeutic technique that makes working with families and individuals more accessible.

" How do you want me to love you?"

*"Romantic love
has been reported present
in nearly all societies."*

Universal love

From Inner Mongolia and Chinese cities, to Papua New Guinea, strip clubs and Mormon polygamous communities, the renowned anthropologist Prof **William Jankowiak** has studied sexual and emotional behavior for more than thirty years. "We, homo sapiens, are not sexually monogamous as a species as much as we are emotionally monogamous", he says. In search of the balance in universal love.

For the longest of times Westerners thought romantic love was a 'disease' that tribal people and other non-Western types seldom experienced due to their being more firmly grounded in the value of bodily sensations. Without formal instruction, non-Westerners were unable to understand, conceptualize, imagine or experience romance. In contrast, Westerners were caught up in a heightened experience of romantic imagination that often manifested itself in a denial of sexuality while embracing an idealized image of pure, albeit chaste, love. When romantic passion was found among non-Westerners it was presumed that it was part of the globalization of ideas, whereby non-Westerners sought to imitate the experience of Westerners. It was thought that if Westerners idealized love, then it must be modern to do so too. From this perspective – and it is a very old one – romantic love is Europe's contribution to world culture.

The only problem with this perspective is that it is not true. We now know that romantic love has been reported present in over 92% of all sample societies. However, in the vast majority of cultures, romantic love was never a reason for marriage. This was an institution that was best left to society elders. One of the things that worried elders was the junior generation meeting, becoming attracted to, desiring and wanting to marry someone unacceptable to the senior generation. To this end, the senior generation worked to monitor and thus regulate the interaction of its youth. In spite of these actions, a number of youth did meet and fall in love. The ethnographic record is filled with stories of love anguish, regret and suicides.

Sex differences

This raises an important question of how non-Westerners, without a rich literary tradition and who live in societies with tradition of arranged marriage, come to experience romantic love? If the origin of romantic love does not lie in a literary tradition, from where does it arise? We now know, based on neuropsychological and hormonal research, that humans have evolved two types of love – one is companionship and the other is romantic passion. Studies of brain functioning find romantic and companionship love located in separate areas of the brain. Moreover, there is a sex difference in their respective origins. For females, romantic passion arises from the mother-child attachment bond, while for males, romantic passion is intertwined with sexual desire. Significantly, once males and females have fallen in love, their experience of love is remarkably similar. When it comes to sexuality, men and women are as remarkably different as they are similar in their experience of love. This is one of life's great paradoxes: how can the sexes differ so much within the erotic domain, while being so similar within the love domain? This is every person's dilemma – how to balance the desire for sexual variety with an equally strong yearning to love and be loved? For men, it is easier with age. There appears to be a relationship between a decrease in testosterone and a preference for a sustained emotional commitment. For women, on the other hand, it is not physiological release that is driving force, but rather the desire to be perceived as sexually desirable. The strength of this desire often pushes woman away from their husbands into the arms of another for no reason other than to feel they are once again desirable.

Papua New Guinea

Whatever a culture's posture towards sex (its patterns of human activity and the symbolic structures that give such activity significance) and the many facets of love, ambiguities, conflicting emphases, perplexities, unclear strictures and downright quandaries litter the cultural landscape. **The diversity of ambivalence, tension and contradiction across the globe is infinite** and, when viewed collectively, bewildering in its range of differences. But what human communities have in common is a universal compulsion to make a working peace with the three-way conflict between romantic/passionate love, comfort/attachment love and physical sex.

Every culture must decide whether to synthesize, separate, blend, discount, stress, or ignore one or the other. For example, **some ethnic groups in Papua New Guinea believe that sexual intercourse is an intensely unhealthy and deeply polluting experience** that should be avoided. However, the fact remains that sex is, in the words of one man, "something that feels so good, but is so bad for you". In a different Papua New Guinean culture, men often run to the river to slice their penis with a bamboo knife to let the contaminated blood flow from their body after a sexual experience. Contradictory or seemingly conflicted attitudes are evident among the Huli of Papua New Guinea, where men abide by traditional taboos in their marriages, while seeking out erotic experiences in their extramarital lives. They can be found in Igbo men's need to develop an intimate comfort or attachment love with their spouse, while also seeking sexual pleasure through sexual variety with a variety of partners.

Sexscape zones

Because the two distinct types of love: companionship love (sometimes called comfort or attachment love) and passionate or romantic love each have their separate logic, many of the social tensions, conflicts and individual moral ambivalence arises from each person or community seeking to balance the twin forces of the two loves. By comfort love I mean a deep affection felt towards those with whom our lives are deeply intertwined. It involves feelings of friendship, understanding and concern for the welfare of another. In contrast, passionate love involves idealization of another, within an erotic setting, with the presumption that the feeling will last for some time into the future. This does not mean companionate love is not without its passions. Although both forms of love are present in every culture, they are often not equally valued, celebrated, or honored. **This results in a tripartite tension that extends beyond love and sex**, being more than the simple contrasting of two desires, but rather a tripartite conflict between the sexual imperative, the romantic and the companionate.

Throughout history, there have been various responses to the tripartite tension. For example, **contemporary American swingers** have institutionalized a set of ritual practices designed to uphold the primacy of the pair bond or comfort love, prevent the formation of a passionate love entanglement and remain open to experiencing sexual pleasure with strangers. For swingers, this is the ideal solution to the competing demands of the tripartite passions. Another contemporary response is found in the development of **sex-tourism trade throughout the Caribbean, Southeast Asia** and other parts of the world.

The construction of sexscape zones enables mostly men to pursue, rather inexpensively, a variety of sexual encounters. In the case of mature European and American women, these zones enable some to construct, however momentary, an imagined romance with someone unsuitable for forming a long-term comfort love relationship.

Societies everywhere have constructed an often uneasy arrangement between the forces of passionate love, comfort love and sexual desire. It is one that requires continuous adjustment at the individual and societal level. **In the domains of love and sex, there can never be a stable society.** The emotional tug between the competing and often contradictory desires ensures that every generation will revisit and renegotiate the traditions used to account for the relationship between love and sex.

The tug of passion

The pull of romance and the tug of sexual passion is nicely delineated in Blanche DuBois' admonishment of her sister, Stella, in Tennessee Williams' play *A Streetcar Named Desire*. Blanche expresses her horror at Stanley Kowalski's obvious sexual appetite as follows: "A man like that is someone to go out with once, twice, three times when the devil is in you. But live with? Have a child by?" In this case, the issues are erotic adventure and excitement, versus the stability of domesticity and family. The irony in Williams' vision is that, while Blanche argues for the latter as the ideal, much of her life has been consumed by the former.

Blanche's problem is not uniquely American: **Chinese literature is full of stories concerned with the difficulty in separating or blending together the two emotions.** In Li Yu's "Be Careful about Love", written prior to European contact, a Qing dynasty emperor is attracted to one woman's beauty, while simultaneously yearning for emotional intimacy with another. Both Blanche's and the Qing emperor's comments are representative of the conflict that lies at the heart of the push/pull tension between erotic attraction and a yearning for deeper emotional attachment.

At various times, sexual passion has been preferred over romantic love, as well as companionship. No ethnographic study has reported that all the passions and affections have been regarded as equally valuable: it is either the sexual, the romantic or the companionship image that is the official ideal and thus the preferred idiom of conversation. **No culture gives equal weight to the sexual, the romantic and the companionate metaphors.** One passion is always regarded as a subset of the other. No matter how socially humane, politically enlightened, spiritually attuned or technologically adapted, failure to integrate sex and love is the name of the game. The paramount passion is easily recognizable from examining conversational idioms. Conflicts over issues of propriety, etiquette and social standing inevitably arise whenever there is a break in the cultural understanding and consensus regarding things sexual and romantic. To some degree, dissatisfaction is everywhere, its dissonance sounds in all spheres of culture.

"Love is the work of the night"

Every sexual encounter need not be about the desire for some kind of transcendental merging with another. Some people desire nothing more than physical gratification without emotional entanglements. Simply put, **sex, the use or objectification of another, can be an act of pleasure**; the norms and guidelines regarding its conduct can, at least, be successful in their clarity of expression. Though regulation itself may not be successful, its regulations can be at least in terms of their intent. For individuals interested exclusively in uncomplicated sexual gratification, the ideal partner is anyone belonging to the individual's preferred sex-orientation who is willing, available and non-judgmental. In this way, sexual desire, in its most objectified form, is a total pursuit of physical pleasure, a perspective captured in Henry Miller's numerous sex scenes that graphically depict the acts of sexual intercourse. For Miller and many men, sexual intercourse can be, at least some of the time, only about heightened physical sensation.

Other times, however, the motivation for seeking sex can be more complicated. **The Central African Aka forgers' pursuit of sexual pleasure** is intertwined with another more important value: reproduction. For the Aka, sexual intercourse is a pleasurable experience that is secondary to their primary goal, which is to have a child. Or in the words of a young Aka woman, "Love is the work of the night; love and play are nice together if it makes a pregnancy." For the Aka, unlike many contemporary Americans and urbanites worldwide, reproduction, not erotic satisfaction, is the higher value.

Good risk

Presently, there is a lively discussion in both scholarly and popular literature over the origins of gender-linked differences in men and women's criteria used to select short-term and long-term partners. In spite of, or maybe because of this discourse, a consensus is emerging that holds that women, in certain contexts, are as open as men to casual sexual encounters. The debate has now shifted to the meaning of 'certain contexts'. Whatever the eventual outcome of these discussions, it is clear that **sexual monogamy does not come easily to mammals, birds, or humans**.

If the pursuit of sexual fulfilment often results in individuals seeking novelty, the love impulse in both its passionate and comfort form engenders an opposite inclination: to find intimacy with familiarity. Unlike sexual gratification, love cannot be bought (or for that matter, arranged, anticipated, or outlawed). If passionate love is bought, it is invalidated. In contrast, sexual release and, thus, satiation, in the absence of a love bond, can result in an immediate disinterest in the other. **People in a state of passionate love discover that sexual gratification does not lessen but intensifies interest in the other**.

The human sex urge is often about more than simply achieving an orgasm. It can be in the desire for tactile contact and intimate communication with another person. However, even when there is little or no prior interest, **sexual orgasm can give rise to stronger feelings of emotional involvement**. It is the desire for physical intimacy, a 'close physical and emotional relationship' that brings erotic interests into social relations, thereby linking eroticism with such interpersonal emotions as affection, trust, insecurity and jealousy. Studies of the relationship between passion and sexuality in Mexico repeatedly found couples losing themselves and with this, all rationality as unions dissolved into emotional transcending ecstasies through sexual interactions. In this way, the pursuit of a 'good risk' (an intense emotional entanglement) may lead to a 'bad risk' in sexual behavior (the loss of 'safe sexual practice').

Strip clubs

The tensions, quandaries and perplexities in balancing love and sex are evident in the way Nevada prostitutes working in legalized brothels interact with their customers. Research on **San Francisco, Stockholm and Amsterdam prostitutes** found a high percent of male customers expected the woman to demonstrate an interest and concern for their well-being. For these customers, the illusion of emotional intimacy is just as, and maybe even more important as being sexually satisfied. A similar pattern is apparent among some male customers at urban strip clubs. In a setting celebrating the objectification of a woman's body, regular customers often strove to develop a 'relationship' with a particular stripper who, for her part, pretended to care about him. Even the domain of the extramarital tryst can quickly transcend the sexual to include the emotional.

These examples illustrate how emotional intimacy can arise out of a highly sexually charged atmosphere. The central finding of mail order brides is that whatever men's and women's initial motivations for entering into the correspondence, most participants sought to develop emotional bonds with each other throughout the courtship process.

Every community must deal with the strong emotional bonds that often result from sex, passionate love and comfort love.
Cultural models are useful in that they provide an explanation of how to integrate the many facets of love and sex into a more unified whole. These models or explanations can be challenged by individuals and interest groups (polyamorists, Christian fundamentalists, libertines and so forth) who offer alternative models as to the proper relationship between the types of love and sex. But this raises a larger and more vexing issue: is the dilemma between sexual desire and passionate love? Or is it between passionate love and comfort love? Or are we dealing with a triangular relationship? Certainly there can be one without the other, a disheartening fact in cultures where the goal is to blend them together.

William Jankowiak is the Barrick Distinguished Professor of Anthropology at the University of Nevada, Las Vegas (USA). He is editor and author of a rich variety of anthropological articles and books, including *Romantic Passion* and *Intimacies*. His main research interests are human sexuality and family systems in complex societies.

Igbo love

"The expectation that love is an important element in courtship and marriage is among the most significant ongoing transformations with regard to sex and gender in Igbo-speaking southeastern Nigeria", says anthropologist Daniel Jordan Smith, **who has been studying for years personal relationships in this originally polygamous ethnic group, one of the largest and most influential in Nigeria. "Love is desired in marriage, but it is not enough."**

Whereas men and women traditionally married young and marriages were mostly arranged by the extended families of the husband and the wife, in contemporary Igboland, increasingly, men and women choose their own spouses. Modern courtship often involves notions of love and most young Igbos marry with the intention of remaining monogamous. In romantically cast premarital relationships, gender dynamics are relatively egalitarian because men and women are viewed as equal partners and the terms of the relationship are negotiated based on ideas of love, trust, and emotional intimacy. While couples themselves now frequently begin the process that leads to marriage, once initiated, families and communities become heavily involved in both the wedding ceremonies and the marriage itself.

Despite recent changes in patterns of courtship and in the criteria for marriage that elevate the importance of love, three norms remain paramount among the Igbo: the social expectation that everyone must marry, the importance of marriage as an alliance between two kin groups and the centrality of parenthood as the foundation for a successful marriage. Love is desired in marriage, but it is not enough.

Rite of passage

Traditional marriage ceremonies, in which the extended families and communities of both the husband and the wife participate, continue to constitute the principal rite of passage marking marriage. Though many couples now choose to be married in their Christian churches, as well as in a traditional ceremony, the traditional ceremony is obligatory, while the Christian ceremony is optional (though, for many, highly desirable). The years after marriage are characterized by great anticipation of pregnancy and childbirth and **nothing is more important in establishing the stability of a marriage than parenthood**. The transformation of a couple's relationship from courtship to marriage, where the roles of mother/father and husband/wife become primary and where many more people are socially invested in the relationship, has significant consequences for the dynamics of gender, tying women to their roles as mothers. In general, the importance of the quality of a couple's personal, emotional relation-among younger couples in more modern marriages, men and women spend a significant amount of time apart and find a large measure of their social satisfaction in same-sex friendships and in interactions with a wide range of kin.

Separate rooms

Traditionally, Igbo husbands and wives did not eat together, husbands and wives had separate sleeping rooms and most social activities were sex segregated. While this is changing in the context of more modern marriages that are based, in part, on 'being in love' (many monogamous couples, for example, now share the same bedroom), even in these relatively modern marriages, a man is more likely to eat separately from his wife and children than with them. In addition, gender roles in the household remain quite polarized, with women almost exclusively responsible for food preparation and childcare.

ship – the importance of love – recedes after marriage, especially after the birth of children.

The degree to which marriage relationships are characterized by love, affection and companionship is highly variable, though, generally, younger couples are much more likely to emphasize these aspects of the relationship than are their elders. In more traditional marriages, affection and companionship are often quite important and can become very deep over time. However, for older Igbos, the idea that a marriage relationship should be the primary locus of intimacy is much less common than among younger couples. Even

Bridewealth payments in Igboland are perhaps the highest of any ethnic group in Nigeria and, once a couple has children, there are few socially acceptable reasons to divorce. In general, falling out of love would not be viewed as a legitimate reason to end a marriage. If a couple does divorce, the children of the union are generally considered to belong to the husband and his lineage. A man may legitimately seek to dissolve a marriage if his wife has been sexually unfaithful, but a woman will be on much firmer ground seeking divorce if she

"Being lucky in love is not the most important issue."

can show that her husband has failed to provide for her and the children. She will receive relatively little social support if she cites problems in their personal relationship or the man's infidelity. Though divorce is heavily frowned upon, in urban areas it is more common now than in any recent time.

Tight bonds

As in many parts of the world, in the Igbo-speaking region of southeastern Nigeria, the expectation that sexual and marital relationships should be based on love is growing. But one of the lessons from observing marriages in Igboland is that **good marriage depends on much more than the personal relationship between spouses.** Love can wax and wane, but when the success

of a marriage is tied to parenthood, the bonds of kinship and obligations to community, it is less likely to dissolve. Of course, whether marriages that stay together even when love lapses are always happy marriages is another question, but for the Igbo in southeastern Nigeria, being lucky in love is not the most important issue.

Daniel Jordan Smith is Associate Professor of Anthropology and Chair of the Anthropology Department at Brown University (USA). His work on Nigeria has been awarded by the American Anthropological Association. His main interest is African studies on which he has published numerous articles and book chapters. He is the co-author of *The Secret: Love, Marriage and HIV*, which presents a five-country comparative ethnographic study.

The culture of passion

"Just like the sacred, love is a product of the imagination, with which the lover tries to close the gap from which he suffers", says Prof Christoph Wulf. He is the perfect guide for a trip through history and culture of the Western concept of love. This finally helps us to understand why we look at love the way we do.

The myth

Ever since the gods cut in two the spherical shape of the human being and this being has had to go through life as man and woman, humans have sought "from two to become one" (Plato). This desire is directed at the restoration of their original state and absorbs their resources. Already in this myth, as described by Plato, it is clear: love originates in a lack. We lack something we believe we once possessed and which we think we need to possess again in order to regain our original inviolability, something that is beyond our own being and that, for this very reason, is the prerequisite for this being. Towards this is directed heavenly Eros, which brings into being the true love that is more than just pure pleasure and which leads one to love in the other not just his or her body but also his or her being and soul. According to this myth the other is the missing part to which the lost androgynous unity points, a unity which is, however, more than the sum of its parts.

Passionate love

Plato and Christ invented love each in their own way. The former's homosexuality and the portrayal of the latter as strangely gender-neutral have undoubtedly influenced the specific concepts of love. In the courtly eroticism of the tenth to twelfth centuries, a new concept of love, the *amour passion*, was invented. It is a heterosexual love, a specific feature of which is to give women a recognized power in the male-female relationship. It defines itself as pure. Although, in the hands of non-noble troubadours, it plays with transgressing the marriage boundary, rejection of this transgression is one of its pre-requisites. Within its framework there arises an eroticism of the eye, of language, of touch. Poets find pleasure in the repression of their desire for sensual satisfaction. They praise the prohibition and, with it, the idea of pure love. In this way, it is the separation of the lovers and chastity that bring the passion of love into being. The lover loves love and, in the beloved, her function of kindling of his own feelings. Uniting with the beloved would mean the end of the images and thus of the love – the sacrificing of imagination to the pleasure of the body. The beloved is different: she is the wholly other and, as such, foreign to the lover. The only way out of the confusion of love remains withdrawal, separation – the discourse of love or death, of the lover or the beloved.

Perfection

This concept of love resurfaces in the mysticism of the following centuries as passionate love for God. The longing that transcends the borders of the personality, with its fundamental non-satiability, is a constituent element in both love towards a beloved and in love towards God. Characteristic of both cases are the idealization and the perfecting of the beloved and of God. **The lover is required to empty himself of all sensations and wishes** other than the love of his beloved, in order to be able to love her totally. Nothing should exist in him other than his love for her. This 'flame of love' in the soul of man is kindled by God, it burns and creates deep wounds in the soul, but with this comes a joy-giving, previously unknown blessedness.

The sense of the sacred

The mystics speak explicitly of the experience of the sacred in the love of God and the troubadours do not describe passionate love differently. Right up to the present day, elements of the holy, all-powerful, awesome and otherness have remained in the concept of passionate love. Like the sense of the sacred, passionate love comes about through reduction, requiring a corresponding control of the emotions through collective control. This control determines which sensations are to be regarded as profane, and which as sublime and sacred. Among the sacred sensations belongs passionate love. **It is a state of arousal, which infects everything around it and spreads.** Man is transcended in it. In the desire for both the sacred and the beloved, he is driven by

" Love is a product
of the imagination."

something he is not, which is different, and from which he promises himself fulfilment. The goal is the fusion with the other, which necessarily fails.

Crystallization

Several centuries later, passionate love has lost none of its fascination. But it has become secular once again. Stendhal, for example, distinguishes between *amour-goût*, love out of inclination, *amour physique*, love out of sensuality and *amour-vanité*, love out of vanity, and defines *amour-passion*, passionate love, as a feeling which resembles a fever and "comes and goes without the slightest influence of the will". The origin of love he explains with a crystallization theory. For this, he develops the following image: "In the Salzburg salt mines, you throw a small leafless branch into the depths of an abandoned shaft. Two or three months later you pull it out, now totally covered with sparkling crystals; even the smallest twig, not bigger than a blue tit's claw, is covered with countless dazzling, sparkling diamonds, so much so that you can no longer recognize the simple branch. I refer to it as crystallizing the activity of the spirit that finds new positive aspects in each trait of a person who is loved." **Passionate love is produced exclusively by the lover.** As long as the lover remains unfamiliar with the beloved, the process of crystallization continues, with the beloved being clothed with the positive aspects in the imagination. The lover cannot but idealize the beloved, dress her out to be

desirable for him. Even where the lover is familiar with the beloved, he cannot but appease ever reappearing doubts with the aid of his imagination. He must try to counteract with his imagination the volatility of his 'love dreams' and cause the sensation to continue. Just like the sacred, love is a product of the imagination, with which the lover tries to close the gap from which he suffers. Like the sacred, love enters into many connections in which it simultaneously manifests itself and withdraws, discloses itself and hides away.

Christoph Wulf is Professor of Anthropology and Education at the Freie Universität Berlin (Germany). His books have been translated into fifteen languages. For his research in anthropology he received the title 'professor honoris causa' from the University of Bucharest. He is Vice-President of the German Commission for UNESCO and editor, co-editor and member of the editorial staff of several national and international journals.

"Sexual orientation develops
across a person's life course."

Sexual orientations

"In most cultures, heterosexual love seems to be the natural one. But love is a construction and our sexual orientation develops across our life course", says Prof **Elisabetta Ruspini**. She has done intensive research on the relationship between love and our sexual orientation(s).

By sexual orientation, we describe a person's romantic, emotional or sexual attraction to another person. It is the 'direction' of one's sexuality and sexual interest: to the opposite sex (heterosexual), the same sex (homosexual), both (bisexual), or neither (asexual). The concept of sexual orientation refers to more than sexual behavior. It includes feelings as well as identity. Sexual orientation develops across a person's life course. Individuals may become aware, at different points in their lives, that they are heterosexual, gay, lesbian, bisexual, or asexual.

Love and heterosexuality seem 'natural' partners in social, sexual and parenthood practices. Usually, what 'love' stands for in most cultures is heterosexual love, but the exact same feelings occur in non-heterosexual relationships. There is, indeed, a strong cultural relationship between love and heterosexuality. Despite recent changes in the theoretical understanding and representations of sexuality, heterosexuality continues to be socially normative. As Johnson (2012) writes, heterosexuality is a largely 'silent' set of practices and identities – it is assumed to be everywhere and yet often remains unnamed and unexplored. However, we may argue that love is a 'social construction' (that is, an idea, concept, or notion that people have accepted and re-produced through social practice) and that the social construction of love is bound up with, and legitimizes, a range of heterosexual practices.

Children

Many stereotypes still surround non-heterosexual parenting, such as "Lesbians and gays are not able to bring up a child"; "Homosexual relations are less stable than heterosexual ones and therefore do not guarantee family continuity"; "The children of homosexual people have more psychological problems than those of heterosexuals".

Research shows that children's health and well being are not linked to the sexual orientation of their parents. The children of gay and lesbian couples are equally likely to grow up as well as those of heterosexual couples. The study by Bigner and Jacobsen (1989) on 33 homosexual fathers and 33 heterosexual residents in Iowa shows no difference in the two groups regarding the level of involvement or intimacy with their children. A study by Charlotte Patterson (2006) suggests that the parental sexual orientation is less important than the qualities of family relationships.

It is generally thought that the transsexuality of one of the parents may be a source of suffering for their children. The main fear is that the transsexual parent, due to his/her problems of identity, may engender in the children confusion and trouble with gender identity. Many parents, therefore, separate in the conviction of finding a remedy for the question, unaware of the fact that the progressive distancing of the father or mother who is making the transition creates more problems than it solves.

A further example concerns asexual parents. Just like anyone else, asexual individuals can choose to form a couple or to have children. In order to become parents, they can choose to have sex, use assisted reproductive technologies, or seek to adopt a child. Parenthood and parental love are today not always dependent upon sexual relationships.

One thing appears clear. For the children, the difficulty does not seem to be their parents' sexual preference, but the attitudes of the socio-cultural context regarding this preference. Children growing up and living in non-heterosexual families have to struggle more against social stigmatization, discrimination and bullying. This leads us to reflect on the problem of homophobia and transphobia, i.e. the expression of fear and contempt for homosexual, bisexual and trans persons. These attitudes may be considered the only reason for parents' sexual orientations having a negative influence on their children.

It is, thus, our attitude that makes the difference. This places a lot of responsibility on women, men, mothers, fathers and social institutions.

The keys

- → **Sexual orientation develops across a person's life course.**
- → **In most cultures 'love' stands for heterosexual love but exactly the same feelings occur in other relationships. Love is a social construction.**
- → **Children's health and well being are not linked to the sexual orientation of their parents. It's the attitude of the others that might cause problems.**

Elisabetta Ruspini is Senior Associate Professor in Sociology at the University of Milano-Bicocca (Italy). There she is also the director of the Center for Media Research 'In Chiaro'. She is the main editor of the series of books *Generi, culture, sessualità (Gender, Cultures, Sexualities)*. Prof Ruspini has extensive teaching and research experience, and has published widely on gender issues.

"Loving yourself
gives more power and life
than accepting oneself."

Love yourself

Being happy to see yourself is not always that easy. It is, however, necessary in order to give and receive love. Isn't that narcissism? "No", says Prof **Mia Leijssen**. "Self-love is being connected with your own inner self and knowing yourself as an individual with specific characteristics, without attaching a value judgment to this." Something that is easier said than done.

This self-reflective function is typically human and distinguishes us from many other living organisms. The tendency to express our 'self', we often articulate with the words "I want…" The discovery of one's own will is a turning point in the individuation process. In this focus on the individual, self-development, autonomy and freedom are all key values. A rich inner life is a major source of satisfaction. A loving environment enables a child to feel that it is entitled to have its own singularity, that there is space in which it can discover what best suits it as an individual, that it is allowed to connect with itself. Connecting with oneself is not that easy in a culture that fills and stuffs us with material things and external activities.

A person's identity can also be completely snowed under by the expectations of others. Individuals who are unable to meet the prevailing expectations of their particular environments are especially vulnerable to 'demoralization'. Demoralization refers to the negative feelings that people feel inside themselves in relating to their circumstances.

Demoralization occurs when we constantly collide with our inability to meet a distorted self-image, constructed mainly on the expectations of others. In this way, self-love is not only undermined, it may even turn into self-aggression, from self-damage to suicide. Children often decide that it is better for them to sacrifice their individuality for the sake of peace, or that the wisest course is to adapt to what strong others desire or require of them, in the hope of earning the love of others. In this way, people lose their own 'selves' in the course of their development.

Behind the mask

The way back is not easy. It is not for nothing that the word 'person' is derived from the Latin word 'persona', which means 'mask'. With the word 'person', we are referring to the set of properties that makes someone say "that's what I am". These are qualities that a person has appropriated in the course of his or her development. This constructed self-image is, at times, a successful lie which has served to obtain approval, acquire social esteem or avoid conflicts. Facing the truth about oneself calls for effort and courage. And yet, acquiring self-knowledge is vital for reconnecting with oneself and experiencing self-love.

'Self-acceptance' is an important stage in many healing processes. But more powerful and life-giving is 'self-love'. **It is an inner attitude whereby a person remains in all circumstances good company for him or herself** and cherishes his or her core essence. Self-love involves peeling off the many outer layers that have come into being in the course of time in order to protect the inner self. This is the essence of self-knowledge: lovingly facing the truth about oneself, so that it is no longer necessary to hide things from oneself or suppress them. This gives the peace of mind of coming to terms with oneself. It goes along with nurturing positive feelings and ideas, not worrying about what cannot be changed, not endlessly dwelling on deficiencies and shortcomings.

No pep talk

This is not the same as 'pep talk' or superficial positive thinking. It is a deeper sense of acceptance that life, as it is given to you, is good. It is a purification process in which the individual recovers contact with the authentic self. Problems no longer elicit condemnation, rather they are best served with an attitude of connection to deeper, underlying motivations that lie there to be discovered in the self. The confidence that the individual had good reason to become what he or she was helps in restoring confidence and self-love. **Not as narcissism, but as legitimate self-knowledge in which painful truths can also be recognized from a position of love.**

There are numerous ways of helping people be loving to themselves. One example of an introspective method for connecting with oneself, sensing where healing is needed and encouraging one's own growth process, is the approach that we call 'focusing'. Such introspection leads to self-knowledge and self-love, but often to a spiritual process and an opening of consciousness, with a loosening of the attachment to 'me as a person'. Here 'love' is being the whole and there is a unity of consciousness in which the experience of being part of a much larger whole predominates. Thus, the experience of a self-love that is not controlled by the ego can be a source of knowledge which lifts man to a superhuman level.

The keys

→ **A loving environment makes us feel that we are entitled to have our own uniqueness and that we can connect with ourselves.**

→ **Our constructed self either snows under our real inner self or is a successful lie. Facing the truth about oneself calls for effort and courage.**

→ **'Self-acceptance' is an important stage in many healing processes. But more powerful and life-giving is 'self-love'.**

Mia Leijssen is Professor of Psychology at the University of Leuven, KUL (Belgium). She teaches psychotherapy and counseling. At European level, she leads an online course *counseling in Existential Well-Being*, with attention to physical, social, psychological and spiritual aspects of human existence. Her main research and publications focus on curative factors in psychotherapy. This has resulted in numerous articles in international journals and several books, including *Leven vanuit liefde* (*Living from Love*). Her academic career is in balanced harmony with nature, music, dance and five grandchildren.

"Embrace our dazzling capacity for unexpected passion."

Bisexual orientations

"We used to think of everyone as divided neatly into two groups: gay and straight", says Dr **Lisa Diamond**. She is well-known for her 18-year longitudinal study of the love life of the same 100 people. Other research affirms her findings. "With respect to sexual orientation, the world is a much more complicated place than we used to think it was."

My research has focused on the health implications of love relationships, and one of the most compelling things that I have learned, not so much from my own research but from working in this field more generally, is the incredible ability of love to promote or hinder our health. As a species, we are born extremely dependent, much more so than other species, and the love of our caregivers is as vital to us as food and water. Babies who do not receive adequate nurturance will not grow properly and will suffer psychological deficits that never recover. As adults, we need love just as badly. Individuals who lack love in their lives, who are truly lonely, suffer profoundly, both physically and emotionally. We need to take love seriously as an element of basic physical and mental health. This includes taking sexuality seriously, as well. Over the years, sexuality has tended to receive short shrift from researchers studying love and relationships, as if it is 'the icing on the cake' of an intimate romantic bond. But **sex is more than just icing – it's baked right into the cake!** A number of large-scale epidemiological studies conducted in a variety of different countries have shown that individuals in long-term relationships who report more frequent and satisfying sexual activity with their partners – whether the activity entails sexual intercourse or other sexually intimate behavior – have longer and healthier lives, independent of other health risk factors. So both love and sex should be taken seriously as promoters of health, and we should treat satisfying love relationships and satisfying sexual relationships as fundamentally important components of a well-lived life.

Flexible system

The other thing that I have learned from my research, and which I think is important for individuals to know, is that love appears to be a more 'flexible' system than sexual desire, when it comes to the gender of our partners. Much of my own research has focused on sexual orientation, and its development and expression over the lifespan. The two most surprising and important things that I have found are that, first, the majority of individuals with same-sex attractions also experience other-sex attractions. In other words, bisexual orientations appear to be more common than exclusive same-sex orientations. Second, most individuals appear to be capable of falling in 'platonic' love (i.e. romantic love without sexual attraction) with just about anyone, regardless of gender.

These two things, taken together, make the world a much more complicated place than we used to think it was, with respect to sexual orientation. We used to think of everyone as divided neatly into two groups: gay and straight. Gay people desired and fell in love with same-sex partners, straight people desired and fell in love with other-sex partners, and that was that. Now we know that mixed patterns of love and desire – to both women and men – are actually quite common across the lifespan. Sometimes they take individuals by surprise: I have interviewed many individuals over the years who report to me that they feel 'different' or 'deviant' because they suddenly discover, late in life, that they have romantic and erotic feelings that are utterly unlike any that they have had before. The message I try to convey to these individuals is one of acceptance and normality. These experiences are actually quite common and there appears to be nothing 'deviant' or 'wrong' with them. The flexibility and adaptability and context-sensitivity of our intimate feelings appear to be a fundamental characteristic of our species. This may throw our lives into temporary disarray, it may prove confusing and startling, but it is part of our human nature. We owe it to ourselves and to one another to be tolerant, loving, accepting and embracing of our dazzling capacity for unexpected passion.

The keys

→ **We need to take love (and sex) seriously as an element of basic physical and mental health.**

→ **Love appears to be a more 'flexible' system than sexual desire, when it comes to the gender of our partners.**

→ **Most individuals appear to be capable of falling in 'platonic' love with just about anyone, regardless of gender.**

Lisa M. Diamond is Professor of Psychology and Gender Studies at the University of Utah (USA). She has received numerous awards for her longitudinal studies on love, sexual development and intimate relationships, summarized in her successful book *Sexual Fluidity*.

Love makes me alive

Google offers, in 0.27 seconds, 1,110,000,000 results for the search term 'love song'. Wikipedia describes a love song as a song about falling in love and the feelings it brings, and/or about heartbreak and how it feels. Dr Robert Neuburger picks out a single line from famous French songwriter Serge Gainsbourg to go to the heart of love.

"What is life without love?" This question in a song by Serge Gainsbourg admirably summarizes the vital, essential role that love plays in enabling us to feel we really live. In saying this, **we need to distinguish between living and being alive.** Living is the little cells that move around, we need to take care of them, feed ourselves, keep healthy. Being alive is something very different, it is a feeling that is fed by love. Often we realize this only when we suffer setbacks. There are times when we are fully alive because our need for love and recognition is being met by our giving and receiving love. This can take two forms. There is 'relational' love, which says "I exist in your eyes, and you exist in mine". And then there is this other link that unites us with another person or persons within circles of belonging, essentially the couple, that I like to call the couple-home, the family, this feeling of love shared with others due to our belonging to the same group.

But sometimes the situation is reversed. We feel abandoned, deceived, betrayed or otherwise. Then we experience a drop in this feeling of being alive, a drop that a certain medicine has pathologized under the name of 'depression'. In reality, it is something quite different, the fact is that we have hit a primitive anxiety, the existential angst against which we struggle daily by building and maintaining bonds of love. This is why the best medicine against depression is not anti-depressants, but 'the cure of love'.

Robert Neuburger is a well-known psychiatrist, couples and family therapist in Paris (France) and Geneva (Switzerland). He is director of the 'Centre d'étude de la famille association' (CEFA). He has published numerous articles and 14 books, including *Exister, le plus intime et fragile des sentiments*.

"Being alive is a feeling fed by love."

"Love will always rebound."

Through the iron curtain

"Love is eternal, to be suppressed by nothing and no one."
It was hard for the young **Tamara Hovorun** to believe these
words, living under the Soviet regime behind the Iron Curtain.
After the dissolution of the Soviet Union in 1991, psychologists
too liberated themselves. Tamara had become one of them,
studying the warmth of love before and after the Cold War.

Psychology is a tradition in my family. My father was a psychologist and I, in turn, passed
the profession to my daughter. I am proud to be part of the very first cohort of psychologists
to graduate from the Kyiv National University (Ukraine) in the early 1970s. I am incredibly
grateful to my professors who, notwithstanding the enormous pressure of Soviet ideology
and without any access to the works of their international colleagues, did their best to give
us well-rounded knowledge of the discipline. My professional discovery of love started
through philosophy. As an undergraduate student, I was fascinated by the fact that love
was a focal point of many philosophical worldviews and that sexual love was at the origin of
not only an individual, but also humanity. One quote that stuck with me through
the years belongs to a Ukrainian philosopher Hryhorij Skovoroda, "Love is eternal,
to be suppressed by nothing and no one."

Suppression of love

I came to fully appreciate the wisdom of these words later on in my professional career. It was the mid-1980s, the period of 'perestroika' and the lifting of the iron curtain. An important part of the process, which is often overlooked by the outsiders, was the rehabilitation of love, specifically sexual and homosexual love. Homosexuality was removed as a criminal offence from the statute book, allowing scores of couples to come to terms with their feelings. Sexuality, too, was slowly shedding its taboo status, making way for the much needed, but often uncomfortable societal discourse. At that time, I had a professional practice at the Kyiv Center for Sexology and Family Counseling and became a witness to the flood of clients who felt liberated and inspired by the shift in ideology. The most important lesson I learned in working with the people who came through my doors is that love was often the only thing that helped them stay physically and emotionally strong in the times of repression. I still remember talking to one couple – two women in their mid-forties – and asking them if either had ever regretted not being of the opposite gender. They responded in unison that they loved each other for exactly who each one was and that their feelings had sheltered them from years of scorn and discrimination. I learned that attempts of the society to suppress love, be it sexual expression of love or homosexuality, have failed. Love will always rebound, as strong as ever.

Freedom of choices

The further democratization of the Ukrainian society has brought with it the democratization of love. My research shows that people of my generation subscribe to the doctrine that love follows the formula of $\frac{1}{2} + \frac{1}{2} = 1$. In other words, love is a union of people who depend on and complement each other. In contrast, the generation of my daughter has come to endorse a new formula, $1 + 1 = 2$. Love is a partnership of self-sufficient individuals who are together because of the want rather than the need. Love is once again about the freedom of choices.

Through the professional experience of working with couples and learning their love stories came another important realization – the ability to sacrifice oneself for the well-being of the other is a signpost of true and mature love. I recall extended psychotherapy with a married couple where a husband fell in love with another woman but wanted to stay committed to the marriage and rekindle the feelings for his wife. When the therapy was coming to an end and the harmony seemed to have been restored, the wife announced she wanted a divorce. Shocked, I asked for an explanation. "I love him as much as I used to ...

perhaps even more. But I want at least one of us to be happy." The love was motivating the wife to set her husband free to discover a new kind of happiness, this time with someone else. Willingness to sacrifice oneself for the well-being of the other is a signpost of true and mature love.

As a practitioner and a researcher, I come to the conclusion time and again that love is incompatible with any kind of forcefulness and suppression, be it interpersonal or societal. It is impossible to make someone fall in love with you. It is equally impossible for society to dictate what love is and is not. Much like the quote from my student youth, love is an antithesis to suppression, an eternal force that continues to liberate and inspire.

The keys

→ **Attempts of the society to suppress love, be it sexual expression of love or homosexuality, have failed. Love will always rebound, as strong as ever.**

→ **Love is about the freedom of choices. It is a partnership of self-sufficient individuals who are together because of the want rather than the need.**

→ **Willingness to sacrifice oneself for the well-being of the other is a signpost of true and mature love.**

Tamara Hovorun is Professor and Chief Scientific Fellow at the Social Psychology Laboratory of the Kostiuk Institute of Psychology in Kyiv (Ukraine) and at the John-Paul the Second Lublin Catholic University in Stalowa Wola (Poland). She has written more than 200 scholarly and popular publications on the psychology of human sexuality, gender stereotypes, sexual education, etc. With a grant from the European Union she created twelve television documentaries on gender. The Ministry of Education awarded her for the popularization of psychology.

Jealous partners

Like love, the experience of jealousy is universal. It is implicated in perhaps a quarter of all murders and is a major factor in domestic violence. Everybody knows the feeling. Dr Gregory White has studied it for over thirty years. Does he know how to cope with it?

It turns out jealousy is not an emotion, per se. Depending on person, relationships, situation and culture, different emotions enter the mix: envy, anger, anxiety, sadness, shame/guilt and heightened sexual and romantic feelings being the most common. It helps to **think of jealousy as a pattern of feelings**, thoughts and actions that fit the 'model' of what jealousy is in a particular culture and for a particular person. If your personal and cultural models are that the jealous person is and should be rageful, then anger will dominate your feelings and actions. If your model is that at least jealousy is a sign of love, then perhaps you will prove your love by demonstrating jealousy.

Two directions

While cultures and individuals do vary a great deal in their models of the usual triggers, emotions and behaviors, these jealousy patterns appear universally to be activated when we assess (perhaps unconsciously) that the real, imagined, or desired relationship between ourselves and our beloved is threatened or damaged by a real or potential rival. There are two directions of threat/damage – one is to our sense of self-worth and identity. Examples include threat (or damage) to our sense of our own physical and emotional attractiveness, status in our community or friendship circles, or that part of identity which is the 'you-me' of being in relationship. The other threat targets the real or potential material and emotional rewards of the relationship (such as sexual pleasure, avoidance of loneliness, financial partnership and shared recreational activities). These twin **threats that drive jealousy are intertwined, but can lead to different actions**. If I compromise myself in a desperate attempt to maintain the relationship, my self-esteem can plummet. If I preserve my self-esteem by starting an affair to prove to myself I am attractive, my primary relationship may be damaged. No wonder that jealousy (*and* romantic love) are two common experiences where even very level-headed people can go at least a little crazy.

Angry men

Overall, research suggests that men and women of any particular culture are about equally likely to get 'jealous' (be in a recognizable jealousy pattern). However, there seem to be consistent gender differences in these patterns. Men, for example, at least in the Western cultures that have provided most of the contemporary research, seem to be more angry and for a longer time when jealous and to focus on the sexual threat they experience, having intrusive fantasies of revenge or images of sexual behavior between a rival and the beloved. Relationships seem harder to repair than if the woman has been jealous. **Women are more likely to be sad and anxious** when jealous, focusing more on the real or fantasied relationship between the beloved and the rival, rather than on sexual acts.

The target

What to do if you are jealous or if you are the target of another's jealousy and your attempts to cope are not working out? First, try to figure out if the jealousy is **symptomatic, reactive or just plain normal**. Romantic jealousy can be symptomatic of delusional states occurring, for example, in deep depression, manic episodes or active schizophrenia; it can also result from dementia or substance and alcohol abuse/dependence. Reactive jealousy is the jealousy magnified by longstanding trauma or inflexibility of personality. Early loss of a parent or intense loss of a first romantic partner can make future romantic threats seem more real and threatening. Some personalities rather chronically scan for threat or loss and then overreact to slight suggestions of a real or perceived rival. People with particularly intense or rigid personalities usually have a number of longstanding interpersonal problems, in addition to jealousy. Symptomatic and reactive jealousies usually require individualized professional help for both the jealous partner and the beloved; **it is unlikely that you can successfully cope with such jealousy on your own**. Trying to fix another's symptomatic or reactive jealousy by accommodating to jealous demands often backfires into increased risk to the fixer's own psychological and physical well-being. Seek advice from professionals to help you sort out what you need to do, but couples counseling alone seems to be of little

help in reducing symptomatic or reactive jealousy. Everything other than symptomatic or reactive jealousy we'll call normal, and most couples have to deal with it from time to time, even in quite long-term relationships. If you have established a good foundation of trust and communication in your relationship, usually the two of you can find your own solution through honest sharing and problem-solving.

Gregory White is both a social and clinical psychologist and is Professor of Psychology at National University, La Jolla in California (USA). He has been involved with the academic study of jealousy for over thirty years. As a psychotherapist he has worked with many individuals and couples caught up in problems of jealousy.

" Romantic love and jealousy are two common experiences that can make us all at least a little crazy."

Six types of givers

Chocolates, flowers, books, a dinner or a drink… We all like to give and to get presents. Dr Tina M. Lowrey studies whether this act is always based on love and uncovers six types of 'givers'.

What we (Cele Otnes and I) found is that givers' motivations fall into various social roles that they play.

1. A Pleaser has the classic goal of giving a gift that the recipient will clearly enjoy.
2. A Socializer attempts to influence the recipient in some way through the gift they choose (e.g. a wife who buys her husband a nice shirt in the hopes he'll pay more attention to the way he dresses).
3. A Compensator buys gifts to make up for some sort of loss the recipient has experienced (e.g. a daughter who buys her widowed father the sort of gift her mother may have given him in the past).
4. A Provider attempts to give useful gifts (e.g. a mother who buys her children socks, underwear and pajamas).
5. An Acknowledger wants the recipient to know the relationship is valued enough to merit a gift.
6. An Avoider is one who chooses not to buy gifts, for a variety of reasons.

We are frequently interviewed by the media, and one of the most unfortunate misrepresentations of our findings is that only the Pleaser is a 'good' gift-giver with pure motivations. What I would like to argue here is that, with only a few minor exceptions, all true giving has love as its motivation (with the obvious exception of someone giving for purely ulterior motives). Yes, the Pleaser's goal is to find a gift that the recipient really wants, and yes, love of the recipient seems to be the primary inspiration for this social role. However negative the Socializer sounds, I believe that love can be the motivation behind this social role as well – if you didn't love

"All true giving has love as its motivation."

the person, you probably wouldn't spend much effort on such an attempt. Compensating someone for their loss is clearly motivated by love for the recipient. Being a provider is, as well. The difficulty in my argument arises for Acknowledgers and Avoiders. Acknowledgers may not deeply love the recipient, but the fact that a gift is warranted communicates that the relationship is of value. Avoiders are more difficult – if one has opted out of gift exchange for negative reasons (e.g. no longer wants to nurture the relationship), than love is clearly absent. But some Avoiders do so for other reasons – they don't want to start a tradition that may burden someone in the relationship, for example, or they would rather show their love in other ways.

Concentration camps

In conclusion, over the years I've come to believe that there is no single 'right' way to give, just as there is no perfect gift, but I do believe that we have a need to give, and that need is based on a need to express our love to others. In research with Jill Klein, we have uncovered instances of giving in the constrained context of Nazi concentration camps. In this research, which is based on an analysis of survivors' memoirs, we have found giving that is clearly motivated by instrumental motives (i.e. giving something in order to receive something in return), but we have also found giving that solely expresses one's need to give in order to feel truly human. For the purposes

of this research, we define 'gift' as anything given to another, tangible or intangible. For instance, there are many examples of a prisoner taking the place of another prisoner during the selection process (where prisoners who were too ill or weak to work were selected to go to the furnaces), simply because they thought the other prisoner may not pass inspection. Although in such instances, the recipient may be a complete stranger to the giver, the overwhelming urge to give of oneself in this way clearly bolsters the argument that we need to give to and express love for one another.

Tina M. Lowrey is Professor of Marketing at the University of Texas at San Antonio (USA). She has done considerable research on gift-giving, together with her colleagues Cele Otnes (University of Illinois) and Jill Klein (Melbourne Business School). She has edited two books and serves on the editorial review boards of several publications, including *The Journal of Consumer Psychology*.

The storyline of love

Prof Rolando Díaz-Loving has spent a lifetime writing the final storyline of love. It is based on reproduction, but tainted and rewritten by culture and specific ecosystems. "I must admit that, given my family name, I must have had a genetic predisposition for this work", he smilingly adds.

Any attempt to understand human behavior needs to account for evolutionary, biological, ecosystem, historical, socio-cultural and psychological components. With this holistic orientation in mind, we have advanced the Bio-psycho-socio-cultural Theory of Couple Relationships in which we specify and research the role played by each component and their interaction in predicting and explaining behavior and its implications for relationship quality. For the bio-psychological components of the theory, the scientific literature up to the 1970s recurrently mentions passion and intimacy as the two central forms of love. These two ways of loving relate directly to the two basic needs of the human species: reproduction and protection; and the behavioral patterns derived from their pursuit. The first is driven by passion; the second is immersed in caring and companionship.

Since the parameters of mating behavior are established by biological characteristics and needs determined by evolution, most psychological work in this realm has centred on looking for the universals of love. However, the variety of behavioral manifestations developed to achieve the goals of reproduction and protection seem tightly meshed to ecosystem and socio-cultural variables. In fact, questions regarding how many, with whom, for how long, how close and why, seem to be constructed on the basic needs of the human species. From these are molded attachment styles derived from the interaction of the basic needs with caring figures, styles that ultimately reflect behavioral variations developed in different historic and geographical niches. These styles are then transformed into norms, beliefs and values, which, in turn, are transmitted to new generations through socialization and enculturation processes. As an example of a norm-based constituent of love, commitment, an aspect derived from culturally constructed norms dating to the onset of agriculture, determines the longevity of a relationship.

Different stages

As to the norms and beliefs that guide behavior when living a romantic, passionate or stable relationship, a sample of Mexicans were asked to indicate what were the appropriate, typical and normal behaviors to engage in with another person in the different stages of a relationship.

"Love is written with tears."

Factor analysis of the responses yielded several statistically robust and conceptually clear dimensions.

Love starts with attraction, in which we can surmise that "one has interest in someone that appears attractive" and "when an attractive person is identified, you should do everything possible to attract their attention". The next steps must include motivation to move towards the target of our affections: love thus contains passion, reflected in the belief that "passion produces sexual desire", "passion burns like brushfire" and "giving in completely to the couple is a sign of passion". Once the relationship has been established, love is also companionship. This form of love includes commitment and maintenance and is expressed as "if you live with someone, you should fulfill certain responsibilities" and "commitment gives formality to a relationship". Lingering in love is always the question of possible loss. As to the historical presence of courtly love and the search for difficult or impossible love, it is found in the romance and sadness dimension which states that "when you are in a romantic relationship, you long to be with your other half all the time" and "when you lose a loved one, you suffer". Where sadness becomes deep, it can lead to tragic love, of the type described in the play *Romeo and Juliet* or in *Love Story*, leading to the understanding that "love is written with tears" and "when a person is not loved, they would rather die".

Finally, if things unravel into the lack of love and detachment, we are advised that "when couples separate, it is because they do not love each other anymore" and "not loving the other half of one's couple means you do not want to be with him/her anymore".

Love is a set of feelings, cognitions and behaviors intended to ensure the reproduction and protection of the species. While their manifestation is certainly built on an evolutionary stage, the final storyline is tainted and rewritten by cultural contingencies that determine the particular manifestations that reflect real, imaginary and even quaint adaptations to specific ecosystems.

Rolando Díaz-Loving is a Professor at the Psychology Department of the National Autonomous University of Mexico (UNAM). His abundant work is an international reference in couple and family relationships and cross-cultural psychology and ethno-psychology. He has written numerous books and articles in scientific journals and has given more than 700 presentations at conferences worldwide. He has received prestigious awards, including the Interamerican Award for Psychology.

*"After being in love,
most often disappointment comes,
and not love."*

Our formula of love

"The question 'What is love?' can only be answered with 'Love is whatever one believes love is' ", says Dr **Zoran Milivojević**. We all follow our own internal logic, our personal 'formula of love'. We will never understand our behavior, emotions and reactions if we do not uncover this hidden, often unreasonable and irrational, logic of love.

Sometimes people repeat behavior in relationships which they themselves believe to be mistaken and harmful. Not only can they not stop behaving in that way, but they are also quite confused because they do not understand why they do so. For example, one client was confused by his behavior in which he tyrannized the person he loved, and he himself called his behavior 'sadistic'. It was typical for him to ask his partners to give up things which were important to them related to their careers, their friends and their families. The analysis of this person showed that his formula of love equated love and sacrifice (*Love = sacrifice*). So this person expected his partner to sacrifice in order to prove that love existed (***If there is sacrifice = there is love***). Such logic enabled him to evaluate the amount of love given by his partner (*small sacrifice = a little love; medium sacrifice = more love; the greatest sacrifice = the greatest love; no sacrifice = no love*).

When he uncovered his dysfunctional formula of love, he began to understand his behavior in love relationships. Then the therapy could move on to changing his internal logic. In this concrete case, it meant that the person had to learn to separate love and sacrifice. Certain formulas of love often come into being during childhood or youth, through personal experience or through the messages a person receives from significant others. This client had learned to equate love and sacrifice by observing his mother who sacrificed herself every day to show her love to her husband and three sons.

The main problem was that he did not differentiate love as such from his idea of love or his idea about relationships. As a result, my client kept trying to force his partners into his concept of relationships, in which the woman had to make constant sacrifices. If he had succeeded, he would finally have felt that he was loved. Since he did not succeed with various partners, he was constantly dissatisfied with his love life. Occasionally, this escalated into aggressive behavior towards his partners, as he demanded that they 'prove' that they loved him.

Thirty logics

In my work, I have described over thirty different dysfunctional formulas, or logics, of love. Here are another two of them.

1. Because of its destructive potential on an individual level, one of the most important formulas is: *partner love = the meaning of life*. When there is a break up, when they are left by someone, people with this kind of logic are not only sad because they have been left by a person whom they still love, but also because they believe that their life no longer has any meaning. Therefore, they can become self-destructive, even suicidal, but they can also be destructive towards the person to whom they have connected the meaning of their life.

2. The formula of love that equates love and being in love, that is love with happiness and pleasure, is especially important because it has come to hold a central place in the collective unconscious of Westerners. Mass media, romance novels and movies have made us believe that real love will bring us constant pleasure and happiness in our relationship. The result is that people believe in the following formula: *love = a pleasant feeling*. On that basis, the more pleasant the feeling and the longer it lasts, people conclude that this certainly must be true love. However, when the pleasant feeling decreases or ceases, they conclude that the love is gone. The result is that many people mistakenly equate love with the fact that they feel good with someone, or, more explicitly, with sex and being in love.

Stop searching

Love and being in love are two feelings which are based on completely different psychological mechanisms. Since these two feelings are experienced in a similar way, many people equate them, or at least think that being in love is the first, obligatory phase of love. Since being in love includes the idealization of the partner, this necessarily leads later to a greater or lesser disappointment in the partner, or in love altogether. That means that being in love is an ephemeral feeling. It also means that, after being in love, most often disappointment comes, and not love.

Since modern Westerners do not know how to choose partners for themselves, except by falling in love, this later leads to unstable relationships, break ups and divorces. Sometimes it seems that our search for a love which brings happiness has actually distanced us from real love. And that is why Westerners need to learn about what love is from those cultures which do not connect love in the first place to happiness and pleasure. When we redefine love, we will stop searching for those things which do not exist in it.

The keys

→ **We all follow our personal 'formula of love', our own internal (often unreasonable and irrational) logic. Uncovering it will help us understand our behavior.**

→ **We have to differentiate 'love' as such from our personal idea of love and relationships.**

→ **Love and being in love are two feelings which are based on completely different psychological mechanisms. We need to learn from those cultures which do not connect love in the first place to happiness and pleasure.**

Zoran Milivojević is a medical doctor specialized in psychotherapy and the director of the Psihopolis Institute in Novi Sad (Serbia). He is President of the Serbian Union of Psychotherapy Associations and board member of the European Association of Psychotherapy. He is the author of several books in Serbian including *Catching a Love* and *The Formulas of love – How Not to Ruin Your Life Searching for Real Love*.

"The family controls whether the sacred rules are followed."

Sacred rules

What about interracial marriages? In the US their number has increased from 0.7% in the 1970s to 4% today. They still represent an absolute minority among the total number of wed couples worldwide, but the divorce rate is sometimes twice as high. **Elena Pruvli** tries to find out why.

The international nature of my career and my lifestyle has given me a unique opportunity to apply the academic frame of intercultural communications to the delicate issues of love and sexuality. I've researched the meaning of sexuality in different cultures (and, I will admit it, included empirical, experimental and even field studies before I met the Love of my Life). Any type of relationship is based on communication. Even if our values and concepts of love are not in contradiction, we still need to be able to encode messages in a way that the recipient can decode them as we intended.

I'm currently involved as an Intercultural Communications coach in an International Red Cross training project. The volunteers, who come from very diverse professional and educational backgrounds, report issues of love, family connections and sexuality as the most difficult to discuss with people from other cultures they are trying to help. **People use the most indirect speech to negotiate a lot of taboos.** Regulations and restrictions already exist while 'just talking' about the subject.

My recent training of career advisors has proved to me that awareness about love and sexuality and the connection of this part of life, with people's careers and professional development, varies dramatically among cultures. That can be a serious barrier in effective communication, when one party seems too cold, official and inhumane, and the other looks like a time-waster with irrelevant subjects.

Rules of love

Everyone who was raised in a tight, stable, closely connected community will understand what I'm talking about. Such cultural groups insist on passing their concept of love unchanged from one generation to another, trying, with different degree of success (as younger members more integrated into the local culture become resistant), to preserve their meaning of love, created mainly when the community was extremely united and interdependent.

Back then, **'rules of love' helped the community to survive. In the process, they became part of something sacred,** which included the community's hierarchy of values and its model of love. The latter was considered to be right for everyone, with little account taken of individual personality traits. Speaking from a female prospective, at the top of the value list in my community were understanding, acceptance, support and even protective misdirection at times. In some other groups, respecting authority, obeying and sacrificing, serving, feeding and praising are listed higher.

Stormy waters

Community concepts contain the set of axioms 'how it should be' and presume that everyone should conform to this not-to-be-questioned model. Both the value priorities and the models of love were shaped by the communities' external environment and, already back then, developed considerably more slowly than the surrounding culture. Today, however, due to increasing globalization, internationalization and liberalization, the integration gap has grown dramatically.

Traditionally 'a decent girl from a good family' was brought up in a 'proper' way to be introduced by a respected community member to an 'acceptable boy'. The couple's extended family would control, throughout their lives, their following of these 'sacred rules', at least outwardly. **In the new era, after absorbing the 'concept of love', young people are thrown into the ocean of life,** with no clear rules or norms. Some of us rush into its stormy waters to work out our own values and models.

Love concept

I would not recommend my path as an example to be copied because I've done a lot of right things, but perhaps in a wrong order. I can't separate my social experience from my professional career, which has involved living in very different cultural environments and meeting a lot of people with very diverse backgrounds and statuses. I would organize the information and ideas they shared with me in a hierarchical order which I can call **the 'pyramid of love rules'.** At the base, we find what place love occupies in the given culture (importance for males, females, priorities towards other facets of life, 'discussability' of love, etc.). The next level is the amount of 'give' of the love concept (what is appropriate in a given culture, what rules are very strictly adhered to, what is flexible and what would be the possible reaction of the society if one broke the rules). Third and fourth is the love concept itself – the hierarchy of the love values and the model(s) of love.

The keys

→ **Any type of relationship is based on communication. Intercultural relationships have more problems in decoding the message.**

→ **Some cultural groups insist on passing their 'sacred rules of love' unchanged from one generation to another.**

→ **The new pyramid of love rules have to take into account the amount of 'give' of the love concept.**

Elena Pruvli is a Westminster (London, UK) graduate. She is Visiting Lecturer at the International Business and Languages department, Hogeschool Drenthe (the Netherlands) and at the Estonian Business School in Tallinn (Estonia). She is an international trainer in Intercultural Communications, teaching Cross-Cultural Management Studies.

LOVE is
is LOVE

whatever
one believes

whatever
one believes

"Love comes and goes without our permission."

In therapy

"As a couple therapist, I refuse to treat people who feel no love for each other", says **Jean-Pierre van de Ven**. "If people want to stay together as a loveless couple, they should consult a lawyer, as do business partners or divorcees. Lawyers can make loveless relationships work, not therapists."

Partners in a romantic relationship love each other, but to love is not the same as having a relationship. **People confuse love and relationships quite easily,** which is understandable, given the interdependence between the two. Love cannot exist without a subject, a person to love. If there is a lover somewhere, you will also find a loved one there. Now you have two people interacting in some way or another, which is a relationship by definition.

Still, we all know by experience the difference between love and relationships, however much overlap there might be. Perhaps we noticed that we did not automatically fall out of love once we decided to end a romantic relationship. (It takes effort, doesn't it, to create and maintain distance between ourselves and the alcoholic, depressive or cheating people who used to be the loves of our lives.) Or perhaps we have experienced, in some other way, that we could not hurry, control or manipulate love even if our lives depended on it.

Stick together

Of course, people can be manipulated, perhaps even into love. And relationships can and should be controlled or, to put it mildly, be the product of mutual agreements. People who do not deal with their life partners do not have a real relationship. It is likely that such persons depend on their partners, or that they boss their partners around. But **love is not simply the sum total of all the agreements romantic partners make** during their shared lives. Love empowers us to make these agreements and love gives us the energy to stick together in hard times. Love makes us braver; love makes us better people; love enables us to give, to care and to accept whatever hand life deals to us. Love is an essential life force. We need love to survive.

Unfortunately, love comes and goes without our permission. It does not care too much about our personal preferences or needs. Love may pop up when we least expect it. Sometimes love disappears for a while and then returns, all fresh and bristling with life and joy. Love can suddenly waver, barely linger, drift off for no apparent reason. And all this without us being able to predict or influence what is going on.

Struggling

If there is love between partners, but they somehow do not get along, this often points to a lack of communication and negotiation skills between them. However logical this idea might be, **distressed couples always focus on something completely irrelevant: love.** They seem to think that all is well as long as love is around. (*"We will be all right, won't we darling, just as long as we love each other."*) This fallacy comes from the countless Hollywood and Bollywood movies, Shakespearean plays and sentimental telenovelas, and from all the love songs that we are exposed to in the course of our lifetimes.

Lies, is what we are made to believe. There is no such thing as living happily ever after, without putting some effort into it. In reality, we have to deal with the person in our living room, at our dinner table, in our bed. We have to negotiate about everything: about the best way to raise our children, about finances, about who will take out the garbage on Sunday evenings. And then, of course, we have to negotiate all the intimacies that belong to sharing our lives with an important other: in what tone of voice do we speak to each other? To what extent do we share information about our individual friends and relatives? How often and in what way do we have sex?

But this all belongs to the domain of our relationships. **Dealing, agreeing and accepting, or fighting, struggling and rejecting have nothing to do with love.** Love is the force that keeps us going, but we cannot keep love going. You can only hope that the force may be with you.

The keys

→ **People confuse love and relationships quite easily.**

→ **There is no such thing as living happily after, without putting some effort into it.**

→ **Love is the force that keeps us going, but we cannot keep love going.**

Jean-Pierre van de Ven is a psychologist. He has a private practice specializing in couple therapy and also works in a psychiatric clinic in Amsterdam (the Netherlands). He used to teach couple therapy at the University of Amsterdam, and currently publishes articles and columns in Dutch national newspapers and magazines. He is the author of *Geluk in de liefde* (*Happiness in Love*) and many books on couple therapy and love. Jean-Pierre van de Ven is married, with three children.

"Foreplay starts outside the bedroom."

Sexual desire

"Love is the answer, but while you are waiting for the answer, sex raises some pretty good questions", is a famous quote of American film director Woody Allen. They are closely linked, but what does sex really have to do with love? Dr **Gurit E. Birnbaum** has spent a lifetime of research from the bedroom to far beyond.

Sex is an integral part of romantic love and adult attachment relationships. Sexual urges and emotional attachments, however, are not necessarily inter-connected. People can feel emotionally attached to someone without being sexually attracted to him or her and vice versa, sexual partners may have sex without being emotionally attached to each other, as in the case of one-night stands. Still, when it comes to romantic relationships, attachments and sex do go together, and romantic partners are typically both attracted to and attached to each other. Thus, within the context of romantic relationships, sex has the potential to represent an intensely meaningful experience, one that may serve as a powerful motivational force across different stages of relationship development. Sexual desire is what brings potential partners together to begin with and determines whether subsequent interaction will or will not take place. Yet, in the end, sexual desire, or more specifically, lack of it, may be what makes partners grow apart.

Short-term

Indeed, sex may affect the future of a potential or current relationship from before it even exists, through the onset of the attachment bonding process, and on through potential detachment and dissolution. In particular, initially, the desire for sex may motivate people to look for either short-term or long-term mating opportunities with potential sexual partners. Once a potential partner is identified, sexual responses to this new acquaintance may serve as a diagnostic test of his or her suitability and compatibility, determining whether future interactions will occur. Increased sexual desire for this potential partner may signify suitability and is therefore likely to motivate the individual to pursue this desirable partner. In contrast, a lack of sexual desire may signal relationship incompatibility and, therefore, would likely to motivate withdrawal from future interactions with this person. Once a suitable partner is found, sexual desire for this partner may motivate the individual to form a relationship that extends beyond a single sexual episode. Then, as the relationship progresses from initial encounters, to casual dating, to steady dating, **sex may serve as a binding force that fosters emotional bonding** between sexual partners and strengthens their emerging relationship.

Signals

In later phases of relationship development, sex may still help maintain the relationship, but become less important to its quality and stability than other aspects of the relationship (e.g. provision of mutual support, warmth and interdependence). Nevertheless, sex may turn out to be especially beneficial to the relationship of most people in anxiety-provoking and relationship-threatening situations, which call for distress regulation and elicit proximity seeking. In these situations, people may use sex to repair their threatened relationships. Even so, relationship restoration is not always feasible, as in the case of major and insoluble relational conflict. Hence, eventually, **sex may tear partners apart.**
For example, prolonged major conflict may lead to a decline in the desire for sex with one's partner that, in turn, may contribute to re-evaluation of his or her suitability. When loss of sexual interest signals incompatibility with partners' relationship goals, it may motivate them to seek resolution of these interpersonal problems, either with the current partner, or by looking for a more suitable one. Sexual desire thrives on rising intimacy and being responsive to your partner's needs is one of the best ways to instil this elusive sensation over time; better than any sexual pyrotechnics.

Alternative route

The effects of sex on relationship quality and longevity may vary, not only across relationship phases and contexts, but also across individuals. For example, frequent and satisfying sexual activity may be most beneficial to the relationship of couples with partners with negative characteristics (e.g. neuroticism, attachment insecurity) or to couples with relationship problems (e.g. poor communication). In these cases, sex may provide an alternative route for serving otherwise unmet needs for support, security and love and compensate for relationship deficiencies. Overall, **sex is important for relationship well-being,** especially when the relationship is more vulnerable (e.g. across the early stages of emerging relationships, under relationship-threatening conditions, and among couples characterized by relationship deficiencies). However, not all depends on sex and other aspects of the relationship, such as intimacy, support and commitment, may be equally important to relationship quality, if not more, in the long run.

Reverse

Of course, influences in the reverse direction, from relationship experiences to sexual functioning, are also possible. For example, being responsive to one's partner's non-sexual needs is as important as being responsive during sex, because for many people, foreplay starts outside the bedroom. But how far outside the bedroom can it go? Well, it can go all the way from one's current relationships to one's parents' home. In other words, both current and earlier attachment experiences shape what people want out of sexual encounters and how they have their needs met. These experiences will determine whether one's relationship will be relatively unrelated to his or her sex life or whether it all depends on sex, for better or for worse.

The keys

→ **Sexual desire thrives on rising intimacy, and being responsive to your partner's needs is one of the best ways to instil this elusive sensation over time.**

→ **Sex is important for relationship well-being, especially when the relationship is more vulnerable. Yet, not all depends on sex: intimacy, support and commitment count as well.**

→ **Being responsive to your partner's non-sexual needs is as important to sexual and relational well-being as being responsive during sex.**

Gurit E. Birnbaum works at the School of Psychology, the Interdisciplinary Center, in Herzliya (Israel). Her research focuses on the underlying functions of sexual fantasies and on the convoluted role played by sexuality in the broader context of close relationship. She frequently contributes to high quality international academic journals. Dr Birnbaum is an Associate Editor of *Personal Relationships* and serves as a member of the editorial boards of the *Journal of Social and Personal Relationships* and the *Journal of Personality and Social Psychology*.

The voice of love

Imagine that you are browsing for new titles at your local bookstore when you hear someone's mobile phone ring in an adjacent aisle. You hear a female voice answer "Hello" and you overhear a minute or two of the conversation. Could you identify whether the woman was speaking to her romantic partner or to a friend based solely on this brief exposure? Dr Sally Farley **examines how love 'leaks' through our voices.**

Many people would argue that they could, in fact, determine if they were overhearing a conversation between lovers, but is this the case? If so, how can we tell? A wealth of research has exposed the many signals that communicate romantic connectedness and love – lovers gaze longer at one another, touch each other more (sometimes more than observers would like!) and stand and sit closer together. They are also more likely to groom one another, by adjusting a tie, pushing back stray locks of hair, or tucking in clothing labels. These signals communicate affection and intimacy to the partner, but they also function to broadcast to the world "this is my romantic partner!" Less attention has been devoted to how our voices change when we communicate with our lovers.

My research with newly-in-love romantic partners has shown that listeners of telephone conversations can determine with greater than chance accuracy whether the caller is speaking with a friend or romantic partner. Although it may not be surprising that individuals can make this distinction after listening to twenty seconds of conversation, often, individuals can make this judgment after hearing very brief segments of speech, such as "how are you?" or a laugh. Furthermore, when callers were speaking to their romantic partners as opposed to their friends, listeners rated their voices as less animated, but more pleasant-sounding, sexier and reflecting more romantic interest. This was the case even though silences were removed from the conversations and listeners heard only one side of the conversations. Observers' skill in decoding this 'romantic tone' underscores the importance of voice as a 'relational marker'. From an evolutionary standpoint, it is important for individuals to quickly identify potential mates by attending to nonverbal cues, so as to avoid wasting energy on unavailable options (because they lack interest, are already 'taken', or do not share our sexual orientation).

Never silent

Another finding of my research is that, when the content of the conversation was masked (and raters could hear the pitch and rhythm of the speech, but not the words), callers were perceived as less popular, less confident and less likable when talking to their romantic partners than when talking to their friends. The tendency for individuals to

Our emotions leak through our nonverbal cues. Whether romantic love should be regarded as an emotion, a drive, or a drug is still under investigation, yet it is revealed in interesting ways through our voices. The way we say things (known to nonverbal researchers as paralanguage) is infinitely more telling than what we say. Remember that our body language is never silent. Rather, body language and voice communicate volumes about people's emotional and motivational states. Love leaks through our voices.

Sally Farley is an experimental social psychologist at the University of Baltimore (USA) whose primary area of interest is nonverbal behavior. Her articles have been published in various journals, including the *Journal of Nonverbal Behavior*. When not chasing her three young children around, she likes to participate in obstacle course trail races.

" Love leaks through our voices."

come across as less socially skilled when they were speaking with their lovers is consistent with the anxiety-laden weight of intense romantic love. When individuals are first in love, their lover is never far from mind. As biological anthropologist Helen Fisher often points out, romantic love is a drive, profoundly affecting the thoughts, feelings and behaviors of those in love. New lovers cannot sate their desire to be with one another, their thoughts are obsessively on one another and they long to touch one another. But these feelings are not uniformly positive. Coupled with the extreme highs (due in part to love's activation of the dopaminergic pathways) comes the fear of loss. **Romantic love puts us in a vulnerable state and our voices betray this vulnerability.**

"Taller men are less jealous than shorter men."

Destructive jealousy

"I'd rather see you dead little girl, than to be with another man" (from *Run for your Life*, The Beatles, 1964). Dr **A. P. Buunk** has studied one of the most intense and destructive emotions related to love: jealousy. How does this normal feeling turn into an obsession?

Jealousy is one of the most intense and potentially destructive emotions in love relationships. It is often difficult to control and may lead to violence, murder and suicide. Jealousy comes in many forms, but implies, by definition always a rival. The rival may be someone who is actually threatening one's relationship. But it may also just be the fear that there is someone vying for one's partner's attention. Jealousy may express itself in all kinds of attempts to prevent the partner from coming into contact with opposite others, for example, by demanding that one's partner not go out alone. The feeling may arise in long-term relationships, but may also occur when one has not yet formed a close relationship but is competing with a rival over someone to whom one is romantically attracted. Jealousy may also be felt for the previous partner of one's loved one, out of fear that one's loved one will go back to him or her.

Threatening rivals

Jealousy may involve a variety of feelings (such as threat, fear, suspicion, distrust, anxiety, anger, betrayal and rejection), cognitions (such as paranoid thoughts and worries about the behavior of one's partner) and behaviors (such as spying on one's partner or rummaging through his or her belongings). While jealousy is a near-universal experience, it has been found to be more pronounced in individuals who are in an anxious way attached to their partner and feel highly dependent on the relationship. Especially among women, jealousy is related to low self-esteem, and women are, in response to a partner's infidelity, more likely to think that they are 'not good enough' and become depressed. Men, on the other hand, are more likely to get drunk and to use violence when they are jealous. Men and women are, in general, most threatened by rivals that are considered attractive to the opposite sex. Therefore, among females, jealousy is evoked more by physically attractive rivals, and, among males, by physically and socially dominant rivals. In addition, individuals tend to report more jealousy as their rivals are perceived to be better on attributes they find important for themselves, such as intelligence, popularity, athleticism and particular professional skills.

High risk

Unlike our closest relatives, the chimpanzees, who have promiscuous sexual relationships, humans engage in more or less stable pair relationships, and males usually invest considerably in the survival of their offspring by food provision and by protection from predators, from other males and from other hostile groups. Because of this, human males have, in the course of evolution, confronted a potential cost not encountered by females, namely that, as a consequence of the infidelity of their partner, they might, unknowingly, invest heavily in another man's offspring without passing on their own genes. Therefore, males tend to focus more upon the sexual aspects of the partner's involvement in extramarital relationships. **The first question men usually will ask their partner when confronted with a rival is: "Are you sexually attracted to him?"** In contrast, when a rival presents herself, women face the risk of having to share their partner's resources with another woman, and, even more threatening, the risk of their partner directing all his support to the rival. Therefore, an emotional bond of one's mate with another female is felt as particularly threatening to women. **The first question women usually will ask their partner when confronted with a rival is: "Are you in love with her?"**

Hormones

Jealousy is clearly related to physical and physiological characteristics. Taller men – who tend to be more dominant and have a higher status – are less jealous than shorter men, who tend to be especially jealous of dominant rivals. Among women, however, the tallest *and* the shortest women are the most jealous, especially of physically attractive rivals. Women of medium height – who tend to be more fertile and more preferred by men – are the least jealous. In addition, more feminine men, that is, men who have prenatally been exposed less to male hormones, tend to be more jealous, especially of dominant rivals, whereas more masculine women, that is women who have been prenatally exposed less to female hormones tend to be more jealous, especially of attractive rivals. In general, women as well as their partners tend to be more jealous when the woman is in the fertile stage of her cycle – the period when competing for the most attractive mate is especially important.

Self-esteem

Jealousy is thus a universal human experience with a strong biological basis, and it is an illusion to think one can eradicate this feeling completely. However, becoming less dependent on one's partner, enhancing one's self-esteem and learning to control one's emotions may contribute to reducing and managing one's jealousy. Of course, there is a difference between obsessive jealousy that may ruin one's life and one's relationships, and the normal jealousy that is an adaptive response to a serious threat to one's relationship, and that alerts the individual to taking action to protect oneself or one's relationship.

The keys

→ **While jealousy is a near universal experience, it is more pronounced in individuals who are in an anxious way attached to their partner and feel highly dependent on the relationship.**

→ **Males tend to focus more upon the sexual aspects of the partner's involvement in extramarital relationships. Women fear more emotional bonds.**

→ **We cannot eradicate jealousy, but becoming less dependent on one's partner, enhancing one's self-esteem and learning to control one's emotions may contribute to reducing and managing it.**

A.P. Buunk is Academy Professor on behalf of the Royal Netherlands Academy of Sciences (the Netherlands). He is an Honorary Professor at various universities in South America. His research now focuses on evolutionary and biological approaches of human behavior, particularly jealousy, intra-sexual competition and parental control of mate choice. He has served on many scientific boards and committees and has over 500 scientific publications in a variety of journals and books.
In 2009, he received the honorable royal distinction of Knight in the Order of the Lion of the Netherlands. He lives part of the time in Spain and in Uruguay. His hobbies include jogging, movies, pop and Latin music, and playing congas.

"Love is the ecology of life."

Ecosexual Love

"We should learn to practice love in as many styles as possible as a human, planetary and cosmic investment in the immense power of love", says Dr **Serena Anderlini-D'Onofrio**. Discover ecosexual love.

Ecosexual love is the love that is beyond gender, number, age, orientation, race and species. It is the style of love that embraces all of life as a partner with equal rights and optimizes local, global and ecosystemic health.

The overall intent of my research about love is to generate awareness around the planet that education to love is the energetic channel for education to peace and democracy. Love is the ecology of life and its power is immense. It is a cosmic force and its energy makes the difference between life and death. An articulate knowledge of how to practice love can be acquired by all those interested in such education. This happens especially when **love is interpreted as an art that one learns with practice**, rather than as a simple need that produces scarcity, or an instinct that produces fear. Therefore my research has been, and continues to be, devoted to generating the paradigmatic shift that will enable interpretations of love as an art to become more accepted and prevalent than they are today.

Erotic expression

The past fifteen years as a Professor of Humanities at the University of Puerto Rico have been conducive of much progress in this direction. My research on practices of love that are fluid and inclusive has charted new fields of knowledge in the humanities and beyond. What I have learned is that bisexuality is the style of love that honors the fluid nature of human sexuality and the practice of which allows one's potential to love a person beyond gender to become expressed. Polyamory is the style of love that honors the inclusive nature of the amorous potential of which the human species is capable. My understanding is that polyamory allows one's ability to extend the practice of love well beyond socially enforced forms of sexual ownership and monogamy. More recently, I have observed ecosexuality emerge as a style of amorous, erotic, sexual and artistic expression that extends love and agency to nature as an equal. **Ecosexuality integrates amorous inclusiveness and sexual fluidity into an embrace that extends to the whole planet where human life is hosted.** Many ecosexuals believe that as one practices the arts of love naturally, the range of emotions one interprets as love expands, as the range of sensations one experiences as pleasure also expands.

Education to love

As a scholar and practitioner of love, I have become convinced that education to love and its multiple, diverse practices is an essential element in the practice of democracy. Education to democracy is education to love, because **"a world where it is safe to love is a world where it is safe to live"**. Education to love is a transformative process that involves the whole person. Educators of love are trained in appreciating the diverse talents students bring to the table, and in supporting the whole person to develop as an artist of love. I believe that the concept of Gaia is of the essence in this context because it integrates biology, physics, mythology, popular culture, critical theory, gender and sexuality into a new paradigm of knowledge that brings the focus on to love as the ecology of life.

The keys

→ **Love is the ecology of life and its power is immense. It is an art that one learns with practice, rather than a simple need or an instinct.**

→ **Bisexuality and polyamory are the styles of love that honor the inclusive nature of the amorous potential of which the human species is capable.**

→ **Ecosexuality is a universal style of amorous, erotic, sexual and artistic expression that extends love and agency to nature as an equal. Education to love involves the whole person.**

Serena Anderlini-D'Onofrio was born in Rome (Italy) and graduated from the University of Sassari in 1979. She earned her PhD in Comparative Literature at the University of California, Riverside (USA) in 1987. She is a Professor of Humanities at the University of Puerto Rico, Mayaguez (Puerto Rico) and a Humanities Fellow at the University of Connecticut, Storrs. She is a scholar, activist, professor, cultural theorist and the author and editor of numerous award-winning books, including *Gaia and the New Politics of Love*, *Bisexuality and Queer Theory* and *Eros: A Journey of Multiple Loves*.

Killing for love

*" How can you kill
the one you love?"*

**"Recently two girls were brutally
murdered on our campus, due to
rejection of friendship proposals",
says Dr Sunil Saini. "It shocked
us that both murderers were their
classmates and showed no remorse
after killing them."**

Romantic relationships are an integral feature
of adolescent development. These relationships
typically begin around 14 to 15 years of age,
initially as an extension of involvement in mixed
gender peer groups. The romantic relationship is
associated with both positive and negative mental
health among adolescent boys and girls.

Psychologists around the world are teaching
lessons on positive psychology, how to live
positively and how to be happy. Happy movies
are being shown in theaters. Spiritual gurus are
preaching on "Love yourself, humanity, etc." in
every corner, particularly in India. The literature
is full of articles on love on internet, TV and print
media. Literature is filled with positive love that
only reflects caring for the partner. Love inspires
people to create great paintings, songs, music
and excel in their respective areas without hurting
his/herself and his/her romantic partner.
But **there is another side of the coin as well.**

Romantic relational aggression in adolescents
is increasing day by day. Watching the daily news
headlines and police records, we see that so-
called love is one of the important reasons for
kidnap, sexual harassment, rape, extra-marital
affairs, breakups, revenge and murder. Honor
killing is a burning issue in India. How can a father
kill his daughter? For the sake of love? Aggression
in romantic relationship can be broadly defined
across a range of behaviors, including physical
assault, kidnapping, acid throwing, rape and even
murder. However, it is also important to consider
the less physical, but still hurtful, relational
aggression in romantic relationships. Examples
include flirting with others to make a romantic
partner jealous, threatening to break up with
a partner if the partner will not comply, or giving
a partner the silent treatment when angry.

**This gap between two sides of love is increasing
day by day** and confuses people about what love
means in their life. We would love to live in a world
full of positive love. But what about the other side
of the coin? There is a great and universal need
to make people learn what is a truly flourishing
relationship, including caring, forgiveness, opti-
mism, empathy, resilience and emotional regulation
and how to manage anger in relationships.

Sunil Saini obtained his PhD in Psychology
from Punjabi University, Patiala (India). He is
a Research Associate of the Guru Jambheshwar
University of Science and Technology.
His research focuses on anger and aggression-
related problems among youth. He is President
of the Indian Association of Health, Research
and Welfare.

"The lower the emotional attachment, the more the love principle mutates towards a credit principle."

The love principle

He used to study the credit, equity and egoism principles, but **Erich Kirchler** has discovered a different and powerful principle in harmonious relationships: the love principle.

It is essential that partners who seek harmonious relationships realize goals through collaboration, which is based on mutual trust. Partners in such balanced relationships not only express themselves, but have an intuitive understanding of each other, resulting in both sides' expectations and needs being met. The dynamics of successful and mutually beneficial decision-making processes rely on relationship harmony and on balanced power relations between the partners. In harmonious relationships, imbalance of power only exists to a small degree in favor of one or the other partner, or else an uneven power distribution between the partners is not used by either of them to obtain egoistic advantages in decision-making.

Partners in unhappy relationships, on the other hand, are inclined to view themselves as economic partners and to calculate what return they can get from the other partner and what they have to contribute to the other partner. Depending on the harmony and power of the partners, their behavior can range along a continuum reaching from altruistic behavior to market-like exchange transactions.

Six pack

Partners in harmonious relationships act in accordance with the 'love principle'.
This principle – rather than the credit, equity or egoism principle – exhibits six particular
characteristics.

1. Happy partners **do not seek to keep a (mental) account of demands and obligations**.
They act spontaneously in a manner which is partner-orientated. While partners in
disharmonious relationships keep account of their demands and obligations and
immediately seek to achieve a balance between the two, partners in happy relationships
orientate themselves above all by the needs of the other person and show consideration.

2. Partners in harmonious relationships are **dependent upon one another in their feelings,
thoughts and actions.** They are affected by the behavior of the other and are, at the same
time, aware that their own actions can affect the other person. The more harmonious
the relationship, the greater the mutual concern and consideration.

3. In economic relationships, give and take are directly linked. If people hand over a part
of their resources, then they expect a corresponding share in rewards from the other person
in return, and the other person feels obligated under the principle of reciprocity.
If a relationship is harmonious, then there is **no requirement for an immediate return
for a pleasure which has been given.**

4. The more harmonious the relationship, **the less interest the partner has in concluding
a trade with the partner.** The relationship in itself acquires a value. Unhappy partners seek
to exploit their opportunities for profit.

5. According to the equity rule of distributive justice, partners are compensated in
proportion to their contributions. In close relationships, however, such rules do not
necessarily hold in the same way. Happy partners **offer one another pleasures as
spontaneous acts.**

6. In economic relationships, only selected types of resources are traded, which are mainly
universalistic. In harmonious relationships, **the main resources traded are particularistic.**
They are not restricted to only a few resources that partners share, but instead a wide
variety of rewarding resources are given and received by the partners.

Egoistic desires

The lower the level of emotional attachment to each other, the more the love principle mutates towards a 'credit principle'. The partners still seek to offer pleasures to each other and look after one another, but they are waiting for a similar effort to be made in return. If the relationship quality diminishes further, then the pattern of interactions mirrors the 'equity principle' in social exchange theory. The partners act increasingly like two business partners. The lower the quality of the relationship, the more important the power differences between the partners. Whereas the power relations in harmonious relationships are unimportant, in 'cooled-off' relationships, the partner who possesses more power will also use the opportunity to control exchange transactions with the other and act according to the 'egoism principle'.

By contrast, relationships between happy partners and between good friends resemble each other in their positivity and altruism. Partners in love and good friends have unconditional positive regard for each other and spontaneously act to please each other; they are less likely to subject their joint actions to the principles of doing business and to consider the costs of their actions. Egoistic desires diminish and are superseded by shared desires. Egoistic maximization of individual benefits, which is generally taken to be the 'dominant strategy' of 'homo oeconomicus', is the rare exception rather than the rule and proves that love really is a many-splendored thing.

The keys

→ **The dynamics of successful and mutually beneficial decision-making processes rely on relationship harmony and on balanced power relations between the partners.**

→ **Partners in harmonious relationships act in accordance with the 'love principle'. This principle exhibits six particular characteristics.**

→ **The lower the level of emotional attachment to each other, the more the 'love principle' mutates towards a 'credit principle'.**

Erich Kirchler is Professor of Economic Psychology at the University of Vienna (Austria). He has been President of the International Association for Research in Economic Psychology and of the Austrian Psychological Association. Erich Kirchler has published over 15 scientific books and more than 300 academic papers.

"Secure individuals have a more positive outlook on life."

Lonely without you

"I am so lonely without you." In popular lyrics, love and loneliness sleep in the same bed. Dr **Daniel Perlman** explains why.

From an attachment perspective, love and loneliness can be seen as phenomena on opposite sides of a coin, yet ones that can both be explained by the same set of ideas. Attachment theory traces back to the genius of British psychiatrist John Bowlby (1907-1990). He defined attachment as "the lasting psychological connectedness between human beings."

Attachment theorists conceptualize *falling in love* as forming an attachment bond and *being in love* as having an attachment partner. They see loneliness as resulting from the absence of a satisfying attachment relationship. So, the essential difference between love and loneliness boils down to having vs. not having an attachment partner.

Anxious

Infants attach to their mothers or other caregivers. This serves an evolutionary function making it possible for individual infants, and the human species as a whole, to survive. In times of stress, they seek closeness with their caregivers. During non-stressful times, securely attached children show an interest in exploring and mastering their environment as well as establishing contact with other people. Attachment theorists call these behaviors "using the caregiver as a secure base".

Not all infants are equally successful, however, in forming a secure attachment with their primary caregivers. Some do form a secure attachment, but others form what have been labeled an anxious-ambivalent or an avoidant attachment. **Securely-attached children have warm relationships with their caregivers,** looking to them for guidance but also venturing out to explore the world. Anxious-ambivalent children are nervous and clingy with their caregivers, seemingly never quite sure their caregiver prioritizes them and will be there for them. Avoidant children are more on their own, paying less heed to their caregivers and relying less on them for guidance or support.

Separation

Attachment theorists believe that children's attachment to their caregivers stems largely from parent-child interaction. The caregivers of secure children tend to be loving, sensitive and responsive. The caregivers of anxious-ambivalent children tend to be inconsistent, almost intrusive at times, but preoccupied with other things and unresponsive at other times. The caregivers of avoidant children tend to be unresponsive and unaffectionate.

If they were limited just to infancy, attachment processes and types would be fascinating and important. But their importance does not stop there. Attachment theorists believe early experiences have long-lasting effects that impact on people's adult personalities and close relationships. Via our early experiences we develop what Bowlby called 'inner working models' of ourselves and of other people. **We develop expectations about whether the significant people in our lives respond to our calls for support and protection** and, similarly, we develop expectations about whether we are the sort of person towards whom our attachment figures are likely to respond in a helpful manner. These inner models can be altered over the life course but they tend to persist, thus connecting early to later experiences.

Many of the dynamics of childhood attachment processes can be observed in adult romantic relationships. Consider two examples. At both age levels, methods are used to maintain proximity and contact (e.g. eye contact, smiling, holding, kissing). Similarly, in both periods, separation causes distress.

Secure

Returning to the theme that love and loneliness can be seen as phenomena explained by the same concepts, securely (vs. insecurely) attached individuals are more successful in love. Their close relationships generally last longer and are more satisfying. Insecurely attached individuals, however, are more likely to be lonely.

Presumably, part of the reason for these different outcomes for secure vs. insecure individuals is their perceptual processes and social skills. Secure individuals have a more positive outlook on life. They feel they are easy to get to know and others will like them. Turning to social skills, **secure individuals are successful in eliciting self-disclosure from others,** reading others' nonverbal facial expressions and conflict management. Perceptions and skills of these sorts undoubtedly foster relationship development.

Experiencing loneliness is undoubtedly a stimulus for many people to seek romantic relationships, to find an attachment partner. To the extent that the causes of loneliness lie within the individual, chronically lonely individuals may face greater challenges in successfully establishing long-term loving ties. It may be easier for individuals who experience transitory forms of loneliness due to circumstantial factors to eventually find long lasting, meaningful love.

Connection

From an attachment perspective, a key to meaningful love is being able to establish a secure attachment. One might think that attachment theory's emphasis on childhood experiences cements our romantic trajectories while we are still in early childhood. That is not, however, necessarily so. Even though there is a tendency for attachment styles to persist, even some individuals who have endured very distressed relationships in childhood function securely as adults. Partially, this may be due to an improvement in a person's circumstances (e.g. a change in household members). Attachment theorists also believe that connecting with a secure partner can help one achieve greater security. From an attachment perspective, an underlying key to alleviating loneliness and finding lasting love is changing one's mental models of self and other. When they are positive, loneliness is likely to dissolve and love be found.

The keys

- → **Love and loneliness can be seen as phenomena explained by the same concepts: securely attached individuals (vs. anxious and avoidant ones) are more successful in love.**
- → **Secure individuals have a more positive outlook on life. Find and focus on the positive in others and in yourself.**
- → **Be responsive and sensitive to the needs of others, for love to flourish, be comfortable depending on others and letting them depend on you.**

Daniel Perlman is Professor of Human Development and Family Studies, University of North Carolina at Greensboro (USA) and is President of the International Association for Relationship Research. His work focuses on loneliness and intimate relationships. He has edited or authored thirteen books.

Love your country

" Expressing love for your country is often associated with aggression."

"I love my country. It's the government I'm afraid of!" says a popular slogan on T-shirts. Millions of people have died (and have murdered) because of some kind of love for their country. It's a powerful emotion. Prof **Christian Bjørnskov** **explains why he and his friends put the national flag on a birthday cake.**

Love has many objects: we love our children, our parents and grandparents, our boyfriends and girlfriends, husbands and wives. Many people would also say that they love their friends and even their colleagues. Likewise, love can take many forms. Our deep affection for grandparents is different from the exalted emotions we feel when we fall in love, and our love for parents and old friends remains despite our knowing their faults and shortcomings.

Even though we express our love in many different ways – from the very public manifestations reflected in Mediterranean and Middle Eastern stereotypes to the very private way Japanese or Finnish love is shown – the feeling is the same and equally human everywhere. Likewise, from Cape Town to Nuuk, or Seattle to Saint Petersburg, love of others is what binds people together and it is a central aim of everyone. Why else would the most popular theme of world literature be the quest for the one love to share one's life with?

Yet one type of love is often frowned upon in large parts of the world: the love of one's country. Expressing a love for one's country and compatriots is far from 'comme il faut' among certain groups in France, where flying the tricolore is sometimes considered support for very right-wing ideology. A similar situation exists in Japan, where the old imperial flag of a rising sun is vigorously used by hardcore nationalists. Expressing such deep positive feelings towards the nation of one's parents or choice is associated, in large parts of society, with aggression. When declaring love of one's country, it is more often than not taken as a negative statement about other countries – if you love Germany, you must hate the rest of the world. However, there need not be anything suspicious about declaring this kind of love. The love of one's country when expressed in Denmark, Norway or Sweden, is markedly different from this stereotype of corrupt love.

A Danish song, written about the 1945 liberation from Nazi occupation, characterized the most visible part of Danish celebrations as "cities blossoming in red and white": accounts from the Allied forces moving into Denmark in those days in May all spoke of seeing 'Dannebrog' – the white cross on a red background that has been the Danish flag since 1219 – everywhere. Yet after twelve gruesome years in which national flags were symbols of repression and war, British soldiers were most astounded by the feeling of seeing thousands of flags waved as symbols of joy instead of aggression. In that lay the difference between warlike aggression and Scandinavian love of one's country – that it was never aggressive.

Love of one's country does not necessarily detract from other countries or populations, nor does it constitute a threat. When conveyed in Scandinavia, **it is an expression of affection towards a very large community of fellow human beings.** Love of one's country in the non-aggressive way practiced in the far European north is a joyous celebration of faith in one's fellow human beings

and flying the Nordic crosses on birthdays and national holidays is simply sharing that love with other people.

Christian Bjørnskov is Professor of Economics at Aarhus University (Denmark). He has published a great deal of work on social trust, subjective well-being and life satisfaction. As a swimming coach, he was responsible for talent development.

Love on Mars

**"I've seen hatred enough in my life",
says Prof** Vid Pečjak. **"I know that
the only answer to it is love." Because
it was often hard to find love, he looked
for it on Mars. And a generation
of kids followed him.**

I was eleven when the Second World War started.
I am not going to describe all the horrors that I saw
in the former Yugoslavia (Slovenia was a part of it).
I was a very sensitive child. At that time, the people
hated each other. Everyone was suspicious of
everyone else, and there was no place for love. At
the end of the war, I was imprisoned and tortured
by the Gestapo. After the war, the communists took
power and hate and suspiciousness continued. I
was arrested again. Later I was freed and I studied
psychology and became a writer. My first book
was a children's book.

"Space flights are merely an escape, a fleeing away
from oneself, because it is easier to go to Mars
or to the moon than it is to penetrate one's own
being." This quote is from the famous psychologist
Carl Gustav Jung. I have only recently discovered
that in the 1950s he was giving lectures in Europe
about Mars and flying saucers, projecting the dream
of reconstructing a new world after the Second
World War. He died in 1961, the year I published
the children's book that would become famous
for generations in our country, *Drew and the Three
Little Martians*.

They were called Manny, Middy and Tinny.
They visited Drew secretly and became his friends.
Later, they even visited Mars together. It was a totally
different world from ours. In addition to differing
from Earth in technology, Mars was a world where
love prevailed over hate. The inhabitants were
happy, especially the children. **Martian law
decreed that people must be happy and love
each other.** Wars were forbidden. The Martians
built the largest playground on their Moon, Phobos.

This playground was famous for its dragons, wolves, dwarfs, fairies, witches and wizards. Although these creatures were all robots, they could move and talk like living organisms. The three little Martians explained to Drew that their planet was peaceful and that it was forbidden for Martians to visit Earth. They said that it would remain so until the wars were forbidden on Earth, too. They had broken the rule because they wanted to see the forbidden planet. But then, after tasting marmalade, they couldn't resist coming back.

Later, I realized that I described an ideal, but fictional, world, just the opposite from the one that I had experienced during and after the war. It was springing from my fantasy, from my wishes. It was only a reaction to my personal past. Since I saw no such society on Earth, I transferred it to somewhere else, to the planet Mars. There is no love on Earth, but there is on Mars. There is no justice on Earth, but there is justice on Mars. There is no friendship on Earth, but there is on Mars. Of course I was not conscious of this transference as I wrote it. I only became aware of this many years later. Now I know that Martian life was only my desperate dream. I was very naive. I also know that such dreaming is no cure for hate. We know that Mars is just a deserted world. But we are all dreaming Drews, looking for love and peace. We know there is no escape, no way to find it on Mars, we will have to create peace and love ourselves. Here and now.

Vid Pečjak worked as Professor of Psychology at the University of Ljubljana, (Slovenia) but has been visiting professor at a number of universities worldwide. He has published about 40 books and 400 papers, mostly on human development, emotions and motivation. He is now retired and lives near the beautiful lake of Bled in Slovenia.

" The only answer to hatred is love."

Conditional love

"I am in love with life and I am fascinated by the social interactions and emotions I study", says Dr Ana Maria Fernandez. "And although I am not a feminist, I admire deeply all the women in experimental social sciences that make their contributions to understanding the human condition from a female perspective that complements the masculine perspective on these topics."

The kinds of love that sustain reproduction, such as parental love, friendships and romantic love, are the object and the engine of our lives. As humans, we are a social species, and loving leads to social exchange, which is necessary for our minimal adjustment to our world. But not all forms of love are equivalent.

Although the satisfaction of our deepest feelings of social exchange is fulfilled by the love of friends and family, we experience deep empathy for and we accept family and friends 'as they are'. This seems to be because our psychological adjustment, as well as our brains, are specialized to seek out and require social bonding from birth to death in order to develop into human beings. My study of evolutionary psychology and the teachings of Leda Cosmides and John Tooby have helped me understand that familial love is moderated by genetic relatedness: we accept more imperfections and give more than we receive to those who are closely related to us. In the case of friendships

and other forms of social bonds, we behave strategically and reciprocally, we expect and give according to what the other means to us socially, and how we think we should be valued by others. Most friendships and family relationships lead to deep feelings of love, but how unconditional they are depends on the degree of relatedness we share, and parental love is the closest and most unconditional form of love we may attain.

Similarly, we inevitably experience and seek out the most fragile sort of love to share our life together with a significant other, who usually

" *We accept family and friends more 'as they are'* *than our partner.* "

When someone is dealing with the loss of a loved one, as is the case of dealing with the loss of romantic love, it can lead to intense feelings of jealousy that may indeed cause irrational aggressive reactions or deep withdrawal and depression. I have studied violations of trust and sex-differences in the situations that trigger romantic jealousy, and the specific emotions that may be involved in the deep affective reaction men and women have when they experience romantic betrayal. My research has led me to hypothesize that **masculine jealousy is dominated by aggressive feelings** that motivate active violence towards the partner or the other. Physiologically, betrayed men seem to experience a boost of active aggression and motivations to attack. Women, on the other hand, feel angry and betrayed, of course, **but the feminine reaction to unfaithfulness is more withdrawal and seeking out social support**. Physiologically, they seem hurt by betrayal, losing active motivation to react towards the partner or indeed anything.

becomes our reproductive partner. As the anthropologist Helen Fisher has documented, our body and our brain are completely affected by desire, sex and romantic love. Paradoxically, **romantic bonds are not an unconditional form of social exchange**, but involve constant evaluation of our current situation, expectations and the possible alternatives we may have if we seek out alternatives, or we stay with our stable partner.

As any emotion, love involves intense psychophysiological reactions that drive the search to attain this state over and over again.

Ana Maria Fernandez is Associate Professor at the Psychology Department of the Universidad de Santiago de Chile (Chile). She has been fascinated by evolutionary psychology since she studied at the University of Texas. This helped her sustain her research on romantic relationships and jealousy while she was doing her master's in experimental psychology and it motivated her doctoral research at the University of Chile and her postdoctoral stay at the Center for Evolutionary Psychology.

"We love life through that which we most love in life."

What is your ikigai?

Over the past twenty years, Dr **Gordon Mathews** has been researching the Japanese concept *ikigai*, meaning 'that which makes your life worth living'. If we can understand what our *ikigai* is, we can lead better lives, being fully aware of where our truest priorities lie.

Ikigai is that which we most love: love of a person, an activity, or a dream that gives meaning to life as a whole. You can sometimes know *ikigai* by the feeling it gives you, although that feeling can be inaccurate, as with those who fall head-over-heels in love with the wrong person, to their later deep regret. Some people might conceivably have several *ikigai*, but most typically it is one thing, one element in your life that makes everything else worthwhile. Surprisingly, people often don't know what this one thing is until push comes to shove. It is our personal reason why we finally put up with life, even in all its myriad routines and unpleasantnesses.

Ikigai is always individual. No one else can tell you what your *ikigai* is. Your spouse may ask you, "Do you love me?" and you may feel forced to answer "yes", just as your boss may push you to work endless overtime; but whether your spouse or your work is your *ikigai*, they can never know—only you can know, within your own heart. Nonetheless, although *ikigai* is always individual, it is never only individual. It is held in the privacy of our heart, but it is always about the world of others. It is most essentially that which links us to the social world in which we live.

Ikigai changes as you grow older. For most teenagers, *ikigai* is their dream of the future, whether being a mother, a rock star, a pro basketball player, a corporate executive, or an anarchist. By the time people are in their thirties, many have made the commitments that define their adult lives, whether in terms of marriage, family and children, or career. Certainly many people break out of these commitments, through divorce and remarriage and job change. Certainly too, many people in the midst of these commitments don't find them to be *ikigai*: "There's got to be more to life than this…" Nonetheless, the majority of people do locate *ikigai* in family, work, hobby, religious belief, or dream. This sometimes remains for decades, through their sixties and seventies and beyond, after which some, if they are fortunate, can continue holding their *ikigai* into the future, while for others, their *ikigai* may begin to fade into the past.

Ikigai **is fundamentally fragile.** Your job which you've lived for ends suddenly and you are out on the street. You wake up next to someone you've been living with for twenty years and suddenly realize "I don't love this person anymore". Your child leaves home and perhaps drifts away in her heart as well. Your spouse dies and, of course, eventually you yourself die. It all comes to an end. If one's *ikigai* ends early, a person can find another *ikigai* with luck and pluck, a person, a calling, a dream, that again makes life worth living. Or some may never find another *ikigai*, perhaps living on, half-heartedly, until they die.

Ikigai **is transcendent.** It is what we most love in life. But what we love never lasts. Life is transient; *ikigai*, love and life itself all vanish in a blink or a century. Christians talk of heaven, but many of us can't believe in such a thing. *Ikigai*, love and life are all so valuable exactly because we experience them so briefly. As far as I can tell, there is no larger meaning to our lives, no transcendent purpose. We're simply here. And being here, being something rather than nothing, is a wondrous thing. But we can't experience that love of life through most of our day-to-day lives because we are trapped in their inevitable tedium. *Ikigai* is what enables us to transcend that tedium, to love life through that which we most love in life, however transient, however fleeting, however brief.

The keys

→ **Everyone has his own *ikigai*: that which makes your life worth living for you.**
→ **Our *ikigai* is individual, changeable, fragile and transcendent.**
→ **If we can understand what our personal *ikigai* is, we can lead better lives, because we can become more fully aware of where our truest priorities lie.**

Gordon Mathews is Professor of Anthropology at the Chinese University of Hong Kong. He has written several books, including the successful *What Makes Life Worth Living? How Japanese and Americans Make Sense of Their Worlds*. His own ikigai is his wife, to whom he has been married for more than thirty years. But he says he is also looking forward to death, to see what, if anything, might come next.

Transcendental love

He was born in Iran and teaches psychology at Harvard University, the University of Toronto and the University of Tehran. He travels the world, researching and giving lectures, training sessions and workshops on a wide variety of subjects, including emotional intelligence and the psychology of negotiation skills. And as you will see, Dr Sayyed Mohsen Fatemi is a poet, too. Here are twenty excerpts on the psychology of transcendental love, 'the epitome of love'.

1. Love abdicates the sovereignty of the self, disengaging one from solipsism, egoism and egotism. Love creates a unique language where meaning is not bounded by utilitarian exchanges and profit-based observation.

2. The language of love does not travel through the flea markets of materialism, consumerism and capitalism. Nor is it halted by impediments, obstructionism and obfuscation.

3. Love illuminates the self and selfhood, bestowing upon self a new world of interpretation: togetherness is the panacea of perfection.

4. Love evokes presence in which multiplicities and fragmentation are replaced by unity and oneness. One cannot love *in absentia:* love demands quintessential presence, dissipating absence and divisibility and opening the way for the celebration of oneness.

5. Of all the mysteries that baffle mind and heart, love tops the list. Love serves the apex of becoming, the peak of progression and the apogee of moving.

6. One can experience the tangible flow of pleasure in the realm of finite joy and jubilance, yet never comprehend the exhilarating rapture of the blossoms of love in their sunrise of arrival.

7. One is entangled, overwhelmed and encapsulated in shimmering lights of love, not by the coercive and manipulative enclosures of parochialism, but by the expansive prompts of oneness. While in its primordial manifestation of passion or lust, love may seem perfunctory and imprisoning, any incarceration is superseded in the sublime crystallization of transcendental love.

8. Love begets and engenders as it glows hot, reinventing and awakening moments of belonging, lingering in the abode of expectations while flourishing in the heat of consummation. Love's be-longing is both being and longing, embedded in time and place and yet longing and craving for a not-yet-arrived stage of becoming.

It denounces the camouflage of disappointment. **Love creates hope and hopefulness.** It flies above the havoc of desperation and helplessness. It befriends faith and prayer, bearing the pearl of emancipation and liberation.

12. Love is not displayed merely in an outcome, but blooms in a process. Love beautifies the emergence of a look, a perspective and a complexion far from the mathematical and linear calculation of a material- stricken mind. It celebrates the possibility of development, a rise of novelty within the manacles of limitations. It creates a window through which the rainbow of meaningfulness can delineate a novel horizon not known by the most meticulous telescopic analysis of the rational mind.

9. The language of love may appear non-sensical, absurd and paradoxical. Its sensitivity may fail to resonate persuasively with the reciprocal orchestration of business-oriented equations.

10. Love goes beyond the mundane streets of habituation, acclimatization and accommodation, introduces new paradigms beyond the familiar domain of sensitivity.

11. Love disowns, in its sublime presentation, the propensity to possessiveness and the predilection for power. It infuses the soul with an incessant flux of appeal, want and ebullience. It enthuses the heart with a continuous grammar of visualization in which the will zealously seeks to experience the galaxy of connectedness. Love removes the roadblock of despondency and despair.

13. Love is understood through ontological engagement. Loving larks in the glory of praxis; it passes through the rivers of practice. **One may know how to love and, yet, be alien to love.** Knowing takes one merely to the path of epistemology from where one can espy the glamour of the scenery and, yet, be far from the lush meadows of practical engagement.

14. Words may find themselves incompetent to elucidate the climax of love. In transcendental love, where lilacs serve as the eloquent harbinger of love, power, paraphernalia and possessiveness are freely relinquished for a choice: to love. The universe recites its verses with Love.

"Love is creational.
It invents and initiates."

15. When noon arrives, when the heat comes up, when heaven and earth are baffled and amazed, when the lady watches the last moment of a farewell, when the little girl becomes parched with thirst for the next visit to her father, when eyes mobilize all their power to accompany the last steps, when the angels' genuflection acknowledges their awe on seeing the epitome of love, one may hear the subtle tintinnabulation of love in the oasis of munificence and compassion, while caught in the barren land of estrangement.

16. Love proceeds briskly, selflessly, purely and ardently. Love can enjoy and, yet, gives away; can possess and yet dis-owns. Love articulates the comprehensibility of oneness and the meaningfulness of connectedness, dissolves pretentiousness and proves authenticity.

17. Love is thirsty and yet eschews monopoly. It loses its hands to prove faithfulness, values and togetherness. Love is not caged and cooped, but liberating and free.

18. Love purifies and beautifies. It can come as an ocean embracing the coasts of comfort and tranquility. Or as a ship navigating the whirlpools of tension and conflict, carrying its passengers on towards the horizon of equanimity and composure.

19. Love is creational; it invents and initiates. It expands spiritual development in a world mired in economic development, effects a radical transformation of consciousness in the apex of mindfulness, testifies to the substantiation of mindfulness in the final moments of reverberation. Love echoes monotheism in the abyss of nihilism.

20. Love circulates in the constant river of tears that accompany the reminiscence of the noon and its glory and glamour. Love is celebrated in the awaiting eyes of pilgrims walking the path of consummation in the hope of response. Love is echoed through the cry of the baby who purifies love of all ostentatious pretentiousness.

Sayyed Mohsen Fatemi (PhD, University of British Columbia) is Associate Professor in the Department of Psychology at the University of Tehran (Iran), a post-doctoral and teaching fellow in the Department of Psychology at Harvard University (USA) and a lecturer in psychology at the University of Toronto (Canada). A frequently published author, he has served as the Vice-President of Iran's Psychology and Counseling Organization, advising in International Affairs. He works in the areas of social and cross-cultural psychology and has been keynote speaker at a number of international conferences, including the World Council for Psychotherapy.

"It's a hunger that seems to be self-nourishing."

The ultimate paradox

We do so like trying to make ourselves think we have everything under control. And then we are hit by love. And by another human being whom we neither know or understand. Psychiatrist **Dirk De Wachter** unveils the ultimate paradox of lasting love.

Life obtains meaning only by being limited in time. The fact that it is death that ultimately gives meaning to life is a paradox that is at once uncomfortable and insurmountable. The same applies to love. That is not unpredictable, hormone-driven infatuation, but the durable form that can transcend this impulsiveness.

The paradox of this love relationship lies precisely in not knowing, in not understanding the beloved. Letting go of the Other, leaving him or her free to be an unknown stranger. French philosopher Emmanuel Levinas (1906-1995) said many wise things about this. I happily draw inspiration from him.

This seems a very difficult task in this era of management, of 'can do', in which the illusion of our control over the world and our destinies also extends to our love lives. **A culture in which we want to shape the other into our image and likeness kills desire.** Letting the Other be, not making him or her the same as oneself, accepting and cherishing the fundamental asymmetry of the human relationship is the unfashionable key to binding attachment.

Hard shell

This apparent contradiction begins already in the relationship between parents and children, in which letting go while remaining attached and recognizing the individuality of the child can provide the basis for its fundamental confidence in later life. This confidence allows the child in time to be able to live with the fundamental unfulfilledness, the never completely coinciding, the constant feelings of difference and inadequacy which form the essence of 'impossible' love as a romantic ideal. **This confidence allows us to constantly be able to fall back on our loneliness,** on our essentially unfulfilled nature, without the beloved being used to fill this deficit. It is precisely this not totally coinciding, the existence of difference, that avoids the symbiotic fusion that kills desire.

The Other (and the beloved *par excellence*) attacks us and disturbs our complacency, breaks through the hard shell of our self-seeking. In this way, the Other is an obstacle to our drifting towards the self-centredness that has become so characteristic of a world in which the Other sometimes degenerates into an instrument of my individual happiness, an exchangeable object of temporary pleasure, of quick consumption enjoyment.

Own shadow

In lasting love, 'impossibility', in the sense of unfulfillability, is precisely the driver of sustained and ever intensifying desire. It is a hunger that seems self-nourishing, able thereby to continue into infinity. Without this profound disturbance brought about by the Other, from the outside, existence threatens to reduce into a self-directed project in which desire disappears. **The breach that the Other causes sheds light on our complacency, revealing to us our own shadow.** This view of ourselves reveals our vulnerability and protects us against ruthless arrogance.

The unfulfilledness of love keeps desire alive and deepens it in turn. It remains a desire for more, the striving continues and is fed. Daring to put our closed individuality on the line – a precarious and risky venture if ever there was – becomes worthwhile because the Other shows us what is missing. It is this that makes love so scary, caught between accident and responsibility, between chance and response, between fear and determination. It's about acting in the direction of goodness, in which a new light can begin to shine.

In love, the Other shows us his or her light, without our wanting to appropriate it.

The keys

→ **The paradox of this love affair lies in not knowing, not understanding the beloved. Letting go of the Other, leaving him or her free to be an unknown stranger.**

→ **It is precisely that not totally coinciding, the existence of difference that avoids a symbiotic fusion that kills desire.**

→ **In love the Other shows us his or her light, without our wanting to take over this light.**

Dirk De Wachter is a professor and psychiatrist-psychotherapist. He heads up the Department of System and Family Therapy at the University Psychiatric Center of the KU Leuven (Belgium). He is a trainer and supervisor in family therapy at different centers at home and abroad. He is the author of the successful book *Borderline Times*, in which he states that the separating line between patients and non-patients is paper-thin.

The four forces of love

"Extraordinary love *is* possible", **says Randy Hurlburt, who has** **over twenty years' experience** **of evaluating love relationships.** **But the secret is the correct applica-** **tion of four universal forces.**

Are great love relationships really impossible? Are pain and confusion inevitable? Consider the couple in this typical story. He has just gone through a divorce. She has had several bad relationships. They both want something stable, and feel they have found the right person. After a year, they are married. A year later, they are fighting. Why? Everyone's story is different, but here are the important and overlooked points that universally affect relationships:

1. Romantic attraction is powerful **but misunderstood.**
Many people get married because of the 'love' they feel. Romantic attraction is powerful, but you can't trust it early on because infatuation and sex masquerade as true attraction and can fade with time. True attraction is the permanent magnetic force that draws people together; it doesn't fade (though it can be dulled by bad treatment…). Attraction is rarely equal for both partners. One person usually wants the relationship more than the other and this causes problems!

2. Emotional maturity is equally important **but often overlooked.**
Romantic attraction certainly is important. But just as necessary, and frequently ignored in the heat of passion, is emotional maturity. This is the ability to conduct a good relationship. On average, adults are only about 60% mature, with one partner typically more mature and the other less mature. Maturity can grow, but it is very slow (think decades). Choosing a mature partner can help avoid a long and painful road.

3. The desire for connection is a strong **motivating force in love relationships.**
Singles are usually lonely. They hunger for the connection that relationships promise. This is natural but…

4. The desire for connection conflicts **with the desire for freedom.**
What most people don't recognize is the conflict between the desire for connection and the desire for freedom. This conflict is often subconscious and only raises its ugly head after a couple years of being together, or after starting to live together, or after getting married. While we can readily discuss our need for connection, openly discussing our need for freedom is more difficult because jealousy, guilt, social pressure and cultural conditioning work together to stifle communication.

"Some partners feel like they are in prison."

As a result, some partners feel like they are in prison and take it out on the other. It is critical for couples to find a balance point, somewhere between total freedom and total connection. Finding a mutually agreeable balance point is often such a difficult task that the partners quit and break up, or stay together and grow apart.

These four competing forces will nearly always create problems. Solving these problems is the key. This requires a *desire* to work together, and it also requires the *ability* to have constructive discussions. As seen above, partners often differ in both desire and ability. Furthermore, problem solving requires knowledge about the subconscious forces at work in relationships, particularly the conflict between freedom and connection. If you are not consciously aware that this is even a problem, how can you discuss it?

Problem solving requires the ability to express feelings in a non-threatening way and to listen

non-defensively to the feelings of one's partner. It requires flexibility to identify out-of-the box solutions and to experiment with them. And it requires patience to hear out your partner over the course of many discussions. If you use these problem solving skills and knowledge of the four forces, you *can* find and keep extraordinary love!

Randy Hurlburt lives and works in San Diego, California (USA). He is an internationally acclaimed relationship coach, speaker and the author of three successful books: *Love Is Not A Game*, *Partners in Love and Crime* and *Dating and Relationship Solutions*. These books include the Romantic Attraction and Emotional Maturity Scales developed by Harold Bessell, PhD. These scales are said to have the potential to predict the future of any relationship.

The challenge to love

Leaving about 16000 people dead and 3000 missing, the Great East Japan Earthquake (March 11, 2011), attendant tsunami and subsequent nuclear power plant disasters marked a turning point in Japan. Also for love and relationships. Natsuyo Iida and Noriko Sakamoto report.

Now referred to in Japan simply as 'March 11', these events have profoundly affected the lives of each person in various ways. When the earthquake hit northeastern Japan, not just the land but we ourselves were greatly shaken. We realized how easily things we took for granted could be lost, that things we believed to be permanent might not last forever and that what was supposed to be safe was not always safe. The world seems to have changed completely since March 11.

Getting through what we have experienced, **many people are rethinking the meaning of life.** Over 80% of 1000 respondents of an internet survey answered that they realized the importance of nature and the value of togetherness with others. Many people have also realized that ties to others are essential to their lives, particularly the ties with families and partners. Some of our friends have decided to visit their parents more often; some go home from work earlier to spend more time with their children. Others have begun to socialize more with neighbors they rarely

spoke with before March 11. In the same survey, over 70% replied that they preferred spending time with their family to working. The Japanese character chosen by the Japanese Kanji Proficiency Society to describe the year 2011 was 'kizuna' (meaning strong ties between people).

More marriages

Research shows the number of women interested in marriage has increased since March 11, apparently to gain a sense of security. According to a survey conducted immediately after the disaster, about 30% of men and 37% of women among the 500 respondents were interested in getting married. Another survey showed that more than 80% of husbands and wives gained greater respect for their partners through the disaster.

On the other hand, some couples decided to break up and get divorced, having discovered differences in values when forced to choose what was most important during the disaster. Perhaps each one of us has been challenged to reflect on our own lives.

The Institute for Studies in Happiness, Economy and Society (ISHES) explores what really matters to people when pursuing true happiness. We believe that the emphasis on economic growth pursued by the world since the last century has been misplaced. The new social interest in reconsidering what is really important is a new opportunity, and we would like to create momentum for more people to pursue true happiness. We will take a deeper look at factors that affect happiness, economy and society, and will be exchanging ideas and information with people who share similar interests.

" Can we only feel love when disasters occur?"

Connected

There is much that is new. Social network services enable us to easily connect, not only with people close to us, but also others we have never met. With new communication tools, people and organizations can deliver information to more people, sometimes much more quickly than the mainstream media. At the time of the disaster, communications through Twitter enabled many support activities in affected areas. Also, through Twitter and Facebook, plenty of messages of love were sent to Japan from all around the world, which encouraged us here very much. We felt we were not alone, but supported by the world.

The March 11 disaster strengthened relationships and a sense of togetherness. Does this mean we can only feel love when disasters like this one occur? Perhaps not. Love is around us in our daily lives, but we often do not notice it. We are connected with others – we simply take the connections for granted. Even every day is not ordinary, but special. And it is a miracle that we can live our lives. These are some of the great lessons we learned from March 11.

Natsuyo Iida is Project Manager of The Institute for Studies in Happiness, Economy and Society (ISHES) in Japan. The institute is engaged in research, information and dialogue on these topics.
Noriko Sakamoto is Communication Director of Japan for Sustainability (JFS), a non-profit organization providing information on development and activities in Japan that lead toward sustainability.

"You don't have to be the most popular person on the dating scene."

The uniquely valuable mate

"How do I *find* the one? How do I know if he or she *is* the one?" Implicit in these questions is that some people make better romantic partners than others: you will be deliriously happy with one partner, but eternally miserable with someone else. **Lucy Hunt** and **Paul Eastwick** hold our hand in our search for 'the one and only'.

Individuals clearly value some characteristics in a partner (e.g. kindness) more than others (e.g. cruelty); nevertheless, this trait-based approach to mate value may be limited. Ask yourself why you are in a good relationship. Is it because everyone would agree that your partner has wonderful qualities? Or is it because your relationship is satisfying, because you experience intimacy with your partner and because you are in love? Consistent with the latter perspective, a close relationships researcher might redefine mate value to refer to a person's ability to provide someone else with a satisfying, intimate, loving relationship. Although it is possible that people with desirable qualities are better able to provide such a relationship, it is also possible that a satisfying relationship derives from the chemistry and compatibility that is shared uniquely between two people. Indeed, the influence of the relationship itself has largely been ignored in the traditional conceptualization of mate value.

Mate value

So how do we test the influence of the relationship on people's perceptions of the mate value of others? First, it is necessary to isolate the effect of individuals' person-level perceptions (e.g. how Candice sees others in general, how others generally perceive Candice) from the effect of the relationship (e.g. how Candice and Adam uniquely perceive one another). Previous studies of mate value only examined the influence of the person (e.g. others' perceptions of Candice in general). However, by implementing a new method of analysis using the Social Relations Model (SRM), we were able to separate the influence of the person from the influence of the unique relationship (e.g. Adam's perception of Candice, specifically). Second, whereas traditional mate value measures ask participants to evaluate others' traits, (e.g. "X is attractive", "X has a good sense of humor"), we developed a new satisfaction-based measure of mate value that reflects relationship satisfaction (e.g. "X and I share important feelings, problems and beliefs with one another", "X makes an effort to spend quality time with me on a regular basis", "X gives me a better life").

Desirable traits

In our studies, participants evaluated themselves and others (acquaintances, friends, current partners) on both traditional trait-based measures of mate value and our new satisfaction-based measure. Consistent with previous research, we found that when evaluating others using trait-based measures, individuals tended to agree on the extent to which someone possessed desirable traits. That is, some individuals had more desirable traits than others. This traditional approach to mate value thus implies that people should strive to be the most consensually desirable person as possible – to possess many romantically sought-after qualities. However, when individuals evaluated each other using the new satisfaction-based measure, they were much more likely to make unique ratings. For example, some individuals felt that Candice was likely to provide them with a satisfying relationship, whereas other individuals who reported on Candice did not. That is, even though some people may have desirable qualities, this fact alone does not mean that they can provide everyone with a satisfying relationship. Her traits notwithstanding, Candice may not be equally compatible with everyone.

Unique fit

Although past research has identified those characteristics that are valued by people in romantic partners, it has overlooked an important element of the relationship experience: the unique perceptions of relationship satisfaction shared by two individuals in a partnership. For even though individuals vary in their desirable traits, they do not seem to vary in their ability to provide a satisfying and fulfilling relationship. In essence, **the 'ability' to provide such a relationship does not seem to be an 'ability' at all**. Rather, satisfying relationships seem to emerge from the good fortune of finding a person with whom you are uniquely compatible.

This new evidence may provide a degree of reassurance to those who are convinced that they are not desirable enough to find a valuable mate. Perhaps the most prudent goal is not to become the most popular person on the dating scene, but instead to find one person who thinks that you *should* be the most popular person on the dating scene. In other words, it does not matter if some or even most people do not perceive you to be a valuable partner; what matters is that you find one person who believes that you are valuable and vice versa. After all, when it comes to romantic relationships, the unique, compatible fit that comes with a satisfying relationship requires just one other person. That it only takes one is perhaps the most reassuring fact of all.

The keys

→ **The influence of the relationship itself has been largely ignored in the traditional conceptualization of mate value.**

→ **Satisfying relationships seem to emerge from the good fortune of finding a person with whom you are uniquely compatible.**

→ **What matters is that you find one person who believes that you are valuable and vice versa.**

Lucy Hunt is pursuing a PhD in Human Development and Family Sciences at the University of Texas at Austin (USA), where she is conducting attraction and relationships research with Dr Paul Eastwick. She is broadly interested in examining relationship maintenance and initial attraction processes.
Paul Eastwick is Assistant Professor in the Department of Human Development and Family Sciences at the University of Texas at Austin. His research interests include attachment, attraction, evolutionary perspectives on mating and the effects of ideal partner preferences on relationship initiation and maintenance.

"Love brings meaning,
rather than satisfaction."

Mature love

"Love is more than just feeling", says Prof **Dmitry Leontiev**.
Beyond the beating heart and the butterflies in our stomach
accompanying romantic love, he discovers the characteristics
of real mature love. A journey beyond oaths, confirmations
and the borders of ourselves.

The role of love in our lives is apparently due to the incomparable emotional richness
and intensity it brings. The feeling of love, often called romantic love or passionate love,
embraces an individual and makes him/her possessed, distorting judgments, plans and l
ife habits. Old descriptions of love as a temporary insanity refer to the individual feeling.

However, love is more than just feeling. Beyond the feeling, love is one of the ontological
foundations of life, on the same scale as life and death. It is a relationship that allows
a mature person who has passed the way of individuation, overcome infantile psychological
symbiosis and transcended narcissistic self-sufficiency, to relate to another person. In fact,
it is loving rather than love, a verb rather than a noun, as Erich Fromm has emphasized.
This is something one can choose and create, taking responsibility for the implementation
of this choice, even if with no warranty as to the outcomes.

This mature, or existential, love challenges one's capacity for responsibility, decision,
inner work and change. It brings meaning rather than satisfaction. This is why not many
mortals are ready to pay this price for this kind of love. The word *existential* means that

it cannot be causally explained and predicted by psychological mechanisms of its generation; it exists as a possibility rather than a facticity, it may or may not come true. Whether to invest oneself in the enterprise and make love grow, or not, is mostly down to the conscious and responsible choice of the involved persons.

Shared space

Mature love is a dialogue. A dialogue is unpredictable and uncontrollable; it is a journey beyond the borders of Me to the foreign territory of the Other. It is due to this unpredictability and uncontrollability that discoveries can be made in this territory that so greatly enrich, change and sometimes even transform us, as is the case in loving relationships. The critical condition is that I disclose myself to the unknown, the unexpected, to the possibility of an encounter with something that would make me change, rather than stay self-defensive, as most of us stay in most relationships.

Another feature of a genuine dialogue is that it creates a shared conversational space between the partners. Words, meanings, values, symbols and worldviews emerge in this space and give shape to this space, just because they are recognized and negotiated as something that unites both people. There are also places, events, people that belong to the shared part of their personal history. **A story of love is the story of the birth and growth of this shared space co-created in mature love relationships,** where both feel at home. There are no borders in this territory of love between the partners – everything is common and both are one. And any sacrifice that is being done by a mature lover, any self-giving, is an investment for the benefit of this common space, rather than for the benefit of an individual partner. One invests oneself in this new shared reality and both enjoy the fruits of this investment. It is self-expansion, rather than self-denial. The loving altruism is a kind of enhanced egoism that is based on the extended personal identity that embraces now the partner as a part of the 'We', the extended 'Me'.

Constant change

A mature love, as any other love, is not always happy, does not always enjoy mutuality. Unshared mature love, however, unlike unshared romantic love, implies a sober determination to carry this burden of an unanswered offer, not only for the sake of winning the reward in a distant perspective, but also for the sake of oneself, of one's growth and authentic passing along one's way. Shared romantic love brings happiness; unshared romantic love brings disappointment. Both shared and unshared mature love bring the sense of meaning and personal growth. It is a trial that makes a person stronger – and shared mature love is a still harder trial than the unshared love.

Romantic love expects much from the beloved; first of all, oaths, confirmations and a lifetime warranty. The paradox of love relationships means, however, that it can survive only in constant growth and change; stagnation makes it fade very quickly. **Mature love does not require confirmations.** It requires something different, namely a constant alertness, a readiness for sensing the other, adjusting to him/her, negotiating at multiple levels, from bodily communication to superordinate values, and the willingness to keep changing. Feelings of love may happen to everyone and do not depend much on the person.

What makes the difference is the way we transform the feeling into the personal responsible enterprise, whether and how we invest ourselves in this life-changing relationship, whether and how we open ourselves to this challenge of unpredictability and the possibility of growth. This shows the measure of humanness we have achieved.

The keys

→ **Mature (or existential) love goes beyond feeling. It brings meaning and it is a verb, rather than a noun.**

→ **Mature love is a dialogue: unpredictable and uncontrollable. In the shared conversational space the other one becomes a part of the extended self.**

→ **Mature love does not require confirmations, but a constant alertness for growth and changes in our self and in the other one.**

Dmitry Leontiev is Professor of Psychology at Lomonosov Moscow State University (Russia). He is Head of the Research Lab of Positive Psychology and Quality of Life Studies at the National Research University Higher School of Economics in Moscow and Director of the Institute of Existential Psychology and Life Enhancement. He has written more than 300 specialized papers and received the award of the Russian Psychological Society for the best book on psychology.

Love in Latin America

Latin America counts some famous winners of the Nobel Prize for Literature: Mario Vargas Llosa (Peru), Octavio Paz (Mexico), Gabriel Garcia Marquez (Colombia), Pablo Neruda (Chile). They often express political commitment and… love. Sociologist Oracio Barradas Meza looks for the fire of love in Mexico. Between machismo and tragedy.

The Mexican contemporary poet Jaime Sabines summarizes it all: "I die of you and of me, I die of both, of this, torn, split, I die, I you die, we die it." Mexican society is eager to find love. From a young age we learn to desire unconditionally, or rather to establish the conditions for desiring and loving. Mexican culture is a metamorphosis of the folklore that Mexicans impress on this feeling that moves surreal passions: love.

Two volcanoes

The legend of Popocatépetl and Iztaccíhuatl can help us give us an idea of how the first Mexicans loved. In the fourteenth century, when the Aztec Empire was at its peak and dominated the Valley of Mexico, it was common practice to subjugate neighbouring towns, imposing a compulsory tax on them. The chief of the Tlaxcaltecas decided to fight for his people's freedom. He had a daughter, Iztaccíhuatl. She fell in love with the young Popocatépetl, a warrior of his people. He asked

the chief for Princess Iztaccíhuatl's hand. The former agreed and promised to receive Popocatépetl with a feast at which he would give him his daughter's hand if the young warrior returned victorious from the battle. Popocatépetl's rival in love, jealous of the love they both professed, told Princess Iztaccíhuatl that her lover had died. She collapsed with grief and, not knowing it was a lie, she died. Returning victorious to his village, hoping to find his beloved, Popocatépetl was told of Princess Iztaccíhuatl's death. He disconsolately wandered the streets, then ordered a tomb to be built in the mountains. Taking his lover in his arms, he carried her to the great tomb, kissed her, lit a smoking torch and knelt in front of his beloved. Since then, they have stayed together, covered by snow and became two large volcanoes.

Bolero

All cultures use different elements to express love. Latin Americans have forged their own style from various resources. The bolero, for instance, is a typical dance, music and love song which expresses multiple emotions like nostalgia and conquest. Serenades at the foot of the balcony take the best verses of songs that have passed from generation to generation. The clarinet sounds in the darkness and accompanies the lines: "I love the street where we were, the night we met. I love the silk of your hands, the kisses we exchanged. I adore you, my life. And I'm dying to have you with me, close, very close to me. Not parting from you,

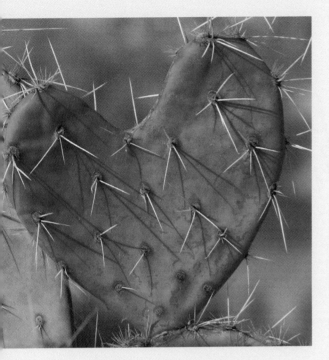

" I die of you and of me."

been reinforced in music, film, television and today the social networks. Life stories are projected on these big stages of entertainment and information. Crisis is not limited to economic and political life; there is also a constant crisis in love. For Mexicans, **loving someone means total surrender, that can turn into possessive and controlling love.** This is not a Mexican rule, but we start from the fact that this degree of possession has to do with the *machismo* present in Latin American culture.

Love as practiced in Mexico remains tragic. **The way to happiness through love lies in suffering.** Mexicans are always suffering for love or enjoying love. All this forms the great escape from a reality in which violence is experienced in the streets, in the many social injustices of every-day life, in the weariness of political corruption, in the lack of opportunity or in the untrammelled ostentation of luxury. In variety shows or in the classicism of fairytale marriages, Mexicans seek an escape and to find the dose that promises them happiness. Love becomes, in this way, the inspiration to build a more human world.

Oracio Barradas Meza is a sociologist from the University of Veracruz (Mexico). He contributes to different magazines and is founder member of the Social Players' Collective. He is webmaster of social blogs and producer of the web radio program AS Radio, examining topics of national interest, culture policy and society.

who are my life, my feeling. You are my moon, you are my sunshine, my night of love. I adore…" **From boleros we can understand that music exalts the sublimest passions,** leaving little to the imagination. This is how we tend to fall in love, but music is not the only item in courtship and infatuation.

Our cinema reinforces the stereotypes and roles to follow. In the film *La Cucaracha* (The Cockroach), María Félix plays a 'brave and gutsy' woman, who upon marrying becomes sweet and servile. The drastic change in the plot exemplies the subjugation of the Mexican woman to the unconditional love for her man.

Machismo

Our history is marked by the violence of a people that is forging itself every day, but has a hard time eradicating the vices it has inherited. These have

"I'm happy that you're happy."

The happiness of the other

"When I meet couples who are in serious difficulty, but are keen to save their relationships, I observe that, in most cases, they try not to be carried away by their feelings. They talk, interact, share their opinions, discuss…" says Dr **Armand Lequeux**. "But that, too, is not enough."

I think they are missing a step, that of listening to each other's basic needs, and then deciding and acting accordingly. Too often they are like the board meeting of a company that has become aware of a problem. It gathers the opinions of the meeting, but fails to go on and implement a strategy to meet the company's needs. Long-term loving is a choice that is renewed every morning. It is expressed in concrete decisions and actions that reflect both partners' sexual and emotional needs. (*"I can never completely fulfill your need to be recognized as unique, but I am mindful of it and I explicitly show that you have a specific and preferred importance for me in all circumstances. You will never fulfill entirely my own need to be loved unconditionally, but you reassure me as much as you can and I do not have to constantly be earning your love. We can never fulfill completely each other's sexual desires, but we can meet in truth in our shared pleasure, while respecting our secret gardens."*)

Distance and proximity

For a couple that wants to succeed in the long term, it is important to continuously vary the intensity of proximity. During the same day, one can experience a state of fusion with one's partner in a sexual relationship, or very intimate exchange and then have, separately, very strong emotional experiences without betraying the priority that each grants to the other. **If we stay glued to each other, we will stifle each other**; if we distance ourselves too much, we will lose each other. It's not so much a question of finding the happy middle path, but rather the good rhythm, the right pendulum movement between distance and proximity. This is like a respiratory movement which supplies the couple with oxygen. (*"What I experience positively outside my relationship gives me joy that reflects on our relationship. The happiness that I know in my relationship has positive effects on the rest of my life."*)

A daily decision

We are not responsible for our partner's happiness. We can, at most, participate in and be glad about it. It may seem obvious that we are happy when our partner receives congratulations, a promotion, praise, or when he or she happens to be particularly lucky in one or another circumstance. However, if we are honest, we have to recognize that **we are often jealous
of his or her good fortune or success**. Indeed, studies on couples who love lastingly have shown that being able to rejoice in the other's happiness is even more important than the mutual help and support we can tender in hard times. (*"I'm happy that you're happy. I look forward to your joy. Thank you for being alive…"*) There are obviously long and pleasant periods in a relationship during which everything seems easy and spontaneous, but in times of crisis or weariness, love is an active attitude, a determination, a decision which one can train oneself to make… every morning. Lasting love is no more natural to man and woman than the rose in the garden.

The keys

→ **It is not enough to interact and to discuss. The missing step is listening to each other's basic needs in order to decide and act accordingly.**

→ **Continuously vary the level of intensity and proximity. Focus not on the happy middle path but rather on the good rhythm.**

→ **Ability to rejoice in the other's happiness is even more important than giving support in hard times. Love is a daily decision.**

Armand Lequeux is a gynecologist and sexologist, Professor Emeritus at the Catholic University of Louvain-la-Neuve (Belgium), Faculty of Medicine and Faculty of Psychology. He is widely recognized for his work and has published several popular books, including *Phallus et cerises, la tendre guerre des sexes* (*Phallus and Cherries, the Tender War of the Sexes*).

"Some people are afraid of humor because they are afraid of intimacy."

The humor style of love

For both men and women, 'humor' is a high priority on the list of characteristics of attractive partners. But there are different reasons to laugh. Prof **Shahe S. Kazarian** has discovered four styles of humoring we often use in relationships. Some are loving. Some are not.

Over the past decade, my collaborative research program with colleagues in Canada and graduate students in Lebanon has been preoccupied, in part, with the link between our styles of relating to family, friends and romantic partners and our styles of humoring. We have focused on two insecure styles of relating to others (anxious and avoidant) and four styles of humoring, two being beneficial (self-enhancing and affiliative) and two being potentially detrimental (self-defeating and aggressive). People with the anxious style of social relating tend to worry that others do not really love them and fear rejection and even abandonment, whereas those with the avoidant style of relating tend to keep an emotional distance between themselves and others because they fear the dependence that may result from emotional intimacy and love. As for humoring, people who use affiliative humor tend to say funny things, to tell jokes and to engage in spontaneous witty banter in order

to amuse others. People who use **self-enhancing humor** tend to have a humorous outlook on life, even when not with others, to be frequently amused by the incongruities in life, to maintain a humorous perspective even in the face of stress or adversity, and to use humor as a coping strategy. People who use **self-defeating humor**, on the other hand, tend to rely on excessive self-disparaging humor, attempt to amuse others by doing or saying funny things at their own expense, and laugh along with others when being ridiculed or disparaged. Finally, people who use **aggressive humor** tend to focus on humor that is critical or manipulative of others as in sarcasm, teasing ridicule and disparagement, or even potentially offensive, such as sexist or racist forms of humor.

In general, we found that people with an anxious style of relating to others use the potentially detrimental self-defeating style of humor perhaps as a means of dealing with insecurities and anxieties they have in interpersonal and love relationships. In essence, these individuals make themselves the butt of their jokes at their own expense so others like them and stay with them. Similarly, we found that people with an avoidant style of relating to others sparingly use humor that enhances closeness in relationships, perhaps as a means of maintaining their emotional distance from others. In essence, these individuals shy away from shared humorous social play and laughter for fear of interpersonal bonding and intimacy.

Lesson One: Rethink your style of relating to others and humorous, as not all social relating and humorous styles are good for your interpersonal relationships or love life. Ideally, you need to nurture a secure, rather than an anxious or avoidant style of relating and to compliment it with humor that is socially bonding rather than self-deprecating.

Childhood roots

More recently, our collaborative research program has been extended to discovering how our upbringing figures in our humorous styles and subjective happiness later in life. We call this the Truth of Love, Humoring and Happiness. We expected adults with warm and accepting caregivers and an abundance of physical and verbal love and affection in childhood to rely more on beneficial styles of humorous and to feel happier than those with rejecting and hostile upbringings. We reasoned that adults, who as children shared love and positive fun with their parents, were more likely to learn and emulate later in life beneficial humorous than those who, as children, lacked love and fun. In general, we found that adults who felt loved and wanted in childhood reported use of self-enhancing and affiliative humor and subjective happiness, whereas those who felt unloved and unwanted reported use of self-defeating and aggressive humor. Taken together, our work on the link between upbringing, humoring and well-being seemed to suggest that our home environments in childhood may be at the roots of beneficial humoring and subjective happiness.

Lesson Two: Warm and accepting home environments are kosher vis-à-vis healthy use of humor and subjective states of happiness. Ideally, we should all strive to invoke warm and accepting social climates to contribute to the trans-generational transmission of love, humoring and happiness.

The keys

→ **Humor is very important in creating loving relationships. However, there are different styles of humor, two being beneficial (self-enhancing and affiliative) and two being potentially detrimental (self-defeating and aggressive).**

→ **Nurture a secure rather than an anxious or avoidant style of relating and complement it with humor that is socially bonding rather than self-deprecating.**

→ **Strive to invoke warm and accepting social climates to contribute to a good transgenerational transmission of love and humoring.**

Shahe S. Kazarian is Chair and Professor at the Department of Psychology at the American University of Beirut (Lebanon). He has published more than two dozen books and book chapters and over sixty papers in peer-reviewed journals on the link between culture and positive psychology generally and attachment styles, humor styles and well-being in particular. He is founding member of the Lebanese Psychological Association and has held multiple academic, clinical and administrative appointments, and professional leadership positions including Professor of Psychiatry, Faculty of Medicine, at The University of Western Ontario. He adds: "I am a Canadian citizen of Armenian heritage with a deep love for life, partly because of my collective identity as a second generation survivor of the Armenian genocide. I love my family and I am proud that we have recently been able to celebrate our fortieth Wedding Anniversary."

"Some couples report having their best sex when making up after arguments."

Passion follows change

"Once in love you're never out of danger, one hot night spent with a stranger… passion", Rod Stewart made it a hit. **Roy F. Baumeister** does the research. He unfolds the relationship between passion and change. And how different introverts and extraverts might react.

Passion and intimacy are two ingredients of love, though different love relationships mix quite different quantities of them. Although good relationships may have both, passion tends to be temporary and to diminish over time, whereas intimacy may increase and remain high for a long period. Thus, as a couple moves from the initial stage of falling in love into the latter part of a fifty-year marriage, there is a shift to make the relationship composed more of intimacy and less of passion.

Our work has concluded that passion often derives from change in intimacy. When two people first meet, both tend to be low. The beginnings of feeling connected bring about an increase in intimacy, and so passion develops too. At some point intimacy is growing quite fast, such as when the two lovers confess their affection for each other, hold long conversations to share their secrets and hopes, and begin to understand each other mentally and physically. This is typically a period of high passion, because intimacy is rising.

Intimacy

After the relationship has solidified for a couple years, intimacy may be high in the sense that the two people understand each other well and care about each other, but it is no longer changing much. The couple has come to know each other's stories and projects, has come to understand each other physically and sexually, and has become able to anticipate each other's emotional reactions and concerns. **Passion drops at this time.** If conflicts emerge and a rift develops, the intimacy may begin to deteriorate, which produces another category of passions, such as anger and resentment. Perhaps ironically, some couples report having their best sex when making up after arguments. These occasions probably indicate a quick and temporary drop in intimacy (during the argument) followed by a sharp rise back up in intimacy (as the fight is resolved and the two reaffirm their positive feelings towards each other), which is sufficient to produce passion. Even though intimacy ends up about where it was before the fight, it feels like it just increased during the transition from fighting (low intimacy) to making up and being nice (high intimacy), and this may be sufficient to trigger some passionate and sexual feelings.

The pattern is not exactly the same for everyone, of course. In mathematical terms, there are different shapes of the curve that links passion to change in intimacy. Extraverts have a sharp rise in intimacy and therefore a sharp rise in passion — but then intimacy quickly levels off, which means that passion dwindles faster among extraverts. In contrast, introverts may be slower to open up, so the initial passion is lower, but perhaps they can sustain passion over a longer period of time. (Sure enough, extraverts tend to have sex earlier in the relationship than introverts.)

New partners

Once intimacy has reached a high level and passion is diminishing, new partners may start to seem more and more appealing — because there is more scope to increase intimacy and thereby generate passion. Extraverts may be especially susceptible to these whirlwind romances because of their quick rise in intimacy. Extraverts may therefore be most prone to stray from the relationship and find new partners. The contrast between the regular, committed partner (high intimacy but very little passion) and the new, exciting one (passion high because of increasing intimacy) makes the new one seem like the truer love, which tempts the extravert to leave the established relationship and start a new one with the new person. Again, evidence confirms that extraverts run through more romances and sex partners than introverts.

Note, however, that it may often be a mistake to leave the committed partner for the exciting new lover. The comparison is between apples and oranges (i.e. between a new relationship which naturally has high passion, versus an established one that consists mainly of intimacy). Once the person has reached a high level of intimacy with the new partner, the passion will wane and the extravert may realize he or she was actually better off with the former partner. The lack of passion in the committed relationship was mistaken for a lack of love, especially when contrasted with the new, thrilling partner.

There may also be differences by gender. By some findings, the same degree of increase in intimacy produces more passion in males than females. Ample evidence indicates that men fall in love faster than women. Men are usually ready for escalating the relationship commitment faster than women, declare their love earlier and are ready for sex earlier. Keep in mind, though, that there are wide differences among individuals within each gender.

The keys:

→ **Passion and intimacy are two ingredients of love, though different love relationships mix quite different quantities of them. Passion follows changes in intimacy.**

→ **Extraverts have a sharp rise in intimacy and passion, but quickly level off. Initial passion is lower with introverts but they can sustain passion over a longer period of time.**

→ **Once intimacy has reached a high level and passion is diminishing, new partners may start to seem more and more appealing.**

Roy F. Baumeister is the Eppes Eminent Professor of Psychology at Florida State University (USA). He received his PhD in social psychology from Princeton in 1978 and completed a postdoctoral fellowship in sociology at the University of California at Berkeley. He has over 500 publications, and his 30 books include the New York Times bestseller *Willpower: Rediscovering the Greatest Human Strength*. The Institute for Scientific Information lists him among the handful of most cited (most influential) psychologists in the world. He has received lifetime achievement awards from the Society for Personality and Social Psychology, from the International Society for Self and Identity and, most recently, the Association for Psychological Science's highest honor, the William James Award.

"Also love the forbidding peaks."

Mountains of love

When you are 'in the flow', you are *in the moment, on fire* **and** *in tune.* **Prof** Mihaly Csikszentmihalyi **is the architect of this concept in modern psychology. Of course there is a strong link between flow and love. But he first takes us to the mountains.**

I recently had the good fortune of spending some time with a group of men from Verona, who are part of a well-known folk choir that specializes in old songs from the Italian Alps. They are men from all walks of life – physicians and plumbers, business-men and teachers – who meet every Tuesday to rehearse and travel all over the world to give performances. They are all amateurs who do this for the simple love of singing together. Because they knew that I had sung those songs when I was a young man, they asked me to join them.

We started with a song from the Western Alps, where the people speak a dialect that is more French than Italian. It is called 'Montagnes Valdostaines'. I had last sung it with a choir about sixty years earlier. As we started with the powerful notes of the first line, I was suddenly surprised by the words, which I had sung so many times before without thinking much about them: "Montagnes Valdostaines, vous êtes mes amours." **Why did these people of the Alps, hundreds of years ago,** call the mountains their love? There seemed no earthly reason for it. The mountains were useless, they kept them from moving around freely, the cows and the sheep got lost among them; in the winters, they buried villages with their avalanches… Yet, looking at the ecstatic expressions on the faces of the mountaineers around me (an expression I was sure also appeared on my face) I had to conclude that there was genuine love expressed in those words. But why?

The second stanza of the song did not clarify matters. In it, the singer explains why he loves the place where he lives: "J'ai ma ceinture… Et mon beret… Mes chants joyeuses, mon amie, et mon chalet…" (I have my belt and my beret, my joyful songs, my girlfriend and my house). OK, you will say, so the song is a piece of propaganda the ruling classes have sold to the helpless shepherds of the Alps, so they can bear their poor and uncomfortable lives. Perhaps, to a certain extent, this is true. The romantic life of the mountain people could serve that purpose. But, as we sang that second stanza, I realized a more profound truth that the song expressed. If you love your house, your girlfriend, your belt and beret – and also the forbidding peaks surrounding your place in the world – you will be doing a lot of loving. Not for any practical reason. The mountains will still be an obstacle, they will still kill you if you are not careful. The belt and beret…

Well, they won't do you that much good either. But what will do you good, if you love them, is that your life will be full of love. What more can we hope for?

In our times, the meaning of 'love' has shrunk to mean the affection between men and women and – hopefully – between parents and children. And not much else. But that is not enough. If we forget that there is so much to love in this world and keep living in an anonymous, alien world, we risk losing our connection to the rest of the cosmos. Yet, it is so easy to fill the awful loneliness of the universe. "All you need", as another song says, "is love".

Mihaly Csikszentmihalyi is Distinguished Professor of Psychology and Management at Claremont Graduate University (USA). He is founding Co-Director of the Quality of Life Research Center that studies positive psychology, and has written numerous articles and books on flow and human strengths.

"We are designed for connection."

Focus on emotion

In developing her Emotionally Focused Therapy over the past thirty years, Dr **Sue Johnson** has become one of the world's principal researchers and clinicians working with love relationships. Modern brainscan analysis supports her approach, which has become a major standard for therapy of couples who seek support in expressing their love. What has she learned about love?

I have learned that love is exquisitely logical – a survival code laid down by millions of years of evolution. It is no longer a mystery and this is very good news because, as our society becomes lonelier and lonelier and social life becomes relegated to an incidental rather than being seen as an essential, we are more and more dependent on our relationship with our mate for support, care, intimacy and fulfilment. I have learned that adult love is an emotional bond, an attachment that is cut from the same cloth as the bond between parent and child. As adults, we need a safe haven and secure base relationship to go to for comfort and reassurance and to go out from into an uncertain world. From the cradle to the grave we are best when we have safe connection with a precious other who, when we call "Are you there for me? – Can I count on you to respond to me?" will answer with a resounding "Yes". When we have this, we can hold onto our emotional balance and become resilient and strong, exploring the world and dealing with challenge and threat.

Hold me tight

For the first time in human history, we really do have a science of love. We have a map to our deepest needs; these are all about having an accessible and responsive attachment figure. The evidence is that, when we have safe emotional connection, the other parts of our relationship, caregiving and sexuality, are most likely to flourish. Emotional safety and responsiveness turn sex into exquisitely coordinated play and fosters sensitive caregiving. Attachment science helps us understand our most basic emotions in love relationships. As mammals, who experience emotional isolation as inherently traumatizing, we experience fear and panic when we cannot get our lover to respond to us, and move into reactive anger to try to force this person to respond. Emotional disconnection cues deep sadness and loss in us and brings fears that we are somehow undeserving of love. A good love relationship is one where partners can turn to each other and risk and reach, asking for their needs to be met. They can help each other deal with their vulnerabilities.

What you understand, you can shape. The Emotionally Focused approach to mending distressed relationships is the gold standard for research in the couple field, and our positive outcome results are, we believe, because we are on target. We know how to not just help couples get caught in less conflict, but how to help couples have Hold Me Tight conversations that, across our sixteen outcome studies, predict recovery from distress at the end of therapy and foster the stability of these results years later. We teach couples to help each other exit from cycles that perpetuate insecurity and disconnection, like blame and withdraw, and move into being able to accept and express their attachment needs to each other in a way that evokes caring and empathy. **Once you can mend the inevitable rifts in your emotional bond, you can have a stable lifetime love.** Our latest studies combine neuroscience, attachment and change in couples relationships, showing in brain scans, that shaping more secure attachment changes how our brains perceive and respond to threats – such as electric shock.

Alice and Peter

So, in their distressed relationship, Alice tells Peter: "You're never here for me. I want emotional closeness, not all the insights and reasons why we don't have it. I'm angry all the time. I push you to get you to respond." Peter says, "I never hear that you want me. I hear that you are disappointed in me and so I move away. It's so painful to be rejected constantly. I shut down." Alice says, "No, you shut me out." Alice and Peter have to learn to deal with their softer feelings in a different way; a way that invites the other in.

When Alice, for example, can talk about her fear that she does not matter to Peter, rather than her rage, he begins to open up and respond. In a Hold Me Tight conversation, Peter says, "I want to learn to be close. I will make mistakes. But you can't go walloping me all the time here. I get so shattered by your criticisms, **I just freeze. I do shut down and shut you out. But I want to come close.** I need you close to me." Alice can reply, "I'm so scared all the time that you do not need me that way I need you. I have to be able to call and have you turn towards me. I need you to reassure me." This kind of connection restores bonds.

My advice? Accept your attachment needs – you are a mammal with a mammalian brain. You are designed for connection. It is not 'weak' to need another. Learn to risk turning to your partner and asking him or her, from a place of softness, to respond to these needs. Your emotions tell you what you need; listen to them. The best gift you can give to your partner is your emotional presence; this is the 'solution' to most couple problems, in fact. Standing together in safe emotional connection, you will bring out the best in each other.

The keys

→ **Adult love is an emotional bond, an attachment that is cut from the same cloth as the bond between parent and child.**

→ **When we have safe emotional connection, the other parts of our relationship, caregiving and sexuality, are most likely to flourish.**

→ **What you understand, you can shape. Accept your attachment needs and help each other exit from cycles that perpetuate insecurity and disconnection.**

Sue Johnson is Professor of Clinical Psychology at the University of Ottawa (Canada), Distinguished Research Professor at Alliant University in San Diego, California (USA) and Director of the International Center for Excellence in Emotionally Focused Therapy. She has received numerous honors for her work, including the Outstanding Contribution to the Field of Couple and Family Therapy Award from the American Association for Marriage and Family Therapy. One of her best known professional books is *The Practice of Emotionally Focused Couple Therapy: Creating Connection*. Her bestseller *Hold Me Tight* has been translated into more than twenty languages. She loves Argentine tango and kayaking on Canada's northern lakes.

Love in Islam

"Love may be one of the most intricate and elusive concepts in all languages and cultural traditions", says Prof Habib Tiliouine. He looks for true lovers and perfect love in the mystics of Islam.

However, legendary love stories such as Shakespeare's Romeo and Juliet continue to inspire people worldwide. Many cases where love, passion, poetry and tragic destinies converge are also reported in ancient and modern Arab and Islamic literature. At least we know the famous poet Antar and his cousin Abla in the pre-Islamic period, Kais and Leila, Jamil and Boutheina, and the less known Hiziya and Sayed in Algeria. Nevertheless, early Muslim scholars would agree to put this type of love under the title of 'profane' love as opposed to a 'sacred' one. A value differentiation between these two types of love is underlined in early Muslim philosophy. In the Platonic way, the latter 'spiritual' love is given much more preference and considered superior compared to the 'natural' one. In some ways, it is recommended that people should long for the 'Highest Beauty', not the 'External Beauty'. In this sense, no beauty excels the absolute beauty of God. Furthermore, beauty of the spirit, the character, or in short, the hidden, may be more important than external and physical beauty.

True lovers

Though early Muslim philosophers, such as Al-Farabi (about 870- 950) and the Brethren of Purity (a group of philosophers of the tenth Century), wrote remarkable treaties about love, Ibn Sina (about 981 – 1037, more widely known as Avicenna) caught much attention. His psychological insights led him to agree with Aristotle that humans possess three types of psyches. The vegetative and animal ones bind humans to earth and seek sensual pleasures. They help them to grow, to reproduce and to acquire knowledge through the senses. The rational psyche, on the other hand, helps them ascend on the way to reach true happiness and connect with God. He insists in his "A treatise of love" that love exists in all three types of psyches. Though he agrees that external beauty has a positive role, exalted and unearthly love remains superior and everlasting compared to the former, which quickly dissipates. 'True' lovers, therefore, are those pious people whose beloved is the Almighty Creator of the universe. God, besides the name of Allah, has 98 other sacred names in the Islamic tradition. None of these names contain anything that may contradict that love is the essence of the universe.

Mercy (*Rahma*) which exists between people, such as the one binding human and animal mothers to their babies, represents a tiny bit of what God holds towards His creatures.

" *There are no limits for love.*"

Perfect love

History teaches us that Rabi`a al-Adawiyya (born about 717) was one of the earliest female mystics in Islam. She completely abandoned a life of materialistic pleasures for the love of God and developed a new theory of love: the Absolute Love, love that refuses to be rewarded. Strategically, people make a difference between the end and the means, but for Rabi`a, no distinction is applicable when it comes to unconditional 'absolute love'.

The Andalusian Ibn 'Arabī (1165- 1240), whose writings are estimated at 15000 pages in modern printing (250 books), is the second figure representing the perfect lover. He writes: "My heart has become capable of every form. It is a pasture for gazelles and a monastery for Christian monks. And a temple for idols and the pilgrim's Ka'ba and the tables of the Torah and the book of the Qur'an. I follow the religion of Love, whatever way Love's camels take. That is my religion and my faith." What made Ibn 'Arabī's heart become multi-formed: fresh grass for animals' sustenance, a monastery for monks, a temple for various types of idols and pilgrims and a reading table for all sacred books? His vision is deeply rooted in the profound understanding of Islam. In short, Ibn 'Arabī holds that **real wisdom cannot come from imitating others**, "but must be discovered by realization, which is the actualization of the soul's

potential." Ibn 'Arabī differs from most philosophers in maintaining that full realization can only be achieved by following in the footsteps of the prophets. Love should not be conceived as a mere dissipating feeling, rather, it is a continuous spiritual ascension through deliberate action. It is an endless process. This is well prescribed in the sacred Books. For Ibn 'Arabī, the cosmos is itself a sacred Book.

It could be concluded that, for these mystics and pious people, love purifies the *soul*, on one condition: it should be unlimited, absolute and particularly not extrinsically driven. There are no limits for love. It embraces the noblest feelings and desires to bring people, in their difference, to go beyond their close selfishness and their materialistic and consumerist inclinations, to live together in harmony and peace. So, keep giving.

Habib Tiliouine is Professor at the Department of Psychology and Educational Sciences, Faculty of Social Sciences, University of Oran (Algeria). He is the Head of the Laboratory of Educational Processes & Social Context. Every 18 months, he conducts a national survey assessing diverse (socio-)psychological aspects related to the life of the Algerian population. He has built up expertise in quality of life studies and well-being in Islamic countries. He has written numerous articles, including *Happiness in Islam* for the Encyclopedia of Quality of Life Research.

"Happiness is found alone
and is then shared."

Happier couples

"Unfortunately, our studies show that marriage is doing rather badly: nearly 50 % of married couples divorce, 30 % live more or less resigned to their fate and only 20 % are happy most of the time", says **Yvon Dallaire**. However, his thirty years of practice as a psychologist specializing in marital therapy have taught him that it is not for lack of love.

Traditional therapies focus on communication ('effective' or 'non-violent') for resolving the many conflicts that are inherent and inevitable in the life of a couple. These therapies work to reduce tension in the short term and to revive love temporarily. But they are ineffective in the long term. The reason is simple: **most conflicts within couples are insoluble.** Discussing unsolvable problems serves only to mire couples in bottomless arguments, with each side trying to convince the other that "I'm right, you're wrong" ("I'm right to want to raise the children permissively and you're wrong to be so authoritarian"; "I'm right to want to save for our old age and you're wrong to want to enjoy your money now"; "I'm right to want to maintain close relations with our in-laws instead of wanting to live by ourselves"; "I think you're not shouldering your fair share of the housework and looking after our children"; "You work too hard and do not invest enough in our personal life"; "And besides, you only think about sex and I wish you would love me for what I am".)

The solution to all these sources of conflict would be that both partners share the same educational principles, the same financial security, the same family spirit. That they also share tasks and want to spend an equal amount of time together. And they have the same libido. Do you understand why I have been saying and writing for many years that marriage is not made to make people happy, but is rather the source of many crises… crises that either enable people to grow or stunt them?

Criticism

There do exist, however, couples who are happy in the long term and not just during the first flush of love, which rarely lasts more than two to three years. How are they different or what do they do differently from the couples who are unhappy or who divorce? Again, the answer is very simple: they agree to go through life living with their disagreements. They have decided to be happy, rather than the one to be right and the other wrong. Rather than using communication to build consensus, they inform each other of their respective views on the many aspects of their relationship and accept that there may be differences. They then negotiate win-win agreements which take into account the views of each side. For example, they negotiate an annual budget which includes a savings account and an account for 'follies'. They then entrust the management of the budget to one of the partners and don't speak any more of money until the following year.

Observing the way happy couples communicate has shown me one of the main secrets of couples that are happy in the long term: they express five to ten times more compliments than criticism or reproach. In other words, they put much more into their love savings accounts than they take out. This is not the 'you' that kills communication as that many experts keep on telling us, but rather what comes after the 'you': "You're brilliant, my love" or "you are so smart, darling" are more likely to maintain a harmonious and respectful than 'you' followed by a criticism: "You don't understand on purpose" or "You're never there for me". These criticisms can only lead to defence and counter-attack, which are the universal dynamic of unhappy couples.

Special guest

As the research findings of positive psychology are showing more and more, only pleasant emotions ought to be expressed, not unpleasant emotions, and much less so frustration. Members of happy couples express their needs and desires, rather than dump their frustrations and criticisms on their partners. In fact, to be happy in our relationships in the long term, we need, first of all, to take 100 % responsibility for our end of the relationship and **stop believing that our partner is responsible for our happiness or unhappiness.** "Happiness is found alone and is then shared" as French actor Benoît Magimel so aptly put it. Taking 100 % responsibility for one's marriage and investing 100 % in this beautiful human adventure that the couple represents is a winning strategy.

Second, no one can be happy in a relationship if they do not develop emotional intelligence. IQ is certainly important for success, but the emotional quotient (EQ) is even more. Conjugal emotional intelligence means not letting negative emotions take the upper hand over positive emotions. We must never forget that the person in front of us is a unique person, the only one of his or her type in the world, and therefore exceptional. Members of happy couples see their partner as a special guest in their lives and take care of this guest. They don't 'fall' in love, they 'rise' into love.

The keys

- → **Most conflicts within couples are insoluble. This means that mere communication therapies are ineffective in the long term.**
- → **Happy couples agree to go through life living with their disagreements. They have decided to be happy, rather than the one to be right and the other wrong.**
- → **Members of happy couples express their needs and desires, rather than dump their frustrations and criticisms on their partners.**

Yvon Dallaire is a psychologist, sexologist and author living in Quebec (Canada). He is the creator of the Psycho-Sexual Approach as applied to couples (L' approche psycho-sexuelle appliqué aux couples, APSAC) and has written numerous books and articles on love and successful relationships.

"A million new people a day are infected."

Love, sex and risk

A million new people a day are infected with Sexually Transmitted Diseases. Less than half are aware of it. In the USA, 25 % of teenage girls are infected. Worldwide, more than 34 million people are living with HIV. Dr **Panos Kordoutis** looks for the kind of love behind this.

Words, expressions and meanings associated with love suggest that there are many kinds of love. Albeit, people involved in romantic relationships experience, for the most part, two major kinds: companionate and passionate love. Companionate love is a deep stable feeling that one's life is intertwined with another, his or her everyday reality, needs and plans. Passionate love is a strong longing for union with a more or less idealized other, accompanied by unstable and contradicting feelings, such as arousal, elation, intimacy, anxiety and sadness.

My research over the past few years has shown that, in youthful relationships, passionate love tends to prevail, although companionate love features are not negligible.
The preponderance of passionate love helps young people overcome realistic obstacles that might have otherwise kept them apart, such as differences in background, values, resources and personality. Lovers see each other through colored glasses; they see more the person they would have liked to love, rather than the one they actually love. Once 'deceptive' passionate love has secured the mutual approach of two young people, chances multiply that companionate love will also further develop. Deceptive or not, passionate love

is the basic mechanism that puts intimate relationships on the go. Moreover, people rejoice in passionate love and younger people, in particular, are attracted to the very idea of having a passionate love relationship.

Erotic moment

Despite its popularity and functionality for starting a relationship, passionate love has a risky side. The strong desire for self-disclosure associated with it is accompanied by the desire to influence the other and accept her or his influence. When in love, personal barriers go down. Although, this process encourages the two 'in love' individuals to move towards 'togetherness', it also weakens their motivation to use self-protecting negotiation skills and rational decision-making. This is of particular concern when it comes to protective behavior during sexual intercourse. The decision to protect oneself against Sexually Transmitted Diseases and unplanned pregnancy is based on knowledge about these risks and the ways of protecting oneself, motivation to do so and negotiation skills (whether one intends to propose protection and stand by one's proposal). Passionate love can hamper the decision to protect oneself and the other from health risks. Protection thoughts and behaviors, such as proposing the use of a condom, seem incompatible to the atmosphere of a passionate love relationship. "How can the person I love be a threat that I have to protect myself from?"; "I cherish the physical contact, the condom is a barrier", "Isn't proposing the use of a condom passing the wrong message that I do not trust my partner?"; "This is a unique erotic moment, why should I spoil it by proposing something anti-erotic". Even when partners individually have made up their mind to use protection, during intercourse they tend to give in to the combined pressure of their partner and the passionate atmosphere. Clearly, in the passionate love context, partners seem to place intimacy and trust above their own and their partner's health.

Care and respect

In my research, decreased protection was observed among young people in both causal and stable relationships that were perceived as passionate. Companionate partners were more likely to use protection; the companionate atmosphere of the relationship encouraged feelings of responsibility and concern for own and other's health and well-being and partners made a point of showing their care for other through the use of protection. Taking into account these findings and the fact that more young people prefer passionate love relationships to companionate ones, I believe that the difficulty of health campaigning to promote safer sex behavior among young people may be related to treating protection as an individual decision, rather than a decision taken within a love relationship, passionate or companionate. If we care to promote safer sex behavior and reduce diseases and unplanned pregnancies, protection should be clearly presented as a behavior in the context of both passionate and companionate love.

Could we also promote companionate love, which is consistent with protective behavior, as a means of increasing protection in youthful relationships? Companionate love and passionate love in relationships are not mutually exclusive. Some companionate love features are present in predominantly passionate youthful relationships. Health education could take advantage of companionate love features to put forth a model of love that mitigates passion with realistic care and respect for the well-being of one's partner. Western culture and particularly the pop culture addressing the younger generations, systematically uphold the influential myth of idealized, passionate love. It is indeed a mesmerizing myth! Yet, we should consider that it may also be detrimental, not just to decisions associated with love and sex, but also with ones associated with sustaining vital individual barriers within relationships of love. Perhaps we need another model of love, one that can compete with the popular myth of passionate love.

The keys

→ **Despite its popularity and functionality for starting a relationship, passionate love has a risky side. Companionate partners are more likely to use protection.**

→ **Protection should be clearly presented as a behavior in the context of both passionate and companionate love.**

→ **Health education could take advantage of companionate love features to put forth a model of love that mitigates passion with realistic care and respect for the well-being of one's partner.**

Panos Kordoutis is Associate Professor at the Department of Psychology of the Panteion University of Social and Political Sciences in Athens (Greece). His research interests and publications include the psychology of interpersonal relationships, intimate relationships and love, as well as the social psychology of health and prevention in the framework of intimate relationships and love.

The invisible wall

The earliest evidence of civilization in Lebanon dates back more than 7000 years. The country has the most religiously diverse society in the Middle East. Dr Aimee Karam **reports on how people try to deal with love when there are so many walls between them. Visible and invisible ones.**

There was an invisible wall. A man was living on one side of it. On the other side, a woman was watching. They found each other on a walking journey, out of the blue. Their eyes met. They felt strong love towards each other and communicated perfectly well. "This wall is a curse", he said. She smiled, but did not get to the core. In her openness to others, she had learned to become a true citizen of the world, far from racism, obscurantism and sectarianism. He practiced his religion vehemently with full duties. She lit a candle anywhere, in a thoughtful gesture towards him and others. For her, it did not matter. **Human ties were above all other rooted beliefs.** For him, he was still wondering as he trained to handle weapons, preparing for the civil war.

There are two paths. The first one is when different identities are open towards a perspective of growth, diversity, wisdom and acceptance. The other one is when the same identities become the platform to nurture closeness, fear and competition, blinding the mind and shutting off any possible dialogue. There were days when people were united, celebrating together. You could have heard the sounds of churches and mosques together. And then, they slipped into madness with one verdict: "You and I, we don't share anything in common."

Strength of life

In this part of the world, love is a challenge among people of different religions and different clans. Education teaches us that the brain is a dynamic entity, capable of developing, evolving and embracing dissonance, opposition and adversities. Young people meet, they are attracted by differences and novelty, but the war inflicted an archaism, an insult to the brain with sequels to repair. Evolution was interrupted and senescence declared. Instead of flourishing diversities, identities became 'killing identities'. However, the strength of life has proved stronger. People have traveled and become exposed, internet and connectivity are everywhere. People are eager to reinvent the world, the way they dream it, the way they vision it. They want to live it in its entire realities, without missing any of its facets. In their twenties they search for intimacy. In their forties they become champions of generativity with a new definition of individuation, fighting cowardice and overcoming divisions.

Some people do not have the guts to go further. For this reason, they deny having made a journey with each other. They find it useless to look in the mirror, as they become convinced that the road ends abruptly and consequently. They just stop. Some others keep on admiring the landscape around them and create the multifacets of human life. They manage to overcome the gaps and mark a victory. **Life is about guts**, some stay in the shelters, others take the plunge and avoid separation.

Powerful trust

The wall became a curse but the curse was just imagined as an inevitable punishment for escaping the rules. He decided to rebel against limitations. She gave him all the trust, the basic trust, the most powerful one. The infinite power dedicated to

illuminate his sky and forget the loss. She taught him the intelligence of acceptance, a glimmer of hope for humanity. They used their communication skills, their memories of the same land, their vision of a prosperous future, the magic of their fusion, they shared hope.

Life in this part of the world is about encompassing limits, learning adaptation and rescripting rules. **It is a push forward for the brain to evolve**, for the emotions to grow and for the sense of freedom to win. As for love, it is above all, the label of many returns, the endeavour and the real core of human life.

Aimee Karam PhD is a Clinical Psychologist at the Department of Psychiatry and Clinical Psychology of St George Hospital University Medical Center, Balamand university, Beirut (Lebanon). She is a founding member of IDRAAC, a non-profit non-governmental organization dedicated to mental health, research and education in Lebanon and the Arab World.

" Love is a challenge."

"When a partner offends,
the other partner wants to get even."

An eye for an eye

Worldwide, we count more than 2.5 million murders a year. Love, sex and intimate relationships are among the top motives. An eye for an eye, a tooth for a tooth. Dr **Johan Karremans** investigates revenge in daily loving relationships. It seems to be part of our nature.

Across the globe, conflicts and offence are an inevitable part of our relationships with others, perhaps especially so in the most loving relationships we have. Although this may be a somewhat pessimistic beginning of a chapter in *The World Book of Love*, it is true: the ones we love most dearly are also the ones who can hurt or offend us most strongly. A partner may say harmful things in the heat of an argument, forget your birthday, or ignore you at a party – there are many possible examples.

Is this troubling? Perhaps most of us would prefer an ideal world in which lovers never quarrel, in which they never say stupid or harmful things to each other during conflict. Yet, conflicts between lovers are a fact of life, but not the problem, per se. **The problem often is how we** *respond* **to our partner's apparent mistakes and negative acts.**
In our own research, we have found plenty of evidence showing that people have a strong tendency to respond in an eye-for-an-eye fashion when they feel hurt, even when that other person is one's romantic partner. Often driven by feelings of justice, when a partner offends,

the other partner wants to get even – or at least this is our initial response. This seems to be part of our nature.

Revenge

However, hitting back makes things worse rather than better, even though people often anticipate that they would feel better if they take revenge. In fact, they don't. We have seen in our own and other researchers' labs that partners who tend to retaliate or avoid their partner in the wake of an offensive act have less satisfying relationships in the long run, and are more likely to break up with their partner. Moreover, not only is a revengeful attitude toward the partner related to negative outcomes for the relationship, it is also related to decreases in personal happiness and even physical health. As one striking example, a study demonstrated that **people who merely think back to a partner's offence in a revengeful manner display increases in bodily stress, such as an elevated heart rate and blood pressure.** Having a vengeful attitude in a romantic relationship and responding in a vengeful manner toward one's partner's misbehaving, can have severe consequences for both the relationship and oneself.

Conflict

So what's the solution? How does one best respond to a partner's negative behavior? Given that, sooner or later, conflicts and offences do arise in most romantic relationships, one of the keys to a long and healthy romantic relationship is the ability to forgive one's partner. Forgiveness is the ability to hold back any negative feelings and urges to retaliate when a partner behaves badly, and instead to respond in a more kind and lenient manner. A decade of scientific research on interpersonal forgiveness has painted a clear picture: partners that are strongly committed to their relationship and who are able to forgive each other, are more satisfied with their relationship in the long run and have more stable relationships. Also, as a general rule, partners who are able to forgive each other (for example, for the other's failure to remember one's birthday), display increases in psychological well-being, both as an immediate result of forgiveness but also over the long run. In short, **forgiveness pays off – both personally and relationally.** This does not mean that we should "forgive everyone, everything, every night before we go to bed", as a famous advice columnist once suggested. There are probably 'unforgivable' offences, such as rape or severe physical violence. Also, forgiving a partner who never shows any signs of remorse does not lead to the same beneficial effects I have described above.

Perspective

I am well aware that it is easier said than done to forgive a partner, as it is often difficult to get rid of the negative thoughts and emotions related to whatever the partner has done wrong. Putting oneself in the partner's shoes can help to promote a forgiving attitude, and the reason is simple. Human behavior, including **a partner's offensive behavior, is driven, to a large extent, by external circumstances**. A partner may have behaved badly – but considering the circumstances in which the behavior took place, often it is sufficient to realize that you may have acted in a similar manner under those circumstances.

By taking the partner's perspective, you may understand that his or her intentions were not so bad after all. Indeed, there are a number of scientific studies that have demonstrated the powerful impact of taking the offender's perspective on our ability to forgive.

There is a lot more to say about forgiveness. In the past decade, researchers have learned a great deal about *what kind of* people generally are more forgiving, *when* people are more – or less – inclined to forgive, and *how* people actually come to forgiveness. But, in short, my own research findings and plenty of other findings by social scientists from many different countries around the world, convey a very consistent message, namely that forgiveness is an indispensible ingredient of a loving and lasting relationship.

The keys

→ **Sooner or later, conflicts and offenses do arise in most romantic relationships.**

→ **Having a vengeful attitude can have severe consequences for both the relationship and oneself. A key to a long and healthy romantic relationship is the ability to forgive.**

→ **Taking the offender's perspective has a powerful impact on our ability to forgive.**

Johan Karremans is Associate Professor at the Behavioral Science Institute of the Radboud University in Nijmegen (the Netherlands). He has published widely in scientific journals on topics such as forgiveness and how romantic partners shield themselves from attractive alternatives. Although he is not sure whether it is because of, or despite of, his knowledge about romantic relationships, he has been happily married for years. He and his wife have two daughters.

"True love
is the divine
unbreakable stone
in each of us."

The breath of love

"What is left for us when nothing is left? When life strips us of all we are composed of, our landmarks, our ways of thinking, our connections to beings and things, our habits? When all is decomposed, what is left?" **Thomas d'Ansembourg** takes us to the state of love. It seems to be only a breath away.

Go outside, now, in front of your house. Notice what surrounds you: walls, houses and streets, cities, villages and roads, churches and palaces, parks, forests and countryside. All that you see was built, raised, maintained and, sooner or later, will be demolished, dispersed, swept away. So, feel in between your fingers the air circulating around you. Feel in your nostrils and your lungs the air circulating within you and keeping you alive, taste that perfect flow: air brings life to everything without attaching to anything; air is essential to most forms of existence, but does not trap itself in any form; air gives itself joyfully to the movement of the world, but does not expect anything in return. Air is powerful; it can overturn or transport everything. Air is tender and sweet, it calms and refreshes. As it is not composed, it will not be decomposed. At the place where you are, now, at this moment, the only thing that is and will be, in five minutes just as in five thousand years, it is not you or the things around you, it is the air and wind that passes.

True love

Now realize that true love is of the same nature, the nature of the Breath which nourishes life in all its forms, infinitely strong, infinitely supple, infinitely renewed, abundant by nature, generous by essence and unable to attach or trap itself in anything. If it is stored, kept, weighed, measured, divided into parts and subject to trade or give and take, it dries, suffocates and dies, because its own nature is to give without measure. Finally, close your eyes and savor your true nature, our deep essence, which cannot be decomposed by anything: we are love. Of course, to savour that state we will have had to travel – often with difficulty – the steps of the human quest. For the child who is born says, "You love me, so I exist." For the adolescent who discovers another says, "I love you, so I exist." Then the spouses say, "We love each other, so we exist." **At those stages, love is always conditional, present with the fear that the condition will slip away….**

But there comes a time when love is no more linked to the very human cycle of relationships, to rituals of giving and receiving, to the separation between I and you, with no attachment to such or such form. There comes a time where we find, beyond humanity, our true nature of unconditional love anchored in that which Christiane Singer called "the divine unbreakable stone in each of us".

The state of love

During the past twenty years in which I have accompanied others through the cycles and seasons of life, I have acquired this conviction, that all, whatever they do, search – sometimes desperately – to taste that state of love which is their only belonging. If they often get carried away on the journey and seem to adopt ways which have the appearance of all the opposites of love, it is simply that they do not know what they are looking for, they do not know who they really are. Nobody has enlightened them on the deep meaning of life. Their education has given them fixed models and representations which, although they do not know it, are suffocating them. And then they attach to forms that they claim as being themselves (my house, my territory, my culture, my image, my religion) and adopt the wrong strategy and misunderstand their needs ("I force myself upon you because I would like you to love me; and behind that need to be loved, I do not know that my real need is to learn to love myself enough to be at peace in my heart and to no longer depend on what you think of me").

Without discernment, we stay in exile of ourselves: separated from ourselves, separated from others, separated from the Whole or God (according the designation you prefer – inevitably impoverished) in a cruel lack of love and unity. From that division of the innermost parts of ourselves emerge all our divisions, from guilt to quarrel, up to war. From that lack of self-intimacy emerges all our compensating systems, from all kinds of greed to addiction and up to mechanisms for monopolizing wealth.

It is our inner work – the work of inner citizenship – which allows us to find our true nature, our deepest impetus and our belonging to love, and to joyfully put ourselves, there where we are, serving the Breath of life.

The keys

→ **True love is of the same nature as the breath which nourishes life.
   Its own nature is to give without measure.**
→ **There comes a time where we find our true nature of unconditional love
   anchored in *the divine unbreakable stone in each of us.***
→ **It is our inner work which allows us to find our true nature and belonging
   to love and to joyfully put ourselves, there where we are, serving
   the Breath of life and love.**

Thomas d'Ansembourg is a lawyer, a writer and a psychotherapist (Belgium). He works as an international trainer and lecturer in human relationships and non-violent communication. His books are international bestsellers and have been translated into 28 languages. They include *Cessez d'être gentil, soyez vrai* (translated as *Being Genuine*). He received the award of the Festival of Psy-Authors in Nîmes (France). Together with Guy Corneau (Quebec), he co-founded the association Cœur.com.

"The meaning of love
is the creation of meaning."

Happy in love

"For modern people, all is clear: love is supposed to make you happy. Every love story starts with a strong element of 'luck'. But that is only the first step towards finding real happiness in love." **Wilhelm Schmid** shows the other steps to take.

When two people have finally, through luck and good fortune, found happiness together in an initial **by-luck-happiness**, a second happiness in this love can be **feel-good happiness**. Lovers can feel good with each together, have pleasure in each other's company, enjoy a great deal of sensuality together and find understanding and comfort in each other. Intentionally seeking this forms part of the work on happiness in love because, unlike happiness that is the fruit of luck, feel-good happiness can not only be helped to happen, but can be made to happen. The sole pre-condition for this is that lovers work to find out and explore by constant experimentation, how and with what they can do each other good. This can be a delicious meal, a long conversation, devoted tenderness, a wonderful evening, a night of passion and much more.

But if love is to last, a third type of happiness is necessary, the **happiness of a full existence**, the ability to play out the full range of human experiences, good and bad, joy and anger. Again, each half of a couple can take steps to promote this happiness. It all depends on the mental attitude derived from asking oneself: "What is characteristic of life and love? Is it not the polarity, the movement between opposites, which shows itself in everything? Am I able, fundamentally, to accept this? Do life and the relationship appear, to me, worthwhile if lived in their full potential polarity?" In this case, a happiness is possible, which has freedom to breathe, because I no longer find myself grasping desperately onto good times, which must not be allowed to end, but am able to accept also the other times of the common life.

Meaning

This three-fold happiness is important for love, but the most important thing is to convey a strong experience of meaning. Where this exists, people can find meaning in love when they are not happy. Meaning is inter-connectedness, and the bond between two persons provides strong inter-connectedness: protecting each other with different strengths and together being stronger than on their own. ("There is a person whom I know and who cares about me, someone with whom I can share ideas and for whom I feel something, even if perhaps right now only anger.") **Love is not the only way to find meaning, but it is a very effective one.** Because of the connections it can hunt down and consolidate, it is a greater provider of meaning in the modern era with its search for meaning, in which so many connections have broken down. The meaning of love is the creation of meaning. Many people see in love the only meaning of life, albeit with the risk that its failure then leads to meaninglessness, calling life into question.

Goodwill

Lovers can experience meaning with one another on several levels: physically, emotionally, mentally and transcendently. The ordering of this sequence is not intended to express the greater or lesser valuation of individual levels. Depending on the interpretation by which lovers are guided, their love can play out on one or several levels, and only they can answer the question of what should be the base level: physical encounter, emotional feeling, intellectual exchange? To equip the relationship with a maximum of both stability and flexibility, it seems reasonable to anchor it on more than one level. In this way, difficulties on one level can be cushioned by a shift to a different one. **Love can breathe best when it can wander backwards and forwards between various levels**, also when one partner moves out to meet the other on his or her own level, because a major difficulty of love is that lovers' needs are not always on the same level. Reinventing love means the same thing as 'letting love breathe', providing a to-and-fro between the closeness to and the distance from one another that everyone needs in order to rediscover him or herself.

Time colors of love

A constant task in modern life is the *synchronization* of ongoing tasks so as to define *common times* when partners can be there for each other, sharing meals, activities, chats, also disputes, for which otherwise only vacations and bank holidays remain. Of course, everyone's time is always too short. It is helpful, with many activities, to be tight-fisted with quarter-hours in order to gain time. It is also helpful to use **golden** hours in which work gets done particularly easily. Everyone can, with experience, identify these hours for himself, in order to squander the saved-up time with everything that both find attractive. Undoubtedly in terms of quantity, it is the **gray** hours that dominate everyday life, but strong contrasts in the picture of life are provided by the **pink** hours of erotic encounter, the **red** hours of strong feelings, the **blue** hours of intense discussion, the **purple** hours of utter self-forgetfulness and also as many as possible **lime-green** hours of simple satisfaction. With this colorful palette, one is best able to endure the hopefully rare **yellow** hours of jealousy and **black** hours of all kinds that complete the color theory of love.

If I want to reduce to a common denominator what I have learned over the many years of work on love, then it is this: in today's modern conditions, love is dependent on two people exhibiting a great deal of goodwill to one another, otherwise nothing works any more. Where once the bond between two people was guaranteed and, indeed, enforced from outside by religion, tradition and convention, it must today come from within, and it is not always just about feelings. Love is also a decision, one that each individual must take for himself. This is the new philosophy of love.

The keys

→ **If love is to last, we have to move from luck and feel-good to a third type: the happiness of full existence.**

→ **The most important thing is to convey a strong experience of meaning, on several levels, to let love breathe.**

→ **Love is a decision. It must come from within and needs a great deal of goodwill towards one another.**

Wilhelm Schmid lives in Berlin and teaches philosophy as Adjunct Professor at the University of Erfurt (Germany). For many years, he has worked as a philosophical counselor at a hospital in Zurich (Switzerland). He has published several books on love, including *Liebe – Warum sie so schwierig ist und wie sie dennoch gelingt* (*Love – Why It Is So Difficult, and How It Nonetheless Succeeds*) and *Die Liebe neu erfinden* (*Rediscovering Love*), republished in paperback as *Die Liebe atmen lassen* (*Letting Love Breathe*).

Love in Vietnam: tinh cam

"Love, like other emotions, does not have an essential core. Love is neither trans-historical nor universal. Love derives its salience from the particular topography of affect within which it is situated", say Harriet M. Phinney and Khuat Thu Hong. Let's take the example of *tinh cam* and love in Vietnam to understand this.

Recognitions of and decisions about whom and what one loves and considers lovable, and when love is appropriate, are malleable, shaped by changing rules, regulations and political economies, and are historically specific.

There are 54 ethnic groups in Vietnam, all of which have their own beliefs and customs regarding love and marriage. The majority ethnic group, the Kinh, who constitute 90 % of the population, exhibit regional diversity as well. In general, the Kinh have a rich literary and folk tradition on love that informs everyday practice. This syncretic tradition, which derives from Confucian, Buddhist and indigenous Southeast Asian beliefs and customs, revolves around an individual's relationship and obligations to the family and extended kinship network – in particular the husband's family. Because people primarily conceptualize themselves in terms of their relations to others, the Kinh concept of the individual is inherently relational rather than atomistic or singular. When considering marriage, each person must generally consider the effects of their decision on the larger extended family. As a result, there may be a difference between whom one falls in love with and whom one marries.

Voluntary love

This disjuncture has roots in pre-revolutionary Vietnamese society (pre-1945) when parents arranged their children's marriages, children had little say in who they married, polygyny was a common practice among high status families, and women were socialized to be self-sacrificing and subservient to men. Confucian family doctrine viewed conjugal love as a sentiment that would develop over time as couples lived, work, aged and became intimate with one another. Bearing and raising children provided the necessary *soi day* (string) to bind a couple, enabling them to live together until "their teeth were loose and hair gray" (*rang long dau bac*).

During the 1920s and 1930s, the desire to marry for love became a focus of intellectual social discourse. With the passage of the first Marriage and Family Law in 1959, arranged or coercive marriages became illegal and 'worthy and voluntary love' became the requisite basis for marriage. Both the bride and groom had to consent to marriage

" Heaven determines who falls in love with whom."

and the minimum marriage age was raised. The shift in marital law and recognition of existing social changes enabled young men and women to explore romantic affiliations in new ways. Nonetheless, due to communist proscriptions and wartime disruption, many lovers were not able to marry. **In many cases, sacrifice of an individual's love for the sake of collective goals (family, nation, etc.) was encouraged and praised.** In this period, romantic love was understood as pure, platonic love; sex was permissible only within marriage.

Predestined

Since the advent of Doi Moi (Renovation) in 1986, rapid social and economic changes have enabled young people to develop premarital romantic attachments and to choose whom they marry. While parental consent is still requisite, parents do not command the same amount of control over whom their children marry as previously. However, choices about whom to marry may not coincide with whom one loves romantically. Instead, **a spouse will be chosen according to whether they are compatible with one's family.** While marriage continues to be the only appropriate domain for sex, premarital sex has increased among many young people; sex has become an integral part of love.

How do people talk about love today? Sharing love is to have *tinh cam* (sentiment/understanding/feelings) with someone. *Tinh cam* entails having sympathy for someone, being supportive, respectful and willing to sacrifice for them, and having true compatibility. When someone has not fallen in love or is not able to marry the person whom he or she loves, they may attribute it to fate. When people do fall in love, it may also be considered fate or *duyen*. *Duyen* translates roughly as 'predestined love'; it recalls the tale of Ong To and Ba Nguyet who, in 'heaven', determine which boy and girl will fall in love with each other.

Harriet M. Phinney, is Assistant Professor of Anthropology, Seattle University, Seattle (USA). She has a broad interest in Vietnam and mainland Southeast Asia, including research on affect and emotion.
Khuat Thu Hong (PhD Sociology) is Co-Director of the Institute for Social Development Studies in Hanoi (Vietnam). She has spent decades researching love and relationships in Vietnam.

"How could you have lied to me like this?"

The shadow of love

How jealous are you? Popular magazines have you do the test asking questions about how possessive you are in romantic relationships. Jealousy is a green-eyed monster hiding to different degrees in most of us. Prof **Ayala Malach Pines** has studied the monster and our ways of getting this shadow of love under control.

The jealous response is triggered when there is a perceived threat to the relationship. The perceived threat may be real or imagined (just as the relationship can be real or imagined). If a man thinks that his wife is interested in other men, even if the threat is a result of his own wild imagination (as is the case in pathological, delusional jealousy), he is going to respond with intense jealousy. On the other hand, if a woman has a close friendship with another man, but her husband feels secure in their marriage and does not feel threatened by this friendship, he is not likely to respond with jealousy.

Blind love

The word jealousy is derived from the Greek word *zelos* which signifies emulation and zeal, and denotes intensity of feelings. Romantic jealousy is the jealousy that emerges in romantic relationships. It evokes different images, emotions and thoughts and is defined very differently by different people. I would like to offer the following definition: jealousy is a complex reaction to a perceived threat to a valued relationship.

This reaction has both internal and external components. The internal component includes certain emotions, thoughts and physical symptoms that often are not visible to the outside world. The emotions associated with jealousy may include pain, anger, rage, envy, sadness, fear, grief or humiliation. The thoughts associated with jealousy may include resentment ("How could you have lied to me like this?"), self-blame ("How could I have been so blind, so stupid?"), comparison with the rival ("I'm not as attractive, sexy, intelligent, successful"), concern for one's public image ("Everyone knows, and laughs at me"), or self-pity ("I'm all alone in the world, nobody loves me"). The physical symptoms associated with jealousy may include blood rushing to the head, sweaty and trembling hands, shortness of breath, stomach cramps, feeling faint, a fast heartbeat and trouble falling asleep. The external component is more clearly visible to the outside world and is expressed in some kind of behavior: talking openly about the problem, screaming, crying, ignoring the issue, using humor, retaliating, leaving or becoming violent.

Feeling like an idiot

The fact that jealousy has both an internal and an external component has an important implication for coping. Even if people can modify the internal component to some extent, most have relatively little control over it, especially over their emotional and physical responses: "I wish I could be cool and rational about it, but the pain is simply too big." "I stood there like an idiot, blood rushing to my face, and couldn't do a thing to stop it." However, people can be trained to have more control over their thoughts. Actually, the premise of cognitive therapy is that we can change our feelings by changing our thoughts.

People have far greater control over the external component of their jealousy than over the internal component. They don't always realize this (and even when they do, they don't always want to admit it), but they can – if they choose to – talk about their feelings, make fun of the whole thing, cry their hearts out, suffer silently and covertly or loudly and visibly, lash out in anger, get out of the relationship, try to make their mate jealous or throw dishes.

When one is overwhelmed by jealousy, it is important to remember that while it may be difficult to control jealous feelings, changing the thoughts that trigger them may help keep the feelings in check. Furthermore, most people have significant control over what they decide to do about their jealousy.

The keys

→ **Jealousy is a complex reaction to a perceived threat to a valued relationship. It has both internal and external components.**

→ **People have far greater control over the external component of their jealousy than over the internal component.**

→ **While it may be difficult to control jealous feelings, changing the thoughts that trigger them may help keep the feelings in check.**

Professor Ayala Malach Pines is a clinical, social and organizational psychologist and author of the book *Romantic Jealousy: Causes, Symptoms and Cures*. This successful book has been translated into nine different languages. She is the Dean of the Faculty of Management at Ben-Gurion University of the Negev (Israel). Her research includes job burnout and couple burnout. She has published ten books, thirty book chapters and more than one hundred research articles.

" Life is when love comes to matter."

The basis of life? Love.

"I contend that meeting is at the origin of life and the proliferation of cells on the Earth's surface. More specifically, we are talking of a romantic encounter", says neuro-scientist Jean-Didier Vincent, **who has spent a lifetime looking for the basis of life. The answer is: love.**

To the solid geometry of crystal, love opposes the fragility of elective affinities between molecules, different and complementary entities that recognize themselves as such; love animated by uncertain forces, the violent necessity of which sweeps along everything in its path, but that a contrary breath is enough to knock down; love that delivers matter to the demon of diversity and to the perverse game of natural selection.

The Goethean aphorism "In the beginning was action", I propose replacing with "In the beginning was Love." This means that **desire is supported primarily by the expression of the flesh in the brain** (emotions and feelings), with action intervening only in the passage to the outward act, in particular sexual intercourse. For this reason, I hold to be true the opinion of Schopenhauer that "Any amorous inclination [...] however ethereal its appearances, is rooted solely in the sexual instinct (desire) and is no more than a more defined, more specialized and, strictly speaking, more individualized sexual instinct." Adopting a strictly naturalist position, I would say then that "life is when love comes to matter".

Desire and aversion

It is not unreasonable to suggest that love and sex, like everything in the field of life, are matters of chemistry. A particular neuro-transmitter, *dopamine*, plays a major role in the genesis of pleasure and desire. Dosing this substance by introducing tiny cannulas into a region of the brain, the *nucleus accumbens*, an important relay of the systems of desire, shows that the presence of dopamine varies not only depending on desire and pleasure, but also on aversion and suffering. These emotions coming from the body are specified by their object that gives them meaning, for example "I am dying of love for A" or "I am full of resentment against B". A neuro-hormone, *oxytocin*, released into both the blood and the basal region of the brain, is involved in orgasm, and further on in the attachment between the two partners, even in the fidelity of the couple. It can therefore be considered, to some extent, as the hormone of monogamy, but equally that of adultery; **sex hormones are not servants of morality in humans,** and in animals remain the humble agents of the mechanics of sex.

Rotten fruit

We must be careful not to assign the exclusive cause to one particular molecule or gene. **The chemistry of our feelings is powerless to solve the existential problems of this strange beast that is the human** (male and female). In order to recognize each other and to stay permanently together (for very variable periods), sensory, visual, tactile and olfactory cues and sweet words, like a marriage hymn, do not need hormones to trigger a passion that, initially at least, considers itself eternal. The extreme sociability of humans imposes a number of rules of conduct that prevent differences between individuals from degenerating into mortal combat, which would weaken the group and very rapidly the entire species. Thus starts to operate a cultural evolution that replaces physical evolution. During childhood, representations of the 'desired other one' are created in the brain; the object of love that remains latent until puberty when hormonal pressures reactivate the cognitive maps which, when vandalized in the young person, will go on to express themselves in the adult in perverse behaviors, the rotten fruit of love, this inexhaustible engine of man's imagination.

Jean-Didier Vincent is a neuropsychiatrist and neuroscientist, born in 1935. He was Professor of Physiology at the Faculty of Medicine of the University of Paris XI. He is a Fellow of the French Institute (Academy of Sciences) and the National Academy of Medicine. Jean-Didier Vincent has contributed greatly to the development of neuroendocrinology which includes the study of interactions between hormones and nervous system. He has written several books, the best known of which is *The Biology of Emotions*.

The intelligence of emotions

The American magazine Foreign Policy named her one of the Top 100 Global Thinkers. She has thoroughly studied the intelligence of emotions. Martha C. Nussbaum on the desiderata for love.

In asking normative questions about conceptions of love, we would do well to begin with the problems the philosophical tradition has identified, namely, with love's links to excessive neediness and a related vengefulness, and to a narrow partiality of concern. And, in fact, the therapeutic accounts I have studied all explicitly address these three problems, claiming to have produced a love that is free of them. We need to assess these claims. My account of early childhood love suggests that, in asking questions about excessive neediness, we would do well to focus on pathological shame, seeing a persisting shame at the very face of one's own needy humanity as a danger sign, a warning that narcissistic projects of manipulation and control may be in the offing. In thinking about love's connection to aggression, we would also do well to focus on the management or containment of disgust. An ascent of love that encourages disgust, with its bounding off of the self from contamination, is unlikely to have surmounted harmful aggression in a stable way.

An adequate assessment of these ascent therapies also requires some positive normative criteria. Although we cannot evaluate these accounts completely without defending a complete ethical theory, we can focus, at least, on the following desiderata, which many otherwise different ethical theories emphasize:

1. Compassion

The view of love (or, rather, the love that is left in someone who lives according to the view) should make room for and support general compassion. We have identified as constituents of compassion: reasonable accounts, that is, of the seriousness of various human predicaments, of our responsibility for these predicaments and of the proper extent of concern.

2. Reciprocity

The view of love (or, rather, the love that is left in someone who lives according to the view) should make room for and support reciprocal relationships of concern in which people treat one another not just as things, but as agents and as ends, and in which they respond to one another with the 'subtle interplay' described by psychoanalyst Donald Winnicott. Any account of love that purports to show how love can become a force for good in society ought to be able to show that it

"Don't treat each other as things but as agents and ends."

can handle this challenge – making room for reciprocity both inside the relationship of erotic love itself and also in other social relationships to which the love is closely linked. Thus, there are actually two questions here: does the love itself contain reciprocity, and does it support other reciprocal relationships? These points are in principle independent, in the sense that a reciprocal love might be so exclusive that it would discourage all other relationships, reciprocal or otherwise, and a love focused on possession, rather than reciprocity might prove compatible with reciprocal relationships in other areas of life. On the other hand, we can see that there is a plausible link between them: for example, if men are encouraged by a normative picture of love to think of women as objects for their use and control, this is not likely to encourage reciprocal relationships between men and women in social and political life. Love gives us understandings of value that we then translate into other spheres.

3. Individuality

Any view of love that is going to be ethically good in itself, or conduce to further social goods, should recognize and make central the fact that human beings are individuals. This is an elusive notion. One aspect of individuality is *separateness*. By this I mean that people have distinct bodies and lives, and lives that are their own to live. Each pursues a separate course of life from birth to death, a separate course of joy and grief, elation and sorrow, that never fuses organically with the life of anyone else (except before a child is born, entering this world of objects). The food given to A does not miraculously arrive in the stomach of B (unless B is that prebirth child); the satisfaction of D does not remove or balance out the misery of C. Nor is this separateness merely spatio-temporal: each person has just one chance at life in this world, a chance to live a life that is that person's life and nobody else's.

A second aspect of individuality is *qualitative distinctness*. All people (also identical twins, and even the clones of the future) have distinct properties, over and above the sheer spatio-temporal differences involved in separateness. They have their own distinct talents and tastes, projects and plans, flaws and virtues, and these are wrapped up together in a way that makes it natural to name each by a proper name.

Of these two aspects of individuality, what I have called separateness seems the more significant, if, by this, we mean separateness not in the mere spatio-temporal sense, but in the richer sense suggested here. However similar people are in socially appealing and any view of love that subverts them is likely to be socially suspect. Indeed, it seems to me that, in insisting on these three features, we need not leave the sphere of political consensus at all: they can be endorsed by a wide plurality of reasonable ethical conceptions. We see, in fact,

their qualitative properties, the fact that each has just one life to live, that person's own life, is a very salient ethical fact. However much influenced by another, or wrapped up in another, only I can live my own life. Consider snowflakes. Each one is qualitatively distinct, or so we are told. So each has that sort of individuality and each is even spatio-temporally distinct. And yet we would not think of snowflakes as having 'individuality' in the sense that we think relevant to our humanity, or to ethics.

These three features seem important for any ethical view that we are likely to find attractive, and they can be shared by ethical views of several different kinds. They are also good features for a view that is likely to support the mutual respect of citizens in a liberal-democratic society – so any view of love that shores them up is likely to be

that several of our ascent conceptions prove supportive of all three features – even though they belong to quite different comprehensive ethical/religious traditions.

Martha C. Nussbaum is Ernst Freud Distinguished Professor of Law and Ethics at the University of Chicago (USA). She is the author of numerous influential books, including *Upheavals of Thought, the Intelligence of Emotions* (in which this chapter is to be found as well). She has forty honorary degrees from colleges and universities in North America, Europe and Asia.

do not let it slide; seek help. If you are not satisfied with how things are going, you owe it to yourself and your partner to tell them how you feel. And listen and be respectful when your partner does the same. If things are becoming ho-hum, take a chance and spice things up. Try a new position, buy some sexy apparel, incorporate sex toys, watch some erotica together, whatever interests you. Maintaining a good sex life takes time, effort and the willingness to take some risks.

Don't stop touching. Regularly touch one another. Cuddle and hold hands more often. Give each other massages. Physical affection communicates appreciation and closeness. Affection can foster sexual intimacy and help carry couples through times when circumstances (like new babies) and health challenges get in the way of an active sex life. A good place to start is to say good morning and good night, hello and goodbye, with genuine warmth and affection–every single time. Banish the perfunctory kiss on the cheek. Think about how dogs greet their best friends on reunion–the big smile, the thumping tail, the wriggling butt. Wouldn't it be nice to come home to that sort of greeting from our romantic partner? We can learn a lot about the value of touch and affection from our furry friends.

These practices do require effort, especially in the beginning. Sometimes we need to act a certain way to start feeling that way. But, as we recapture more loving feelings and behaviors, the rewards will follow.

The keys

→ **Love can last. To keep love alive in the long term, we must cultivate the same sorts of feelings and behaviors that came so easily in the beginning.**

→ **Be decent, appreciate your partner, break out, keep your sex life alive and don't stop touching.**

→ **Lasting love requires some effort. We need to act a certain way to start feeling that way.**

Kim Bartholomew is Professor of Psychology at Simon Fraser University (Canada). She has spent over twenty years conducting research and teaching in the field of close relationships. Her research has explored attachment processes in adult relationships, abusive relationships, same-sex relationships and, more recently, sexuality within relationships.

Love on the Internet

"In the West more than half of the dating between people in their thirties takes place via emotional or sexual partnering sites", says Prof Pascal Lardellier. He studies the Networks of the Heart: sex, love and seduction on the Internet.

When sociologists examine how love stories begin nowadays certain facts stand out.

An initial observation is that, over the past forty years, the number of singles in Western societies has been constantly rising. The number of adults living unpartnered has doubled since 1970. Everyone, male and female, feels under a strong pressure: to develop and succeed professionally, and, at the same time, under often insistent pressure from family and friends, to earn the wherewithal to 'support a couple'. Because the couple remains a social norm and the basis of the family. In fact, it has never been so difficult for people to meet emotionally in these days of triumphant communication media. This is a curious paradox.

Closed eyes

'In the old days', we met in real life first, before falling in love and thinking of living with someone. But the advent of the Internet significantly changed the rules of the traditional romantic encounter. And everyone seeking love quickly realized the benefit they could derive from this 'relational technology', enabling them to seduce while free from the burden of the body and social conventions. Falling in love on the Internet often takes the form of becoming attached to someone whom you first meet 'from the inside'; it is loving an 'intimate stranger'. In short, it reverses the logic of seduction and birth of feelings.

Another finding: researchers are discovering in digital networks, the same sociological logic that existed previously: the tendency to go for people who are like ourselves, and producing pairs belonging to the same social categories, the same religion and sharing similar values. In fact, we find socio-cultural affinities once again playing a key constitutive role in the formation of many couples. This seems all the more surprising given that Internet interaction always starts between anonymous persons. Love appears to be not as blind as we might have thought. Cupid enables us to find our other half with closed eyes on the web.

Prisoners of the Net

Of course, the Internet is a real solution for finding one's 'soulmate', but provided you do not remain a prisoner of the virtual. It is important to open up, to move frequently to the other side of the screen, remembering that in Ovid's *Metamorphoses,* Pygmalion engaged in a virtual relationship (even then!), with her beautiful statue Galatea.

"Love appears to be not as blind as we might have thought."

And moving from one mirage to another, Narcissus preferred his image to the tender inclination of the muse Echo, and drowned as a result.

But we still love 'for real' nowadays, **however great the temptation to stay hidden behind the screen, which ultimately protects.** Of course, we will still continue to meet in real life, to desire bodies, to start beautiful *In Real Life* stories. But we will increasingly use ICT and its providential resources in order to meet and love. Nowadays, in the West, more than half of the dating between people in their thirties takes place via emotional or sexual partnering sites.

Behind the screen

When everything is in flux, it is good to return to the wisdom of the ancients. Between *The Art of Love*, Ovid's manual of uninhibited seduction, and Plato's *Symposium* and its beautiful account of the origin of fusional relationships, love hesitates, choosing sometimes one and sometimes the other, influenced also by the mores of the particular era. The 'emotional Net' permits us to opt for the emotional-sexual model of 'interchangeability'. But for a short time only. Because however cynical or disillusioned, many singles on the Internet retain the intuition that a unique and very special person lurks just behind the screen, and that they will finally be brought into contact, like the two halves of Plato's androgyne. **Love is the intensity**

of shared vibrations. In the Internet Age, love-seekers of both sexes try to trap Venus or Cupid with technology. Occasionally, the latter deign to offer them to share these vibrations. At this stage in the game, it is up to our Net lovers to invent a story, to learn to become a couple. It's there that the hardest part begins. For Internet, which binds, is quick to untie. And the story of love relationships, never finished, continues to be written…

Pascal Lardellier is a Professor at the University of Burgundy in Dijon (France) and an author and lecturer. He specializes in the social uses of the Internet. On this subject, he has published *Le coeur NET. Célibat et amours sur le Web* (*The Networked Heart. Celibacy and Love on the Net*), *Le pouce et la souris. Enquête sur la culture numérique des ados* (*The Thumb and the Mouse. Survey of Teenage Digital Culture*) and *Les réseaux du coeur. Sexe, amour et séduction sur Internet* (*Networks of the Heart. Sex, Love and Seduction on the Internet*). He gives frequent lectures on these topics and writes columns in several newspapers and magazines.

"Love is."

Loving is being

"Love is so inextricably associated with other human experiences – intimacy, sex, marriage, spirituality, desire – that it's hard to think about or feel love as the sheer experience it is and the way it transforms a person", says **Jasmeet Kaur.** Loving is being.

Based on my work and my own personal experiences over the past 22 years, I believe that what all of us are trying to reach through these various relationships is the enduring phenomenon of loving, and that the journey to reach it contains immense personal growth and transformation. It is a state of being. For me, loving is feeling fully alive and caring towards another person where the other's needs and selfhood feel as important as one's own. It is not static, and defies precise definition, but rather unfolds different feelings and aspects of one's identity and grows over time.

Four phases

Different phases emerge in the process of reaching loving as a state of being: falling in love, feeling loved, feeling unlovable and loving itself. The initial '**falling in love**' is only a starting phase. Actually, it is just the first rush of feelings of liking and attraction and the joy of being seen as 'special' to another person and finding someone who is special to oneself. In a way, one is more in love with one's evoked feelings of aliveness, affection, openness and desire. This state shifts as the two involved people become more intimate with each other. Being treated as special by another person makes one 'feel loved' – a delicious and seductive feeling. One is in the receiving position and it brings up three intense processes: a) the desire for all of one's needs to be met by the loved one, including fulfilment of past unmet needs, to keep 'feeling loved'; b) the desire for constant fusion and sameness, so that one never feels alone or vulnerable; c) disturbing and unpleasant feelings and fears (jealousy, greed, hurt, selfishness, etc) which reveal one's imperfections – the feelings and the reality of imperfections can be unbearable. Obviously, the other cannot satisfy all our desires and expectations, nor protect us from our distressing feelings, and thus we start seeing the other's limitations and realness. If there is no inner acceptance of one's imperfections, it leads to feeling that one is unlovable. Here begins an intense struggle, change process and understanding of loving itself.

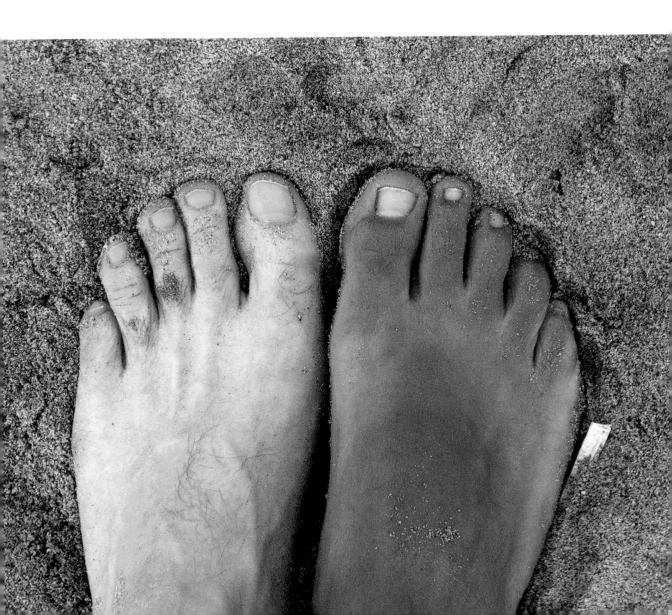

Surrender

When we allow ourselves to just experience and deal with these processes and not be immersed in or submerged by them, we begin the process of self-acceptance and move away from fervently wanting the other to change or take away all our unwanted feelings. There is an ally inside us – our love for the other also creates a desire to want the best for him/her. Staying in touch with this gives a strength to learn to bear our stresses and inner storms. The withstanding of discomforts, disappointment or intense wishes happens by keeping in mind those equally alive moments of tenderness and passion which we have felt for the other. To see time as a merging continuum where we allow the good of the past to co-exist with the painful of the present (or vice versa) enables us to accept our full self and take in the whole of who our beloved is. Once we like and accept our real self, we begin seeing and valuing our beloved as they are, being tolerant of their desires and flaws.

The notion of surrender is pivotal for loving another. Surrender is to give oneself up to the phenomenon of love and all the experiences it brings with it. This lessens the identification with one's ego and allows for deep acceptance. **The ego disappears as one surrenders** and becomes open to all the feelings and experiences which come up in the intimate relationship without resisting or rejecting any, abandons trying to control and steer things only in the direction one wants or finds pleasurable. The transformation from being identity-bound, self-defined to a fluid, receiving-and-giving person happens only when we surrender to the flow. Loving becomes an ongoing state of being when we feel care for the other's humanness as much as our own and celebrate the connectedness that exists. Loving another actually changes us and introduces us to our tenderness, compassion, transcending of self-absorption, openness, acceptance and tolerance.

East and West: cultural shades of love

Some differences in recognizing and defining love exist between all cultures. Compare, for instance, the Indian culture and the Anglo-Saxon cultures of North America and Europe (broadly called 'East' and 'West' respectively). In Eastern culture, there is more emphasis on 'being', while the Western focus is more on 'doing' and this is also true in the domain of love. The 'being' focus consists of connecting with one's internal experiences and consciousness and holding the loved one in one's awareness. This way presupposes that one's external actions will flow in a natural caring way when one is 'being loving' inside. In Western culture, the dominant focus is on doing or not doing things for the other, demonstrating, expressing and changing behavior or the environment outside in order to feel the love. The action and active dimensions of love and creating external spaces of love are given greater higher focus.

Another difference is in the way love is examined by a majority of thinkers, researchers and helping professionals. In the West, it is explained or broken up into discrete, smaller dimensions in an analyzing, categorizing/organized manner, while in the East the attitude or inner experience of love is explored and talked about as an overall stance or phenomenon. These perspectives are then communicated widely in mainstream society, which influences how people begin identifying and viewing love.

These differences can become troublesome when two people from different cultures experience love for each other. Both partners feel love, but they express it in different ways and also expect to see it in the form in which they recognize love, based on their internal cultural imprints. Being implicit, these definitions of love are rarely recognized in the early stages. It is more liberating to look for each other's definitions of love and ways to express them. In the words of leading 21st century thinker and psychoanalyst, Sudhir Kakar: "Love is not about something. It is."

The keys

→ **Four different phases emerge in the process of reaching loving as a state of being: falling in love, feeling loved, feeling unlovable and loving itself.**

→ **The notion of surrender is pivotal for loving another: the ego disappears.**

→ **In the East, there is more emphasis on 'being' while the West focuses more on 'doing' and this is also true in the domain of love.**

Jasmeet Kaur is a psychotherapist and group dynamics trainer in New Delhi (India). She holds a BA degree (honors) in Psychology from Delhi University India and MSc in Marriage, Family and Child Counseling from California State University USA. She returned to work in India in the early 1990s, making her one of the first formally-trained couples therapy professionals in India. She has served on the governing boards of the Indian Society for Applied Behavioral Science and Indian Association for Family Therapy. In 2012, she chaired an international conference on Intimate Relationships and Couples Therapy in India.

"We are walking a path full of mystery and excitement."

The magic formula

The magic pill, the mystery drink and the enchanted glance: we all love to believe they exist. Dr **Xiaomeng Xu** has examined whether there is evidence-based and universal advice for long-lasting love: the magic formula.

One of the interesting questions about romantic love is whether or not it differs significantly across cultures. Past research using questionnaires has found differences between people from East Asian cultures (e.g. China) and those from Western cultures (e.g. USA), in that Easterners tend to talk about romantic love in more reserved ways, emphasizing pragmatic concerns such as security and family values, rather than things like passion and excitement. However, because how we talk about our feelings is influenced by our culture, it is difficult to know whether or not cross-cultural differences exist in how people actually *experience* love, or just in the way they talk about that experience. Because Chinese culture tends to value reserve and modesty, Chinese people may just not be as expressive about their feelings when asked on a questionnaire. At the same time, American culture may subtly push Americans to be especially expressive about their feelings.

Brain activity

I became very interested in this question and wanted to use a non-questionnaire based method to really look at whether the *experience* of love is cross-culturally different.

Researchers had already started looking at early-stage love using neuroimaging techniques, but these studies had only been done with Westerners. Therefore, I decided to use functional Magnetic Resonance Imaging (fMRI) in an Eastern culture to see if brain activity differed or not, cross-culturally. Luckily, I had some wonderful collaborators who helped me carry out this study, which we conducted in Beijing, China. We found that for Chinese people who had fallen in love, their brain activations while looking at a picture of their romantic partner were almost identical to those of Americans. We were able to conclude then that despite significant differences between how Chinese and Americans talk about love, **what's actually going on in the brain when they fall in love is pretty much the same.** Other researchers have gone on to extend these findings and show that brain activations associated with falling in love are quite similar for men and women, and for heterosexual and homosexual people. So, despite the infinite nuances in how we express and define love, the experience seems to be rather universal.

Happily Ever After

I often get asked for relationship advice, as if we might have found some magic formula that ensures the Hollywood version of Happily Ever After. While love is fundamentally similar, no matter who you are, decades of research tells us that there is no 'one right path' for love to take. Some people fall in love quickly and intensely; others fall in love slowly, perhaps even over many years. Romantic relationships can evolve over time with many ups and downs, or they can stay very much the same as they always were. You may end up as the cute old couple who hold hands and walk together in the park and share a very companionate kind of love. You may end up as the old couple who are still all over each other decades after they first got together. Or you may end up having a very rich and diverse social network of friends and family that your romantic partner is just one part of. There are many possibilities ranging far and wide with almost infinite variations in between, all of which can be just as valid, satisfying and wonderful. Therefore, **it is important to be careful when comparing your relationship to other relationships**, particularly those in movies or in the media (which tend to be less realistic). While other relationships may be inspiring, always thinking about how things 'should' be, or trying to pursue a 'perfect' relationship, can be detrimental, especially if these sorts of comparisons lead you to feel like a failure. Many things influence relationship quality and whether or not a relationship lasts, including factors outside of the relationship (health problems, financial hardships, other stressors and traumatic events, etc.) and it does not necessarily reflect a personal deficit if your relationship does not work out, or works out differently from how you perceive the relationships of those around you.

The best chance

There *is* some general advice the literature can give on how to help a fledgling romance attain a better chance of survival or help a more established relationship retain its lustre:

→ Be respectful.

→ Be affectionate.

→ Communicate often and well.

→ Have social connections and support outside of your relationship with each other.

→ Do fun and exciting things together.

→ Have complementary goals and help each other move towards them.

But here's the thing: there are no fast and hard rules that can guarantee how things will turn out. Each relationship is a special story and your individual narrative will be no exception. Only you can experience it and only you can know if it is right. Enjoy it, knowing that you are taking part in a universal and fundamental human experience, but also that you are walking down a unique path, full of mystery and excitement, and the potential for incredible meaning and happiness.

The keys

→ **Despite significant differences between how we talk about love, our brain activities when falling in love are pretty much the same for men and women, heterosexuals and homosexuals, Chinese and Americans.**

→ **Every path and relationship is different. Don't compare (particularly not to what you see in movies and media).**

→ **General advice to give your relationship a better chance of survival includes respect, affection, communication, connection, fun and goals.**

Xiaomeng (Mona) Xu was born in Fuling (China) and moved to the USA when she was five. She grew up in New York City and attended college at New York University where she worked as a research assistant in the Couples Lab and promptly fell in love with close relationships research. She went to graduate school at Stony Brook University (USA), receiving a PhD in Social Health Psychology in 2011, and has conducted research in Beijing (China) with The Chinese Academy of Sciences.

Love
is not the
question(*)

(*)

Love is the answer

Sex in love

"Sex is the physical expression of love."

Being a sexologist in Singapore, Dr Martha Tara Lee meets a great variation of couples in her therapy. What is her best advice? "To have the loving relationship and mind-blowing sex you have always wanted, you need to return to love. Love is not the question, it is the answer."

Sex, love and intimacy are regarded as interrelated. Since sex is often viewed as the physical expression of love, the lack of sex in a relationship can pose problems, especially with regards to feeling loved and accepted unconditionally. While sex is not the most important thing in a relationship, the lack of sex can become an issue if one partner feels it is one. This is especially pronounced where unequal power dynamics are created, from one partner being the sole breadwinner and the other being a homemaker, financially dependent on the other; or even from couples who work alongside each other in the same company (usually their own). This is usually complicated with their own questioning of male-female roles and the usually unspoken expectations imposed upon their partner.

More than once I have been touched by the manifestations of love evident between the couple sitting before me – from the way they link fingers, gaze into each other's eyes or smile from the heart. It's almost akin to subconsciously saying "It's us against the world" as they brace themselves for

their session with me. I have also sat mainly silent witnessing the onslaught of tears, shouts and yelling as couples express the pain from the depths of their soul. I continue to be amazed by the resilience we humans possess. I have come to recognize that I am most useful when it comes to helping my clients reconcile within themselves the kind of person they want to be, before discussing the relationship they desire to be in (including the sexual aspect). From there, I will facilitate greater understanding of the ways they long to be loved.

In short, they need to take steps in being whole and complete themselves (inside) before they can begin to express and reach out to their partner (inside to out). The saying, "You need to learn how to love yourself before you can love another" certainly rings true. After all these years, here are some tips relating to love I would like to recommend to you.

1. Exercise extreme self-care. Self-care refers to taking care of your needs, listening to your body and resting when you are tired instead of over-extending yourself. Care for yourself as a parent would take care of a child.

2. Practice self-love. Self-love consists of your internal dialogue or self-talk and how you treat yourself when you mess up. While we often look externally for validation of worthiness, this unconditional love for self stems from the understanding that you can only be truly good for somebody else when you can first love and accept yourself.

3. Commit to honesty. A lot of relationships fall apart, or the sex within them is not very good anymore because couples have fallen into a rut and begin to take each other for granted. Be honest with yourself about your happiness level and take steps in being real with your partner in growing the relationship from strength to strength.

4. Open to intimacy. Intimacy involves removing your protective layers and facades, revealing yourself, connecting mentally, emotionally and sexually with your partner. It could mean getting to know each other all over again, exploring non-sexual areas, before working up to primary erogenous zones such as breasts and genitals.

5. Play nice. Any kind of abuse – whether physical, emotional, physiological – does affect intimacy. Once the intellectual and emotional sharing in the relationship stops, feelings of love, intimacy and passion in sex will end soon after. Genuine praise, appreciation and small gestures of kindness expressed can go a long way in maintaining closeness and nurturing love in relationships.

Martha Tara Lee is Founder and Clinical Sexologist of Eros Coaching in Singapore. She provides sexuality and intimacy coaching for individuals and couples, conducts sexual education workshops and speaks at public events in Asia. She holds a doctorate in Human Sexuality from the Institute for Advanced Study of Human Sexuality, as well as certificates in practical counseling, life coaching and sex therapy.

"Love is not exclusive, lasting or unconditional."

If your body could speak

What is love? People worldwide answer this question in countless different ways, often reflecting both the culture in which they were raised and their own unique life lessons on intimacy. Yet, what if your body could speak up and tell you how *it* defines love? **Barbara L. Fredrickson** presents a new approach: Love 2.0

As a scientist who studies human emotions, I think your body's definition of love is especially valuable. To uncover it, I examine how this powerful and deeply cherished emotional state evolved across millennia in our human ancestors, and how, today, it continues to affect you physically, in ways you may not have recognized.

Micro-moments of good feeling – whether they arrive in bursts of enthusiasm, pride, or joy, or unfold more quietly as gratitude, inspiration, or serenity – share in common that they open up your mindset. When you feel good, in other words, you can literally see more and appreciate the bigger picture that surrounds you. These moments of broadened awareness are consequential in that they help you discover and build useful traits and habits, which become ingrained aspects of your character that you can draw on to cope with the challenges that life inevitably brings. Put differently, positive emotions, although fleeting, have value. They broaden your outlook and build your resources for survival. This is the evolutionary logic that I have distilled into my broaden-and-build theory of positive emotions.

Shared positivity

Many times you feel good in isolation, all on your own. An individual achievement brings an inner sense of accomplishment and pride. A puzzle or game draws your interest and holds you in fascination as you consider its many aspects. Other times, you feel good *with* others. As you check out of the grocery store, you share a laugh with the cashier about the face you see peering up at you from the uncommonly gnarly tomato in your basket. On your way to pick up your mail, you happen upon a neighbor you've not seen in a while and pause to chat. Within minutes, you find yourselves swapping lively stories with one another about the fascinations you share. At work, you and your teammates celebrate a shared triumph with hugs and high fives. On your morning jog, you smile and nod to greet fellow runners and silently wish them a good day. You share a long embrace with a family member after a trip that has kept you apart for too many days. While all positive emotions broaden-and-build and transform you for the better, **moments of shared positivity carry special significance.** They seem to have the capacity to drive your growth, well-being and physical health in more profound and far-reaching ways.

This is how I see love. Love, as your body sees it, occurs in those micro-moments in which you and another connect over a shared positive feeling. Any positive emotion then – joy, interest, serenity, inspiration – can be instantly transformed into a moment of love when shared by two or more people simultaneously. Shared positive emotions create a powerful state of positivity resonance, in which one person's good feelings trigger and are triggered by those of another.

Synchrony

Beyond shared positivity, micro-moments of love are also characterized by a behavioral and biological oneness or synchrony. When two or more people share a positive emotional moment, research suggests, they begin to mirror each other's nonverbal gestures, as well as their inner biochemistry. They begin to move 'as one' in both seen and unseen ways. They also become momentarily and earnestly invested in each other's well-being. They come to care about and take care of each other.

I see love as the supreme human emotion in which positivity and mutual care momentarily resonate between and among people in deeply biological and kinematic ways. **Micro-moments of connection like this are like nutrients that nourish your health, well-being and spiritual growth.**

This new way of seeing love breaks open infinite opportunities to experience this life-giving state. Far from being a rare state felt toward that small set of people with whom you share the bonds of commitment, love can be found in *any* micro-moment of positive connection forged between you and another – even a stranger. Love, then, is not exclusive, lasting or unconditional, but is instead a forever renewable resource that can infuse and energize *any* interpersonal connection that honors certain preconditions. Those preconditions include a sense of safety, together with physical and temporal co-presence, perhaps most significantly face-to-face eye contact. A better understanding of love's preconditions can help you appreciate that love need not remain an unpredictable and elusive state. This is what I've aimed to offer in my work on *Love* 2.0. With practice, you can learn to generate love anytime you wish and, in doing so, steer you and those with whom you connect toward health, happiness and your higher ground.

The keys

- → **All positive emotions broaden-and-build and transform you for the better.**
- → **Love, as your body sees it, occurs in those micro-moments in which you and another connect over a shared positive feeling.**
- → **Love is a forever renewable resource that can infuse and energize *any* interpersonal connection that honors certain preconditions.**

Barbara L. Fredrickson is Professor of Psychology and Director of the Positive Emotions and Psychophysiology Lab at the University of North Carolina (USA). She is a leading scholar studying positive emotions and human flourishing. Her research is funded by the US National Institutes of Health and has influenced scholars and practitioners worldwide, in education, business and healthcare. Dr Fredrickson has published more than one hundred peer-reviewed articles and book chapters and the international bestsellers *Positivity* and *Love 2.0*.

"The magic words of love are the positive ones said aloud."

Love does not retire

Love does not look at age or count wrinkles – quite the contrary.
With age, conceptions of the value of love become deeper.
Emotions, or social and mental abilities, are not bound to age either.
After intensive research in Lapland, Prof **Kaarina Määttä**
finds the seven stepping stones to a lasting love.

Every young couple believes their love will last forever. But divorce rates are high.
Still, there are marriages that last. How do they manage? I put the question to hundreds
of Finnish couples who have been together for a long time. Here is their how and why.

Four reasons why

1. A satisfying relationship makes an excellent health insurance. Those people who are
content with their intimate relationship live not only healthier but also longer. In addition,
a satisfying relationship seems to work as an efficient wall against stress. Loneliness,
as well as the absence of intimate relationships and trustworthy conversation partners,
is a health risk.

2. Parents' good relationship is the best lap for a child. A good relationship is a significant
prerequisite of parenthood. It is important to support parents' mutual relationship because
it reflects in children's well-being, security and balanced development.

**3. A good relationship provides intimacy when living in a society of competition
and performance.** Human relationships have become narrower and scarcer, which goes
towards increasing the attractiveness of an intimate relationship. People need intimacy,
affection and privacy. An intimate relationship functions well in this task. When things
at home are OK, one is able to take care of work tasks and do better in life overall.

4. A satisfying intimate relationship averts painful divorce. The frequency of divorces has not turned them into light or easy human experiences. Divorcing is a painful experience. On the other hand, divorce should not lead to incrimination: sometimes divorcing is the only right and reasonable solution.

Seven steps how

1. Accepting dissimilarity and change. People would prefer building their lives conformable to their own hopes and needs and mold the other to suit them too. The relationship will flourish if both are allowed to have their own individuality and dissimilarity and are even encouraged to develop these. Accepting changes requires compromises, flexibility and bargaining but it is not necessary to compromise on everything. One has to make clear what one is ready to bargain for. A martyr's life is not satisfying.

2. The ability to enjoy everyday life. Tolerating everyday life is valuable for surviving and succeeding in life. The treasure trove of everyday life is accessible to everyone, but finding it is not easy if one only aspires after great experiences and luxurious enjoyments. There is no feast without daily life; neither can one experience moments of joy without having experienced sorrow. Indeed, love may be the most valuable in everyday life when people are drained by work and feel fatigue. In the family, both children and adults need love, especially when they do not seem to deserve it.

3. Confessions of love and the ability to make happy. Lovers look at the other with admiration and gratefulness. How to make the partner happy, alight and excited over and over again? The magic words of love are the positive ones said aloud: *"thank you"*, *"it's magnificent that you did this"*, *"you're wonderful"*, *"you're important to me"*. There is no reason to hold back these expressions of gratitude and admiration. They will not be worn away or lose their effect, even when used abundantly. Even the smallest positive gesture may be a tonic and foster positive atmosphere.

4. Conscious commitment to the partner. Work tasks will not go well if one does not concentrate on them. Likewise in marriage, the guarantee of a lasting relationship is the will and ability to devote and engage to it. Then spouses can trust each other's promises to stay together and this trust turns into strength. Strong love is focused on the future and ahead of them; spouses see their common future when they share both the daily life and the most glamorous dreams.

5. Self-appreciation. When people are in balance with themselves, it is easier to accept others' mistakes and flaws. Both can be themselves and feel good, exactly as they are. In a harmonious intimate relationship, it is a resource for spouses to have the trustful feeling of standing at each other's side, steady as bedrock and making each other feel certain and significant – and thus, they strengthen each other's ability to control their lives.

6. Lightening the vicissitudes. Support and comfort received from the other are precious in love. The marriage will last if the spouses are ready to calm down, soothe and stand by each other's side, open new vistas, encourage and look for the better life that could arise from even the most unbearable situations. At its best, the burdens feel lighter to bear together.

7. Tolerating and settling disagreements. No one is perfect, nor can anyone manage to avoid arguments or disagreements. It is crucial how well spouses get along, tolerate, or are possibly able to solve the inevitable conflicts. In a lasting relationship, there are more harmonious periods than there are conflicts. Problems come and go as long as positive things weigh more in scale. Therefore, it is important to create shared pleasures in the marriage and offer the partner those unique moments and excursions that make love attractive to both.

The keys

→ **Emotions or social and mental abilities are not bound to age. With age, conceptions of the value of love become deeper.**

→ **There are good reasons to stick together for a long time: it's healthy, good for the kids, stimulates performance and… averts from a painful divorce. But neither is a martyr's life satisfying.**

→ **Seven steps stimulate a long relationship: accepting, enjoying, confessing, commitment, self-appreciation, lightening and tolerating.**

Kaarina Määttä is Professor of Educational Psychology at the Faculty of Education, University of Lapland, in Rovaniemi (Finland). She has become famous and recognized in Finland as 'The Love Professor', due to numerous television and media appearances. She has studied human relationships and love in its various forms, based on thousands of Finnish people's experiences over the years. She has written dozens of articles and eight books about the theme in both Finnish and English, for example *The Fascination of Falling in Love*, *Love in Later Life* and *The Secrets of Long Marital Relationships*.

"All relationships are temporal.
They do not freeze at their most pleasurable periods."

What we know about love

Prof **Ellen Berscheid** was born in 1936 and has spent a lifetime studying why and how people fall in love. In 1974 an American senator called it scandalous that universities received money for that kind of 'stupid research'. But Berscheid continued and received distinguished awards for her internationally respected work. Now she has retired and writes: "My contribution to this book is intended to be my last professional writing. You asked me to do it in 1000 words. This is the best I can do. Finally, I have written 1058 words. Feel free to edit as you wish." We didn't change a word: what we finally know about love.

My work of almost fifty years in social psychology has focused on understanding interpersonal relationships, particularly close relationships. Most scholars agree that two people are in a relationship if each influences the other's activities, including the other's thoughts, feelings and emotions and other, more easily observable, behaviors. The relationship is viewed as close if the partners exert a great deal of influence on each other; that is, the partners are highly interdependent. An understanding of close relationships, including how and why they are formed, or why some endure and others dissolve, as well as the many phenomena that occur within them, is not possible without an understanding of one of the most fascinating of these phenomena: love.

People use the word 'love' to describe their thoughts, feelings and emotions and other behaviors experienced with their relationship partner. Research documents that no two individuals use the word in exactly the same way. The meaning of the word 'love' (i.e. the feelings and thoughts it represents) not only is likely to differ among individuals, but even for a single individual, the word may carry very different meanings as it is used in different relationships. Even in a single relationship, the meaning of the word 'love' may vary each time the individual uses it. The myriad meanings of the word love is a common source of misunderstandings between partners who do not appreciate that the meaning of the partner's statement "I love you" may differ from the meaning they attribute to it.

Romantic love

Because the meaning of the word 'love' is amorphous, scholars have attempted to identify commonalities among the situations in which people use the word and have offered a number of categorization schemes of different varieties of love. Four varieties appear to be relatively distinct and one of these, which is included in virtually all categorization schemes, is romantic love, often also called 'passionate love', 'erotic love' or 'being in love'.

Romantic love usually appears in a new relationship in which there is uncertainty about the partners' willingness to continue the relationship *and* the individual feels sexual desire for the partner. Sexual desire appears to be a necessary component of romantic love; that is, people who are not sexually attracted to their partner are not likely to describe their feelings for the partner as romantic love or themselves as being in love. Although necessary, sexual desire alone is not sufficient for people to describe their feelings as romantic love; rather, evidence suggests that sexual desire must be accompanied by another type of love: companionate love.

Companionate love

Companionate love is sometimes called 'friendship love' or, simply, 'strong liking' for the partner. This variety of love is based on commonality of interests, goals, background and other similarities. People who experience both sexual desire for their partner and *also* strongly like the other are most likely to describe themselves as being 'in love' with their partners. As long as the partners continue to share commonalities, which they often do, companionate love remains relatively stable. Sexual desire for the partner, however, appears to wane over time as the partner's novelty and uncertainty about the partner's feelings diminish and also as a result of conflict, which generally accompanies increasing closeness. In addition, as the partners themselves grow older, biological changes may decrease sexual desire. Unfortunately, some people attribute the waning of sexual desire for their partner as evidence that their partner is inadequate, or they themselves are inadequate, or there is something 'wrong' with the relationship. Rather, it is highly unusual for the intense sexual desire typical of young people in young relationships to be sustained over time; it is normal for romantic love to wane and for other types of love to gain in importance for the endurance of the relationship. One of these, commonly overlooked, is compassionate love.

Compassionate love

Compassionate love, sometimes called 'caregiving love', 'altruistic love', or 'selfless love', refers to concern for the partner's well-being and responsiveness to the partner's distress with support and help, even when such attempts are costly to the individual and even when positive feelings for the partner are absent. Such supportive behavior is usually present at the beginning of romantic relationships, as well as in friendships and other types of relationships, but it, too, may wane over time, as a result of conflict in the relationship or an increasing reluctance to provide too frequent and costly care to the partner. Because people tend to maintain close relationships as they believe their well-being is enhanced by the relationship, accumulating evidence that their partner has little or no concern for their welfare, or even is destructive of it, is likely to sound the death knell of the relationship.

Attachment love

Compassionate love is important for the endurance of the relationship for another reason: it appears to be the process by which, over time, attachment love for the partner may develop. It is clear that people are biologically wired to form attachment bonds to a person who provides care, comfort and protection. Attachment love, which grows slowly over time, is likely to occur under the radar of the partners, but once the bond is formed, it is likely to persist, even if romantic love and companionate love have vanished. Attachment love depends only on long familiarity and a history of receiving comfort and protection from the other over a substantial period of time. Because most people are not aware that an attachment bond is being formed, many are surprised when they feel severely distressed when permanently separated from their partner, especially when they no longer like or love that person in other ways – indeed, may now dislike the other intensely and have initiated the separation through divorce or other means.

In summary, all relationships are temporal. They change over time as a result of changes in the social and physical environments in which they are embedded and also as a result of biological and other changes in the partners themselves. Consequently, the varieties and intensities of love present in the relationship will also change over time. Unfortunately, relationships do not freeze at their most pleasurable periods – which for many people in romantic relationships is the period at which romantic love is most intense. For those whose relationships endure over time, the comforts of companionate love, compassionate love and attachment love are likely to increase in their importance for the partners' happiness and well-being.

The keys

→ **The meaning of the words "I love you" differs among all individuals and even a single individual may give it a different meaning in different relationships.**
→ **Four varieties appear to be relatively distinct: romantic, companionate, compassionate and attachment love.**
→ **All relationships are temporal and the varieties and intensities of love present in the relationship will also change over time.**

Ellen Berscheid is a social psychologist. She received her PhD in Psychology from the University of Minnesota (USA) in 1965 and remained at Minnesota throughout her professional career. In 2005 she went into phased retirement following the death of her husband. She is Regents' Professor of Psychology Emeritus, having fully retired in 2010. Her professional work has focused on close relationships, particularly phenomena associated with interpersonal attraction. She is the author of The Psychology of Interpersonal Relationships and numerous articles on love. Ellen Berscheid was elected Fellow of the American Academy of Arts and Science and has received various awards, including the American Psychological Association's Distinguished Scientist Award.

"

Dear Leo.

My contribution to this book is intended to be my last professional
writing because my present circumstances are not conducive to
scholarly work; keeping two young dogs happy and healthy,
dealing with bugs eating the roses, deer eating the begonias
and buckthorn invading my lake bank, in addition to reading
wonderful books. I never had time to read before and keeping track
of issues of health and home leave little time for anything but my
family who live nearby. Thank you for the kind and gracious words
on my work. Good luck and success with The World Book of Love.
Thank you for your invitation to contribute to it.

Ellen.

"

"And in the end,
the love you take
is equal to
the love you make."

— THE BEATLES —

THE

BERKELEY BOWL COOKBOOK

RECIPES INSPIRED BY THE EXTRAORDINARY PRODUCE OF CALIFORNIA'S MOST ICONIC MARKET

LAURA McLIVELY

PHOTOGRAPHS BY ERIN SCOTT

PARALLAX
PRESS

BERKELEY, CALIFORNIA

Parallax Press
P.O. Box 7355
Berkeley, California 94707
parallax.org

Parallax Press is the publishing division of
Plum Village Community of Engaged Buddhism, Inc.
Copyright © 2018 by Laura McLively

Printed in China

Photographs © 2018 Erin Scott
Food styling by Lillian Kang
Cover and text design by Debbie Berne

ISBN: 978-1-941529-96-6

Library of Congress Cataloging-in-Publication Data
is available upon request.

1 2 3 4 5 / 22 21 20 19 18

To Mom
for teaching me how to cook and how to love

Contents

66 **SQUASH BLOSSOM**
Sweet Corn and Chive-Stuffed
Squash Blossoms

69 **BANANA BLOSSOM**
Banana Blossom with Glass Noodles
and Crispy Garlic

71 **SNAKE BEAN**
Smokey Snake Beans

73 **PURPLE CAULIFLOWER**
Purple Cauliflower Quesadillas
with Curry Crema

75 **CRANBERRY BEAN**
Three Sisters Succotash with Crispy Sage

76 **CHESTNUT**
Roasted Chestnut Chocolate Torte

SPORES AND SUCCULENTS

80 **SEA BEAN**
Sea Bean and Soba Salad

82 **WOOD EAR MUSHROOM**
Wood Ear and Israeli Couscous Consommé

83 **NOPAL**
Charred Cactus and Black-Eyed Pea Chili

85 **HEDGEHOG MUSHROOM**
Hedgehog Mushroom Toast

88 **MOREL MUSHROOM**
Morel Pot Pies with Asparagus and Peas

89 **ABALONE MUSHROOM**
Abalone Mushroom Schnitzel

90 **ALOE VERA**
Aloe Vera Mango Ceviche

92 **PURSLANE**
Purslane with Chilled Melon and Feta

93 **MATSUTAKE MUSHROOM**
Matsutake Miso Soup

95 **FIDDLEHEAD**
Fiddlehead Tempura with
Sriracha Crème Fraîche

96 **ALBA PIOPPINI**
Meyer Lemon–Marinated Pioppini and
Frisée Salad

STEMS

100 **LONG CHOY SUM**
Tortilla China

102 **BẠC HÀ**
Garlic Soup with Bạc Hà

103 **YELLOW GARLIC CHIVE**
Nori Packets with Yellow Garlic Chives

105 **CARDOON**
Moroccan Cardoon Stew

106 **RHUBARB**
Vanilla Rhubarb Jam

108 **WHITE ASPARAGUS**
White Asparagus with Preserved Lemon

109 **RAMP**
Ramped-Up Mushrooms

111 **GREEN GARLIC**
Green Garlic Soup with Lemon
Cardamom Yogurt

112 **LEMONGRASS**
Lemongrass Coconut Ice Cream

113 **KOHLRABI**
Kohlrabi Ramen

ROOTS AND TUBERS

116 **PURPLE POTATO**
Purple Potato Galette with Tarragon

118 **DAIKON**
Savory Daikon Pancakes with
Ginger Maple Syrup

120 **MALANGA**
Malanga Masala Latkes

122 **SATSUMA SWEET POTATO**
Chipotle-Roasted Satsuma Tacos
with Cilantro Yogurt

123 **GOLDEN BEET**
Golden Beet Tamales with Red Pepper Sauce

125 **WATER CHESTNUT**
Greek Spaghetti with Water Chestnuts

126 **WATERMELON RADISH**
Watermelon Radish and Pineapple Carpaccio

129 **BURDOCK ROOT**
Burdock Root Pizza

130 **JICAMA**
Forbidden Rice Bowls with Stir-Fried Jicama

132 **HORSERADISH**
Port Roast with Horseradish Crisp

133 **SALSIFY**
Creamy Salsify Soup with Salsify Chips

134 **LOTUS ROOT**
Spiced Lotus Chips

136 **PARSLEY ROOT**
Curry-Roasted Parsley Root with
Feta-Yogurt Sauce

137 **SUNCHOKE**
Sunchoke Farro with Roasted Apricots

138 **CELERIAC**
Celeriac Ravioli with Celery Leaves
and Lemon Oil

141 **YUCA**
Buñuelos de Yuca

SAVORY FRUITS

144 **MOQUA**
Moqua Pisto with Fried Egg

146 **ANAHEIM CHILE**
Anaheim Chile and Corn Chowder

147 **WINTER MELON**
Tom Yum Soup with Winter Melon

149 **PLANTAIN**
Thai-Style White Curry with Plantain

151 **MILPERO**
Roasted Milpero Salsa Verde

154 **BLUE HOKKAIDO SQUASH**
Spiced Rice with Blue Hokkaido

155 **ARMENIAN CUCUMBER**
Falafel Waffles with Armenian
Cucumber Slaw

158 **INDIAN EGGPLANT**
Stuffed Mini Eggplants

159 **SINGUA**
Singua Paneer Curry

161 **INDIAN BITTER MELON**
Indian Bitter Melon Tonic

162 **CHAYOTE**
Chayote Pozole

165 **CHERRY BOMB PEPPER**
Stuffed Cherry Bomb Peppers

166 **GREEN PAPAYA**
Green Papaya Gazpacho

167 **CARNIVAL SQUASH**
Carnival Spice Cake

SWEET FRUITS

Introduction

I remember the first time I saw an African horned melon at Berkeley Bowl. I was steering my overloaded shopping cart around the bend of the citrus aisle when it caught my eye: a spiky, neon-orange hand grenade straight out of a science fiction movie. On top of the pile, one was cut in half to display its even more scandalous interior of lime-green slime. Cautiously taking a whiff, I was surprised by its cucumber-like scent. I was intrigued but couldn't imagine what one would do with such a thing. It wasn't until a decade later that I actually took one home to try. It tasted extraordinary: a tangy burst with hints of melon and banana.

Hundreds of unusual fruits and vegetables at Berkeley Bowl, like the African horned melon, had remained in my "no try zone" for too long. Like many cooks, I had gravitated toward familiar ingredients. Growing up in California with a mother from Spain and a father of Greek descent, I cooked dishes rooted in the Mediterranean and Latin traditions of my childhood. However, after dabbling with the horned melon, I became determined to expand my culinary horizons. After all, foods unfamiliar to *me* are as much a part of someone else's everyday diet as tomatoes are in my family.

During my next shopping trip, I stood among wiry-haired rambutans and tubers taller than a toddler, in one of the most extensive produce sections in the country, and made a personal commitment—a quest of sorts—to try every unfamiliar fruit and vegetable from Berkeley Bowl and to create a recipe honoring each of their unique qualities.

This was the start of my journey as a food explorer, and in the spring of 2014, I started the blog *My Berkeley Bowl* to chronicle this adventure. I embraced the successes—and mishaps—of cooking with foods I had never tasted before. Despite a few nettle stings and cactus spine impalements, each of the mysterious fruits and vegetables in this book deserves the culinary spotlight. I stirred the lime-green juice of the African horned melon into a fizzy gin cocktail. I dipped wily rambutans into pools of white chocolate and tackled the three-foot-long burdock root until I found my new favorite pizza topping.

The Berkeley Bowl Cookbook is a collection of my favorite discoveries from this adventure and a tribute to the family-run market where my quest was born. I drew inspiration for these plant-based recipes from the dishes of my childhood, travels, and imagination, as well as from the experience of living in one of the most culturally diverse areas in the nation. While I want you to enjoy them, I also hope this book opens the door for you to use these extraordinary fruits and vegetables in your own go-to dishes and way of eating.

You don't need to live in Berkeley to get your hands on these ingredients. Latin American, Asian, and specialty groceries, as well as farmers' markets all over the country, stock these items in abundance. Sourcing this unusual produce is part of the adventure, so seek out ethnic food purveyors and chat with local growers at your weekend farmers' market. Perhaps you're thinking about planting some new varieties in your vegetable garden, or maybe you subscribe to a community supported agriculture (CSA) box and keep getting things you don't know how to prepare. Whatever your reason for picking up this book, my hope is that it helps deepen your appreciation for the many treasures the world gifts to us in its seeds, fruits, flowers, and roots.

Thank you for joining me on this food adventure.

Laura McLively

The Berkeley Bowl Story

It's a typical September afternoon at Berkeley Bowl, and the produce section is buzzing. Twelve hundred varieties of fruits and vegetables stretch out in a sea of color. Customers dodge each other's shopping carts that glow green like gardens on wheels, sprouting with leafy pea shoots and Taiwanese spinach. Shoppers block the aisles as they stoop to pick through bins of wine-colored cherries from local farms. A college student furrows his brow at the shiny eggplants stacked three rows high, with names like *albino* and *graffiti*. A gray-haired woman wrangles a thorny bunch of cardoons that refuse to fit in the dangling scale. Intrepid shoppers brave the crowds and chaos because, here, you can find *anything*.

But most shoppers are here for the mother lode: eight towering tons of tomatoes at their peak. Swarms descend on the bins of fiery reds, oranges, and yellows of late summer's treasures: Roma, Sugar Plum, Sun Gold, Early Girl, and dozens of heirloom varieties such as crimson- and green-striped Zebra tomatoes and the heavy, juice-laden Pineapple tomatoes. Only a few weeks of the season remain, but customers will find consolation as fall ushers in its own delights: piles of pears and apples compete for space with speckled pumpkins and wart-covered squash, while exotic fungi with pine needles still clinging to their gills file into a forty-foot display.

Such is the bounty of this produce mecca that attracts humble home cooks and world-famous chefs alike. Food journalist Mark Bittman has called it the "ultimate grocery store," while Yotam Ottolenghi, inspired by his visit to the "epic Berkeley Bowl Market," created a multicolored cauliflower dish for his cookbook, *NOPI*. It was even the setting for the first season of *Top Chef*, with contestants crossing the San Francisco Bay to spend a heart-racing thirty minutes gathering the ingredients they believed would take them to the top.

It's hard to imagine that this world-renowned market began as a small, family-run grocery in a former bowling alley. The founders and owners, Glenn and Diane Yasuda, opened the original location back in 1977 because they lived just behind it, a circumstance that reminded them of the family-owned shops of their former residence in Japan. Glenn hails from a family of Southern California farmers and Diane from a family of grocers, so this venture was a natural choice. Diane was pregnant

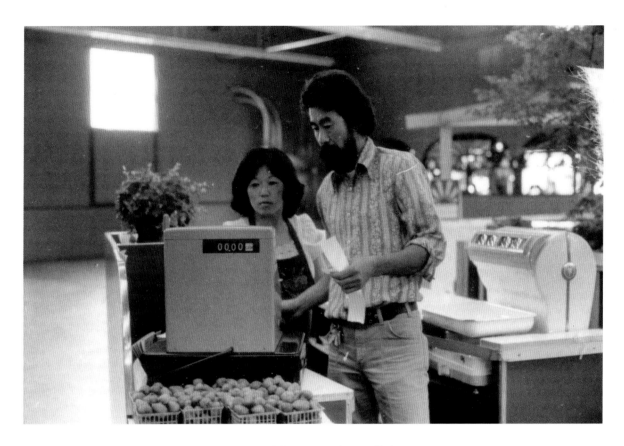

with their son Gen at the grand opening, and forty years later, all three continue to run the family business.

How did this mom-and-pop produce shop become what the *Los Angeles Times* has called "one of the nation's most renowned retailers of exotic fruits and vegetables"? Ironically, it's the very smallness of the Berkeley Bowl family business that has propelled it to big-shot status in the produce world. While large grocery franchises purchase enormous quantities of (mostly unripe) produce that make a long, bumpy journey from centralized warehouses, Glenn often buys from small farmers, working directly with sellers and growers to source items at their peak. When he chooses a juicy, ripe strawberry in the morning, he knows what it will taste like to his customers later that day.

Every day since 1977, Glenn has arisen in the darkness, bundled up in the cold morning fog, and climbed into his car in search of the best fruits and vegetables he can find. At 2:30 a.m., he heads west across the Bay Bridge to a wholesaler in South San Francisco, making his way back east to Oakland's Jack London Square market by sunrise. He ducks in and out of each warehouse, greeting workers by

▲ The produce aisles of Berkeley Bowl in 1977

name and taking the time to sample orange sections, snap green beans, and smell melons before placing his order. Even now, in his eighties, Glenn continues to run this circuit himself, insisting "it's important for the sellers to see me, to keep that relationship going."

In addition to Glenn's daily dawn pilgrimages, Berkeley Bowl sources much of its produce directly from growers. Organic produce manager Nick Christopher, who started as a dishwasher in the Berkeley Bowl kitchen twenty years ago, regularly visits thirty or so small farms throughout northern California to learn how the soil, weather, and farming practices affect the quality of the produce. An ambassador of Glenn's emphasis on relationships, Nick sees the direct benefits when, for instance, farmers ask *him* what they should plant. By prompting growers to cultivate items such as mizuna, dinosaur kale, and Buddha's hand, Nick helps Berkeley Bowl keep up with customer demand and ensure farmers a market for these niche products.

In 1987, David "Mas" Masumoto of Masumoto Family Farm in central California was on the verge of bulldozing his Suncrest peach trees, planted two

▲ Berkeley Bowl soon outgrew its original location in a former bowling alley on Shattuck Avenue

decades earlier by his father, because demand had plummeted. This juicy heirloom variety was prized for its perfect peachy flavor, but because it bruised easily, produce brokers favored more commercially viable varieties that could travel long distances and last for weeks on shelves. In a last-ditch effort to save his family heirloom, Mas published an article that summer in the *Los Angeles Times*, "Epitaph for a Peach." He wrote, "A bulldozer will crawl in, rip each tree from the earth and toss it aside; the sounds of cracking limbs and splitting trunks will echo through my fields . . . No one wants a peach variety with wonderful taste." Fortunately, Glenn Yasuda did. He started purchasing the juicy, flavorful, easily bruised peach directly from Mas, who has credited Berkeley Bowl as one of the forces that saved his farm.

With the motto of "If we can find it, we'll buy it," there's nothing too obscure for Berkeley Bowl, although Glenn and Diane concede they don't always know what people do with spongy stalks of bạc hà, nopal cactus paddles that brandish sharp spines, or taro leaves the size of elephant ears. From the beginning, they've been committed to stocking whatever produce meets the demands of their incredibly diverse customer base (more than 112 languages are spoken in Berkeley, according to US census data). Sometimes this means offering unfamiliar items long before they've caught on in the culinary world, such as the "exotic" cilantro, which three decades ago, Glenn couldn't sell a case of in a week. But Berkeley's international, culinarily curious community "will try anything," Glenn says, so it pays to be a step ahead.

Berkeley Bowl offers foods long before most other stores sell them and even before many consumers know they want them. While Glenn and Diane are certainly in tune with food trends and customer demand, they don't have an agenda beyond simply providing a service to the customer. Nick Christopher, however, recognizes that the relationship between Berkeley Bowl and overall culinary trends is perhaps symbiotic. He cites the example of galangal, an aromatic root that has slowly earned attention as more customers develop an interest in East Asian cooking. "Someone comes to us long before galangal is popular because they know we're going to have that specialty thing. Then we may start purchasing more, maybe open up a bigger display or move it to an area with more traffic, and then people might discover it who weren't even looking for it."

Whether intentional or not, there's no doubt that Berkeley Bowl has inspired curious eaters to try a host of extraordinary—if unfamiliar—fruits and vegetables. Many come looking for apples or tomatoes but get swept away by fuchsia-streaked cranberry beans or plump, purple okra. Boundaries of familiarity are broken even among shoppers, as they chat about how to cook this long, skinny burdock root or that banana blossom with its tightly packed petals, some even exchanging recipes.

Despite two locations and more customers than they can handle, Berkeley Bowl has retained its quirky independence. Generation after generation continue to shop at "The Bowl," as it's affectionately known by regulars, even while luxury markets pop up all around it. On this September afternoon, a man with graying dreadlocks and a home-sewn shopping bag comes through the sliding doors alongside a family chatting in Spanish, a woman in a hijab, and a grandmother dressed in her Sunday best. They're all headed for that bin of perfect tomatoes, but chances are they'll leave with some other unexpected edible treasures. Such is the magic of Berkeley Bowl.

▸ The Yasudas (Glenn, Diane, and their son Gen) continue to run the family business, with two locations and more than 400 employees

Kitchen Notes

While no special knowledge is needed to work with the fruits and vegetables showcased in this book, these pointers will help you navigate the wondrous world of extraordinary produce.

Seasonality

Many of the fruits and vegetables in this book have a short window of availability, or are produced in far-off regions during the off-season. While the sidebars at the bottom of each recipe will give you a general idea of seasonality and provide off-season suggested substitutions, you can also learn about availability by asking produce stockers or farmers at your local market. They will know best what's happening in your region. At Berkeley Bowl, handwritten signs above each item indicate where it was grown so you can decide if you want to buy those redcurrants in winter from Chile or wait until California's summer harvest.

Safety, Storage, and Selection

Some of these fruits and vegetables are prickly, while others must be cooked before consuming. Look to the sidebars at the bottom of each recipe for safe handling information as well as tips on how to select and store unfamiliar items.

Substitutions

You can still use these recipes even if you can't find the featured ingredient. I've listed substitutions in the sidebars whenever possible, but feel free to read the flavor/texture notes and swap in something you think works well.

Knives

When working with so many fruits and vegetables, it's crucial to keep your knives sharp. Not only will this give you precise slices, but it will keep you safe and prevent your hands from getting tired. Ask at your local knife store or knife sharpening service about the best tools and techniques for sharpening, as this varies based on the type of knife. It also helps to have a good vegetable knife. My go-to is my nakiri knife—a lightweight Japanese knife with an ultrafine blade and flat edge designed specifically for chopping vegetables. The blade is too fragile for very coarse, dense vegetables like galangal and butternut squash, so I keep a sharp chef's knife close by for heavy-duty chopping.

Buy Extras

If you're cooking a recipe with a fruit or vegetable you've never tried before, consider buying a few extras. It's nice to be able to taste the new ingredient and learn how it behaves without worrying about not having enough for the actual recipe. Also, if you've never selected items like fresh water chestnuts or rambutan, you never know if there may be a "bad egg" in the batch, and you'll be glad to have a few backups on hand.

Spice Safety

The recipes in this book frequently call for spicy peppers and chiles, so it's important to practice spice safety. Keep a pair of latex or food service gloves handy for handling spicier chiles like Thai chile or habanero. For milder chiles like serrano or jalapeño, a good handwashing with soap and warm water immediately after handling will suffice.

Other Kitchen Equipment

Unless you have perfectly precise knife skills, there's no better tool than a **mandoline** for uniformly slicing vegetables to a specific width, such as to make chips or slaws. Just be very careful during use, as the super sharp blades don't distinguish between a carrot and your finger.

One of my favorite pieces of kitchen equipment is a **microplane.** It's the perfect tool for getting a fine grate from citrus zest, hard cheese, garlic, chocolate, nutmeg, or other hard spices. Finally, if you don't already have a **fine mesh strainer**, pick up this handy kitchen tool at a local hardware store, kitchen supply, or flea market. I recommend getting a few different sizes—tiny strainers are great for dusting desserts with cocoa or powdered sugar, and the larger ones come in handy for draining beans, washing fruits or vegetables, pressing the liquid out of a pulp, or straining a fine puree or stock.

Oil Options

Many of the recipes in this book are inspired by the Spanish and Greek dishes of my childhood, and so rely on good, robust olive oil. For the healthiest and tastiest results, choose cold-pressed, extra-virgin olive oil, preferably organic. For sautéeing, roasting, or stewing, select an earthy olive oil that can withstand some heat, such as the *Hojiblanca* varietal. For drizzling on top of raw dishes, I usually opt for a bright, grassy *Piccual*. Skip the olive oil when cooking or frying at high heat, and instead choose a heat-stable, neutral oil like peanut, sunflower, or coconut oil.

A Word on Salt

The quantities for salt I provide in these recipes are meant to be a loose guide, but always taste your dish along the way and adjust the seasoning to your liking. Unless otherwise specified, I cook with a fine-grain sea salt because I prefer its flavor over refined table salt, as well as the feel of the nonuniform grains between my fingers. If substituting table salt, you will likely need to reduce the quantity. If using a coarser salt like Kosher, you will need to increase the quantity. But as always, taste your food and adjust the seasoning to suit your own preference.

Stocking Up

Many recipes in this book call for discarding the tops or stems of perfectly good vegetables, such as leeks, green onions, or lemongrass. I encourage you to throw these into a pot to make your own vegetable stock, or stash them in a bag in the freezer until you have enough to simmer up a homemade stock. Many of the dishes call for vegetable *broth*, by which I mean salted and seasoned vegetable stock. So if you're using homemade stock, make sure to salt and season it until it tastes like a full-flavored vegetable broth before using it in the recipe.

LEAVES

Catalan-Style Gai Lan with Raisins and Pine Nuts

Gai lan, also known as Chinese broccoli, is well-suited for this Spanish-style preparation from the province of Catalonia. Its slightly bitter greens and sweeter stems complement the bitter, sour, and sweet flavors of toasted garlic, lemon, and raisins. Serve as a side dish or tapa.

Serves 4 to 6

2 tablespoons olive oil

4 cloves garlic, peeled and thinly sliced

2 bunches gai lan (2 pounds)

¾ teaspoon salt

Freshly ground black pepper

2 tablespoons raisins

2 tablespoons pine nuts, toasted

1 lemon, halved

Availability year-round at Asian markets and specialty markets

Selection select firm stalks with deep green leaves and unopened flower buds like broccoli

Storage refrigerate in a plastic bag for up to 1 week

Substitutions broccolini

Heat the olive oil in a large skillet over medium heat. When the oil is hot but not smoking, add the garlic and fry for 1 to 2 minutes, until the garlic has turned lightly golden. Remove from the heat and remove the garlic with a slotted spoon, allowing it to drain on paper towels. Leave the garlic-infused oil in the skillet and set aside for later use.

Separate the leaves from the stalks of the gai lan. Roughly chop the leaves, and slice the stalks into ¼-inch pieces. Heat the skillet with the garlic-infused oil over medium heat. Add the gai lan stalks and sauté for 5 to 7 minutes, until just tender. Add the gai lan leaves and sauté for 3 to 4 minutes, until the leaves are wilted and tender. Stir in the salt, pepper, raisins, and pine nuts and remove from the heat. Drizzle with the juice from half the lemon and taste for seasoning. Drizzle with a little olive oil and garnish with the crispy garlic and a lemon wedge.

Lemon Sorrel Butter

Fresh sorrel, a leafy herb with a tartness akin to lemon or green apple, is the basis for this compound butter. Add a pat or two to brighten roasted vegetables, peas, or pasta, or spread onto toast or scones.

Serves 4

½ cup salted butter, softened

16 sorrel leaves, stems removed and minced

¼ teaspoon salt

Pinch of freshly ground white pepper

Zest from 1 small lemon

2 teaspoons freshly squeezed lemon juice

Availability year-round at well-stocked groceries and farmers' markets, with peak in spring and summer

Selection look for bright green, unwilted leaves with a fresh scent

Storage wrap in a paper towel and refrigerate in a plastic bag for up to 3 days

Substitutions other bright, fresh herbs such as lemon mint, basil, or parsley

Combine all the ingredients in a bowl and beat with a wooden spoon until fully incorporated.

Transfer the butter mixture onto a piece of wax paper or plastic wrap and roll into a log-shape, twisting the ends to secure.

Refrigerate until solid, about 2 hours.

Consume within 2 weeks.

CHRYSANTHEMUM GREENS

Chrysanthemum Greens and Turnip Fried Rice

Also known as shungiku, these frilly greens are the edible leaves of the well-known flowering plant, chrysanthemum. While the young leaves can be eaten raw, the more mature leaves found in most markets have a slightly bitter bite that are better suited for cooked dishes. Here, the herbaceous, grassy greens complement the sweet nuttiness of turnip and brown rice.

Serves 4

3 teaspoons toasted sesame oil

2 large eggs, lightly beaten with a pinch of kosher salt

2 tablespoons peanut oil

5 green onions, white and green parts finely sliced

1 turnip, small diced

1 cup shiitake mushrooms, small diced

1 small red bell pepper, small diced

2 cloves garlic, minced

1 tablespoon minced fresh ginger

3 cups cooked brown rice or long-grain rice

1 bunch chrysanthemum greens, thick stems discarded and leaves roughly chopped

3 tablespoons soy sauce

½ teaspoon salt

Edible flower petals such as chrysanthemum and marigold petals, for garnish (see *Note*)

Heat 1 teaspoon of the sesame oil in a large wok or nonstick skillet over medium-high heat. Pour in the beaten eggs and swirl to form a very thin omelet. Once the eggs have set, flip the omelet and cook for 30 more seconds before removing from the wok. Slice into 1-inch pieces and set aside.

Heat the peanut oil in the same wok over high heat. Add the green onions and turnip and stir-fry for 1 minute. Add the mushrooms, bell pepper, garlic, and ginger, and stir-fry for 2 minutes, or until the vegetables are just tender. Add the remaining 2 teaspoons of the sesame oil and the rice, and stir-fry for 2 to 3 minutes, until the rice begins to stick slightly to the wok. Fold in the chrysanthemum greens along with the omelet pieces, soy sauce, and salt, and cook until the greens are just wilted, about 2 minutes. Serve immediately garnished with the edible flower petals.

Note: Edible flower petals can be picked from your garden, and are also sold at farmers' markets and specialty markets like Berkeley Bowl.

Availability year-round at Asian markets, specialty markets, and farmers' markets

Selection choose deep green, unwilted leaves with crisp stalks; also called shungiku or chop suey greens

Storage refrigerate in a plastic bag for up to 5 days

Substitutions other herbaceous greens such as dandelion greens, turnip greens, or stinging nettles

Corn Tortillas with Epazote Leaf

These flavorful, chewy corn tortillas are so simple to make there'll be no turning back to the dry, easily cracked store-bought versions. Epazote leaf, a pungent herb that has been used in Latin American cooking and medicine since the Aztecs began using it, finds a new purpose here: Imprinted onto the surface of each tortilla, the jagged leaf imparts aromatic flavors of citrus, pine, and oregano. You can eat these straight out of the skillet, or as a base for a quesadilla or taco, such as Chipotle-Roasted Satsuma Tacos (page 122).

Makes 1 dozen

22 epazote leaves (about 1 bunch)

1⅓ cups hot water

¼ teaspoon salt

2 cups masa harina (see *Note*)

Availability year-round at Latin American markets and specialty markets

Selection look for bright green, unwilted leaves with a strong aroma of pine, citrus, and oregano

Storage store with stems in a glass of water and leaves covered in a plastic bag, and refrigerate for up to 1 week

Substitutions while there is no true substitute for the flavor of epazote, you can roll a small sprig of Mexican oregano into the tortillas

Set aside the largest 12 epazote leaves for imprinting the tortillas. Mince the remaining 10 leaves and place them in a mixing bowl with the hot water. Allow to steep for 5 minutes before adding the salt and masa harina. Mix with a fork for 2 minutes, or until the mixture becomes a smooth dough. If the dough seems dry, gradually add and mix in more water a few drops at a time.

Roll the dough into about 12 balls the size of a golf ball. Place the dough balls on a sheet of wax paper and cover with a damp towel to keep them from drying out while you work. Place a ball between two additional sheets of wax paper and use a flat-bottomed pie pan or plate to flatten it into a disc shape. Lift the top sheet of the wax paper, place an epazote leaf on top of the disc, and replace the wax paper. Use a rolling pin to lightly roll the dough into a 5-inch or 6-inch tortilla. Set aside and repeat until all the tortillas have been rolled out.

Preheat a griddle or cast-iron skillet over medium-high heat. Cook the tortillas in batches for about 50 to 60 seconds per side, until they are very lightly golden in places. Transfer the tortillas to a dampened, folded towel to keep them soft and warm until ready to serve.

Note: Masa harina is a very finely ground corn flour used to make tamales and tortillas. It is sold in the bulk-bin section at Berkeley Bowl as well as in packages from brands like Maseca and Bob's Red Mill.

Treviso Spring Rolls with Black Tahini

Treviso has the long, graceful leaves of endive with the burgundy color and bitter bite of radicchio. It's just the thing to add color and crunch to these Vietnamese-style spring rolls stuffed with fresh herbs and juicy vegetables. A nutty black tahini dipping sauce complements the bright and bitter flavors of this dish. Serve as an appetizer, or combine with Tom Yum Soup with Winter Melon (page 147) or Thai-Style White Curry with Plantain (page 149) for a light meal. Black tahini is fabulous on toast, vegetables, or fruit, so you may want to double the recipe and stash it in a jar in the fridge.

Makes about 1½ dozen

BLACK TAHINI

¾ cup black sesame seeds

1 tablespoon honey

½ teaspoon salt

⅓ cup vegetable oil

SPRING ROLLS

3 tablespoons rice vinegar

1 tablespoon chile garlic sauce (see *Note*)

1 tablespoon soy sauce

1 (14-ounce) package extra-firm tofu

3 tablespoons vegetable oil

1 tablespoon sesame oil

2 heads Treviso

1 mango, peeled and julienned

1 large red bell pepper, seeded and julienned

Preheat the oven to 350°F. To make the black tahini, place the sesame seeds on a baking sheet and bake for 6 to 7 minutes, until the seeds are lightly toasted and fragrant. Allow the seeds to cool completely. Place the seeds in a food processor and process on high until they break down into a sticky meal. Add the honey and salt. With the food processor on high, slowly drizzle in the oil until the mixture is smooth and glossy.

To make the spring rolls, combine the vinegar, chile garlic sauce, and soy sauce in a small bowl and set aside. Drain the tofu and slice it lengthwise into three even slabs. Wrap the slabs in a lint-free towel or paper towels. Place a cutting board on top of the towel and press down firmly to squeeze excess liquid from the tofu. Heat the vegetable oil and sesame oil in a large skillet over high heat. Add the tofu slabs and fry for 4 to 5 minutes on each side, until golden brown and crispy. Remove from the skillet and allow to cool before slicing the tofu into ¼-inch strips. Place the strips in a bowl and drizzle with half the vinegar mixture to marinate. Slice off the top 3½ inches of the Treviso heads and set aside. Finely slice the rest of the Treviso and toss with the remaining vinegar mixture to make a slaw.

1 bunch green onions, white and green parts finely sliced

1 bunch fresh mint, stems removed

1 bunch fresh Thai basil, stems removed

20 dried spring roll wrappers (or rice paper) (see *Note*)

Availability year-round at specialty markets and farmers' markets

Selection choose bunches in the shape of small romaine lettuce, with crisp, purple-red leaves and bright white ribs

Storage wrap in a paper towel and refrigerate in a plastic bag for up to 3 days

Substitutions radicchio, endive

To assemble, fill a large bowl with hot water. Dip a spring roll wrapper in the hot water until it is softened and flexible, about 10 to 30 seconds. Use both hands to carefully lay the wrapper flat on a nontextured surface. Place a Treviso leaf on the bottom half of the rice paper and top with a rounded tablespoon of the Treviso slaw. Add a piece of the marinated tofu and a slice or two of the mango and bell pepper. Top with a few green onion slices, a mint leaf, and a basil leaf. Roll the bottom edge of the wrapper away from you to enclose the filling, folding each side toward the center as you go, like a burrito, until forming a tight roll. Repeat with the remaining spring roll wrappers.

Serve immediately with the black tahini as a dipping sauce, or cover tightly with plastic wrap and refrigerate. The spring rolls are best if consumed within 8 hours.

Note: A popular brand of chile garlic sauce that's not too difficult to find is Huy Fong. Dried spring roll wrappers are commonly sold in packages in the Asian foods section of Berkeley Bowl and other well-stocked grocery stores.

image appears on following page

Stinging Nettle Filo Bites

Anyone who's ever been stung by wild nettles while hiking or gardening knows this is one well-armored weed. But all it takes is a little heat to disarm nettles of their sting, and they become a tender, edible green. Their spinach-cucumber flavor is a nice match for feta and walnuts wrapped in flaky filo dough.

Makes 2 dozen

8 ounces stinging nettles (about 10 cups, lightly packed)

2 tablespoons olive oil

2 shallots, minced

2 cloves garlic, minced

1 tablespoon freshly squeezed lemon juice

1 teaspoon salt

Freshly ground black pepper

8 walnut halves

⅔ cup crumbled feta cheese (about 3 ounces)

⅓ cup ricotta cheese

½ pound filo dough sheets, thawed

4 tablespoons salted butter, melted

Availability year-round at specialty markets and farmers' markets, with peak in spring and summer

Selection choose bunches of deep green, unwilted, leafy nettles

Storage refrigerate in a plastic bag for up to 1 week

Safety wear thick rubber gloves or gardening gloves while handling raw to prevent stings

Substitutions fresh spinach

Wearing thick dish gloves or gardening gloves to avoid stinging, strip the tender leaves from the tough nettle stems, discarding the stems. Heat the olive oil in a skillet over medium heat. Add the shallots and sauté for 7 to 8 minutes, until softened. Add the garlic and sauté for 1 to 2 minutes, until the garlic is fragrant but not browned. Add the nettle leaves and sauté for 3 to 4 minutes, until wilted and tender. Stir in the lemon juice, salt, and pepper, and turn off the heat. Set aside.

Place the walnut halves in a food processor and pulse until coarsely chopped. Add the nettle mixture and pulse for 10 to 15 seconds, until the mixture resembles a very coarse pesto. Stir in the feta and ricotta cheeses, and set aside.

Preheat the oven to 400°F. Place the filo sheets under a damp towel to keep them from drying out and cracking between batches. Place one filo sheet on a large cutting board. Use a pastry brush to lightly brush the sheet with the melted butter. Place a second sheet on top. Use a chef's knife or pizza cutter to slice through both filo sheets lengthwise into three long strips. Place 1 tablespoon of the nettle mixture at the bottom of each strip. Fold the corner of the strip over the filling, forming a triangle, and then continue folding the strip in a triangular fashion until reaching the end of the strip, as if folding a flag. Repeat with the remaining filo strips and filling until all the nettle mixture is used up.

Place the triangles, seam-side down, on a baking sheet and brush the tops lightly with butter. Bake for 10 to 15 minutes (see **Note**), until golden brown and crispy. Serve hot.

Note: You can also freeze the filo bites before baking them. When ready to use, simply place them directly on the baking sheet and bake at 350°F for 20 to 25 minutes.

Breakfast Pea Shoots and Polenta

These garlands of soft green leaves and wild tendrils are young pea shoots, plucked before their spring peas have formed. Both the leaves and stems have a tenderness and fresh snow-pea flavor that are enhanced through stir-frying, as in this breakfast served with creamy polenta and topped with a fried egg.

Serves 2

2 cups salted vegetable broth

1 cup water

½ cup polenta (coarse cornmeal)

¾ teaspoon finely minced fresh savory (or rosemary)

1 tablespoon plus
1 teaspoon mild olive oil

6 ounces fresh pea shoot tendrils

⅓ teaspoon sea salt

Pinch of freshly ground black pepper

¼ teaspoon red pepper flakes

2 eggs

⅓ cup grated Parmesan cheese

Whisk together the vegetable broth, water, polenta, and savory in a small saucepan. Bring to a boil before lowering the heat to simmer for 10 to 15 minutes, until thick and creamy, stirring frequently to avoid sticking. Remove from the heat and cover to keep warm until ready to serve.

Heat 1 tablespoon of the olive oil in a large skillet over high heat. Add the pea shoots and use tongs to toss them in the hot oil. Stir-fry for 3 to 4 minutes, until the pea shoots are wilted and tender. Sprinkle with the salt, black pepper, and red pepper flakes and toss to coat evenly. Remove the pea shoots from the skillet and set aside. Add the remaining 1 teaspoon of the olive oil to the skillet and fry the eggs until the whites are set and the yolks are still runny.

Just before serving, stir the Parmesan cheese into the polenta mixture, and thin with additional water if necessary to achieve a grits-like consistency. Spoon the polenta into two serving bowls. Mound the pea shoots over the polenta and top with a fried egg. Sprinkle with sea salt and black pepper and serve immediately.

Availability year-round at Asian markets, specialty markets, and farmers' markets, with peak in spring

Selection choose crisp, bright green leaves with juicy stems and curlicue tendrils; shoots should be 6 to 8 inches long and sold loose in a bin (not as the small "microgreen" shoots sold in plastic containers)

Storage wrap in a paper towel and refrigerate in a plastic bag for up to 3 days

Substitutions other tender stir-fry greens such as spinach

Matcha Mousse with Opal Basil Syrup

Opal basil, a variety of sweet basil, imparts its deep purple hue to a syrup that pops against vivid green *matcha* in this silky, airy mousse. People don't expect to find basil in their dessert, but its sweet, herbal taste is surprisingly lovely against the bitterness of matcha (see *Note*).

Serves 6 to 8

SYRUP

½ cup boiling water

2 tablespoons sugar

4 opal basil leaves

MOUSSE

¼ cup water

½ cup sugar

4 opal basil leaves

1 tablespoon matcha powder, plus more for garnish

2 egg whites

2 cups heavy whipping cream

Availability year-round at specialty markets and farmers' markets

Selection choose fragrant, unwilted leaves with deep purple color

Storage place the bottoms of the stems in a small glass of water and keep in a dark, cool place for up to 5 days

Substitutions purple basil, sweet basil (syrup will not be purple)

To make the syrup, place the boiling water, sugar, and basil leaves in a blender or food processor and pulse until the leaves are broken down. Let stand for 10 minutes while the basil infuses. Strain the mixture through a cheesecloth into a small saucepan, and bring to a boil. Reduce the heat to simmer for 5 minutes, or until the syrup has been reduced to about 3 or 4 tablespoons. Chill the syrup in the refrigerator until ready to serve.

To make the mousse, place the water, sugar, and basil leaves in a small saucepan and bring to a boil, stirring to dissolve the sugar. Turn off the heat and allow to sit for 10 minutes while the basil infuses. Discard the basil leaves. Whisk in the matcha powder until it is completely dissolved.

In another bowl, beat the egg whites with a whisk or electric mixer until stiff peaks form. Gradually add the matcha mixture until incorporated and set aside. In a separate bowl, beat the heavy whipping cream with a whisk or electric mixer until stiff peaks form. Gently fold the whipped cream into the egg white–matcha mixture until completely incorporated and smooth. Cover and refrigerate for 1 hour or overnight.

To serve, spoon the mousse into six ramekins. Drizzle with the opal basil syrup and garnish lightly with matcha powder.

Note: Matcha is a fine powder made from green tea and is sold in the bulk-bin section of Berkeley Bowl as well as in Asian or specialty markets.

Grilled Cheese with Mizuna, Dates, and Goat Brie

An Asian green from the mustard family, mildly bitter mizuna is wilted in balsamic vinegar and paired with dates in a rich and gooey grilled cheese sandwich. Goat milk Brie's complex flavor and soft texture pairs well with this mustardy green, but it's hard to go wrong with any creamy, flavorful cheese.

Serves 4

1 tablespoon olive oil

1 large bunch mizuna (about 10 ounces), tough ends removed and roughly chopped

½ teaspoon salt

Freshly ground black pepper

2 teaspoons aged balsamic vinegar

4 teaspoons salted butter

8 slices crusty levain or sourdough bread

8 ounces goat milk Brie, cut into thin slices

6 large dried Medjool dates, pitted and sliced (¼ inch)

Availability year-round at well-stocked groceries, Asian markets, and farmers' markets

Selection choose bunches of unwilted green leaves

Storage refrigerate in a plastic bag for up to 5 days

Substitutions arugula, young mustard greens

Heat the olive oil in a skillet over medium heat. Add the mizuna and toss in the hot oil for 1 to 2 minutes, until wilted. Stir in the salt, pepper, and vinegar and allow to cook uncovered for 1 minute, or until the liquid has mostly evaporated. Remove the mizuna from the skillet and set aside.

Wipe out the skillet and return to the stove over medium heat. Spread the butter on one side of each slice of bread. Place a slice of bread, butter-side down, in the skillet. Top with a quarter each of the mizuna, Brie, and dates. Top with a second piece of bread, butter side up.

Cook for 2 to 3 minutes on each side, until the cheese is melted and the bread is golden and toasty. Repeat with the remaining six slices of bread. Slice each sandwich in half diagonally and serve immediately.

Summer Salad with Rau Ram Chimichurri

Like a spicy, musky version of cilantro, rau ram emboldens a tangy chimichurri sauce that is good on just about anything. The sauce is drizzled over a salad of juicy nectarines and tomatoes with thinly sliced white onion for crunch. Double the recipe for the chimichurri if you want leftover sauce for Purple Cauliflower Quesadillas (page 73) or roasted vegetables.

Serves 4 to 6

CHIMICHURRI

1 cup lightly packed rau ram leaves

1 cup lightly packed parsley leaves

¼ cup olive oil

2 tablespoons red wine vinegar

2 tablespoons freshly squeezed lemon juice

½ teaspoon salt

3 small cloves garlic

SALAD

1 small white onion, halved and finely sliced

½ teaspoon salt

1 tablespoon red wine vinegar

1 pound baby potatoes (waxy variety such as new potatoes), unpeeled and quartered

1½ pounds heirloom tomatoes, sliced into wedges

2 nectarines, sliced into wedges

10 rau ram leaves, roughly chopped

To make the chimichurri, combine all the ingredients in a food processor or blender and pulse on high for 10 to 20 seconds to form a dressing.

To make the salad, place the onion, salt, and vinegar in a large salad bowl and stir to combine. Let stand to allow the onion to mellow while you prepare the potatoes.

Bring a pot of salted water to a boil. Add the potatoes and cook for 7 to 8 minutes, until tender but not mushy. Drain the water and run the potatoes under cold water to stop the cooking. Drain well. Add the potatoes to the onion mixture, along with the tomatoes, nectarines, and rau ram leaves. Mix gently to combine. Drizzle with the chimichurri and serve.

Availability year-round at Asian groceries and specialty markets

Selection look for bunches of blade-shaped, green leaves with a purple crescent at the base; also sold as Vietnamese coriander/cilantro/mint, hot mint, laksa leaf

Storage refrigerate in a plastic bag for up to 5 days

Substitutions cilantro

Beans and Greens

This dish makes a great weeknight supper using whatever greens are on hand. But for this preparation, Taiwanese spinach is particularly well-suited because it gets tender but not stringy when cooked. The hollow stems are as succulent as the leaves, especially after they soak up the tangy vinegar. Home-cooked beans to accompany them are ideal, but good-quality canned beans, such as those produced by Strianese, can be a lifesaver if you're pressed for time. Serve with crusty bread for sopping the juices.

Serves 4 to 6

1 pound Taiwanese spinach (about 3 bunches)

3 tablespoons good-quality olive oil

2 red onions, sliced thinly

⅓ cup white balsamic vinegar

¼ cup water

3 cups cooked or canned butter beans

1 teaspoon salt

Freshly ground black pepper

¼ teaspoon red pepper flakes

Availability year-round at Asian markets, specialty markets, and farmers' markets

Selection select bunches of deep green, unwilted leaves with hollow stems that are usually connected at the base

Storage refrigerate in a plastic bag for up to 4 days

Substitutions spinach, chard, or other mild leafy greens

Separate the leaves from the stems of the spinach. Chop the spinach leaves into 1-inch ribbons and chop the stems into ½-inch pieces.

Heat the olive oil in a large, flat-bottomed skillet over medium heat. Add the onions and sauté for 5 to 7 minutes, until softened and browned. Add the spinach stems and sauté for 2 to 3 minutes. Add the spinach leaves along with the remaining ingredients and stir.

Simmer on low for 5 to 10 minutes, until the greens are soft and the beans have a vinegary flavor.

Taste and adjust seasoning as desired. Serve warm or at room temperature with a drizzle of olive oil.

Toasted Salad Savoy with Pears and Goat Cheese

Salad Savoy, the youngest vegetable in this book, is a cross between kale and cabbage and was first developed in 1983. With bright purple centers bursting from within frilly green leaves, it's a beauty fit for a flower bed. Fortunately, this crunchy, nutritious plant is more than just a pretty new face. Here, its mild broccoli flavor is enhanced by toasting the leaves and tossing them with pears and goat cheese.

Serves 4

1 pound purple Salad
Savoy (see *Note*)

1 tablespoon olive oil

Salt

2 ounces goat cheese, crumbled

1 pear, halved and thinly sliced

1 tablespoon aged
balsamic vinegar

Freshly ground black pepper

Availbility year-round at well-stocked groceries and farmers' markets

Selection choose heavy heads with crisp leaves streaked with bright purple

Storage refrigerate in a plastic bag for up to 1 week

Substitutions white Salad Savoy, curly kale or Redbor kale

Separate the frilly leaves from the stems of the Salad Savoy, discard the stems, and separate into two even batches. Heat half of the olive oil in a large flat-bottomed skillet over high heat. Cooking in two batches to avoid steaming the leaves. Add half the leaves to the skillet and coat them in the hot oil.

Allow them to toast in a single layer for about 2 minutes, tossing them every 30 seconds or so, before removing them from the skillet. Add the remaining olive oil to the skillet, and cook the second batch of leaves.

Arrange the leaves on a serving plate, sprinkle with salt to taste, and toss. Top with the goat cheese and pear slices. Drizzle with the vinegar and sprinkle with the pepper. Serve immediately.

Note: Salad Savoy is not the same as savoy cabbage.

Spanish-Style Chinese Cabbage on Manchego Toast

The key to this melt-in-your-mouth cabbage is the tenderness of the Chinese variety, whose ruffled leaves are slow-fried in a healthy dose of olive oil. Spooned onto crispy toast with the robust flavors of Manchego cheese, garlic, and sweet paprika, this tapa will transport you straight to a cozy bar in Spain.

Serves 4

1 Chinese cabbage
(about 2 pounds)

3 tablespoons olive oil,
plus more for brushing

4 cloves garlic, peeled
and thinly sliced

¾ teaspoon salt

¾ teaspoon pimentón dulce
(sweet Spanish paprika)

8 slices crusty French
bread, ½ inch thick

¾ cup grated Manchego cheese

Availability well-stocked groceries

Selection heavy cabbage with crisp, tightly packed leaves; also sold as Napa cabbage

Storage refrigerate covered in plastic wrap for up to 1 week

Substitutions savoy cabbage

Slice the cabbage in half lengthwise and then again to form quarters. Cut out the core at the base, discard it, and then chop the cabbage into half-inch strips.

Heat the olive oil in a large, deep skillet over medium heat. Add the garlic and cook for 2 to 3 minutes to lightly toast. Add the cabbage and sauté for 15 to 20 minutes, until very tender. Turn off the heat and stir in the salt and pimentón dulce. Taste the cabbage and adjust seasoning as desired before transferring it to a serving bowl. Top with a pinch of pimentón dulce and a drizzle of olive oil before setting aside to cool slightly.

Preheat the oven to 375°F. Place the bread slices on a baking sheet in one layer. Brush the top of each slice lightly with olive oil using a pastry brush and sprinkle with the Manchego cheese. Bake for 6 to 8 minutes, until the cheese is melted and the bread is lightly toasted. Arrange the slices of Manchego toast around the cabbage so guests can serve themselves.

Shiso Limeade

It's fun to marvel as clear shiso tea transforms into a shocking bubble-gum pink upon adding lime juice. The secret is anthocyanin, the natural pigment in shiso leaves that turns pink in acidic conditions. There are many kinds of shiso, but the minty, lemon flavor and two-toned, heart-shaped leaves of Chinese shiso make it especially nice in this refreshing drink.

Serves 6

1 cup packed Chinese shiso leaves, plus a few leaves for garnish

2 liters boiling water

⅓ cup freshly squeezed lime juice

Lime slices, for garnish

Availability year-round at Asian markets and specialty markets

Selection look for bunches of heart-shaped leaves that are dark green on the front and purple on the back

Storage refrigerate in a plastic bag for up to 1 week

Substitutions mint leaves (but they will not turn pink)

Place the shiso leaves in a large heat-resistant jug or jar and pour the boiling water over the leaves.

Let the tea steep for 10 to 15 minutes, depending on the desired strength. Strain out the leaves and discard.

Stir in the agave syrup and lime juice, and watch as the tea magically takes on its bright pink color.

Chill before serving over ice, garnished with a lime slice and a shiso leaf.

image appears on following page

FLOWERS, SEEDS, AND PODS

Romanesco Slaw with Chili-Lime Pepitas

With a taste and texture similar to its relative, the cauliflower, Romanesco is well-suited to many preparations. To preserve its vibrant chartreuse hue and satisfying crunch, eat it raw, as in this slaw of contrasting colors with spicy pumpkin seeds.

Serves 4 to 6

3 tablespoons apple cider vinegar

2 tablespoons freshly squeezed lime juice

3 tablespoons mild olive oil

1 teaspoon sea salt

2 teaspoons honey

½ head of purple cabbage, shaved

3 green onions, white and green parts thinly sliced

2 jalapeño peppers, seeded and thinly sliced

1 Romanesco

1 green apple, cored and thinly sliced

½ cup cilantro leaves, stems removed

CHILI-LIME PEPITAS

⅓ cup roasted pepitas (pumpkin seeds)

½ teaspoon chili powder

½ teaspoon paprika (mild to hot)

¼ teaspoon ground cumin

½ teaspoon salt (omit the salt if using salted pepitas)

1 teaspoon fresh lime zest

Whisk together the vinegar, lime juice, olive oil, sea salt, and honey. In a large salad bowl, toss the dressing with the cabbage, green onions, and jalapeño peppers and allow to marinate in the refrigerator for at least 4 hours or overnight.

To make the chili-lime pepitas, toss the pepitas in a small skillet with the chili powder, paprika, cumin, and salt over medium heat until fragrant and lightly toasted (about 3 minutes). Turn off the heat and add the lime zest, tossing to coat. Allow to cool.

When ready to serve, separate the florets of the Romanesco. Set aside the smallest, bite-sized florets for later, and chop the larger ones into ¼-inch pieces. Add the chopped Romanesco, apple, and cilantro leaves to the cabbage dressing and mix well. Top with the chili-lime pepitas and small Romanesco florets just before serving.

Availability year-round at well-stocked groceries and farmers' markets

Selection choose vibrantly colored, unblemished heads with crisp leaves

Storage store head-up in a plastic bag in the refrigerator to prevent bruising

Substitutions green cauliflower, broccoli, or conventional cauliflower

Purple Okra Pickles

Okra is a polarizing pod, beloved or abhorred for its slippery, seedy centers. For those in the latter camp—or for those still unsure—pickled okra is a game changer. The pods retain their crunch and trap the delicious brine between their squishy seeds for a satisfying play of textures. This purple- and red-streaked variety looks beautiful packed into a jar with pink peppercorns, though the brine steals their color over time. Serve as a sandwich sidekick or cheese plate addition.

Makes 4 cups

1 cup rice vinegar

⅓ cup water

1½ tablespoons salt

1 tablespoon sugar

1 spicy small dried chile (such as guindilla)

¾ teaspoon mustard seeds

¾ teaspoon coriander seeds

¾ teaspoon pink peppercorns

2 dill sprigs

2 cloves garlic

1 pound fresh purple okra

Availability year-round at specialty markets and farmers' markets, with peak in summer

Selection firm, dry, deeply colored pods between 2 and 6 inches long

Storage refrigerate in a paper bag for up to 3 days

Substitutions green okra

Bring the vinegar, water, salt, and sugar to a boil. Meanwhile, pack a sterilized quart-sized canning jar with the chile, mustard seeds, coriander seeds, peppercorns, dill sprigs, garlic cloves, and as much okra as will fit snuggly in the jar.

Okra shrink and float when pickled, so to get the most in the jar, pack one layer with the stems down and one with the stems up, pushing them down to pack them in well.

Pour the vinegar mixture over the top and seal the jar with a fresh canning lid.

Store in the refrigerator or process in a canner for shelf-stable storage. Either way, the okra will be ready to enjoy after about 10 to 14 days.

Tangy Tamarind Mustard

Tamarind pods have a sticky, sweet-and-sour flesh that plays a central role in the traditional food and drink of India, Southeast Asia, and Latin America. In this recipe for coarse mustard, tamarind pulp imparts tang along with a complex, fruity flavor. The hardest part about making homemade mustard is waiting to dig into it—it has to be stowed away in the fridge for at least a week before consuming to allow the bitter oils released by the mustard seeds to mellow. But once ready to go, this spread will upgrade any sandwich, charcuterie, or cheese plate.

Makes 2 cups

¾ pound whole tamarind pods, as plump as possible

1¼ cups boiling water

¼ cup apple cider vinegar

¼ cup yellow mustard seeds

¼ cup black mustard seeds

½ teaspoon salt

2 tablespoons maple syrup

Availability year-round at Asian, Latin American, and specialty markets

Selection look for brittle pods with plump, sticky flesh (pods may be cracked open in places); they are sold loose or in pre-packaged boxes

Storage store in a sealed plastic bag at room temperature for up to several months

Substitutions pre-packaged tamarind paste

Peel away the hard shells and strings from the tamarind fruit, and discard the shells. Place the fruit in a blender and add the boiling water. Place the lid on the blender and set aside for 20 minutes to allow the tamarind to soak. Pulse the blender three or four times to loosen the flesh from the seeds, without breaking down the hard seeds. Pour the contents of the blender through a fine-mesh strainer set over a small bowl. Press and stir the pulp with the back of a spoon to release the pulp and juices into the bowl, leaving behind the seeds and tough fibers. There should be about 1 cup of strained pulp.

Add the vinegar, yellow mustard seeds, and black mustard seeds to the bowl and stir to combine. Cover with plastic wrap and allow to sit at room temperature for 8 hours or up to 2 days. Remove the plastic wrap and pour the contents of the bowl into a food processor. Add the salt and maple syrup and blend on high for about 30 seconds to break down some of the mustard seeds and create a creamy consistency (the mustard will still be very grainy). Transfer the mustard to a pint-sized glass jar, secure the lid, and store in the refrigerator for at least 1 week before consuming to allow the initially bitter taste to mellow. Enjoy within 3 months.

Spring Chickpea Tabbouleh

With nubby green skin and a flavor reminiscent of garden peas, fresh chickpeas bear little resemblance to their canned or cooked counterparts. These chickpeas are tossed straight out of the pod with plenty of herbs and lemon juice in this springtime bulgur salad. Shelling peas can take a while, so gather some friends or family around the counter to help.

Serves 4

1 cup bulgur

¾ pound fresh chickpea pods, shelled

3 tablespoons minced chives

¾ teaspoon salt

2 tablespoons freshly squeezed lemon juice

2 tablespoons olive oil

3 tablespoons minced fresh mint

Lemon wedges

Availability specialty markets and farmers' markets in spring and summer

Selection look for pods that are green and stiff

Storage refrigerate in a plastic bag for up to 1 week

Substitutions fresh English or garden peas, fava beans, edamame

Place the bulgur in a large bowl and pour boiling water over it until it is covered by about an inch of water. Cover and let stand for 20 minutes to absorb. Strain and press out any excess water before combining with the remaining ingredients.

Season to taste and serve cold or room temperature with a lemon wedge.

Sweet Corn and Chive-Stuffed Squash Blossoms

Even though this recipe uses only five ingredients, these stuffed squash blossoms look and taste deceptively gourmet. With molten centers of ricotta and corn and elegantly tied up with fresh chives, there isn't a better way to savor the tender zucchini flowers that mark the start of summer. It's impossible to decide whether these are better baked or fried, so take your pick—or try both.

Serves 4 to 6

1 ear of sweet corn

1 cup ricotta

2 tablespoons fresh minced chives

¾ teaspoon salt

1 teaspoon freshly squeezed lemon juice

12 squash blossoms

Extra fresh chives for tying the blossoms

OPTIONAL (FOR FRYING)

Vegetable oil

Cornmeal

Pinch of salt

1 egg, beaten

Lightly boil or steam the sweet corn for 2 minutes. Slice off the kernels and combine with the ricotta, minced chives, salt, and lemon juice.

Carefully reach into the squash blossoms to pinch off the stamens. Fill each blossom with about 2 tablespoons of the corn ricotta mixture and twist the top of the blossom. Fold a chive in half for extra strength and carefully tie it around the top of each blossom to secure them closed.

For tender, delicate baked blossoms: Preheat the oven to 350°F. Place the stuffed blossoms on an oiled baking dish and bake for 10 minutes. Serve immediately.

For rich, crispy fried blossoms: Heat 1 inch of oil in a large skillet over medium-high heat. Combine the cornmeal with the pinch of salt. Dip the stuffed blossoms in the beaten egg and dredge in the cornmeal. Fry in the skillet for about 1 minute per quarter turn until all sides are golden brown. Serve hot.

Availability well-stocked groceries and farmers' markets from late spring to summer

Selection vibrant yellow-orange flowers that are tightly closed

Storage refrigerate wrapped in a paper towel in a plastic bag for up to 2 days

Preparation do not wash the squash blossoms with water; simply wipe away dust with a damp towel

Substitutions flexible leaves such as Swiss chard

Banana Blossom with Glass Noodles and Crispy Garlic

While bananas are by far the most consumed fruit in the United States, few consumers are familiar with the other edible part of this plant: the maroon, tear-shaped blossom that emerges from the center of a banana cluster. It's quite popular in Southeast Asia where the entire blossom is eaten cooked and raw in salads, soups, and curries. This recipe utilizes the tender, white heart of the banana blossom, which is similar in texture and flavor to a mildly bitter bamboo shoot. Here it's stir-fried and served inside the plant's beautiful, boat-shaped petals.

Serves 4

1 lemon

1 banana blossom

6 ounces glass noodles (also sold as rice vermicelli, cellophane noodles, or mung bean noodles)

3 tablespoons coconut oil

6 large cloves garlic, thinly sliced

1 (1-inch) nub ginger, peeled and minced

2 Thai chiles, minced

1 large carrot, peeled and grated

1 small red bell pepper, seeded and julienned

3 green onions, white and green parts finely sliced

3 tablespoons unseasoned rice vinegar

¼ cup freshly squeezed lime juice (about 2 limes)

1 tablespoon brown sugar

1 teaspoon salt

1 cup lightly packed chopped cilantro leaves

½ cup lightly packed chopped Thai basil leaves

Fill a bowl with cold water and add the juice from the lemon. Trim the stem from the banana blossom at the point where it meets the base of the petals. Remove the dark outer petals from the banana blossom, and wash and set aside the four largest and prettiest petals for serving the salad in. Discard the remaining dark petals and tiny florets between each layer until you reach the heart, which consists of tightly packed white petals. Slice the heart in half lengthwise and, using a very sharp knife or mandoline, slice the heart into very thin strips (⅛ inch) and immediately place the strips in the lemon water to prevent discoloration.

Break the glass noodle bundles into 3 to 4 pieces each. Bring a saucepan of water to a boil, add the noodles, and turn off the heat. Let the noodles soak for 5 minutes, or until the noodles are softened. Drain the noodles in a colander and rinse with cold water. Drain well and set aside.

Heat the coconut oil in a large wok or skillet over medium heat. Once the oil is hot but not smoking, add the garlic. Fry for 1 to 2 minutes, until the garlic has turned slightly golden. Remove the garlic with a slotted spoon and allow it to drain on paper towels. Set aside.

continued on the following page

Availability year-round at Asian markets and specialty markets, with peak in fall and winter

Selection choose heavy blossoms with tightly packed, maroon leaves free of deterioration; also sold as banana flower

Storage refrigerate wrapped tightly in plastic wrap for up to 4 days

Substitutions bamboo shoots

Return the wok to the stove with the garlic-infused coconut oil and increase the heat to medium-high. Drain the sliced banana blossom heart and add it to the wok along with the ginger and chiles. Stir-fry for 2 to 3 minutes.

Add the glass noodles and stir-fry for another 2 minutes to coat the noodles in the hot oil before removing from the heat. Stir in the carrots, bell pepper, and green onions. In a separate dish, combine the vinegar, lime juice, brown sugar, and salt and pour over the noodles. Add the cilantro and Thai basil and toss to combine.

To serve, fill the four dark petals with the noodle mixture and top with crispy garlic.

Smokey Snake Beans

Also called yard-long beans for their extraordinary length, snake beans are prized for their chewy, grooved texture that traps the sauce in stews and stir-fries. Simmered with caramelized shallots, tomatoes, and spices, the beans soak up this smokey sauce with a taste of southern barbecue. Serve over steamed rice or with freshly baked cornbread.

Serves 4 to 6

4 tablespoons olive oil

4 large shallots, thinly sliced (about 1½ cups)

2 cloves garlic, minced

1 teaspoon minced fresh ginger

¼ teaspoon ground allspice

¼ teaspoon red pepper flakes

1 teaspoon paprika (mild to hot)

1 tablespoon tomato paste

1 tablespoon balsamic vinegar

1 teaspoon Worcestershire sauce

1 cup water

1 teaspoon sea salt

1 bunch snake beans (about 1½ pounds), chopped into 2-inch pieces

2 to 3 tomatoes, chopped

To make the sauce, heat 3 tablespoons of the olive oil in a large skillet over low heat. Add the shallots and allow to cook slowly for about 15 minutes, stirring occasionally, until very soft and caramelized. Increase the heat to medium and add the garlic and ginger; sauté for 3 minutes. Add the allspice, red pepper flakes (to taste), paprika, and tomato paste and sauté for an additional 1 minute to release the flavors. Stir in the vinegar, Worcestershire sauce, water, and sea salt and bring to a simmer for 1 minute. Pour the sauce into a food processor or blender and blend until smooth.

Heat the remaining 1 tablespoon of olive oil in the same skillet over high heat. Add the snake beans and stir-fry for 3 to 5 minutes, until just tender but still chewy. Add the tomatoes and stir-fry for 1 additional minute. Pour in the sauce and simmer for 3 to 5 minutes to allow the beans to soak up the flavors of the sauce. Serve hot with cornbread or steamed rice.

Availability year-round at Asian groceries, specialty markets, and farmers' markets, with peak in summer and fall

Selection sold in bunches labeled as yard-long beans; they should be thin and floppy but not limp, free of bulges, and with light green or deep green, grooved skin

Storage refrigerate in a plastic bag for up to 3 days

Substitutions okra, green beans

Purple Cauliflower Quesadillas with Curry Crema

Who knew the cauliflower section of a grocery store could be such a thrill? A flash of lime green, a shimmer of orange, a gleam of amethyst—the variety of colors are like a painter's palette. These seemingly unnatural colors are a result of varying levels of natural antioxidant pigments, like beta-carotene and anthocyanin. No artificial food colorings or genetic modifications here, just Mother Nature at work. In this recipe, the contrast of royal purple with yellow curry is particularly beautiful, but choose whatever cauliflower catches your eye. This dish pairs nicely with a fresh green salsa, such as Sour Plum Salsa on page 193 or Roasted Milpero Salsa Verde on page 151.

Serves 4

1 purple cauliflower

1 tablespoon olive oil

1½ teaspoons salt

1 cup sour cream

2 teaspoons curry powder

¾ teaspoon turmeric

1 tablespoon freshly squeezed lime juice

4 large corn tortillas (about 8 to 10 inches)

4 ounces Oaxaca cheese or other white melting cheese, shredded

2 ounces *queso fresco,* crumbled

Availability year-round at well-stocked groceries and specialty markets

Selection look for bright purple, heavy heads free of discoloration

Storage refrigerate in a plastic bag for up to 1 week

Substitutions cauliflower of any color

Cut the florets from the cauliflower core and chop them into bite-sized pieces. Heat the olive oil in a large skillet over medium-high heat and add the cauliflower. Sauté for 5 minutes, or until the cauliflower is lightly browned. Add 2 to 3 tablespoons of water and cook an additional 5 to 7 minutes, until the cauliflower is fully softened and the water is completely evaporated. Stir in ¾ teaspoon of the salt and set aside.

Meanwhile, make the curry crema by combining the remaining ¾ teaspoon of salt with the sour cream, curry powder, turmeric, and lime juice. Set aside.

Preheat the oven to 200°F. Heat a skillet (preferably cast-iron) over medium heat. Brush the skillet lightly with oil and place a tortilla in the bottom of the skillet. Sprinkle a quarter of the Oaxaca cheese and a quarter of the *queso fresco* over half of the tortilla and top with a quarter of the cauliflower mixture. Fold over the other half of the tortilla and press down with the back of a spatula. Once the cheese is melted and the bottom of the quesadilla is golden and crispy in places, about 2 minutes, use the spatula to flip the quesadilla and cook for an additional 2 minutes. Remove the quesadilla and place it directly in the oven to stay warm, using a piece of tinfoil underneath to catch any melting cheese. Repeat until you have made all four quesadillas. Serve with a dollop of the curry crema.

Three Sisters Succotash with Crispy Sage

The Native American story of the three sisters honors the significance of corn, beans, and squash. For centuries, native people have planted these crops in concentric rings, with corn providing a pole for the soil-enriching beans to climb, while the prickly squash leaves shade the soil and keep out predators. This easy recipe brings the three sisters together again in a homey succotash featuring a stunning, heirloom bean. Although cranberry beans lose their magenta speckles when cooked, their plump, creamy texture more than makes up for it.

Serves 4

1 pound fresh cranberry bean pods, shelled

1 teaspoon salt

2 tablespoons olive oil

12 sage leaves

1 bunch green onions, white and green parts sliced

1 red bell pepper, seeded and diced

1 ear fresh corn, kernels sliced off

1 yellow summer squash, diced

1 zucchini squash, diced

1 cup vegetable broth

Salt and freshly ground black pepper

Bring a small pot of water to boil and add the shelled beans and salt. Simmer for 15 minutes, or until the beans are fully cooked and tender. Drain.

Meanwhile, heat the olive oil in a large skillet over medium heat. When the oil is hot, tip the skillet so the oil pools on one side of it and add the sage leaves. Let the leaves fry in the pooled oil for about 1 minute, or until they darken in color but do not burn. Remove them from the oil and place them on a paper towel for later.

Turn the heat up to medium-high and add the green onions and bell pepper to the skillet. Sauté for 1 to 2 minutes. Add the corn, summer squash, and zucchini, and sauté for 1 more minute. Add the beans, vegetable broth, and salt and pepper (to taste), and let simmer for 5 minutes, or until the vegetables are *al dente*, the stock is partly evaporated, and the flavors are melded. Serve hot, garnished with the crispy sage leaves.

Availability year-round at well-stocked groceries and farmers' markets, with peak in late summer and fall

Selection choose plump, vibrantly colored pods

Storage refrigerate in a plastic bag for up to 1 week

Substitutions other fresh shelling beans, dried cranberry beans (but cooked completely)

Roasted Chestnut Chocolate Torte

Few things evoke the festive feel of winter holidays like the aroma of fresh roasted chestnuts, the basis for this chocolate torte. Rich, moist, and laced with espresso, this decadent dessert is best shared with a crowd and topped with a dollop of fresh whipped cream.

Serves 16 to 20

36 whole chestnuts (see *Note*)

¾ cup salted butter

8 ounces dark chocolate
(70 to 75 percent cacao),
roughly chopped

½ cup warm espresso
or strong coffee

¾ teaspoon vanilla extract

4 eggs, separated

1 cup sugar

Fresh whipped cream

Availability well-stocked groceries in winter

Selection heavy, firm nuts with glossy mahogany shells

Storage refrigerate in a perforated plastic bag for up to several weeks

Substitutions packaged, pre-peeled chestnuts, or other tree nuts such as ground almonds or hazelnuts

Preheat the oven to 425°F. Fill a pot with water and bring to a boil. Meanwhile, place a chestnut on a folded dish towel to hold it steady and cut an X about ⅛ inch deep into the rounded side of the chestnut with a sharp knife. Repeat with the remaining chestnuts.

Add the chestnuts to the boiling water and boil for 5 minutes. Drain well and immediately place them on a baking sheet. Roast the chestnuts for 18 to 20 minutes, until the shells curl away and reveal the golden flesh inside. Remove them from the oven, and wrap the hot chestnuts in a kitchen towel to allow them to steam for 5 minutes. While still warm, peel away the outer shell and papery skin from each chestnut. Place the chestnuts in a food processor and pulse to form a fine meal. You should have about 1½ cups of chestnut meal.

Turn the oven down to 325°F and grease a 9-inch or 10-inch springform pan. Place the butter and chocolate in a large glass bowl and gently heat in a double boiler until completely melted. Remove from the heat and stir in the chestnut meal, espresso, and vanilla extract.

Beat the egg yolks with the sugar until smooth and creamy. Stir in the chocolate batter. In another bowl, beat the egg whites until they form stiff peaks, and gently fold them into the chocolate batter. Pour the batter into the springform pan and bake for 30 to 35 minutes, until a toothpick inserted into the center comes out with moist crumbs attached. Let the torte cool slightly before removing it from the pan. Serve with a dollop of fresh whipped cream.

Note: You can also buy packaged, preroasted, and prepeeled chestnuts. If you use those, omit the roasting and simply grind the chestnuts to a fine meal.

SPORES AND SUCCULENTS

Sea Bean and Soba Salad

Bursting in the mouth with a salty pop, sea beans are a playful addition to salads and stir-fries. Here, the tiny aquatic succulents are tossed with buckwheat (soba) noodles and sesame in a bright and satisfying salad.

Serves 4

10 ounces dry soba noodles

2 tablespoons sesame oil

1 tablespoon black sesame seeds

2½ cups sea beans, chilled

5 green onions, white and light green parts finely sliced

6 to 8 Thai basil leaves, finely sliced

1 cup seeded, thinly sliced medium-spice red chile (such as Fresno)

2 tablespoons freshly squeezed lime juice

2 tablespoons rice vinegar

2 tablespoons soy sauce

2 teaspoons honey

1 tablespoon fresh minced ginger

Availability year-round at specialty markets and farmers' markets

Selection look for crisp, bright green sea beans that snap when bent; also sold as salicornia, pickleweed, or saltwort

Storage wrap in a damp paper towel and refrigerate in a plastic bag for up to 1 week

Substitutions chopped sugar snap peas

Cook the soba noodles in boiling water for 1 minute less than indicated on the package directions, or until they are *al dente*. Immediately drain and rinse with cold water to stop the cooking. Drain well and toss with the sesame oil. Cover and refrigerate for at least 1 hour or overnight.

Heat a small skillet over medium heat. Add the sesame seeds and toast until fragrant, shaking the skillet to avoid burning (about 1 minute). Set aside to cool.

To serve, place the noodles in a large serving bowl and add the sea beans, green onions, Thai basil, and chili. In a separate bowl, mix the lime juice, vinegar, soy sauce, honey, and ginger. Pour over the soba noodles and vegetables, and toss to coat evenly. Sprinkle with the toasted sesame seeds and serve immediately.

Wood Ear and Israeli Couscous Consommé

As chef Deborah Madison says in *The Greens Cookbook*, "A clear, simple soup or broth that contains a single vegetable, and perhaps some rice or pasta, has an invaluable place at the beginning of a large dinner." And so it is with this winter warmer, where frilly, seaweed-like mushrooms trap a chive-flecked broth between their folds.

Serves 4

1½ cups water

4 cups salted vegetable broth

½ teaspoon salt

1 cup dried mushrooms (such as porcini and/or shiitake)

2 sprigs fresh oregano

½ cup Israeli couscous

3 ounces fresh wood ear mushrooms (about 1½ cups)

¼ cup minced fresh chives

———————————

Availability year-round at well-stocked groceries and Asian markets

Selection look for dark brown or black mushrooms with a flexible, rubbery texture

Storage refrigerate in a paper bag for up to 1 week

Substitutions cloud ear mushrooms, dried and rehydrated wood ear mushrooms

In a saucepan, combine the water, vegetable broth, and salt. Cover and bring to a boil. Add the dried mushrooms and oregano sprigs; cover, turn off the heat, and allow to sit for 30 to 40 minutes. Pour the contents of the saucepan through a fine-mesh strainer into another saucepan, pressing down on the solids to extract as much of the broth as possible.

Bring the strained broth to a boil. Add the couscous, and cover and lower the heat to simmer for 7 minutes. Rinse the wood ear mushrooms and pinch off and discard the stiff nub at the base. Roughly chop the mushrooms, and add them to the saucepan to simmer with the couscous for an additional 2 minutes.

Taste and adjust the salt content as desired. Serve immediately while the couscous is still *al dente*. Sprinkle generously with the chives.

Charred Cactus and Black-Eyed Pea Chili

Nopales are the large, spiny leaves or "paddles" of the prickly pear cactus (see Prickly Pear Sorbet on page 201 for another take on this succulent). Although common in gardens and parks throughout California and the Southwest, many cooks don't realize that these torturous-looking leaves are in fact food—after removing the spines, of course. Nopales are popular in Latin American cuisine for their crisp, juicy texture and tanginess, like a lemony green bean. Here, they are first charred along with poblano peppers to add a smokey note to a black-eyed pea chili. As always with homemade chili, it's even better the next day once all the flavors have melded.

Serves 8 to 10

2 cups dried black-eyed peas

3 nopales (cactus leaves)

2 large fresh poblano peppers (see *Note*), halved and seeded

1 large red bell pepper, halved and seeded

2 tablespoons olive oil

1 large yellow onion, finely chopped

4 large cloves garlic, minced

1 bay leaf

1 tablespoon plus 1 teaspoon chili powder (preferably New Mexico chili powder)

1 tablespoon dried Mexican oregano

2 teaspoons ground cumin

½ teaspoon ground cayenne

4 Roma tomatoes, chopped

2 teaspoons salt

3 cups salted vegetable broth

ingredient list continued on following page

Place the black-eyed peas in a saucepan and fill with water to cover the peas by 4 inches. Cover the saucepan and bring to a boil. Turn off the heat and allow the peas to soak for at least 4 hours or overnight. When ready to make the chili, drain and rinse the peas in a colander and set aside.

While wearing thick rubber gloves, use a large, flat-bladed knife on its side to shave off any spines or rough spots from the nopales. Place the nopales on a large sheet pan in a single layer and arrange the poblano peppers and bell pepper around them, cut-side down. Place the pan under the broiler very close to the flame for 7 to 10 minutes, until the nopales are bubbled and browned in places (you can also place the nopales and peppers directly on a barbecue grill). Turn the nopales over, leaving the peppers cut-side down so the skin can blacken, and broil for an additional 7 to 10 minutes. Remove the pan from the oven and place the peppers in a sealed paper bag to steam. Chop the nopales into ½-inch squares and set aside along with any juices from the broiling pan. When cool enough to touch, peel away the skin from the peppers and chop the peppers into ¼-inch squares and set aside.

continued on the following page

Chopped cilantro

Sliced avocado

Sour cream

_____

Availability year-round at Latin American markets and specialty markets

Selection choose nopal leaves 7 to 10 inches long, with bright green, firm skin with or without spines; they can also be found prechopped in plastic bags sold as *nopalitos* at Berkeley Bowl and other markets

Safety wear thick rubber gloves while handling nopales that are not de-spined

Storage refrigerate in a plastic bag for up to 10 days

Substitutions green bell pepper, prechopped nopalitos

Heat the olive oil in a large Dutch oven or pot over medium heat. Add the onion and sauté for 7 to 8 minutes, until softened and translucent. Add the garlic, bay leaf, chili powder, oregano, cumin, and cayenne and sauté for 3 minutes to release the flavors. Add the black-eyed peas, nopales, peppers, tomatoes, salt, and vegetable broth and bring to a boil. Simmer, uncovered, for 25 to 35 minutes, until the black-eyed peas are tender. Taste and adjust the level of salt and spices to your liking. Serve hot, garnished with the cilantro, avocado, and sour cream.

Note: Poblano peppers are sometimes sold as pasilla.

Hedgehog Mushroom Toast

This wild mushroom gets its name from the tightly packed teeth on the underside of its broad cap, like the spines of a hedgehog. A close relative of the similarly rust-colored chanterelle, hedgehog mushrooms' nutty flavor begs to be sautéed in butter. Here they're spooned onto crisped toast and brightened with a dollop of farmer's cheese and fresh herbs for a simple supper or appetizer.

Serves 3 as a main course,
6 as an appetizer

1 pound hedgehog mushrooms, roughly chopped

2 tablespoons salted butter

¾ teaspoon salt

Freshly ground black pepper

3 tablespoons white wine or champagne

3 tablespoons minced curly-leaf parsley

3 (½-inch-thick) slices of levain or sourdough bread (6 to 7 inches wide)

⅔ cup Russian-style farmer's cheese (or *fromage blanc*)

1 tablespoon minced fresh chives

Olive oil, high quality

To clean the mushrooms, trim any brown spots and brush away any debris using a damp towel. Melt the butter in a large cast-iron skillet over medium-high heat. Add the mushrooms and sauté for 5 to 7 minutes, until they are fragrant and most of the liquid has cooked off. Stir in the salt, pepper, white wine, and half of the parsley. Cook for 1 more minute before removing the mushrooms from the skillet. Reserve the juices in the skillet for later use.

While the mushrooms are cooking, toast the bread in a toaster or in the oven until lightly golden. Wipe the toasted bread along the bottom of the cast-iron skillet used to cook the mushrooms to soak up the flavors. Arrange the toasted bread, flavored side up, on a cutting board and top with the farmer's cheese. Spoon the mushrooms on top of the cheese and sprinkle with the remaining parsley and the chives. Finish off with a drizzle of the olive oil and some pepper before slicing each piece of toast in half and serving immediately.

Availability specialty markets and farmers' markets from fall to early spring

Selection look for firm, golden-colored mushrooms free of soft spots, with a nutty aroma; also called sweet tooth mushrooms

Storage refrigerate in a paper bag for up to 3 days

image appears on following page

Preparation do not wash mushrooms in water; use a damp towel to remove dirt

Substitutions other meaty, wild mushrooms such as porcini or chanterelles

Morel Pot Pies with Asparagus and Peas

Morel mushrooms are intricately beautiful fungi, like the long, lacy spires of a gothic cathedral. This spring treat has a meaty, woodsy taste that begs to be baked into a flaky pot pie with a sherry gravy. Fresh asparagus and peas with a healthy scoop of fresh herbs keep things light and bright under the rich pastry top. Serve with a simply dressed salad of spring greens.

Serves 4

1 (9 by 9-inch) square of frozen puff pastry dough (½ pound), thawed but chilled

3 tablespoons butter

2 large shallots, minced

1 large Yukon gold potato, peeled and small diced

½ pound fresh asparagus, sliced into 1-inch pieces

6 ounces fresh morel mushrooms (about 20 mushrooms), sliced into ½-inch pieces

1 cup shelled English peas (about 14 ounces of pea pods)

1 teaspoon salt

Freshly ground black pepper

1 tablespoon all-purpose flour

1½ cups salted vegetable broth, hot

2 tablespoons sherry

2 teaspoons freshly squeezed lemon juice

¼ cup heavy cream

1 tablespoon minced fresh chives

1 tablespoon minced fresh chervil

1 beaten egg

Preheat the oven to 400°F. Heat 1 tablespoon of the butter in a large skillet over medium-low heat. Add the shallots and sauté for 7 to 10 minutes, until softened. Increase the heat to medium and add the potato and asparagus. Sauté for 4 to 5 minutes, until the potatoes are not quite tender. Add the mushrooms and peas and gently sauté another 1 to 2 minutes. Stir in the salt and pepper. Divide the vegetables among four 1-cup ramekins and set aside.

Return the skillet to medium heat and melt the remaining 2 tablespoons of butter. Whisk the flour into the butter to form a paste and continue whisking for 1 to 2 minutes, until the mixture turns a pale tan color. Slowly add the hot broth, whisking it into the flour mixture until it is completely incorporated. Add the sherry and simmer for 1 to 2 minutes, until the gravy has thickened slightly. Turn off the heat and stir in the lemon juice, cream, chives, and chervil. Divide the gravy over the four ramekins of vegetables. Brush the rims of the ramekins with the beaten egg using a pastry brush. Set aside the remaining egg for later use.

Slice the thawed pastry dough into four equal squares. Press the dough squares onto the tops of the egg-brushed ramekins to create a seal, and brush the dough lightly with the remaining egg. Place the ramekins on a rimmed baking sheet and bake for 25 to 30 minutes, until the pastry is puffed up and golden. Serve immediately.

Availability specialty markets and farmers' markets in spring

Selection select tender, non-brittle morels with an earthy aroma; avoid those with soft spots or a sour smell

Storage refrigerate in a paper bag for up to 2 days

Substitutions other earthy, woodsy mushrooms such as porcini or chanterelles

Abalone Mushroom Schnitzel

Abalone mushrooms take after their shellfish namesake in more ways than one: smooth and ivory-colored; disc-shaped; and, with its buttery, mild shellfish flavor, begging to be breaded and pan-fried. Purists will eat them simply with a squeeze of fresh lemon, but these mushrooms are also tasty with marinara sauce or baked in a killer "mushroom parmesan."

Serves 4 to 6

1½ cups unseasoned breadcrumbs, preferably homemade (see *Note*)

¾ teaspoon garlic powder

1 tablespoon fresh minced parsley

1 tablespoon finely grated Parmesan cheese

1 teaspoon salt

2 eggs, beaten and in a small bowl

2 large abalone mushrooms, sliced in ⅓-inch "cutlets"

Oil for frying (corn, canola, or other mild-flavored oil)

Sea salt

Lemon wedges

Combine the breadcrumbs, garlic powder, parsley, Parmesan cheese, and salt in a small bowl and set next to the bowl of beaten eggs. One by one, dip the mushroom cutlets first in the beaten eggs and then in the breadcrumb mixture to coat evenly. Set aside on a tray or baking sheet until all the mushroom cutlets have been breaded.

Heat about an inch of oil in a large skillet over medium-high heat. When the oil is hot but not smoking, add the mushroom cutlets one batch at a time to avoid crowding the skillet. Fry for 2 to 3 minutes on each side, until the breading is golden brown. Remove to drain on paper towels and sprinkle lightly with sea salt. Repeat with the remaining batches. Serve hot with a squeeze of fresh lemon.

Note: To make homemade breadcrumbs, slice half a sourdough baguette and place on a baking sheet. Bake at 250°F until the slices are dried out (about 15 minutes). Allow to cool before grinding in a food processor to form medium-fine crumbs (makes about 2 to 3 cups of crumbs). Store the leftovers in an airtight container at room temperature.

Availability specialty markets and farmers' markets in winter

Selection choose large, ivory-colored mushrooms with firm flesh and gills free of slime; they should smell mild and buttery

Storage refrigerate in a paper bag for up to 4 days

Preparation do not wash mushrooms in water; use a damp towel to remove dirt

Substitutions fresh king oyster mushrooms, fresh porcini mushrooms

Aloe Vera Mango Ceviche

Many people are familiar with the clear gel of the aloe vera leaf as a topical salve to treat burns and skin irritation, but throughout Latin America, it's commonly blended into a medicinal drink to boost digestive health, immune function, and even blood sugar control. Once rinsed of its slippery sap, aloe has a succulent but surprisingly firm texture similar to raw fish, making it ideal for a vegan "ceviche." Its clean taste is a springboard for the brightness of mint, bell pepper, lime, and green onion in this refreshing starter. Adjust the amount of serrano chile to suit desired heat level.

Serves 4 to 6

1 large aloe vera leaf

3 tablespoons freshly squeezed lemon juice

¾ teaspoon salt

3 green onions, white and green parts finely sliced

1 small mango, diced

½ cup red bell pepper, minced

1 serrano chile, seeded and minced

1 firm avocado, diced

3 tablespoons minced fresh mint leaves

2 tablespoons freshly squeezed lime juice

Corn tortilla chips for serving

Lime wedge, for garnish

To extract the aloe vera gel, lay the leaf flat on a cutting board. Slice off the bottom inch of the leaf base as well as the top third of the leaf, which is too narrow to extract any gel. Pressing the leaf down so it flattens against the cutting board, insert a large knife into the base between the gel and the green rind on the cutting board side. Carefully move the knife along to separate the gel from the rind. Flip the leaf over and repeat with the other side, leaving a long fillet of clear gel. Slice the gel fillet into ½-inch cubes and place in a colander. Run under cold water to rinse away any yellow latex (sap). Place the rinsed aloe vera cubes in a bowl and combine with the lemon juice and half of the salt. Cover and refrigerate for at least 3 hours or overnight.

To serve, place the aloe vera in a colander and rinse under cold water until the aloe is no longer slippery. Drain well and combine with the remaining salt and the green onions, mango, bell pepper, serrano chile, avocado, mint, and lime juice. Taste and adjust seasoning as desired. Serve immediately with crispy tortilla chips and garnished with a lime wedge.

Availability year-round at Latin American markets and specialty markets

Selection choose firm, plump leaves with smooth, green skin free of blemishes

Storage refrigerate for up to 1 week

Safety ensure the gel fillet is rinsed well of yellow latex (sap), which can cause indigestion

Substitutions while there is no substitute for fresh aloe vera gel, this recipe can be made with any favorite ceviche ingredients (tomato, cucumber, avocado, etc.)

Purslane with Chilled Melon and Feta

A crisp and juicy succulent that tastes a bit like watercress, purslane won't wilt in salads. Here it's paired with melon and feta for a summery dish best enjoyed by chilling the fruit and purslane beforehand. Serve immediately after tossing to prevent the melon from releasing its juice.

Serves 4 to 6

2 bunches purslane
(about 1 pound)

1 small ripe honeydew melon, sliced into cubes and chilled

½ red onion, very thinly sliced

3 tablespoons freshly squeezed lemon juice

2 tablespoons olive oil

¾ teaspoon salt

½ cup crumbled feta cheese

Availability Latin American and Middle Eastern groceries, specialty markets, and farmers' markets

Selection look for dark green, crisp leaves with reddish stems; also sold as Mexican parsley or verdolaga

Storage refrigerate in a plastic bag for up to 2 days

Substitutions mâche, watercress

Pinch the leaves off the purslane and discard the stems. Wrap the leaves in a paper towel and place in a sealed container. Chill the leaves in the refrigerator for at least 30 minutes.

To assemble, combine the purslane leaves with the melon, onion, lemon juice, olive oil, and salt and toss to coat.

Crumble the feta over the top and serve immediately.

Matsutake Miso Soup

Slices of matsutake mushrooms are just the thing for those yearning for more from miso soup. Meaning "pine mushroom" in Japanese, this distinctively flavored delicacy with a spicy-musky aroma can stand up to the complex flavor of miso broth. Sip a nourishing bowl and imagine these fragrant white mushrooms growing quietly on the forest floor.

Serves 4

1 (5 by 5-inch) square kombu (dried seaweed) (see *Note*)

2 small matsutake mushrooms (about 5 ounces)

6 cups water

¼ cup miso paste

¼ cup dried wakame

3 tablespoons mirin

3 tablespoons soy sauce or tamari

6 ounces firm tofu, drained and sliced into bite-sized pieces

2 green onions, white and light green parts thinly sliced

Availability Asian markets, specialty markets, and farmers' markets from midfall through winter

Selection select mushrooms with a fresh, peppery aroma with firm, white flesh, although some rust color is okay

Storage refrigerate in a paper bag for up to several days

Preparation do not wash mushrooms in water; use a damp towel to remove dirt

Substitutions porcini, although they will not have the same spicy aroma

Lightly wipe the square of kombu with a damp cloth to remove the extra salt and place it in the bottom of a saucepan. Use a mushroom brush or damp cloth to remove any dirt from the matsutake mushrooms. Trim the discolored ends from the mushrooms, leaving about 1½-inch sections of stalk intact. Use the edge of a knife to scrape off any discolored skin from the remaining stalks. Thinly slice the mushrooms lengthwise into ⅛-inch sections and add them to the saucepan with the kombu. Cover with the water and bring to a boil. Boil for 1 minute before turning off the heat and discarding the kombu.

Add the remaining ingredients to the hot broth, stirring until the miso paste is completely dissolved. Taste and adjust the level of salt or miso to your liking. Serve hot.

Note: Kombu is usually sold in sealed packages at Asian markets and specialty markets.

Fiddlehead Tempura with Sriracha Crème Fraîche

With their playful coils, mild-asparagus taste, and fleeting season, it's easy to see why fiddleheads are considered a delicacy—especially when one considers they are each a furled frond of a young ostrich fern hand-foraged from a forest floor. Coated in a light, crispy tempura batter and served with a spicy dipping sauce, this spring treat elevates snacking to a new level.

Serves 6 as an appetizer

SRIRACHA CRÈME FRAÎCHE

½ cup crème fraîche

1 to 2 tablespoons Sriracha

1 teaspoon fresh lime juice

½ teaspoon honey

TEMPURA

1 cup all-purpose flour

¼ cup plus 1 tablespoon cornstarch

1 egg, beaten

1 cup club soda

½ pound fiddleheads

Canola oil for frying

2 tablespoons sesame oil

Togarashi (see *Note*)

Sea salt

Availability specialty and farmers' markets in midspring

Selection choose firm, tightly furled, bright green fronds

Storage refrigerate in a sealed plastic bag for up to several days

Safety blanch before consumption to eliminate potential bacteria

Substitution asparagus

To make the Sriracha crème fraîche, combine all the ingredients and set aside until ready to serve.

To make the tempura, combine the flour with 1 tablespoon of the cornstarch in a mixing bowl, and refrigerate it along with the beaten egg and club soda until you are ready to make the tempura batter—cold ingredients will ensure a light, airy tempura.

Set a pot of salted water to boil. Meanwhile, clean the fiddleheads by swishing them around in a bowl of cold water to remove any dirt or brown papery skin, and trim the ends. Blanch the fiddleheads in the boiling water for 7 minutes (see Safety note below). Drain and put in an ice bath to stop the cooking. Drain well and pat dry.

Heat at least 1 to 2 inches of canola oil plus the sesame oil in a skillet over high heat. Dredge the fiddleheads in the remaining ¼ cup of cornstarch and shake off the excess. Combine the beaten egg with the club soda and pour into the flour mixture. Using a pair of chopsticks or a fork, stab at the flour for no more than 20 to 30 seconds to loosely combine it with the liquid but maintain lumps and pockets of dry flour.

Turn the heat under the skillet down to medium and, working quickly, dunk a fiddlehead in the batter using chopsticks or small tongs and drop it into the hot oil. Repeat with the other fiddleheads but do not crowd the skillet. Fry for 1 to 2 minutes, until the fiddleheads turn lightly golden and crispy. Drain on paper towels and immediately sprinkle lightly with the togarashi and sea salt. Fry the remaining batches. Serve immediately with the Sriracha crème fraîche as a dipping sauce.

Note: Togarashi is a Japanese spice blend sold in the Asian foods section of Berkeley Bowl and in Asian markets.

Meyer Lemon–Marinated Pioppini and Frisée Salad

Marinating these bite-sized mushrooms in Meyer lemon juice preserves their bright white color and brings out their mildly sweet, nutty flavor. A type of shimeji mushroom that sprouts up in clusters, their delicate stalks and gilled caps look elegant strewn atop a bed of crisp frisée, shaved carrot, and white onion. A hard-boiled egg adds just the right note of richness.

Serves 2 as a main course,
4 as a side dish

MARINADE

⅓ cup mirin

2 tablespoons rice vinegar

1 tablespoon water

1¼ teaspoons salt

2 strips Meyer lemon peel

6 ounces alba pioppini mushrooms

2 teaspoons freshly squeezed Meyer lemon juice

1 teaspoon olive oil

SALAD

1 large head frisée, torn into bite-sized pieces

1 purple carrot, peeled and shaved

¼ white onion, finely sliced

1 tablespoon olive oil

¼ teaspoon salt

2 hard-boiled eggs, sliced into wedges

Freshly ground black pepper

1 teaspoon freshly squeezed Meyer lemon juice

To prepare the marinade, place the mirin, vinegar, water, salt, and lemon peel in a small saucepan and bring to a boil. Immediately add the mushrooms and gently coat in the liquid. Lower the heat and simmer for 2 to 3 minutes, until the mushrooms are slightly softened. Remove from the heat and stir in the lemon juice and olive oil. Cover and refrigerate for 2 to 3 hours, or overnight, until chilled.

To make the salad, combine the frisée, purple carrot, and onion in a large salad bowl. In a separate bowl, whisk together 2 tablespoons of the pioppini marinade, olive oil, and salt until combined. Pour over the frisée salad and toss to coat. Scatter the egg wedges and the marinated mushrooms over the top. Top with the pepper and lemon juice and serve immediately.

Availability year-round at Asian markets and specialty markets

Selection choose pioppini with bright white color free of discoloration; also called white beech, buna shimeji, and white shimeji

Storage refrigerate in a paper bag for up to 1 week

Preparation do not wash mushrooms in water; use a damp towel to remove dirt

Substitutions white enoki mushrooms, brown pioppini (but they will not have the same color effect on the dish)

STEMS

Tortilla China

Every Spanish family has its own way of making the perfect tortilla which in Spain, is a kind of omelet made with olive oil and vegetables—most typically potatoes and onions (the more well-known Mexican tortilla is a completely different entity). The simplicity of tortilla preparation and flavor is a springboard for whatever ingredients are on hand. This particular recipe brings together East and West with the addition of Chinese flowering cabbage, or choy sum. Its tender white stalks and mustardy leaves yield a moist tortilla with loads of flavor for a twist on the classic Spanish dish.

Serves 6 to 8

¼ cup plus 1 tablespoon olive oil

2 bundles long choy sum (about 1¼ pounds)

1 yellow onion, chopped

1 small russet potato, peeled, halved lengthwise, and thinly sliced (⅟₁₆ inch thick)

7 eggs

3 tablespoons milk

1½ teaspoons salt

¾ teaspoon ground cayenne

Availability year-round at Asian markets and specialty markets

Selection look for fleshy white stalks with dark green oval leaves, with or without small yellow flowers; also called Chinese flowering cabbage

Storage refrigerate in a plastic bag for up to 1 week

Substitutions bok choy, green chard

Heat ¼ cup of the olive oil in a very large skillet over medium-high heat. Separate the green leaves from the white stalks of the choy sum and set aside the leaves. Chop the stalks into ¼-inch pieces and add them to the skillet along with the onion. Sauté for 7 to 8 minutes, until soft and translucent. Lower the heat to medium and add the potato slices. Sauté for 10 to 15 minutes, until the potato slices are tender. Roughly chop the choy sum leaves and add them to the skillet. Sauté for 2 to 3 minutes, until the leaves are wilted and tender. Turn off the heat.

In a large bowl, whisk the eggs, milk, salt, and cayenne to combine. Gently fold the choy sum mixture into the egg mixture. Heat the remaining olive oil in a 9- or 10-inch nonstick skillet over medium heat. Pour in the egg and choy sum mixture, and immediately lower the heat to medium-low. Let cook undisturbed until the sides have started to set and the bottom has turned golden brown, about 6 to 8 minutes (the middle will still be runny).

To flip the tortilla, loosen the tortilla edges with a rubber spatula, brace a large plate over the top of the skillet, and then carefully and quickly flip the skillet over so the tortilla is on the plate. Return the skillet to the stove and carefully slide the tortilla back into the skillet, tucking in the sides with a spatula and shaking the skillet gently a couple of times to prevent sticking. Cook for 2 to 3 minutes more for a moist tortilla or 4 to 5 minutes for a firmer one.

Tilt the skillet to slide the tortilla onto a serving plate. Slice into wedges and serve warm or at room temperature with a simple green salad.

Garlic Soup with Bạc Hà

This recipe is a take on *sopa de ajo*, a traditional peasant's soup made with just a few staples: loads of garlic, stale bread, poached eggs, and pimentón dulce (sweet Spanish paprika). In this version, an unlikely Asian vegetable with a spongy, porous quality stands in for the bread, soaking up the bone-warming broth. Vietnamese and Japanese cultures have long used bạc hà in this way, taking advantage of its texture and mild taste to absorb the flavor of the soup. It's customary to serve garlic soup after welcoming in the New Year, providing good luck and warm bellies on the cheap for weary partiers. But this quick and filling soup goes down easy any night of the year.

Serves 4

1 stalk bạc hà (about 8 ounces)

2 tablespoons olive oil

6 to 7 large cloves garlic, peeled and finely sliced

2 teaspoons pimentón dulce

6 cups salted vegetable broth, heated

4 eggs

Availability year-round at Asian markets and specialty markets

Selection look for firm, bright green stalks with spongy white ends in the refrigerated section; also known as doc mung, taro stem, elephant ear stem, and hasu-imo

Storage refrigerate in a plastic bag for up to 1 week

Safety do not consume raw; oil your hands or wear food preparation gloves when preparing

Substitutions stale baguette

Bring a small pot of lightly salted water to a boil. Coat your hands with oil or wear food preparation gloves (see *Note*), trim each end of the bạc hà, and then remove the peel by grabbing a strip from the top of one end and peeling it all the way down the stalk. Trim any brown spots or ridges. Slice the bạc hà on the diagonal into ⅓-inch slices, cutting the larger pieces in half as the stalk gets wider toward the base. Drop the slices into the water and boil for 10 minutes. Drain and set aside.

Heat the olive oil in a saucepan over medium heat. Add the garlic and gently fry for 1 or 2 minutes, until lightly golden, being careful not to let it burn. Remove from the heat and stir the pimentón dulce into the hot oil. Add the heated vegetable broth and boiled bạc hà. Return to medium heat and simmer for 5 minutes.

Just before serving, reduce the heat to low so the soup ceases to simmer. Crack open the eggs one at a time and use a ladle to carefully lower them one by one into the broth. Allow the eggs to poach in the hot soup for 6 to 7 minutes, until the egg whites are set, before turning off the heat and ladling the soup into serving bowls.

Note: Because the calcium oxalate can cause irritation, oil your hands or wear gloves when preparing bạc hà and boil it completely before adding it to the soup.

Nori Packets with Yellow Garlic Chives

Grown without sunlight to keep them from turning tough and green, these vampires of the chive world have a mellow flavor somewhere between garlic and onion. Yellow garlic chives become tender and juicy when stir-fried and are delectable piled on sushi rice wrapped in nori, for a nibble inspired by the Japanese snack *onigiri*. Don't wrap up the nori packet until it's almost in your mouth, or the nori will lose its crispiness. These have plenty of flavor on their own, but they are also tasty dipped in wasabi and soy sauce.

Makes ½ dozen

1 cup sushi rice

1 cup water

2 tablespoons unseasoned rice vinegar

1 tablespoon mirin

2 teaspoons sugar

1 teaspoon salt

2 tablespoons peanut oil

1 pound yellow garlic chives, chopped into 1-inch pieces

1 tablespoon minced fresh ginger

¾ teaspoon sesame oil

1 tablespoon soy sauce

6 sheets of nori

Availability Asian markets and specialty markets, with peak in spring and summer

Selection choose flat, unwilted stalks and leaves with pale color

Storage refrigerate in a paper towel for up to 1 week

Substitutions slowly cooked yellow onion with green garlic chives

Rinse the sushi rice under cold water in a fine-mesh strainer until the water runs clear. Drain well. Place the rice in a small saucepan and add the water. Cover with a lid and bring to a boil before lowering the heat to simmer for 18 minutes. Without removing the lid, turn the heat off and let the rice sit for 10 minutes while it absorbs the steam.

While the rice is cooking, warm the vinegar and mirin in a saucepan over low heat, and stir in the sugar and salt until completely dissolved. When the rice is done, sprinkle the vinegar mixture over the rice and gently stir to coat, being careful not to break or mash the rice. Spread the rice out on a baking sheet or a sheet of parchment paper and let it sit at least 20 minutes, or until the moisture evaporates and the rice cools completely.

Heat the peanut oil in a large skillet or wok over medium heat. Add the chives and ginger and stir-fry for 5 minutes, or until the chives are tender. Stir in the sesame oil and soy sauce and turn off the heat. Allow to cool.

To assemble, spoon about ⅓ cup of rice onto a sheet of nori, top with a spoonful of the chives, and fold in the corners of the nori like an envelope to make a packet. Eat immediately or store the rice and chives separately from the nori for a picnic or snack at a later time.

CARDOON

Moroccan Cardoon Stew

Cardoons may look like weeds or prehistoric celery, but those who take the time to prepare them are rewarded with tender stalks and the earthy taste of artichoke, its close relative. In this hearty stew, cardoons soak up the seductive spices and herbs of the Mediterranean, the region that first brought us this edible thistle. Serve alongside couscous or with pita bread for unabashed sopping.

Serves 4 to 6

Juice from 1 lemon

1 bunch cardoons

2 tablespoons olive oil

1 yellow onion, thinly sliced

½ teaspoon saffron threads

1 tablespoon minced fresh ginger

½ teaspoon ground turmeric

¾ teaspoon ground cumin

¼ teaspoon ground cinnamon

4 cloves garlic, peeled and minced

2 tablespoons brown sugar

2½ cups water

1 cup white wine

1½ teaspoons salt

Freshly ground black pepper

5 red potatoes (about 1 pound), unpeeled and cut into bite-sized cubes

4 Roma tomatoes (about 1 pound), chopped

⅔ cup assorted olives, pitted

8 dried prunes, pitted and halved

½ cup chopped cilantro, for garnish

½ cup chopped parsley, for garnish

Add the lemon juice to a large pot of moderately salted water. Remove the bottom 1 inch from the cardoon bunch and discard. Use a paring knife to strip the leaves and trim the edges of each stalk to remove the small thorns. Peel back the strings as you would celery. Chop the cleaned stalks into 1½-inch pieces and immediately place them in the pot of lemon water to prevent discoloration. Cover the pot and bring to a boil. Boil for 30 minutes to remove any bitterness and then drain.

Heat the olive oil in a large Dutch oven or deep skillet over medium heat. Add the onion and sauté for 7 to 10 minutes, until the onion is softened and translucent. Meanwhile, grind the saffron, ginger, turmeric, cumin, cinnamon, garlic, and brown sugar with a mortar and pestle until they form a paste. Add the paste to the onions and sauté for 2 minutes to release the flavors. Add the boiled cardoons, water, wine, salt, pepper, potatoes, tomatoes, olives, and prunes, and simmer uncovered for 20 to 30 minutes, until the potatoes and cardoons are tender. Taste and adjust salt level as desired.

Serve garnished with the cilantro and parsley alongside couscous.

Availability Middle Eastern markets and farmers' markets from January to June

Selection heavy stalks with silvery green color; also sold as cardoni or cardo

Storage refrigerate in a plastic bag for up to 1 week

Substitutions artichokes

Vanilla Rhubarb Jam

Sadly, rhubarb often plays second fiddle to strawberries in pies and pastries. Here, these tangy, berry-red stalks headline in a foolproof jam with just a hint of vanilla bean. Slather it onto toast with fresh goat cheese or butter in the morning, or spoon it onto vanilla ice cream for a dressed-up dessert.

Makes about 1 cup

½ vanilla bean

3 cups finely chopped rhubarb (about 3 to 4 large stalks)

½ cup sugar

1½ tablespoons freshly squeezed lemon juice

Availability well-stocked groceries and farmers' markets, with peak in spring and summer

Selection firm, plump stalks with deep red color

Storage refrigerate in a plastic bag for up to 1 week

Substitutions frozen rhubarb, tart plums

Slice open the vanilla bean and scrape the seeds into a small saucepan, tossing in the whole vanilla bean as well. Add the remaining ingredients and bring to a simmer.

Simmer on low, uncovered, for 20 minutes. Pour into a 12-ounce jar and secure a clean lid.

Store in the refrigerator and enjoy within 1 month.

White Asparagus with Preserved Lemon

In northern Europe, white asparagus is a rite of spring. Nicknamed "edible ivory," its velvety texture and delicate flavor are a result of a laborious and dark upbringing: Grown beneath the soil to keep out the sun's rays, they don't develop the toughened stalks or strong flavor of their green counterparts. In this recipe, poached asparagus are drizzled with a simple vinaigrette to bring out their mild earthy flavor.

Serves 2 to 4

1 bunch white asparagus

1 teaspoon salt

¼ of a preserved lemon (see *Note*), pulp discarded

2 teaspoons chopped fresh parsley, for garnish

VINAIGRETTE

1 teaspoon Dijon mustard

2 tablespoons olive oil

2 teaspoons freshly squeezed lemon juice

⅛ teaspoon sherry vinegar

⅛ teaspoon salt

Freshly ground black pepper

Availability specialty markets and farmers' markets in spring

Selection choose thick, firm stalks with tightly closed tips

Storage wrap the cut ends in a wet paper towel and refrigerate in a plastic bag for up to 3 or 4 days

Substitutions jarred or canned white asparagus (omit cooking)

Lay the asparagus on a flat surface and use a vegetable peeler to peel away the fibrous outer skin, starting an inch below the head. Cut off and discard the bottom inch.

In a deep skillet wide enough to fit the asparagus lying down, heat 2 inches of water with the salt and bring to a boil. Add the asparagus and simmer for 10 to 12 minutes, until the tip of a knife pierces it easily. Carefully remove the asparagus from the water and drain well on paper towels. Set aside to cool.

Meanwhile, place the ingredients for the vinaigrette in a small-lidded container and shake until emulsified.

To assemble, arrange the asparagus on a serving plate. Dice the preserved lemon peel into small bits and scatter over the top. Drizzle with the vinaigrette and garnish with the parsley. Serve at room temperature.

Note: Preserved lemon can be purchased at specialty and Middle Eastern groceries, or made from scratch with kosher salt and two weeks' time.

Ramped-Up Mushrooms

Some may wonder why something that looks like a common green onion can prompt such a frenzy at farmers' markets in the few weeks of spring they're available. A perfect marriage of garlic and onion, with tender leaves that can be eaten in their entirety, this wild leek is a flavor-seeker's dream. The bite-sized mushrooms in this recipe, stuffed with a ramps-based pesto that packs a punch, make the quintessential appetizer. For heartier fare, serve them atop creamy polenta.

Serves 4 to 6

½ cup walnuts

¼ cup plus 2 tablespoons olive oil

1 bunch ramps (about 8 ounces), roots removed and roughly chopped

1 tablespoon freshly squeezed lemon juice

1 teaspoon salt

⅓ cup grated Parmesan cheese

18 portobellini or brown button mushrooms

Freshly ground black pepper

⅓ cup dry white wine

1 tablespoon reduced balsamic vinegar (see *Note*)

Availability specialty and farmers' markets in early spring

Selection choose ramps with bright green, unwilted leaves and crisp, green onion–like stalks and bulbs, with or without roots attached

Storage wrap in a damp paper towel and refrigerate in a plastic bag for up to 3 days

Substitutions other common pesto ingredients such as basil, chives, and garlic

Heat a skillet over medium heat. Toast the walnuts in the skillet for 2 to 3 minutes, stirring regularly so they don't burn. Remove them from the skillet and set aside. Heat 1 tablespoon of the olive oil in the skillet over medium heat. Add the ramps and sauté for 2 minutes, or until just wilted and deep green. Remove the skillet from the heat and let the ramps cool slightly.

Place the ramps and walnuts in a food processor or blender, and add ¼ cup of the olive oil, the lemon juice, ½ teaspoon of the salt, and the Parmesan cheese. Process or pulse the mixture until it comes together to form a pesto-like paste. Taste for seasoning and add more salt or lemon juice as desired.

Pinch off and discard the mushroom stems, leaving a hollow in the underside of the mushrooms. Heat the remaining 1 tablespoon of olive oil in the skillet over medium heat. Add the mushrooms, hollow-side down, and sprinkle with the remaining ½ teaspoon of salt and some pepper. Cook undisturbed for 5 to 6 minutes, until softened and slightly browned. Turn the mushrooms over so the hollow is facing up. Add the wine and swirl it to coat the mushrooms. Simmer for 2 minutes to reduce the wine. Fill the hollow of each mushroom with a dollop of the ramps mixture, cover the skillet, and reduce the heat to low. Cook for 7 to 10 minutes, until the mushrooms are cooked all the way through. Drizzle a serving platter with the vinegar and arrange the mushrooms on top. Serve warm.

Note: Purchase store-bought balsamic reduction, or make your own by simmering ½ cup balsamic vinegar with 1 tablespoon honey in a sauce-pan until the mixture is reduced to a quarter of its original volume.

Green Garlic Soup with Lemon Cardamom Yogurt

The beauty of this voluptuous soup is the balance between the earthy green garlic purée and the sweet tang of spiced yogurt. Enjoy it on a chilly night in early spring, when tender, young garlic shoots first appear in markets. Alternatively, serve chilled to take advantage of a warm spell.

Serves 6 to 8

2 leeks

2 bunches green garlic (about 1 pound)

3 tablespoons olive oil

2 small yellow potatoes, peeled and diced

6 cups vegetable broth

1 teaspoon salt

2 bunches fresh spinach (about 10 ounces), roughly chopped

1 lemon

1 cup Greek yogurt

¼ teaspoon ground cardamom

Availability well-stocked groceries and farmers' markets in spring

Selection choose bunches with dark green leaves, long white or purple bases, and intact roots with a mild garlic smell

Storage wrap in a damp paper towel and refrigerate in a plastic bag for up to 1 week

Substitutions ramps, spring onions

Slice the leeks and green garlic (white and light green parts only) and swish them around in a large bowl of cool water to loosen the dirt and allow it to settle at the bottom. Use a small strainer or slotted spoon to skim the leeks and green garlic, transferring them to a colander to drain and being careful not to disturb the dirt at the bottom of the bowl.

Heat the olive oil in a large heavy-bottomed pot over medium-low heat. Add the leeks and green garlic and sauté for 10 minutes, or until soft and fragrant. Add the potatoes, stock, and ¾ teaspoon of the salt, and bring to a boil. Cover and let simmer for 20 minutes, or until the vegetables are soft. Stir in the spinach and immediately turn off the heat.

Meanwhile, grate the zest of the lemon into the Greek yogurt. Stir in the cardamom, the remaining ¼ teaspoon of the salt, and the juice of half the lemon (see **Note**).

Purée the soup using a handheld (immersion) blender or standing (standard) blender. Taste for salt content and adjust as desired. Serve with a generous dollop of the lemon cardamom yogurt.

Note: If omitting the yogurt from this recipe, add the cardamom, salt, and lemon juice directly to the soup.

Lemongrass Coconut Ice Cream

Luxuriously creamy and infused with the zing of fresh lemongrass, this four-ingredient frozen treat will keep ice cream lovers asking for more.

Serves 4

3 stalks lemongrass

2 (14-ounce) cans coconut milk (regular, not light)

¾ cup granulated sugar

3 slices peeled ginger (about the thickness of a coin)

Availability year-round at well-stocked groceries and Asian markets

Selection look for long, light green stalks that are heavy for their size

Storage refrigerate for up to 2 weeks, or chop and freeze in a plastic bag for up to several months

Substitutions lemon verbena

Remove the outermost layer of the lemongrass stalks and trim the ends, leaving about 5 inches of the thickest part of the stalk. Give the stalks a couple of whacks with the flat side of a wide knife to loosen the layers a bit, and then slice them thinly.

Combine all the ingredients in a small saucepan and stir gently over medium heat until the mixture just begins to simmer. Remove from the heat and let stand for 15 minutes to allow the lemongrass and ginger to infuse. Pour the mixture into a container and refrigerate until completely chilled through, about 4 hours or overnight.

Strain the mixture and discard the contents of the strainer. Turn on the ice cream maker, pour in the mixture, and follow the manufacturer's instructions for processing time or process until the ice cream is thick and creamy, generally about 15 to 20 minutes. Serve immediately for a softer ice cream, or transfer to a freezer-safe container and freeze for at least 3 hours for a firmer consistency.

Kohlrabi Ramen

The purple or green "bulb" at the end of a kohlrabi is often mistaken for the root but is, in fact, a swollen stem with a satisfying taste and crunch comparable to broccoli. An emblem of versatility, its leaves, stalks, and stems are delicious raw, roasted, or stir-fried, as they are atop this richly flavored, miso-based ramen.

Serves 4

BROTH

1 tablespoon peanut oil

1 yellow onion, chopped

4 cloves garlic, peeled and chopped

4 cups salted vegetable broth

4 cups water

1 cup dried shiitake mushrooms

2 tablespoons soy sauce

2 tablespoons yellow or white miso paste

KOHLRABI RAMEN

8 ounces ramen or Japanese noodles

2 tablespoons peanut oil

2 kohlrabi, greens and stems chopped, and bulbs peeled and cut into bite-size pieces

1 spicy red chile (such as Fresno)

2 tablespoons minced fresh ginger

2 cups fresh shiitake mushrooms, stems removed and sliced in half

1 teaspoon sesame oil

3 tablespoons soy sauce

2 soft-boiled eggs, halved

3 green onions, white and light green parts finely sliced

To make the broth, heat the peanut oil in a large saucepan over medium heat. Add the onion and garlic and sauté for 8 to 10 minutes, until the onion is golden but not browned. Add the stock, water, dried mushrooms, and soy sauce. Cover, bring to a boil, and then reduce the heat and simmer for 25 to 30 minutes. Stir in the miso paste and process the stock in a blender until smooth.

To make the kohlrabi ramen, cook the ramen according to package directions. Heat the peanut oil in a large wok or skillet over high heat. Add the kohlrabi, chile, ginger, and fresh mushrooms and stir-fry for 5 to 6 minutes, until the kohlrabi is tender but still slightly crisp. Stir in the sesame oil and soy sauce. Taste and adjust seasoning as desired. Divide the ramen into four deep bowls. Ladle the hot broth over the ramen. Top each bowl with the stir-fried vegetables, half a soft-boiled egg, and some green onion, and serve.

Availability year-round at well-stocked groceries and farmers' markets

Selection look for crisp, dark green leaves and heavy bulbs free of cracks

Storage refrigerate the bulbs and tops separately in plastic bags for up to 2 weeks

Substitutions broccoli stems and crowns, turnips with intact greens

image appears on page 4

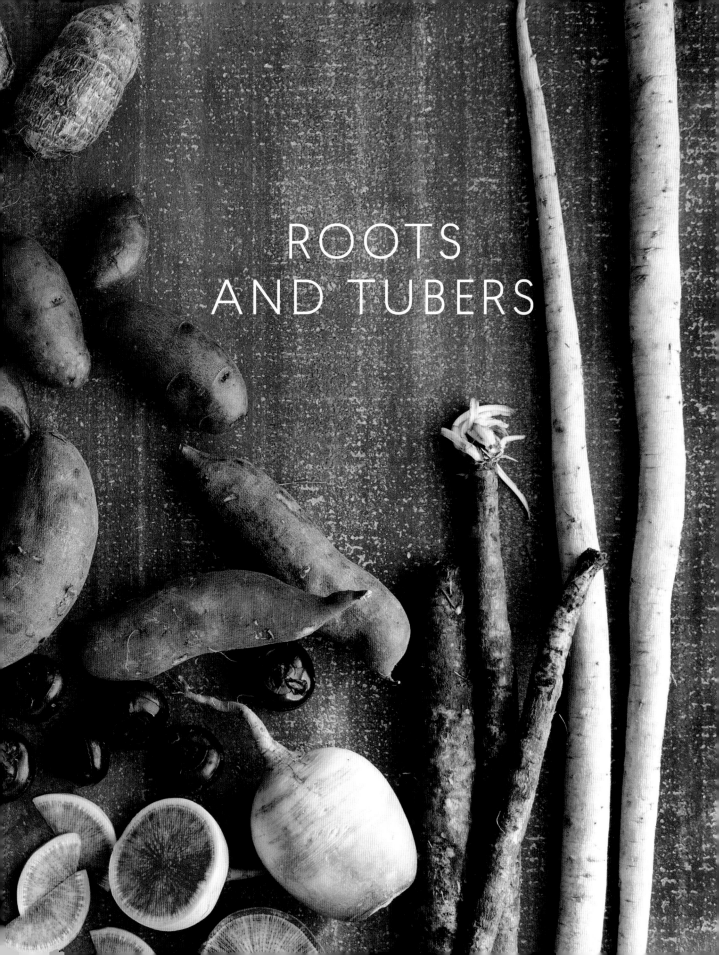

ROOTS
AND TUBERS

Purple Potato Galette with Tarragon

Fanned out across a flaky pastry smeared with caramelized shallots, this deep royal purple potato is a showstopper. A sprinkling of fresh tarragon and a dollop of sour cream balance the galette's richness. Serve for brunch or lunch alongside lightly dressed mixed greens.

Serves 6 to 8

2 tablespoons plus
1 teaspoon olive oil

4 large shallots, peeled
and thinly sliced

1 tablespoon fresh
chopped tarragon

½ teaspoon salt

Freshly ground black pepper

10 ounces purple potatoes
(about 4), unpeeled

1 9-inch pie dough (homemade
or store-bought)

1 egg, beaten

Sour cream for serving

Availability year-round at well-stocked groceries, specialty markets, and farmers' markets

Selection look for firm potatoes with delicate, deep purple skin, about the size of a new (young) potato

Storage store in a dark, cool place for up to several weeks

Substitutions other colorful root vegetables, such as carrots or beets

Heat 2 tablespoons of the olive oil in a skillet over low-medium heat. Add the shallots and sauté on low for 20 minutes, or until the shallots are soft and caramelized. Turn off the heat and stir in half of the tarragon, half of the salt, and some pepper. Set aside to cool slightly. Use a mandoline or a sharp knife to cut the potatoes into ¹⁄₁₆-inch-thick slices. Set aside.

Preheat the oven to 375°F. Use a rolling pin to roll the pie crust thinner and into a 13-inch circle. Line a baking sheet with parchment paper and place the crust on it. Spread the shallots over the pie crust, leaving a border around the edge (about 1½ inches). Starting from the outer edge of the shallots, place the potato slices on top the shallots in overlapping layers, spiraling inward.

Use a pastry brush to brush the potatoes with the remaining olive oil and sprinkle the remaining salt. Fold the border of the dough up and over the potatoes, pressing down in loose pleats. Brush the exposed dough with the beaten egg and bake for 28 to 32 minutes, until the crust is golden and the potatoes are tender.

Sprinkle the remaining tarragon over the galette and serve with dollops of cold sour cream.

Savory Daikon Pancakes with Ginger Maple Syrup

The Berkeley Bowl Cookbook would not be complete without a recipe for daikon, which is pictured on the store's logo. This super-sized, versatile radish is a staple in Japan, where daikon roots and greens appear in diverse ways on almost every restaurant menu: pickled, stir-fried, fermented, boiled, grated, battered, fried, roasted, steamed, and raw. Grated daikon root with steamed daikon greens make for a moist, savory pancake with a mild radish flavor. Drizzled with a sweet and spicy syrup, these pancakes make a bold statement for brunch, or even for dinner. If you can't find daikon root with the greens intact, buy them separately or substitute other cooking greens, such as mustard or kale.

Serves 4

PANCAKES

1 bunch daikon greens or other winter greens (about 6 ounces)

1 small daikon root (about 12 ounces), peeled

1 cup all-purpose flour

1 teaspoon salt

1½ tablespoons baking powder

2 teaspoons ground ginger

3 tablespoons olive oil

¾ cup milk

2 eggs, whites and yolks separated

2 serrano chiles, seeded and minced

2 green onions, white and green parts finely sliced

Heat a large, flat-bottomed skillet with a lid over medium heat. Strip the leaves from the daikon greens and discard the stems. Place the leaves in the skillet with ¼ cup water, cover, and cook for 3 to 4 minutes, until the leaves are wilted and tender. Drain the leaves in a strainer and allow to cool before pressing them into a ball between your hands and squeezing out as much moisture as possible. Roughly chop the pressed leaves and set aside.

Grate the daikon root using the large holes of a box grater; there should be about 2 cups of grated daikon. Press the grated daikon into a ball between your hands and squeeze out as much moisture as possible. Set aside.

Place the flour, salt, baking powder, and ginger in a mixing bowl and whisk to combine. Add the olive oil, milk, and egg yolks and whisk until smooth. Use a rubber spatula to fold in the chopped daikon leaves, grated daikon root, chiles, and green onions until well combined. In another bowl, beat the egg whites using a whisk or an electric mixer until stiff peaks form. Gently fold the egg whites into the daikon batter with a rubber spatula.

GINGER MAPLE SYRUP

½ cup maple syrup

¼ cup low-sodium soy sauce

1 teaspoon ground ginger

1 teaspoon sesame oil

1 teaspoon freshly squeezed
lime juice

Availability year-round at well-stocked groceries, Asian markets, and farmers' markets

Selection choose firm daikon with smooth white skin and bright green, unwilted leaves

Storage refrigerate the root and greens in separate plastic bags for up to 4 days

Substitutions turnip with intact greens

Preheat the oven to 200°F. Wipe out the skillet used to wilt the daikon leaves. Add enough olive oil to the skillet to lightly coat the bottom and place the skillet over medium-high heat. When the oil is hot but not smoking, form pancakes by adding ¼ cup-fulls of batter to the pan, pressing the batter down to flatten slightly and ensuring the pancakes do not touch. Allow to cook for 2 to 3 minutes on each side until golden and slightly crispy on the outside. Transfer to a plate and keep warm in the oven while you continue making pancakes, adding oil to the pan as needed, until the batter is used up. You should have about ten to twelve pancakes.

While the pancakes are cooking, combine all the ingredients for the ginger maple syrup in a small saucepan over high heat. Bring to a simmer for 1 minute before turning off the heat. Serve two to three pancakes per person and drizzle with the warm syrup.

Malanga Masala Latkes

Malanga, a starchy root from Central America, has a "glueyness" that helps bind the ingredients without the need for eggs. It is finely grated and mixed with herbs and spices so that the resulting crispy fritters are a cross between two fried favorites: Indian samosas and Jewish latkes. Top with sour cream and chutney for a sweet-and-sour nosh, or serve with a green salad as a light meal.

Serves 4

1 large malanga blanca (about 12 ounces), peeled and grated (see *Note*), about 2 cups

⅓ cup minced red bell pepper

⅓ cup petite peas

1 jalapeño pepper, seeded and minced

2 green onions, minced

2 tablespoons freshly squeezed lemon juice

1 tablespoon minced cilantro

1 teaspoon garam masala

¼ teaspoon ground cayenne

½ teaspoon salt

Coconut oil for frying

Sour cream and chutney for serving

Availability year-round at Latin American markets and specialty markets

Selection malanga can be club-shaped or oval with hairy brown skin free of soft spots or cracks

Storage refrigerate in a perforated plastic bag for up to 1 week

Substitutions taro, yuca, malanga lila

Mix the malanga, bell pepper, peas, jalapeño pepper, green onions, lemon juice, cilantro, garam masala, cayenne, and salt in a bowl until well combined.

Add enough coconut oil to a large, flat-bottomed skillet until it coats the bottom and place over medium heat. When the oil is hot but not smoking, spoon about ¼ cup of the malanga mixture into the hot oil and flatten slightly with the back of the spoon. Repeat until you fill the bottom of the skillet (this recipe makes about eight latkes but may require two batches depending on the size of your skillet).

Fry the latkes for 4 to 5 minutes on each side, until they are golden brown and crispy.

Drain on paper towels and serve hot with sour cream and chutney, or with harissa yogurt sauce (page 156).

Note: Malanga is slippery, so use a paper towel to help hold onto the root when you're grating it.

Chipotle-Roasted Satsuma Tacos with Cilantro Yogurt

The purple-skinned, cream-fleshed satsuma sweet potato has a nutty, chestnut-like flavor and texture that's brought out through roasting. Spiced with chipotle and tossed with eggplant, peppers, and onions, this nontraditional taco filling is topped with a bright and tangy cilantro yogurt. Roll out some fresh Corn Tortillas with Epazote Leaf (page 38) for the most authentic flavor. These tacos also pair well with Roasted Milpero Salsa Verde (page 151).

Serves 4 to 6

1 large satsuma sweet potato, unpeeled, scrubbed, quartered lengthwise, and sliced (about ¼ inch thick)

1 large white onion, halved and sliced (about ⅓ inch thick)

1 Chinese eggplant, halved lengthwise and sliced (about ½ inch thick)

1 large red bell pepper, quartered, seeded, and sliced (about ⅓-inch strips)

2 tablespoons olive oil

1 teaspoon ground coriander

¾ teaspoon ground cumin

1½ teaspoons salt

pepper (see *Note*)

12 corn tortillas, warmed

CILANTRO YOGURT

1 cup Greek yogurt

1 tablespoon lime juice

¼ cup lightly packed minced cilantro leaves

1 serrano chile, seeded and minced

½ teaspoon salt

Preheat the oven to 425°F. In a large bowl, toss the sweet potato, onion, eggplant, and bell pepper with the olive oil, coriander, cumin, salt, and chipotle pepper (add the chipotle pepper gradually until the desired heat intensity is achieved) until evenly coated. Spread the vegetable mixture in a single layer on a large rimmed baking sheet. Roast for 25 to 35 minutes, tossing the vegetables halfway through with a spatula to ensure even roasting, until lightly browned and tender. Taste and adjust salt and spices as desired.

Combine all the ingredients for the cilantro yogurt. Spoon the roasted vegetables onto the tortillas and top with a generous dollop of the yogurt.

Note: Ground chipotle is sold in the spice section of Berkeley Bowl or specialty spice stores, but you can also buy whole, dried chipotle peppers and grind them in a food processor or coffee grinder.

Availability year-round at well-stocked groceries and farmers' markets, with peak from late summer to early spring

Selection choose firm potatoes with purplish skin free of cracks, with ends that taper; also sold as Japanese sweet potatoes

Storage store uncovered in a cool, dry place for up to 2 weeks

Substitutions sweet potato

Golden Beet Tamales with Red Pepper Sauce

The classic pairing of beets and goat cheese is taken a step farther in these revisionist tamales. Tucked into moist roasted-corn masa and wrapped in beet leaves for steaming, the entire golden beet plant is used. A brilliant red pepper and tomato sauce complements the filling's earthy-sweet flavor. Unlike banana leaves and corn husks that traditionally encase tamales, these tender beet leaves are eaten rather than discarded.

Serves 4

FILLING

4 golden beets (about 1 pound), with a total of at least 12 larger leaves intact

1 tablespoon olive oil

¾ teaspoon salt

2 ounces goat cheese

MASA

1 ear of corn

1 teaspoon olive oil

½ cup butter

½ cup salted vegetable broth

2 cups masa harina (see *Note*)

1 teaspoon salt

½ teaspoon baking powder

SAUCE

4 Roma tomatoes, halved

2 red bell peppers, halved and seeded

2 cloves garlic, unpeeled

1 tablespoon olive oil

1 teaspoon salt

To make the filling, cut the stems off the beets and remove the leaves from the stems. Select the largest and best 8 to 10 leaves, setting them aside for later. Mince any remaining leaves as well as the stems. Peel the beets and dice them into ¼-inch cubes. Heat the olive oil in a skillet over medium-low heat. Add the diced beets, minced leaves and stems, and salt. Sauté for 15 to 20 minutes, until the beets and stems are very tender. Remove from the heat; crumble the cheese over the top and gently toss to distribute. Set aside.

To make the masa, slice the kernels from the ear of corn and toss with the olive oil. Spread the kernels on a baking sheet and place under the broiler for 5 minutes, or until some of the kernels are lightly charred. Put the kernels, butter, and broth in a blender and blend on medium for 1 minute, or until smooth. Combine the masa harina, salt, and baking powder in a large bowl. Add the kernel mixture to the bowl and stir with a wooden spoon until smooth. Wipe off the baking sheet to use it later. Place a steaming basket in a pot with a lid, add a couple inches of water, and bring to a boil.

To assemble the tamales, lay the beet leaves on a work surface with the vein of the leaf running horizontally and the smooth side face down. Using your fingers, press enough masa (about the size of a ping-pong ball depending on the size of your leaves) onto each leaf to cover it in a layer that is about ¼-inch thick. Spoon about a tablespoon of the filling along the middle of the masa. Fold the leaf in half lengthwise and seal the masa around the filling. Tuck in the edges of the leaf and place seam-side down in a covered steamer for 30 minutes.

continued on the following page

Availability year-round at well-stocked groceries, specialty markets, and farmers' markets

Selection select heavy, firm beets with deep orange-gold color; leaves should be deep green and as large as possible

Storage refrigerate beets and green tops separately in plastic bags for up to 4 days

Substitutions other beet varieties; if you cannot find intact beet greens, use one large chard leaf per two small tamales

To make the sauce, while the tamales are steaming, toss the tomatoes, bell peppers, and garlic with the olive oil and salt on a baking sheet. Arrange the tomatoes and peppers skin-side up and place under the broiler for 8 to 10 minutes, until the skins of the tomatoes and peppers are lightly charred. Allow to cool before removing as much of the charred skin of the tomatoes and peppers as possible and peeling the garlic. Place in a blender, including any juices, and blend on high until smooth. Taste and adjust seasoning as desired.

Divide the sauce among four plates and place two to three tamales on top of the sauce. Serve warm.

Note: Masa harina is a very finely ground corn flour used to make tamales and tortillas. It is sold in the bulk-bin section at Berkeley Bowl as well as in packages from brands like Maseca and Bob's Red Mill.

Greek Spaghetti with Water Chestnuts

Pasta tossed in browned butter, grated cheese, and freshly ground black pepper is comfort food beloved by many Greek Americans. Water chestnuts, which retain their crisp texture even when cooked, contrast the pasta's richness in a new take on "Greek spaghetti." Although purists would argue against it, sprinkle with some fresh minced parsley, oregano, or thyme if so inclined.

Serves 4

1 pound dry spaghetti

1 dozen fresh water chestnuts

5 tablespoons salted butter

3 ounces grated mizithra cheese (or other hard cheese such as kefalotyri or Parmesan)

Salt and freshly ground black pepper

Availability year-round at Asian groceries

Selection select very hard water chestnuts with sheened skin free of soft spots; purchase more than needed as they can still have soft spots on the inside

Storage refrigerate in a paper bag for up to 1 week

Substitutions canned water chestnuts

Cook the spaghetti *al dente* and drain well.

While the pasta is cooking, use a paring knife to peel the water chestnuts and remove any soft or discolored spots. Slice into ¼-inch discs.

Melt the butter in a skillet over medium-high heat. Add the water chestnuts and sauté for 4 to 6 minutes, until they turn lightly golden and the butter begins to brown.

Toss with the pasta and cheese and season with salt and pepper to taste.

Serve immediately.

Watermelon Radish and Pineapple Carpaccio

The inspiration for this snack comes from Oakland's largely Latino neighborhood of Fruitvale, a few miles south of Berkeley Bowl. Here, vendors roll carts down the sidewalk laden with fresh chopped mango, cucumber, jicama, and watermelon. The chilled fruit is delicious with a pinch of salt, drizzle of lime, and a dash of chili powder. Watermelon radish, named for its lime-green skin and fuchsia flesh, is quite peppery and densely textured. It's a perfect match for slices of sweet, juicy pineapple. No utensils are required.

Serves 6 to 8

Ice water

2 watermelon radishes

1 small pineapple

2 limes

Flaked sea salt

Chili powder

Availability year-round at well-stocked groceries

Selection choose firm radishes with lime-green skin to enjoy the watermelon effect when cut open

Storage wrap in a damp paper towel and refrigerate in a plastic bag for up to 5 days

Substitutions fresh beets or other large radishes, such as the black Spanish radish

Fill a bowl with ice water. Slice the radishes very thinly using a mandoline or sharp knife. Place in the ice water for 5 minutes, or until the slices curl slightly. Meanwhile, cut the skin from the pineapple and slice the flesh into thin rounds. Drain the radish slices well.

Arrange the pineapple rounds and radish slices on a serving platter and juice the limes over the top.

Sprinkle lightly with the salt and chili powder and serve immediately.

Burdock Root Pizza

The mildly sweet, artichoke-heart flavor of this pan pizza comes from burdock, a skinny taproot with an impressive length—up to 3 or 4 feet! This recipe highlights the versatility of an unlikely pizza ingredient that is used both in the creamy garlic sauce and as a topping.

Serves 4 to 6

1 pound fresh pizza dough (homemade or store-bought), at room temperature

¾ teaspoon salt

12 to 14 ounces burdock root (about 2)

¼ cup cream

1 small clove garlic, peeled

Freshly ground black pepper

Olive oil

1½ cups shredded fontina cheese (about 4 ounces)

½ small red onion, thinly sliced

3 sprigs fresh thyme

Availability year-round at Asian groceries, specialty markets, and farmers' markets

Selection look for firm, light brown roots about 2 to 3 feet in length and the diameter of a quarter

Storage wrap smaller sections of burdock root in damp paper towels and refrigerate in a plastic bag for up to 4 days

Substitutions artichoke hearts

Place the pizza dough on a floured work surface, cover with a damp towel, and allow to rest while you prepare the burdock root.

Place 2 cups of water and ½ teaspoon of the salt in a small pot and bring to a boil. To make the long roots easier to work with, cut the burdock into two sections. Working quickly to prevent discoloring, peel off the thin brown skin and slice into ⅛-inch-thick discs, immediately dropping the discs into the boiling water as you slice them. When all the burdock has been added to the boiling water, cover and lower the heat to simmer for 25 minutes. Drain well.

Place half the burdock in a food processor or blender and add the cream, garlic, remaining salt, and some pepper. Blend on high until smooth.

Preheat the oven to 425°F. Grease a cookie sheet or 14-inch pizza pan with the olive oil. Roll or stretch the pizza dough, using a rolling pin or floured hands, to match the shape of the pan. Lift the dough and press it to fit into the greased pan. Spread the burdock cream mixture over the top of the dough and sprinkle with the remaining burdock slices. Top with the cheese and red onion. Using kitchen scissors, snip the thyme leaves evenly over the top. Bake for 18 to 22 minutes, until the crust and the cheese are golden. Serve hot.

Forbidden Rice Bowls with Stir-Fried Jicama

It's hard to say why it's more fun to pluck a variety of colorful, carefully arranged ingredients from a bowl than to eat them off a plate, but this dish is no exception. At the heart is jicama root, which stays juicy-crisp and mildly sweet even after tossed in Moroccan spices and stir-fried. Paired with nutty black rice, slivered mango, and a creamy tahini-harissa dressing, this bowl bursts with flavor.

Serves 4

RICE

¾ cup forbidden rice
(also called black rice)

1½ cups water

½ teaspoon salt

3 strips of fresh lemon zest

DRESSING

⅔ cup plain yogurt

2 tablespoons tahini

2 teaspoons harissa paste

3 tablespoons freshly
squeezed lemon juice

⅔ teaspoon salt

STIR-FRIED JICAMA

1 small jicama (about 1 pound)

1 tablespoon olive oil

1½ teaspoons ras el
hanout (see *Note*)

1¼ teaspoons salt

TOPPINGS

⅓ cup toasted cashews

2 carrots, peeled and grated

1 cup cilantro leaves,
stems removed

1 ripe mango, peeled and sliced

To make the rice, combine all the rice ingredients in a small saucepan, cover with a lid, and bring to a boil. Allow to simmer on low for 35 minutes. Turn off the heat, but leave the lid on for an additional 15 minutes to continue steaming.

Meanwhile, combine all the ingredients for the dressing and mix until smooth. For the stir-fried jicama, peel the jicama and dice into 1 inch by ½-inch rectangles. Toss with the olive oil, ras el hanout, and salt. Heat a skillet over high heat, add the jicama mixture, and stir-fry for 5 minutes, until the jicama is lightly golden in places. Remove from the heat and set aside.

Carefully arrange the rice, jicama, and toppings in four serving bowls. Drizzle with the dressing and serve immediately.

Note: Ras el hanout is a Moroccan spice blend sold in the spice aisle of Berkeley Bowl and other well-stocked groceries.

Availability year-round at well-stocked groceries, Latin American markets, and farmers' markets, with peak from fall to spring

Selection look for smaller jicama that is heavy for its size with smooth, firm skin free of wet or moldy spots

Storage store uncovered in a cool, dry place, as moisture will cause it to mold

Substitutions fresh water chestnuts

Celeriac Ravioli with Celery Leaves and Lemon Oil

Once rid of its craggy roots and dirt-caked crevices, celeriac's bright white flesh tastes like mellow, mildly sweet celery. Its leaves have a more concentrated celery flavor with a vegetal, almost herbal undertone. In this recipe, the root is puréed with mascarpone for a smooth and delicate ravioli filling. The cooked ravioli are then tossed with lemon oil and sautéed celeriac leaves to bring out the best of both the root and the leaves. You can assemble these in a matter of minutes with the help of gyoza wrappers, or make your own pasta dough if so desired.

Serves 4

1 large celeriac root, with stems and leaves intact

⅓ cup mascarpone cheese

½ teaspoon salt

24 round gyoza (or pot sticker) wrappers

1 egg, beaten

3 tablespoons lemon-infused olive oil

Sea salt and freshly ground black pepper

Availability year-round at well-stocked groceries and farmers' markets

Selection choose large, heavy, and firm celeriac with unwilted stalks and bright green leaves attached

Storage refrigerate in a plastic bag for up to 1 week

Substitutions celery top leaves combined with puréed root vegetable such as potato or turnip

Trim the stems from the celeriac root. Remove ⅔ cup of leaves from the stems and set aside; discard the stems and remaining leaves. Place a steaming basket in a pot with a lid, add a couple inches of water, and bring to a boil.

Use a knife to peel the celeriac root. Discard the peel. Dice the celeriac into ½-inch pieces and place in the steaming basket. Steam, covered, for 10 minutes, or until tender. Place the steamed celeriac root in a food processor along with the mascarpone and salt. Pulse on high for 15 to 20 seconds, until smooth.

Lay the gyoza wrappers on a lightly floured surface. Place 1½ teaspoons of the celeriac mixture in the middle of each wrapper. Working one by one, lightly moisten the edge of one side of the wrapper with the beaten egg using a pastry brush or your finger. Fold the wrapper in half, pushing out any air before pressing the two edges together to seal. Repeat with the remaining wrappers until all the celeriac mixture has been used.

To cook the ravioli, bring a large pot of salted water to a boil. In two batches, gently drop the ravioli into the boiling water and cook for 2 minutes, or until *al dente*. Use a slotted spoon to carefully remove.

While the ravioli are cooking, heat the olive oil in a large skillet set over medium heat. Add the celery leaves and toss in the hot oil for 1 minute, or until wilted. Turn off the heat and immediately add the cooked ravioli to the skillet, tossing gently to coat. Divide among four warmed plates and sprinkle with sea salt and pepper.

Buñuelos de Yuca

The basis for this light, crispy fritter is yuca, a mildly sweet tuber that is a widespread staple in tropical regions. The recipe is a new take on the classic treat served at holiday festivals throughout Spain and Latin America. Enjoy hot with a cup of café con leche.

Makes 2 dozen

1 large yuca (about 1 pound)

1 cup shredded mozzarella or Oaxaca cheese

¼ cup cornstarch

2 tablespoons granulated sugar

½ teaspoon salt

¾ teaspoon anise seed

Oil for frying (corn, canola, or other mild-flavored oil)

Zest from 1 lemon

½ cup granulated sugar for dusting

Availability year-round at Latin American, Asian, and African markets; also sold as cassava and manioc

Selection look for shiny, uncracked skin and pure white flesh absent of dark flecks or streaks

Storage store in a cool, dry place for up to 1 week

Safety do not consume raw

Substitutions other starchy, mildly sweet vegetable such as taro or potato

Bring a large pot of water to a boil. Meanwhile, cut the yuca into three sections to make peeling easier. Cut each section in half lengthwise and then use a paring knife to slice away the waxy peel and light pink skin in strips. Place the chunks of yuca into the pot and boil for 15 to 20 minutes, until the yuca pierces easily with a fork but is not overly mushy. Drain and allow to cool. Remove the tough, yellowish vein that runs through the middle of the yuca and discard.

Place the boiled yuca, cheese, cornstarch, 2 tablespoons of sugar, salt, and anise seed in a food processor. Pulse for 20 to 30 seconds, until the mixture comes together to form a uniform dough.

In a 4-quart saucepan, heat 3 to 4 inches of frying oil over medium-high heat. Grease your hands and a tray with some oil, and roll sections of the dough into smooth balls about 1 tablespoon in size between your hands before placing them on the greased tray. Mix the lemon zest with the ½ cup of granulated sugar in a small bowl and set aside.

Test if the oil is hot enough by dropping a small piece of dough into the oil and making sure it bubbles and sizzles. Working in batches, drop several of the yuca balls into the hot oil and fry for 3 to 4 minutes, until golden brown, loosening them from the bottom of the pot if they stick at first. Remove them with a slotted spoon and place them on paper towels. While they are still hot, roll the buñuelos in the lemon sugar and set aside. Continue frying the remaining batches and rolling them in the lemon sugar. Serve while still hot.

SAVORY
FRUITS

Moqua Pisto with Fried Egg

Pisto is Spain's version of ratatouille, a simple vegetable dish simmered in nothing more than olive oil to honor the taste of summer vegetables at their peak. Whether spooned onto bruschetta, baked in an empanada, or topped with a fried egg as in this recipe, pisto always tastes rustic and fresh. In this version of pisto, moqua, also known as fuzzy melon, is added. Beneath the moqua's fine fuzz is a delicate, juicy flesh with a mild zucchini flavor. It makes an excellent companion to vegetables like peppers, onions, and tomatoes, absorbing their flavorful juices as they simmer. Serve with fresh, crusty bread for sopping.

Serves 6

¼ cup olive oil

2 yellow onions, small diced

2 cloves garlic, minced

1 green bell pepper, seeded and diced

1 red bell pepper, seeded and diced

3 tablespoons tomato paste

1 small eggplant, diced

1 moqua (about 1 pound), peeled and diced

10 Roma tomatoes, diced

1¾ teaspoons sea salt

6 eggs

Fresh minced parsley, for garnish

Heat the olive oil in a large skillet over medium heat. Add the onion and sauté for 7 to 8 minutes, until softened and translucent. Add the garlic and green and red bell peppers. Sauté for 5 to 6 minutes, until softened. Stir in the tomato paste and cook for 1 to 2 minutes before adding the eggplant, moqua, tomatoes, and salt. Simmer uncovered over low heat for about 1 hour, or until the vegetables are tender and most of the liquid is absorbed, stirring occasionally to prevent scorching. Taste and adjust seasoning as desired.

When ready to serve, fry the eggs in a little olive oil until the white is set and the yolk is still runny. Serve the pisto warm topped with a fried egg and garnished with the fresh parsley.

Availability year-round at Asian markets and specialty markets

Selection choose firm moqua with light green, spotted skin covered in small fine hairs; also sold as fuzzy melon, *mo gwa* or *mo qua*

Storage refrigerate in a plastic bag for up to 1 week

Substitutions zucchini, summer squash

Anaheim Chile and Corn Chowder

Anyone who has ever eaten canned "diced green chiles" has—even if unknowingly—tried Anaheim chile. Popular in Latin cuisine for its bright, sweet flavor and mild spiciness, it makes a killer addition to a chunky corn chowder spiked with buttermilk.

Serves 6

2 tablespoons butter

1 large white onion, minced

2 cloves garlic, minced

3 Anaheim chiles, seeded and finely chopped

1 celery stalk, finely chopped

2 small Yukon gold potatoes, peeled and diced

2 ears corn, kernels sliced from the cob (about 2 cups)

1 teaspoon ground coriander

1 teaspoon salt

Freshly ground black pepper

¼ teaspoon red pepper flakes

4 cups salted vegetable broth

1 cup whole milk

¾ cup lowfat buttermilk

Availability year-round at well-stocked groceries, Latin American markets, and farmers' markets

Selection choose chiles with glossy, bright green skin free of soft spots

Storage refrigerate in a paper bag for up to 5 days

Substitutions other mild green chiles such as poblano

Melt the butter in a large Dutch oven or pot over medium heat. Add the onion and sauté for 6 to 7 minutes, until softened.

Add the garlic, chiles, celery, potatoes, and corn and sauté for 3 to 4 minutes to soften the vegetables slightly. Add the coriander, salt, black pepper, red pepper flakes, and vegetable broth and bring to a boil.

Cover and reduce the heat to simmer for 10 to 15 minutes, until the potatoes and corn are tender. Use a hand blender to partly purée the soup, leaving much of the vegetables chunky (or, alternatively, pulse in a blender for a few seconds).

Stir in the whole milk and buttermilk, taste the soup, and adjust the level of salt or spice as desired.

Serve hot with freshly ground black pepper to taste.

Tom Yum Soup with Winter Melon

A few minutes simmering in an aromatic broth, and this hard, savory gourd transforms into a translucent, melt-in-your-mouth delicacy. Slicing rather than chopping it gives the appearance of crescent moons floating elegantly in this Thai-inspired soup. Note that *tom yum* relies on a balance of tangy, spicy, and sweet, so adjust the amount of chile, lime, sugar, and salt to suit your tastes.

Serves 4

6 cups water

2 stalks lemongrass

1 (1-inch) piece galangal (see *Note*), sliced into thin discs

1 to 2 Thai chiles (depending on desired heat level), sliced lengthwise and seeded

5 kaffir lime leaves

½ cup dried shiitake mushrooms

3 shallots, thinly sliced

3 cloves garlic, minced

2 tablespoons palm sugar (or brown sugar)

1½ pound-section of winter melon

7 fresh shiitake mushrooms, thinly sliced

3 tablespoons freshly squeezed lime juice

3 green onions, white and light green parts finely sliced

2 small Roma tomatoes, sliced into 6 wedges each

8 sprigs fresh cilantro, stems removed

Bring the water to a boil in a saucepan with a lid. Remove the outermost layer of the lemongrass stalks and trim the ends, leaving about 8 inches of the thickest part of the stalk. Give the stalks a couple of whacks with the flat side of a wide knife to loosen the layers a bit, and then slice into ½-inch pieces. Tie up the lemongrass, galangal, chiles, lime leaves, and dried shiitake mushrooms in a piece of cheesecloth, and drop into the simmering broth along with the shallots, garlic, and sugar. Cover and simmer for 20 minutes. Remove the cheesecloth bundle and discard.

Meanwhile, prepare the winter melon by scooping out the seeds with a spoon. Cut into ½-inch-thick crescents and slice away the thin rind; you should have about 6 to 8 slices. Add the winter melon to the broth along with the fresh shiitake mushrooms. Cover and return to a boil. Simmer for 6 to 8 minutes, until the winter melon starts to turn translucent and pierces easily with a fork. Remove from the heat and add the lime juice, green onions, tomatoes, and cilantro. Taste and adjust the level of salt, sugar, and lime juice as desired. Divide the soup among four bowls and serve hot.

Note: Galangal is a peppery, branched root like a very pungent version of ginger. It is usually sold near fresh ginger in specialty and Asian markets.

Availability Asian markets and specialty markets in winter

Selection due to its immense size, it's usually sold in slices or sections in a refrigerated display similar to sectioned watermelons; also called ash gourd

Storage refrigerate covered in plastic wrap for up to 1 week

Substitutions zucchini, moqua/ fuzzy melon, unripe honeydew melon (eliminate the sugar in the recipe)

Roasted Milpero Salsa Verde

Wrapped in crinkly, paper-like husks like their relative, the tomatillo, the smaller and more flavorful milpero look like marbles swirled with purple, brown, and green. Roasting is a great way to heighten their tangy sweetness, as in this quick and easy salsa. Serve with tortilla chips or spoon onto enchiladas or huevos rancheros as you would salsa verde.

Makes about 1½ cups

1 pound milpero, husks removed and washed well

4 small cloves garlic, skin still on

8 green onions, ends trimmed

2 jalapeño peppers, halved and seeded

1 green bell pepper, halved and seeded

2 tablespoons olive oil

½ teaspoon sea salt

1 lime

Availability year-round at Latin American markets

Selection choose milpero that are firm beneath papery husks free of mold

Storage refrigerate in a paper bag for up to 5 days

Preparation wash well to remove the sticky sap before using

Substitutions tomatillos

Line a roasting pan with parchment paper and spread the milpero, garlic, green onions, jalapeño peppers, and bell pepper in the pan. Drizzle with the olive oil and sprinkle with the salt. Broil for 5 to 8 minutes, until the vegetables begin to lightly char in places. Flip the vegetables over with a spatula or tongs and broil for another 5 to 8 minutes on the other side. Remove from the oven and let cool before peeling the garlic.

Place all the contents and juices from the roasting pan into a food processor. Add the juice from the lime and pulse until you have a chunky salsa. Taste for salt and lime, and adjust seasoning as desired.

1 small red bell pepper

2 small zucchini squashes

1 ear fresh corn

1 tablespoon coconut oil

2 tablespoons chopped fresh cilantro, for garnish

Lime wedges, for garnish

Availability year-round at well-stocked groceries and Latin American markets

Selection choose firm, yellow plantains with very few brown spots; avoid entirely green or brown plantains

Storage store at room temperature but avoid over-ripening

Substitutions sweet potato, yuca (also sold as cassava and manioc)

contents of the strainer. Cover and reduce the heat to simmer until the plantains are tender like a boiled potato, about 6 to 12 minutes depending on the ripeness. Add the bell pepper, zucchini, and corn and cook an additional 2 minutes, or until the vegetables are just tender. Serve hot, garnished with the cilantro and a lime wedge.

Note: Galangal is a peppery, branched root like a very pungent version of ginger. It is usually sold near fresh ginger in specialty and Asian markets.

Thai-Style White Curry with Plantain

This curry manages to be at once flavorful and delicate, a far cry from the thick, overpowering curry sauces that need rice or naan to cut the heaviness. The secret is caramelized plantains, which impart a hint of starchy sweetness to a white curry broth infused with aromatics and whole spices. Choose plantains that are yellow with very few brown spots rather than completely green or brown.

Serves 4

1 teaspoon coriander seeds

¼ teaspoon cumin seeds

2 whole cloves

1 tablespoon coconut oil

½ white onion, diced

4 white button mushrooms, chopped

1 (1-inch) nub ginger, peeled and minced

2 slices peeled galangal (see *Note*), ⅛ inch thick

Bottom 4 inches lemongrass stalk, sliced lengthwise and then into thirds

2⅔ cups water

1 (14-ounce) can coconut milk

3 kaffir lime leaves

1 small Thai red chile, sliced lengthwise (including seeds)

1½ teaspoons salt

2 plantains, yellow but not brown

ingredient list continued on following page

To make the white curry, place the coriander seeds, cumin seeds, and cloves in a 4-quart saucepan over medium heat. Heat for 2 to 3 minutes, until fragrant, shaking the saucepan about every 30 seconds to prevent burning. Add the coconut oil and onion, and sauté for 5 to 6 minutes, or until the onion is soft and translucent. Add the mushrooms, ginger, galangal, and lemongrass, and sauté for 4 to 5 minutes, until the mushrooms are softened. Add the water, coconut milk, lime leaves, chile, and salt, and bring to a boil. Reduce the heat and simmer, uncovered, for 10 minutes. Turn off the heat and set aside while preparing the vegetables.

Slice off both tips of the plantains. To remove the peel, make a shallow incision along the length of the plantain peel and pull each side back. Slice into ⅓-inch rounds. Quarter and seed the bell pepper, and slice it julienne style. Slice the zucchini in half lengthwise, and then slice each half again lengthwise into thirds. Chop into 1½-inch pieces. Slice the corn off the cob.

Heat the coconut oil in a large skillet over medium heat. Place the plantain slices in a single layer in the oil and allow to cook undisturbed for 2 to 3 minutes per side, until lightly golden and crisp. Pour the white curry through a fine-mesh strainer held over the skillet and discard the

continued on following page

Spiced Rice with Blue Hokkaido

Blue Hokkaido, a squash with silvery blue skin and rich ocher flesh, stands out in this explosion of texture and color. Aromatics, acids, and herbs all come together with the squash's nutty sweetness in a dish that's hearty enough to stand on its own.

Serves 6

1 small blue Hokkaido squash, unpeeled, seeded, and cut into 1-inch cubes

3 tablespoons olive oil

Salt and freshly ground black pepper

1 yellow onion, diced

2 cloves garlic, minced

1 cinnamon stick

1 star anise pod

1 teaspoon coriander seeds

5 cardamom pods

½ teaspoon turmeric

Pinch of saffron

1½ cups uncooked basmati rice

2½ cups water

¾ teaspoon sea salt

3 tablespoons freshly squeezed lemon juice

⅔ cup fresh chopped parsley

Seeds from one pomegranate

¼ cup roasted hazelnuts, chopped

Preheat the oven to 400°F. Place the Hokkaido squash on a baking pan and drizzle with 1 tablespoon of the olive oil. Sprinkle with the salt and pepper and toss to coat. Roast for 15 to 20 minutes, until the squash is tender.

Meanwhile, heat the remaining 2 tablespoons of the olive oil in a large lidded skillet over medium-low heat. Add the onion and sauté for 10 minutes. Add the garlic, cinnamon stick, star anise pod, coriander seeds, cardamom pods, turmeric, and saffron, and sauté for 1 to 2 minutes to release their flavor. Add the rice and stir to coat in the oil and spices. Add the water and sea salt, and bring to a boil. Cover the skillet and simmer on low heat for 15 minutes. Turn off the heat and keep the lid on to let the rice steam for an additional 10 minutes.

To assemble, place the squash, rice, lemon juice, and parsley in a large bowl and toss to coat. Taste for salt and pepper, and adjust seasoning as desired. Top with the pomegranate seeds and hazelnuts. Serve slightly warm or at room temperature.

image appears on previous page

Falafel Waffles with Armenian Cucumber Slaw

Although actually a type of melon, the Armenian cucumber tastes like the ultimate cucumber: extra crisp and mildly sweet. Its deep ridges are striking when sliced thinly in this refreshing slaw, which sits atop a unique union of two world cuisine favorites—falafel and waffles.

Serves 4 to 6

SLAW

1 Armenian cucumber, unpeeled

4 colorful carrots, peeled

1 small white onion, thinly sliced

½ cup fresh chopped parsley

3 tablespoons freshly squeezed lemon juice

2 tablespoons red or white wine vinegar

3 tablespoons olive oil

½ teaspoon salt

WAFFLES

2 cups cooked chickpeas (fresh or canned)

2 eggs

1 cup milk

¼ cup olive oil

3 green onions, chopped

2 large cloves garlic, chopped

1 teaspoon salt

2 tablespoons freshly squeezed lemon juice

ingredient list continued on following page

To make the slaw, use a mandoline or a sharp knife to slice the Armenian cucumber and carrots very thinly, about the thickness of a dime. Place in a mixing bowl with the remaining slaw ingredients and toss to combine. Set aside.

To make the waffles, preheat a waffle iron to the highest setting and preheat the oven to 200°F. Place the chickpeas in a large bowl filled with water. Rub the chickpeas lightly between your palms to loosen the skins, which will float to the top. Skim off the skins using a slotted spoon before draining the chickpeas.

Place the chickpeas in a blender or food processor along with the eggs, milk, olive oil, green onions, garlic, salt, lemon juice, cilantro, parsley, cumin, coriander, and cayenne. Blend for 20 to 30 seconds to form a fairly smooth batter. Add the baking powder and flour, and blend on low for a few seconds until combined.

Brush the hot waffle iron with oil or cooking spray and pour in the batter. Cook the waffles for 7 to 10 minutes, depending on the waffle iron, until golden brown. Transfer the waffles directly to a wire rack in the oven to stay warm while preparing the remaining waffles.

continued on following page

½ cup fresh chopped
cilantro, packed

½ cup fresh chopped
parsley, packed

2½ teaspoons ground cumin

1½ teaspoons ground coriander

1 teaspoon ground cayenne

1 tablespoon baking powder

1 cup all-purpose flour

HARISSA YOGURT SAUCE

1 cup plain Greek yogurt

1 tablespoon harissa paste

2 tablespoons freshly
squeezed lemon juice

¼ teaspoon salt

Combine the harissa yogurt sauce ingredients (harissa paste to taste) while the waffles are cooking, and set aside.

Top each waffle with the slaw, drizzle with the yogurt sauce, and serve immediately. Leftover waffles can be refrigerated or frozen and then reheated in a toaster.

Availability Middle Eastern markets and farmers' markets in summer

Selection select firm cucumbers with unblemished skin

Storage wrap in a dry paper towel and refrigerate in a plastic bag for up to 5 days

Substitutions English cucumber, Persian cucumber

Stuffed Mini Eggplants

Bite-sized and bursting with roasted garlic and fresh oregano, these stuffed Indian eggplants make great finger food for a cocktail party or a picnic. This egg-sized variety has mildly sweet flesh and none of the bitterness associated with larger types. If you can't find Indian eggplant, slice and roast half of a large Italian or globe eggplant, and hollow out the other half to serve the filling in as a dip for crispy pita chips.

Makes 18

1 dozen Indian eggplants

2 tablespoons olive oil

1 teaspoon salt

Freshly ground black pepper

3 large cloves garlic, peeled

⅓ cup plain Greek yogurt

1 tablespoon freshly squeezed lemon juice

2 tablespoons toasted pine nuts

2 tablespoons chopped fresh oregano, for garnish

Paprika (mild to hot), for garnish

Availability year-round at Asian markets and specialty markets, with peak in spring

Selection choose heavy, firm, egg-sized fruits with deep purple flesh free of scarring or soft spots

Storage keep in a dark, cool place for up to several days, or refrigerate in a plastic bag for up to 1 week

Substitutions other small eggplant varieties such as fairy tale or mini graffiti eggplant, or one large globe or Italian eggplant

Preheat the oven to 375°F. Cut the eggplants in half lengthwise and toss with 1 tablespoon of the olive oil, ½ teaspoon of the salt, the pepper, and the garlic cloves. Line a baking sheet with parchment paper and place the eggplant halves (face down) and garlic cloves on the baking sheet. Bake for 20 to 25 minutes, until the eggplants and garlic cloves are tender. Remove from the oven and let cool.

Use a melon baller or small spoon to carefully scoop the flesh out of the eggplant halves, leaving intact a ⅛-inch border of flesh in the skins so they maintain their shape. Set the skins aside for filling later.

Place the scooped-out flesh in a food processor along with the roasted garlic, yogurt, lemon juice, and remaining ½ teaspoon of the salt and 1 tablespoon of the olive oil. Pulse on high for 15 to 20 seconds, until the mixture is creamy. Taste and adjust seasoning as desired. Stir in the toasted pine nuts.

Use a small spoon to fill about 18 of the eggplant skins with the eggplant mixture, discarding the remaining 6 skins. Arrange on a serving plate and garnish with the fresh oregano and a light dusting of paprika.

Singua Paneer Curry

While most people only recognize this plant when it's dried and hung in the shower, the younger form of luffa (or loofah as it's sometimes known) is actually a delicious gourd with a zucchini-like taste. Its deep ridges make a beautiful sun shape when sliced, and its spongy texture soaks up sauces, as in this Indian-style curry with tender bites of paneer.

Serves 4

¼ cup coconut oil

4 large shallots, minced

2 cloves garlic, minced

1 (1-inch) nub ginger, peeled and minced

8 curry leaves

1 tablespoon tomato paste

1 teaspoon garam masala

1 teaspoon curry powder

1 teaspoon ground coriander

1 teaspoon salt

2 singua gourds

1 to 2 jalapeño peppers, sliced into thin rounds

4 Roma tomatoes, chopped

1½ cups water

1 (14-ounce) package of paneer, sliced into 1 by ⅓-inch rectangles

Heat the coconut oil in a Dutch oven or large, deep skillet over medium-low heat. Add the shallots and sauté for 10 to 15 minutes, until softened and caramelized.

Meanwhile, prepare the singua by using a vegetable peeler to lightly peel the ridges. Slice the singua into ⅓-inch rounds and set aside.

Add the garlic, ginger, curry leaves, tomato paste, garam masala, curry powder, coriander, and salt to the shallots and sauté for 2 minutes to release the flavors. Add the jalapeño peppers and sliced singua, and sauté for 3 minutes. Add the tomatoes and water, and stir to combine. Raise the heat to bring the sauce to a boil, and then lower the heat to simmer for 10 minutes, or until the sauce is thickened and the singua is tender. Add the paneer and allow to cook an additional 5 minutes, or until the paneer is soft. Serve hot over steamed basmati or brown rice.

Availability year-round at Asian markets and specialty markets

Selection choose unblemished, light green luffa the size of a large cucumber that give slightly to pressure; also sold as sin qua and Chinese okra

Storage refrigerate in a plastic bag for up to 5 days

Substitutions zucchini

Indian Bitter Melon Tonic

While Indian bitter melon is too astringent for some palates, the quinine in it makes it ideal for homemade tonic. Simmered with citrus fruit and juniper berries, this easy-to-make tonic comes out bright, complex, and bittersweet. Mix it with club soda over ice for a spritzer, or with gin in a jazzed-up version of the classic cocktail.

Makes 16 ounces concentrate for about 8 to 10 drinks

5 ounces Indian bitter melon (about 2 small melons)

1 large grapefruit

1 lemon

6 juniper berries

4 cups water

1⅓ cups granulated sugar

Availability year-round at Asian groceries and specialty markets

Selection choose small, bright green melons with firm spikes

Storage wrap in a paper towel and refrigerate in a plastic bag for up to 5 days

Substitutions regular bitter melon (not spiky)

Slice the bitter melons in half lengthwise, and scoop out and discard the pulpy seeds (a melon baller works well). Slice into ¼-inch slices and place in a saucepan. Use a sharp knife to slice the zest from the grapefruit and lemon in strips, avoiding as much of the white pith as possible. Add the strips of zest to the saucepan, along with the juice from the grapefruit and lemon. Use the flat side of a wide knife to lightly press the juniper berries so they open up and release their aroma, and add them to the saucepan. Add the water, bring to a boil, and simmer uncovered for 20 minutes.

Pour the liquid through a fine-mesh strainer and discard the solids. Pour the strained liquid back into the saucepan and add the sugar. Boil uncovered for another 15 to 20 minutes, until the liquid has been reduced by about half. Pour into a lidded pint jar and allow to cool. Store the tonic in the refrigerator for up to 1 month.

Note: To make a spritzer, mix equal parts bitter melon tonic and club soda and pour over ice. Garnish with a slice of bitter melon and a lemon or lime wedge. To make a gin tonic, pack a highball glass with ice and add equal parts bitter melon tonic, gin, and club soda. Stir and garnish with a slice of bitter melon and a lime wedge.

Chayote Pozole

With origins that trace back to the Aztecs, pozole is a traditionally slow-cooked hominy stew topped with fresh garnishes like shaved cabbage and radish. This quick, light version uses slices of chayote squash, also a traditional Aztec food, instead of pork to soak up the tomatillo-based broth. The pear-shaped gourd comes in varieties ranging from smooth to spiny. To avoid the need for peeling, choose the "common chayote" with smooth, lime-green skin.

Serves 6

1 pound tomatillos, halved

1 celery rib, roughly chopped

5 green onions, white and light green parts roughly chopped

3 cloves garlic, peeled

2 jalapeño peppers, seeded

1 pasilla chile, seeded and chopped

1 bunch fresh cilantro, stems removed and roughly chopped

1 teaspoon dried oregano

¼ cup roasted pumpkin seeds

5 cups salted vegetable broth

2 cups white hominy

2 chayote squashes, quartered and sliced into ¼-inch-thick, bite-sized pieces

Salt

GARNISHES

Chopped fresh cilantro

Lime wedges

Sliced radish

Sliced avocado

Shredded purple cabbage

Minced white onion

Minced jalapeño

Crushed tortilla chips

Place the tomatillos, celery, green onions, garlic, jalapeño peppers, pasilla chile, cilantro, oregano, and pumpkin seeds in a blender, and add 1 cup of the vegetable broth. Blend until smooth.

Pour into a soup pot and add the remaining vegetable broth and the hominy. Bring to a boil and then simmer uncovered on low heat for 15 minutes.

Add the chayote and simmer an additional 15 minutes, or until the chayote pierces easily with a fork.

Salt to taste.

Serve hot pozole in deep soup bowls, topped with your favorite garnishes.

Availability year-round at well-stocked groceries and Latin American markets

Selection choose firm chayote with smooth, unblemished skin

Storage store in a plastic bag and refrigerate for up to several weeks

Substitutions zucchini

Stuffed Cherry Bomb Peppers

Bite-sized cherry bomb peppers sizzle against their creamy Gorgonzola filling in this three-ingredient appetizer. Assemble ahead of time and roast just before serving. Don't be deterred by the word "bomb" in the name—most of the spiciness is in the discarded seeds, while the flesh of this cherry-shaped pepper is of medium heat.

Makes 16

1 small cauliflower, cut into florets and core discarded

2½ ounces Gorgonzola cheese

Sea salt and freshly ground black pepper

16 cherry bomb peppers

1 teaspoon olive oil

Availability specialty markets and farmers' markets, mainly in summer

Selection look for bite-sized peppers with firm, bright red skin; also sold as red cherry chile peppers

Storage refrigerate in a paper bag for up to 1 week

Safety although these peppers are only medium-heat level, wash your hands after handling and avoid touching your face

Substitutions fresh piquillo peppers

Steam the cauliflower florets until soft, about 15 minutes. Blend in a food processor to make about 1½ cups of cauliflower purée. Add the cheese and process until smooth. Add the sea salt and black pepper to taste.

Toss the cherry bomb peppers in the olive oil and sprinkle with a pinch of sea salt and black pepper. Slice the tops off the peppers and set them aside for later.

Scrape out the seeds using a melon baller or small spoon. Fill the peppers nearly to the top with the purée using a pastry bag or a squeeze bottle, and then press the tops back on the peppers, securing with a toothpick.

Place the stuffed peppers on a baking sheet and broil close to the flame for about 10 to 15 minutes, turning the peppers every few minutes, until softened and blistered in places.

Allow to cool for a few minutes before removing the toothpicks and serving.

Green Papaya Gazpacho

The refreshing tang of green papaya is blended into this tropical version of a summertime favorite. Serve in bowls for a light meal on a warm day, or pour into small glasses for an eye-catching appetizer.

Serves 6

1 clove garlic

⅓ cup olive oil

¼ cup white balsamic vinegar

⅓ cup freshly squeezed lime juice

¼ teaspoon ground cumin

1½ teaspoons salt

3 cups water

1 cucumber, peeled and sliced

1 green bell pepper,
seeded and sliced

½ green papaya, peeled, seeded,
and cubed (about 3 cups)

1 small avocado, flesh only

1 jalapeño pepper,
seeded and sliced

Availability year-round at well-stocked groceries and Asian markets

Selection choose very firm, football-sized papayas with smooth, green skin

Storage store at room temperature for up to 1 week

Substitutions cucumber

Place the garlic, olive oil, vinegar, lime juice, cumin, and salt in a blender, and blend until frothy and emulsified.

Add the remaining ingredients in batches and blend on high until smooth.

Pour the contents of each batch into a large bowl or pitcher to serve as a mixing container.

Once all the ingredients have been blended and poured into the mixing container, stir and adjust the seasoning by adding more salt, more acid (lime juice or vinegar), or more water depending on your preference.

Once the seasoning is to your liking, put the mixture back into the blender to blend through one more time to obtain a smooth and creamy texture.

Serve chilled.

Carnival Spice Cake

With splashes of orange and green and a nutty flavor tinged with maple, this aptly named squash embodies the delights of a fall carnival. Here, it is baked into a moist, dense cake sprinkled with fresh cranberries and autumnal spices. Indulge in a slice for breakfast or with afternoon tea for a true taste of the season.

Serves 12

2 cups all-purpose flour

2 cups whole wheat flour

1½ teaspoons baking powder

2 teaspoons baking soda

2½ teaspoons cinnamon

1 teaspoon ground cloves

1 teaspoon ground ginger

1 teaspoon sea salt

2 cups carnival squash purée (see *Note*)

1 cup granulated sugar

1 cup packed brown sugar

¾ cup canola oil

1 cup unsweetened applesauce

¾ cup water

1 cup chopped fresh or frozen cranberries

⅓ cup roasted pumpkin seeds

2 tablespoons Demerara or turbinado sugar

Preheat the oven to 350°F. Grease and flour a 9-inch tube cake pan with a removable bottom. Combine the all-purpose flour, whole wheat flour, baking powder, baking soda, cinnamon, cloves, ginger, and salt in a bowl. In a separate, large mixing bowl, whisk the squash purée, granulated sugar, brown sugar, canola oil, applesauce, and water until smooth. Add the flour mixture and the cranberries to the sugar mixture, and fold until just combined. Pour into the cake pan and sprinkle the top with the pumpkin seeds and Demerara sugar. Bake for 50 to 60 minutes, until an inserted toothpick comes out clean. Allow to cool before removing the sides of the cake pan and serving.

Note: To make the carnival squash purée, first preheat the oven to 375°F. Cut the squash in half and scoop out the seeds. Place cut-side down in a baking dish and add about ½ inch of water. Cover the baking dish with foil and bake for 30 to 40 minutes, or until the squash is very soft when pierced with a fork. Scoop out the cooked squash with a spoon and mash with a fork or blend in a food processor until you have a smooth purée.

Availability year-round at well-stocked groceries and farmers' markets, with peak in fall and winter

Selection choose firm squash free of cracks and soft spots

Storage store in a cool, dark place for up to several weeks

Substitutions acorn squash

SWEET
FRUITS

REDCURRANT

Redcurrant Almond Clafoutis

Studded with fresh redcurrants shimmering like rubies, this dessert looks deceptively fancy. The truth is, making *clafoutis* is as quick and simple as frying pancakes. This French dessert traditionally consists of fresh cherries and a custard-like batter that puffs up during baking, ultimately deflating with all the pomp and circumstance of a soufflé. While the French don't tend to alter traditional recipes, I think they'd agree that the tangy pop of these sparkling berries bursting in the mouth is heavenly against the rich custard and almond paste.

Serves 6 to 8

3 eggs

½ cup plus 1 tablespoon granulated sugar

⅛ teaspoon salt

½ teaspoon vanilla extract

2½ tablespoons salted butter, melted

½ cup whole milk

½ cup all-purpose flour

¾ cup redcurrants (4.4-ounce package), stems removed

2 tablespoons crumbled almond paste

Availability specialty markets and farmers' markets in late summer

Selection look for bunches of plump, translucent-red berries with stems intact

Storage refrigerate for up to 3 days, or freeze for later use

Substitutions frozen redcurrants, other tart berries such as raspberries or sour cherries

Preheat the oven to 325°F.

Butter a 9-inch cast-iron skillet or pie pan. In a mixing bowl, whisk together the eggs, sugar, salt, vanilla extract, and melted butter until creamy.

Add the milk and flour and whisk until smooth like pancake batter. Pour the batter into the skillet and sprinkle the redcurrants and almond paste evenly over the top.

Bake for 30 to 35 minutes, until the clafoutis is puffed up and golden brown around the edges (the clafoutis will deflate once you remove it from the oven).

Allow to cool slightly before dusting with powdered sugar. Serve warm.

Broiled Pomelo with Cinnamon Crème Fraîche

The goliath of the citrus world, pomelo looks like an oversized grapefruit, at two to four times its size. While many assume the pomelo and the grapefruit, both rose-colored inside, are interchangeable, the pomelo actually has a sweeter taste and less bitterness as well as a firmer flesh that's well-suited for broiling. Its thick layer of white pith on the cross-section looks striking against the broiled cinnamon sugar topping, crowned with a dollop of cinnamon crème fraîche.

Serves 4

2 pomelos

4 teaspoons brown sugar

½ teaspoon ground cinnamon

Pinch of salt

½ cup crème fraîche

Availability well-stocked groceries and Asian markets in winter and spring

Selection firm with smooth yellow or green skin; also sold as pummelo or shaddock

Storage room temperature for a few days or refrigerate in the crisper drawer for 1 to 2 weeks

Substitutions grapefruit

Cut the pomelos in half, slicing across the equator, not across the poles. Slice a ¼-inch disc from the bottom of each half so that they sit flat. Place the pomelo halves on a broiling pan.

Mix together the brown sugar, ¼ teaspoon of the cinnamon, and the salt in a small bowl. Sprinkle the sugar mixture over the tops of the pomelo halves. Place the pomelo halves under the broiler a few inches from the flame. Broil for 5 minutes, or until the sugar is melted and lightly browned in places. Allow to cool slightly before running a serrated knife at an angle along the border of the pith to separate it from the fruit inside (for ease of consumption), being careful not to cut straight through the bottom.

Stir the remaining cinnamon into the crème fraîche. Top each pomelo half with a dollop of the cinnamon crème fraîche. Consume by scooping out each segment of flesh with a small spoon, avoiding the bitter membranes.

Persimmon Gingersnap Smoothie

The flavor of Fuyu persimmon evokes the essence of fall, with hints of cinnamon, pear, and brown sugar. Its pumpkin-orange color makes a striking smoothie spiced with ginger and molasses. For a decadent treat, top with fresh whipped cream and freshly grated nutmeg or allspice.

Serves 2

2 large Fuyu persimmons (about 10 ounces), peeled and quartered

¾ cup unsweetened almond milk

¼ cup freshly squeezed orange juice

1 heaping teaspoon molasses

1 heaping tablespoon minced crystallized ginger (about 2 crystallized ginger discs), plus more for garnish

⅛ teaspoon freshly ground allspice, plus more for garnish

⅛ teaspoon ground cinnamon

1 tablespoon almond butter

1 cup ice cubes

Availability well-stocked groceries and farmers' markets from mid-fall through winter

Selection select firm, tomato-shaped fruit with orange, glossy skin free of soft spots

Storage store at room temperature for up to several weeks

Substitutions pumpkin purée (sweetened to taste)

Place all ingredients in a blender.

Cover and blend on high for 30 to 60 seconds, until smooth and creamy.

Serve in two chilled glasses, garnished with crystallized ginger and allspice.

Buddha's Hand Scones

With hardly any flesh or juice inside, this poetically named citrus fruit is prized for its floral-scented rind and pith. Baked into this slightly crisp scone with a moist crumb, the subtle taste of Buddha's hand is reminiscent of the orange-blossom water used in baked goods throughout the Mediterranean region. Use leftover chopped Buddha's hand to flavor tea or ice water, or make a decadent marmalade.

Makes 10

2 cups all-purpose flour

½ teaspoon salt

2½ teaspoons baking powder

3 tablespoons granulated sugar

½ cup unsalted butter, frozen

¾ cup plus 2 tablespoons cold buttermilk

¼ teaspoon vanilla extract

¾ cup finely chopped Buddha's hand, skin and pith

1 tablespoon Demerara or raw sugar

Availability well-stocked groceries and farmers' markets in late fall and winter

Selection firm with fragrant, yellow skin free of blemishes

Storage store at room temperature to enjoy the fragrance for up to several days

Substitutions Meyer lemon rind or orange rind with a couple drops of orange blossom water

Preheat the oven to 425°F. Mix the flour, salt, baking powder, and granulated sugar in a large bowl. Working quickly so the butter stays chilled, grate the frozen butter into the dry ingredients using the large holes of a cheese grater. Lightly work the butter into the dry ingredients with a fork or pastry cutter until the mixture resembles a coarse meal.

Add ¾ cup of the buttermilk, the vanilla extract, and the Buddha's hand to the flour mixture and stir until just moistened and can be formed into a ball. Place the dough ball on a lightly floured surface and flatten it into an 8-inch circle using your hands. Use a sharp knife dipped in flour to cut the circle into ten wedges.

Place the wedges at least 1 inch apart on a baking sheet lined with parchment paper. Brush each wedge with the remaining buttermilk and sprinkle with the Demerara sugar. Bake for 15 minutes, or until the scones are golden. Remove from the oven and let cool slightly on a wire rack before serving.

Cherimoya Panna Cotta

Beneath the reptilian green skin of this dinosaur egg–shaped fruit, cherimoya has a custard-like flesh so sweet and creamy Mark Twain called it "the most delicious fruit known to man." With hints of vanilla, banana, and papaya, this melt-in-your-mouth fruit from the Andes was made for a velvety white panna cotta.

Serves 6

1¼ cups half and half

⅔ cup coconut milk

1 tablespoon powdered gelatin

¼ cup sugar

1 star anise

1 large, ripe cherimoya

Availability Latin American groceries and specialty markets from late fall to spring

Selection heavy fruit with brownish-green skin that yields to pressure like a ripe avocado would

Storage ripen at room temperature, and then refrigerate in a plastic bag for up to 1 week

Substitutions guava or pear with cream-colored flesh

Lightly grease six ramekins with vegetable or coconut oil and set aside. Place the half and half and coconut milk in a small saucepan and sprinkle the gelatin evenly over the top. Allow to sit for 5 minutes. Place the saucepan over medium-low heat and add the sugar and star anise, whisking constantly to prevent scalding. When the mixture just begins to simmer, turn off the heat and let stand for 15 minutes before discarding the star anise.

Cut the cherimoya in half and scoop the flesh into a bowl using a spoon. Squish the flesh between your fingers to remove and discard all the black seeds. Purée the cherimoya flesh in a blender or food processor. You should have about 1 cup of purée.

Whisk the cherimoya purée into the gelatin mixture until smooth. Pour through a fine-mesh strainer into the ramekins. Place the ramekins in the refrigerator for at least 3 hours, or overnight, until set and chilled through.

To serve, run a spatula around the inner edges of the ramekins to loosen the sides of the panna cotta and invert onto a dessert plate, or simply enjoy it directly out of the ramekin.

Kiwano Cooler

Also known as kiwano, the African horned melon is perhaps the most unusual-looking fruit in this cookbook. Those who brave its neon-orange spikes and dig into its oozing green insides will be rewarded with a taste so tangy and fresh that it's tempting to just eat it straight from the spoon, seeds and all. Its flavor brings to mind cucumber, melon, and banana, with a tartness well-suited for this fizzy cocktail.

Serves 1

½ African horned melon, plus 1 slice for garnish

2 teaspoons sugar

5 mint leaves

1 tablespoon freshly squeezed lime juice

1½ ounces gin

Ice cubes

3 ounces club soda

Availability year-round at specialty markets, with peak in summer

Selection heavy fruit free of soft spots

Storage keep refrigerated because chilling intensifies the flavor

Substitutions cucumber, honeydew melon

Scoop the green jelly and seeds out of the African horned melon and place in a blender. Pulse on low to burst the juices from the seeds.

Strain the juice into a cocktail shaker or lidded jar, pressing the pulp down to express as much juice as possible. Add the sugar and mint and muddle a few times to release the flavor of the mint.

Add the lime juice, gin, and some ice cubes and shake vigorously for 20 seconds.

Strain the mixture into a glass packed with ice and top off with the club soda.

Stir and garnish with a slice of African horned melon.

Braised Leeks with Blood Oranges

This recipe pays tribute to Spain by utilizing only ingredients that spring from its soil: blood oranges, leeks, thyme, mustard, sherry vinegar, and, of course, olive oil. In the country's northern region, leeks are often served whole and at room temperature to highlight their velvety texture, a quality that is accentuated here through braising.

Serves 4

6 large leeks, roots and dark green tops removed

2 tablespoons olive oil

½ cup dry white wine

½ cup salted vegetable broth

6 sprigs fresh thyme

2 blood oranges

DRESSING

1 teaspoon Dijon mustard

2 tablespoons olive oil

1 tablespoon freshly squeezed lemon juice

1 teaspoon sherry vinegar

Salt and freshly ground black pepper

Availability well-stocked groceries in winter

Selection firm with smooth orange skin

Storage room temperature for a few days or refrigerate in the crisper drawer for 1 to 2 weeks

Substitutions Cara Cara oranges, navel oranges, grapefruit

Preheat the oven to 375°F. Remove the tougher, outermost layers of the leeks and discard. Slice them in half lengthwise and run under cold water to remove all the grit, being sure to rinse between the layers. Place the leeks cut-side down in a single layer in a 9 by 13-inch roasting pan.

Drizzle with the olive oil, wine, and vegetable broth (the liquid should come about halfway up the leeks), and snip the thyme sprigs over the top.

Roast for 35 to 45 minutes, flipping the leeks over halfway through, until they are completely tender and lightly browned. Allow to cool to room temperature.

Using a sharp knife, cut away the peel and pith from the oranges. Cut between the membranes to remove the fruit in segments. Arrange the leeks and thyme sprigs on a serving platter and scatter the oranges on top. Whisk together the ingredients for the dressing, taste and adjust seasoning as desired, and drizzle over the top.

Serve at room temperature.

Gooseberry Sweet-and-Sour Tofu

The secret to this sweet and tangy sauce is the cape gooseberry, a sun-colored fruit the size of a cherry tomato with a tart, pineapple flavor. Like their close relative, the tomatillo, gooseberries grow inside a thin, papery husk that is sometimes still attached, depending on where they are purchased. Otherwise, look for a package of bright golden berries labeled under one of its many other names: golden gooseberries, Chinese lanterns, husk cherries, goldenberries, or Peruvian ground cherries. Snacking on these little fruits is unavoidable, so consider buying extra.

Serves 2 to 4

1 package cape gooseberries (about 6 ounces)

1 teaspoon seasoned rice vinegar

1 tablespoon freshly squeezed lime juice

¼ teaspoon sesame oil

¼ teaspoon salt

1 (1-pound) package extra-firm tofu, drained

2 tablespoons peanut oil

1½ cups sliced sweet peppers

3 slices peeled ginger (about the thickness of a coin)

3 green onions, white and light green parts finely sliced

Chopped cilantro and lime wedges, for garnish

Blend the gooseberries, vinegar, lime juice, sesame oil, and salt in a food processor or blender until smooth. Pour into a small saucepan and simmer on low for 5 minutes to reduce slightly. Remove from the heat.

Cut the tofu in half lengthwise. Wrap the two rectangles in a clean dish towel and press down firmly with your hands to squeeze out excess liquid. Heat 1 tablespoon of the peanut oil in a large wok or nonstick skillet over medium-high heat. Add the sliced tofu and cook undisturbed for 5 minutes on each side, or until golden brown and slightly crispy. Remove the tofu from the skillet and cut it into smaller bite-sized cubes.

Heat the remaining 1 tablespoon of peanut oil in the skillet. Add the peppers and ginger and stir-fry for 3 minutes, or until the peppers are just tender. Add the gooseberry sauce, cubed tofu, and green onions to the skillet and mix gently to coat evenly. Garnish with the cilantro and lime wedges. Serve immediately alongside steamed rice.

Availability year-round at well-stocked groceries and farmers' markets, with peak season in late summer and fall

Selection choose berries with bright golden color and plump texture like cherry tomatoes

image appears on following page

Storage room temperature for a few days, or refrigerate for up to 2 weeks

Substitutions pineapple, sun gold tomatoes

Dragon Fruit and Lime Curd Tart

Dragon fruit, also known as pitaya in Latin America, is actually a cactus fruit with fuchsia skin and green-tipped scales that protrude like the fins of a tropical fish. Inside, the fruit is studded with tiny black seeds that provide a crunch similar to that of poppy seeds. Thin slices of the fruit top this dramatic tart, showcasing the fuchsia rind against the white speckled flesh. Tangy lime curd and a buttery shortbread crust complement the fruit's watermelon-like flavor.

Serves 12

½ cup freshly squeezed lime juice

½ cup granulated sugar

3 eggs

½ cup heavy whipping cream

1 cup flour

⅓ cup powdered sugar

1 cup salted butter, softened

¼ teaspoon almond extract

1 very large dragon fruit,
or 2 small ones

Availability Latin American markets and specialty markets in summer and early fall

Selection heavy fruit with bright fuchsia skin free of soft spots

Storage refrigerate in a plastic bag for up to 5 days

Substitutions prickly pear, kiwi

To make the lime curd, place the lime juice, granulated sugar, eggs, and cream in a small saucepan. Heat gently over very low heat, stirring constantly with a rubber spatula to ensure the bottom doesn't stick, for about 10 minutes, or until the mixture thickens. Pour the mixture into a bowl and secure plastic wrap over top. Chill in the refrigerator for at least 2 hours, or overnight.

Preheat the oven to 350°F. Combine the flour and powdered sugar in a mixing bowl. Add the butter and almond extract and use a pastry cutter or large fork to work the butter and extract through the dry ingredients until it all comes together in a loose dough. Use your fingers to press the dough into the bottom and sides of a 10-inch loose-bottomed tart pan, trimming the edges with a knife. Bake for 10 to 15 minutes, until the crust is golden. Remove from the oven and cool completely. The crust can be wrapped tightly in plastic wrap and stored in a cool place overnight.

To assemble, pour the lime curd into the cooled crust and spread evenly to cover the bottom. Slice the thin outer peel from the dragon fruit, leaving as much of the dark pink rind intact as possible. Slice the fruit into ⅛-inch discs and layer them in a fan shape atop the tart. Serve immediately or cover tightly in plastic wrap and refrigerate for later.

Sour Plum Salsa

These pucker-inducing plums are simply just plums picked before they are ripe, when they are still green and hard like miniature Granny Smith apples. High in acid and low in sugar, sour plums are popular in many Middle Eastern and Asian cultures as a tart and crunchy snack, pickle, or palate cleanser. Here, they fill the role traditionally played by tomatoes in a tangy salsa that captures the freshness of spring. Serve atop tacos, with tortilla chips, or alongside Purple Cauliflower Quesadillas (page 73).

Makes about 4 cups

1 large English cucumber, peeled and finely diced

1⅓ teaspoon kosher salt

1 pound sour green plums, pits removed and small diced

½ white onion, finely diced

4 tablespoons freshly squeezed lime juice

1 to 2 serrano chiles, seeded and minced

½ cup minced cilantro leaves

Availability Middle Eastern markets and specialty markets in early spring

Selection bright green, hard fruit the size of cherries; also sold as janerik

Storage store in a cool, dark place for up to 2 weeks

Substitutions unripe green mango, tomatillos, milpero tomatillos

Mix the cucumber with 1 teaspoon of the salt and place in a strainer set over a bowl in the refrigerator for 20 to 30 minutes or up to 1 hour.

Meanwhile, combine the rest of the ingredients along with the remaining ⅓ teaspoon of the salt in a serving bowl.

Remove the cucumber from the refrigerator and press the cucumber against the sides of the strainer using your hands or the back of a spatula to remove excess liquid.

Add the cucumber to the plum mixture and stir to combine.

Taste for salt, lime, and spice and adjust to your liking.

image appears on page 72

Moscato-Poached Quince

The perfume scent of quince tempts one to simply hold the fruit forever beneath one's nose. But quince aficionados know what a shame that would be. Long bouts of roasting, poaching, or cooking turn this dense, pale fruit into a tender treat with a distinctive rose hue, such as in *membrillo* (quince paste), its most common preparation. In this recipe, quince is bathed in sweet Moscato wine and is an elegant finish to a heavy meal. The coffee beans, an old trick from Spain, mellow the brightness of wine-poached fruit. In the United States, we put ice cream on everything, but leave these unadulterated so you don't overpower the delicate taste of bliss.

Serves 4 to 6

4 quinces

1 bottle of pink Moscato (or rosé champagne or wine)

⅔ cup sugar

8 coffee beans

Availability well-stocked groceries and farmers' markets, with peak in fall

Selection hard fruit with a perfume fragrance and completely yellow skin free of bruises

Storage store in a cool, dark place for up to 1 month

Substitutions Bosc pears, but decrease poaching time

Peel and quarter the quinces and cut away the hard cores. Place the quinces in a saucepan with the remaining ingredients, weighing the quinces down with a heatproof plate so they are submerged in the wine.

Bring to a boil and then lower to simmer for 20 to 25 minutes, until the quinces pierce easily with a fork. Remove the quinces from the liquid using a slotted spoon and set aside in a bowl.

Continue to simmer the poaching liquid for 10 more minutes to allow it to reduce slightly and turn a deeper pink color. Pour the liquid over the quince and let cool slightly before chilling in the refrigerator for at least 3 hours or overnight.

Serve well-chilled in small dishes with the syrup and a couple of coffee beans.

Passionfruit Zabaglione

Passionfruit juice is so flavorful and concentrated that it's almost liqueur-like, requiring very little to infuse its powers. It brings zabaglione to new heights, permeating the frothy egg yolks with its tropical notes. The result is at once light and rich. Let the foam overflow down the sides of the cup for a decadent display.

Serves 4

6 to 10 passionfruits

7 teaspoons sugar

6 egg yolks

Availability year-round at specialty markets, but sporadically due to weather conditions

Selection choose plump fruits that are heavy for their size, with dark purple, dimpled skin

Storage ripen at room temperature (until dimpled), then refrigerate in a paper bag for up to 1 week

Substitutions mango nectar, store-bought passionfruit nectar

To extract the juice from the passionfruits, slice them in half and scoop the juicy pulp into a fine-mesh strainer set over a bowl. Stir and press the pulp against the strainer using the back of a spoon to release the juice from the pulp and seeds. You should have about 7 tablespoons of juice. Discard the pulp and seeds.

Bring to a boil an inch of water in a large pot. Combine the passionfruit juice, sugar, and egg yolks in a large copper or glass mixing bowl and set the bowl over the top of the pot, ensuring it is not touching the water.

Use a balloon whisk to whisk the mixture quickly and constantly, incorporating as much air as possible and ensuring the eggs don't cook onto the sides of the bowl. It should take about 2 to 3 minutes to froth the mixture, triple its original volume, and reach a warm temperature.

Immediately pour it into four warmed dessert cups or martini glasses and serve.

Pickled Kumquats

Whether popped into the mouth whole or prepared in a recipe, kumquats are a bursting mouthful of citrus during the darkest months of the year. Pickled with a hint of spice, these tangy morsels are a wonderful addition to a bitter green salad or paired with a strong cheese.

Makes about 2 cups

¾ pound kumquats

¾ cup rice vinegar

¼ cup water

6 black peppercorns

4 cardamom pods

½ teaspoon salt

⅓ cup sugar

Availability well-stocked groceries and farmers' markets from November to March

Selection look for firm flesh with bright-orange skin

Storage room temperature for a few days or refrigerate for up to 2 weeks

Substitutions sliced calamondin orange, sliced tangerine

Slice the kumquats into 3 to 4 discs each and pop out any visible seeds. Place the fruit with the remaining ingredients in a small saucepan and bring to a boil. Reduce the heat and simmer for 2 minutes. Pour into a pint-sized jar and cover with a lid. Chill overnight before consuming. The pickled kumquats can be stored in the refrigerator for up to 2 weeks.

Starfruit Almond Torte

Slices of starfruit crown this densely textured almond torte, inspired by a medieval legend in which shepherds were guided by a bright star to the site of the remains of St. James, or Santiago. The site in northwestern Spain is now the final destination of one of the world's most famous pilgrimages, Santiago de Compostela, and to this day slices of almond cake are served to pilgrims after enduring weeks of travel on foot. Starfruit, also known as carambola in Southeast Asia, is easily recognized by its five ridges that form a star shape when the fruit is sliced crosswise. Its crisp yet juicy flesh has the tartness of green apple, grape, and pineapple, which plays beautifully with this sweet almond dessert.

Serves 10 to 12

1 starfruit

1 tablespoon brown sugar

8 ounces blanched almonds (about 1½ cups whole almonds or 2 cups slivered almonds)

6 eggs, at room temperature and separated

1⅓ cups granulated sugar

Zest from 1 lemon

¼ teaspoon almond extract

¼ teaspoon salt

Availability year-round at Asian markets and specialty markets, but sporadically due to weather

Selection choose heavy fruit with firm yellow flesh free of soft spots; fruit is ripe when ridges turn slightly brown

Storage ripen at room temperature and then refrigerate for up to 1 week

Safety those with impaired kidney function should avoid starfruit

Substitutions thinly sliced pineapple or green apple

Slice off the very ends of the starfruit and trim off any brown spots along its five ridges using a paring knife. Cut into ¼-inch slices. Butter the bottom and sides of a 10-inch or 11-inch springform cake pan. Sprinkle the brown sugar over the base of the pan and arrange the starfruit slices in a single layer on top of the sugar. Preheat the oven to 350°F.

Place the almonds in a food processor and pulse until you have a fine meal; you should have about 2 cups. In a large mixing bowl, beat the egg yolks and granulated sugar until smooth and creamy. Stir in the lemon zest, almond extract, and salt.

In a clean mixing bowl with clean beaters, beat the egg whites until stiff peaks form. Gently fold them into the egg yolk mixture until incorporated, being careful not to overmix. Fold in the ground almonds until just incorporated. Pour the batter over the starfruit slices in the cake pan and bake for about 40 to 45 minutes, until the middle feels springy when lightly touched. Remove from the oven and let cool.

Run a knife around the outside of the torte to ensure it is not stuck to the sides of the pan before releasing the springform pan and inverting it onto a serving plate. Carefully lift off the bottom of the springform pan to reveal the starfruit-topped cake below, using a spatula to release any pieces that may have stuck. Serve small slices of the dense, flavorful cake.

Prickly Pear Sorbet

It's hard to believe so much color and flavor come from this little red fruit that grows atop the nopal cacti throughout California and the Southwest. The prickly pear's deep magenta flesh makes a lush, jewel-toned sorbet. In this version, the fruit's sweet, watermelon-like flavor is offset with a subtle kick of spice.

Serves 4 to 6

7 to 8 ripe red prickly pears

1 cup water

⅔ cup sugar

4 tablespoons freshly squeezed lemon juice

3 tablespoons freshly squeezed lime juice

1 serrano chile

Availability Latin American groceries from August to December; also sold as red tunas or red cactus fruit

Selection deep magenta, uniformly colored fruit that is firm but yields to pressure

Storage store at room temperature until ripe, then refrigerate for up to 4 days

Safety wear gloves while handling to avoid invisible but prickly spines

Substitutions watermelon

To extract the juice, slice the prickly pears in half lengthwise and use a spoon to scoop out the flesh, getting as close to the skin as possible. (Caution: Prickly pears can have invisible spines on their skin, so consider wearing rubber or gardening gloves while handling them.) Pulse the prickly pear flesh in a blender for 5 to 10 seconds to separate the flesh from the seeds. Pour the contents of the blender through a fine-mesh strainer. Stir for several minutes to extract as much juice as possible and discard the seeds and thick pulp that remain. There should be about 1⅔ to 1¾ cups of juice.

In a small saucepan, heat the water and sugar until the sugar completely dissolves. Remove from the heat and stir in the prickly pear juice, lemon juice, and lime juice. Using a fine grater or microplane, grate the sides of the serrano chile all the way around, avoiding the seeds in the middle. Add half the chile to the juice mixture and taste for spiciness. Grate and add more chile if desired. Refrigerate the mixture until completely chilled through, about 3 hours or overnight.

To make the sorbet, turn on the ice cream maker and pour in the chilled prickly pear mixture. Follow the manufacturer's instructions or process until the sorbet is thickened and velvety in consistency, about 15 to 20 minutes. Serve immediately for a softer sorbet. For firmer consistency, transfer the sorbet to a container and freeze for at least 3 hours, allowing the sorbet to soften for a few minutes at room temperature before serving.

Seasonal Menus

Spring Luncheon

White Asparagus with Preserved Lemon (page 108)

Sunchoke Farro with Roasted Apricots (page 137)

Green Garlic Soup with Lemon Cardamom Yogurt (page 111)

Sweet Corn and Chive-Stuffed Squash Blossoms (page 66)

Cherimoya Panna Cotta (page 184)

Backyard Summer Bash

Kiwano Cooler (page 186)

Watermelon Radish and Pineapple Carpaccio (page 126)

Green Papaya Gazpacho (page 166)

Chipotle-Roasted Satsuma Tacos with Cilantro Yogurt (page 122)

Corn Tortillas with Epazote Leaf (page 38)

Roasted Milpero Salsa Verde (page 151)

Prickly Pear Sorbet (page 201)

Warming Fall Supper

Malanga Masala Latkes (page 120)

Creamy Salsify Soup with Salsify Chips (page 133)

Meyer Lemon–Marinated Pioppini and Frisée Salad (page 96)

Port Roast with Horseradish Crisp (page 132)

Roasted Chestnut Chocolate Torte (page 76)

Winter's Brunch

Shiso Limeade (page 55)

Buddha's Hand Scones (page 183)

Toasted Salad Savoy with Pears and Goat Cheese (page 52)

Purple Potato Galette with Tarragon (page 116)

Broiled Pomelo with Cinnamon Crème Fraîche (page 172)

Tapas Night

Indian Bitter Melon Tonic (page 161)

Ramped-Up Mushrooms (page 109)

Stuffed Cherry Bomb Peppers (page 165)

Spanish-Style Chinese Cabbage on Manchego Toast (page 54)

Tortilla China (page 100)

Buñuelos de Yuca (page 141)

LEAVES: ❶ Mizuna ❷ Opal Basil ❸ Stinging Nettle ❹ Chrysanthemum Greens ❺ Chinese Cabbage ❻ Epazote ❼ Rau Ram ❽ Gai Lan ❾ Treviso ❿ Salad Savoy ⓫ Pea Shoot ⓬ Shiso ⓭ Sorrel

FLOWERS, SEEDS, AND PODS: ❶ Fresh Chickpea ❷ Purple Cauliflower ❸ Romanesco ❹ Snake Bean ❺ Cranberry Bean ❻ Chestnut ❼ Banana Blossom ❽ Tamarind

SPORES AND SUCCULENTS: ❶ Aloe Vera ❷ Abalone Mushroom ❸ Alba Pioppini ❹ Wood Ear Mushroom ❺ Purslane ❻ Hedgehog Mushroom ❼ Sea Bean ❽ Nopal ❾ Morel Mushroom ❿ Fiddlehead

STEMS: ❶ Green Garlic ❷ Rhubarb ❸ Cardoon ❹ Ramp ❺ Kohlrabi ❻ Bạc Hà ❼ Long Choy Sum ❽ White Asparagus ❾ Yellow Garlic Chive ❿ Lemongrass

ROOTS AND TUBERS: ❶ Celeriac ❷ Parsley Root ❸ Daikon ❹ Jicama ❺ Horseradish ❻ Sunchoke ❼ Yuca ❽ Golden Beet ❾ Lotus Root ❿ Malanga ⓫ Purple Potato ⓬ Satsuma Sweet Potato ⓭ Water Chestnut ⓮ Watermelon Radish ⓯ Salsify ⓰ Burdock Root

SAVORY FRUITS: ❶ Indian Eggplant ❷ Singua ❸ Plantain ❹ Chayote ❺ Armenian Cucumber ❻ Moqua ❼ Milpero ❽ Green Papaya ❾ Carnival Squash ❿ Blue Hokkaido Squash ⓫ Indian Bitter Melon

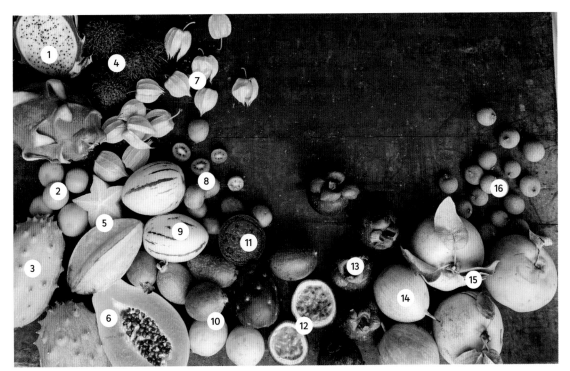

SWEET FRUITS: ❶ Dragon Fruit ❷ Kumquat ❸ African Horned Melon ❹ Rambutan ❺ Starfruit ❻ Papaya ❼ Cape Gooseberry ❽ Kiwi Berry ❾ Pepino Melon ❿ Guava ⓫ Prickly Pear ⓬ Passionfruit ⓭ Mangosteen ⓮ Fragrant Pear ⓯ Quince ⓰ Longan

Acknowledgments

This book would not have been possible without the support, cooperation, and enthusiasm of Glenn and Diane Yasuda, the founders and owners of Berkeley Bowl. Thank you for creating the special place that inspired this journey of discovery. I'd also like to acknowledge the dedicated Berkeley Bowl staff, particularly Nick Christopher for sharing his time and expertise.

A resounding thank you to my publisher Rachel Neumann for believing in me and for giving me the chance to bring this idea to life. From the start, you honored this cookbook's potential by ensuring it had the very best team behind it: Art and Production Director, Terri Saul; Cookbook Designer, Debbie Berne; and all the amazing people at Parallax Press. I especially want to thank my editor, Allison Serrell, for gently guiding me through my first book, pushing me to reach higher, and always having my back. And finally, to Jason Kim, a true friend and the first person to tell me I could be a published author.

Thank you to photographer Erin Scott for capturing the essence of Berkeley Bowl and bringing these recipes to life. I'll cherish the days I got to spend on set, watching you and food stylist Lillian Kang work your magic by turning piles of produce into works of art.

To my gang of committed and talented recipe testers, I'm still overwhelmed by your dedication and generosity in sharing in the creation of this project with me. You have each given a piece of yourself to this cookbook: Alix Wall, Allison Serrell, Amalia Wille, Amy Walters, AnnaLise Hoopes, Anya Dubin, Barbara Wille, Becky Conway, Bonnie Trinclisti, Brandon Rennels, Caitlin and Josh Jachimowicz,

Catherine and Mike Byrne, Colin Anthony, Constance Lively, Dara Wells-Hajjar, Elizabeth Mueller, Hagar Scher, Hisae Matsuda, Katherine Kodama, Kathy Grandfield, Leslie Kossoff, Lisa Moresco, Luke and Jilli Taylor, Maggie Evans, Mary Gee, Mary Hoopes, Melissa Cannon, Meredith Heuer, Minnie Reichek, Nancy McNeil, Paul French, Rachel Neumann, Rebecca Dienner, Rose Anthony, Shauna Pirotin, and Susan Patton Fox. I especially want to thank Basha Starr, Tracy Apple, and Jeanine Lively who, between the three of you, tested the entire book. Thank you for your endless support, candid feedback, and discerning palates that allowed me to feel confident sending these recipes out into the world.

The support of my friends and family played an immeasurable role in lifting me through the joys and challenges of this project, so thank you to all of you. I could not have done this without the love and support of two people in particular. To my mom, Jeanine Lively, who nurtured my desire to cook and to create, and taught me everything I know when it comes to cooking. You are my true hero, and I will forever cherish the time we've spent together in the kitchen. And to my husband Mike, who spent a good part of the last two years scrubbing pans, standing in line at Berkeley Bowl, proofreading text, taste-testing numerous versions of the same dish, providing honest feedback, and calming me through several meltdowns on the floor of our kitchen. You did it all with ceaseless joy, compassion, and love. I'm eternally grateful to have you by my side.

Index

213

About the Author

Laura McLively is a registered dietitian and food writer based in Oakland, California. An avid home cook, Laura is the creator of *My Berkeley Bowl*, a food blog about cooking with unusual fruits and vegetables. She is a frequent contributor to the food and recipe sections of the *East Bay Times* and the *Mercury News*.

Recognized as the birthplace of California cuisine and farm-to-table dining, Berkeley is at the nexus of America's natural food revolution. This sumptuous cookbook celebrates a vast diversity of produce from different cultures and cuisines, all available at Berkeley Bowl, California's legendary market.

With recipes including Green Garlic Soup with Lemon Cardamom Yogurt, Hedgehog Mushroom Toast, and Starfruit Almond Torte, avid home cook and registered dietitian Laura McLively highlights the versatile and unique qualities of the beautiful, plant-based bounty available to vegetarians and meat eaters alike.

These recipes will guide you in using fruits and vegetables you may have never tasted or tried to prepare, including crunchy sea bean spindles, tubers bigger than a toddler, dazzling redcurrants, and lush rambutans.

Berkeley Bowl is a mecca for great chefs from all around the world. With the recipes in this cookbook, even if you live far from Berkeley Bowl, you'll be able to create showstopping dishes that explode with flavors and textures and offer a true culinary adventure for all your senses.